# Church History

## faith first

Legacy Edition

**Teacher Guide**

RESOURCES FOR CHRISTIAN LIVING®

www.FaithFirst.com

"The Ad Hoc Committee to Oversee the Use of the Catechism, United States Conference of Catholic Bishops, has found the doctrinal content of this manual, copyright 2007, to be in conformity with the *Catechism of the Catholic Church.*"

**NIHIL OBSTAT**
Reverend Msgr. Robert M. Coerver
Censor Librorum

**IMPRIMATUR**
† Most Rev. Charles V. Grahmann
Bishop of Dallas

June 20, 2006

The Nihil Obstat and Imprimatur are official declarations that the material reviewed is free of doctrinal or moral error. No implication is contained therein that those granting the Nihil Obstat and Imprimatur agree with the contents, opinions, or statements expressed.



Send all inquiries to:
RCL • Resources for Christian Living
200 East Bethany Drive
Allen, Texas 75002-3804

Toll Free 877-275-4725
Fax 800-688-8356

Visit us at **www.RCLweb.com**
**www.FaithFirst.com**

Printed in the United States of America

**20547** ISBN 0-7829-1128-5 (Student Book)

**20550** ISBN 0-7829-1131-5 (Teacher Guide)

1 2 3 4 5 6 7 8 9 10

06 07 08 09 10 11 12

**ACKNOWLEDGMENTS**

Scripture excerpts are taken or adapted from the *New American Bible with Revised New Testament and Psalms* Copyright © 1991, 1986, 1970, Confraternity of Christian Doctrine, Inc., Washington, DC. Used with permission. All rights reserved. No part of the *New American Bible* may be reprinted without permission in writing from the copyright owner.

Excerpts from the English translation of the *Catechism of the Catholic Church* for the United States of America © 1994, United States Catholic Conference, Inc.—Libreria Editrice Vaticana. English translation of the: *Catechism of the Catholic Church Modifications from the Editio Typica* Copyright © 1997, United States Catholic Conference, Inc.—Libreria Editrice Vaticana.Used with permission.

Excerpts from *General Directory for Catechesis,* Copyright © 1997, United States Conference of Catholic Bishops, Washington, DC. Used with permission. All rights reserved. No part of this work may be reproduced or transmitted in any form without the permission in writing from the copyright holder.

Excerpts from the *National Directory for Catechesis,* Copyright © 2005, United States Conference of Catholic Bishops, Washington, DC. Used with permission. All rights reserved. No part of this work may be reproduced or transmitted in any form without the permission in writing from the copyright holder.

Excerpts from the *Compendium of the Social Doctrine of the Church,* Copyright © 2004, United States Conference of Catholic Bishops, Washington, DC. Used with permission. All rights reserved. No part of this work may be reproduced or transmitted in any form without the permission in writing from the copyright holder.

Excerpts from *Sharing the Light of Faith* Copyright © 1979 United States Conference of Catholic Bishops, Washington, DC. Used with permission. All rights reserved. No part of this work may be reproduced or transmitted in any form without the permission in writing from the copyright holder.

Excerpts are taken or adapted from the English translation of the *Roman Missal* © 1973, International Committee on English in the Liturgy, Inc. (ICEL), and from the English translation of *A Book of Prayers* © 1982, (ICEL). All rights reserved.

English translation of "The Nicene Creed," "The Apostles' Creed," "Sanctus," "Benedictus," "Gloria Patri," and "Magnificat" by the International Consultation on English Texts (ICET).

Excerpts from *Catechesi Tradendae: Catechesis in Our Time* Copyright © 1979, Daughters of St. Paul; excerpts from *Evangelii Nuntiandi: On Evangelization in the Modern World* © 1975, Daughters of St. Paul, Boston, MA.

Excerpts from the *Dogmatic Constitution on the Church* (Lumen gentium), *Decree on Pastoral Office of the Bishops in the Church* (Christus Dominus), *Decree on Ecumenism* (Unitatis redintegratio) from *Vatican Council II: The Conciliar and Post Conciliar Documents,* New Revised Edition, Austin Flannery, O.P., Gen. Ed., Copyright © 1975, 1986, 1992, 1996 by Costello Publishing Company, Inc. Used with Permission.

Excerpt from Pope Paul VI, homily at Shrine of Namugongo 1969.

Footnotes can be found on page 152.

# Faith First Legacy Edition Development Team

Developing a religion program requires the gifts and talents of many individuals working together as a team. RCL is proud to acknowledge the contributions of these dedicated people.

*Program Theology Consultants*
Reverend Louis J. Cameli, S.T.D.
Reverend Robert D. Duggan, S.T.D.

*Advisory Board*
Judith Deckers, M.Ed.
Marina Herrera, Ph.D.
Elaine McCarron, SCN, M.Div.
Reverend Frank McNulty, S.T.D.
Reverend Ronald J. Nuzzi, Ph.D.

*Contributing Writers*
*Student Book and Teacher Guide*
Christina DeCamp
Judith Deckers
Reverend Robert D. Duggan, S.T.D.
Mary Beth Jambor
Reverend Steven M. Lanza, S.T.L.
Eileen A. McGrath
Susan Stark

*Director of Creative Development*
Jo Rotunno

*National Catechetical Consultant*
Kate Sweeney Ristow

*Managing Editor*
Susan Smith

*Art & Design Director*
Lisa Brent

*Electronic Page Makeup*
Laura Fremder

*Production Director*
Jenna Nelson

*Designer*
Tricia Legault

*Project Editors*
Patricia A. Classick
Steven M. Ellair
Craig W. O'Neill

*Web Site Producers*
Joseph Crisalli
A. C. Ware

*General Editor*
Ed DeStefano

*President/Publisher*
Maryann Nead

# CONTENTS

# Welcome to Faith First Junior High!

# faith first®
## Legacy Edition

## *Teaching the Timeless Truths of Our Faith Every Year*

*Faith First* is unique, effective, and comprehensive.

The *Faith First* kindergarten through junior high scope and sequence* is a spiral approach to learning our Catholic faith. The four pillars of the *Catechism of the Catholic Church*—Creed, Sacraments, Morality, and Prayer—are taught and developed on every grade level every year. This ensures that the beliefs of our faith are introduced to and reinforced for the young people as they grow, develop, and mature in their faith.

This educationally sound method means that each teacher will build upon and reinforce what students have learned previously in other grades. The result is age-appropriate learning on all topics of the faith.

**See the complete junior high scope and sequence chart on pages 33–37.*

Each text provides:
- **Doctrine Chapters**
- **Scripture Chapters**

In junior high the liturgical season lessons are found in the *Called to Prayer and Liturgical Lessons* booklet.

### *Doctrine Chapters*

While catechesis is much more than simply "teaching religion," providing students with a comprehensive understanding of the Catholic faith is essential to good catechesis. In the *Faith First* doctrine chapters, the students come to understand what we believe as Catholics and how to live out those beliefs.

## *Scripture Chapters*

The Scripture chapters in each unit of the *Faith First Junior High Legacy Edition* student books help the young people come to know and understand the Word of God. Each of these complete lessons has three distinctive elements:

**Bible Background**
The Scripture story is put into context for the young people by teaching about the author, the setting, and the background of the people in the story.

**Reading the Word of God**
The young people read or listen to a story from the Scriptures, followed by a brief summary that recalls what happened in the Scripture story.

**Understanding the Word of God**
This section explores the meaning of the story and helps the young people see how God's love, presence, help, and Revelation guide us in our daily lives.

## *Liturgical Season Lessons*

Seasonal lessons give young people the opportunity to celebrate and prayerfully participate in the liturgy every Sunday. These resources are found in *Called to Prayer and Liturgical Lessons* (see page 20) and are reproducible for your convenience.

**Advent and Christmas**
Four Advent lessons help young people joyfully prepare to celebrate the Incarnation and Christ's rebirth in our hearts at Christmas, followed by two lessons on the Christmas Season.

**Lent**
Six lessons guide the young people through Lent and help them turn their minds and hearts to God through prayer, fasting, and almsgiving. Through Scripture stories and the presentation of Lenten traditions, the young people recall Christ's sacrifice on the cross and prepare to celebrate new life in Christ.

**The Triduum and the Season of Easter**
Together, you and the young people journey through Holy Thursday, Good Friday, and the Easter Vigil. Then six Easter season lessons celebrate the joy of Christ's Resurrection and the new life we receive through the Sacraments of Christian Initiation. Your journey through the liturgical year concludes with a lesson on the coming of the Holy Spirit at Pentecost.

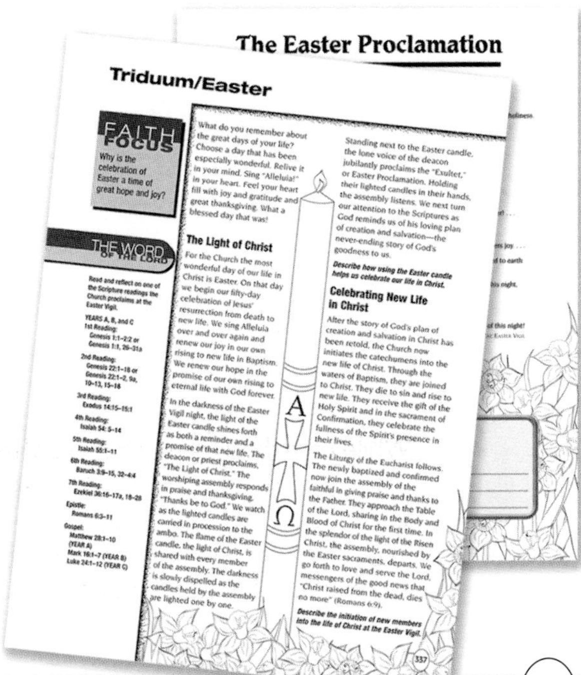

Online resources for teens, catechists, and parents.

# Features of the Student Book

*Each chapter of* Faith First *has consistent features that direct learning, develop religious literacy, reinforce content, and encourage integration of faith and life.*

# The Church Grows: A.D. 50–A.D. 400

2

FAITH FOCUS

Why did the Gospel spread so widely during the first three centuries?

FAITH VOCABULARY

**Gentile**
**presbyters**
**apologists**
**apostolic succession**
**Council of Jerusalem**
**Deposit of Faith**
**heresies**

***What clubs or organizations do you belong to? What do you know about their history and development?***

Have you ever been a member of a newly formed club or organization? Initially, there are just a few people with a lot of spirit. As the organization grows it draws up rules, forms a governing body, attracts new members, and becomes a visible part of your community. Something similar happened to the Church in her first four hundred years. By the end of the fourth century, the structure of the visible institution of the Church that we know today began to emerge.

***What do you know about the events and people that were part of the story of the Church in the first four centuries of her existence?***

Ruins at Corinth on the Peloponnese peninsula in southern Greece.

*And every day the Lord added to their number those who were being saved.*
Acts of the Apostles 2:47

19

### Chapter Opener

The first page of every chapter features a photograph that illustrates in some way the focus of the chapter. This page also contains questions to assess what the young people already know about the subject to be learned.

### Faith Focus

Prepares young people for learning the content of the chapter with an introductory question.

### Faith Vocabulary

Enables you to build religious literacy and vocabulary by defining and explaining important faith words and concepts.

### Timeline

This feature includes a list of key events and people, such as Fathers of the Church, Doctors of the Church, saints, Popes, and others who have played a significant role in the period of Church history presented in a chapter. An inclusive timeline is included on page 146 of the student text.

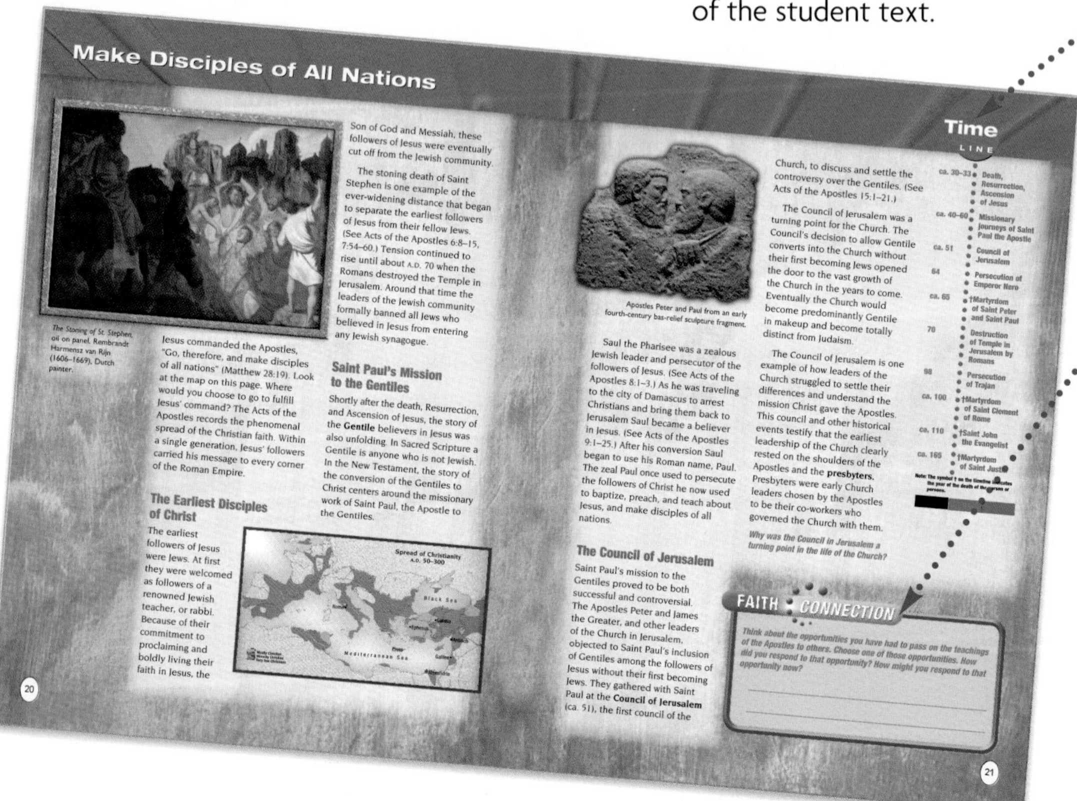

## Make Disciples of All Nations

*The Stoning of St. Stephen,* oil on panel, Rembrandt Harmensz van Rijn (1606–1669), Dutch painter.

Jesus commanded the Apostles, "Go, therefore, and make disciples of all nations" (Matthew 28:19). Look at the map on this page. Where would you choose to go to fulfill Jesus' command? The Acts of the Apostles records the phenomenal spread of the Christian faith. Within a single generation, Jesus' followers carried his message to every corner of the Roman Empire.

### The Earliest Disciples of Christ

The earliest followers of Jesus were Jews. At first they were welcomed as followers of a renowned Jewish teacher, or rabbi. Because of their commitment to proclaiming and boldly living their faith in Jesus, the Son of God and Messiah, these followers of Jesus were eventually cut off from the Jewish community.

The stoning death of Saint Stephen is one example of the ever-widening distance that began to separate the earliest followers of Jesus from their fellow Jews. (See Acts of the Apostles 6:8–15, 7:54–60.) Tension continued to rise until about A.D. 70 when the Romans destroyed the Temple in Jerusalem. Around that time the leaders of the Jewish community formally banned all Jews who believed in Jesus from entering any Jewish synagogue.



### Saint Paul's Mission to the Gentiles

Shortly after the death, Resurrection, and Ascension of Jesus, the story of the **Gentile** believers in Jesus was also unfolding. In Sacred Scripture a Gentile is anyone who is not Jewish. In the New Testament, the story of the conversion of the Gentiles to Christ centers around the missionary work of Saint Paul, the Apostle to the Gentiles.

20

Apostles Peter and Paul from an early fourth-century bas-relief sculpture fragment.

Saul the Pharisee was a zealous Jewish leader and persecutor of the followers of Jesus. (See Acts of the Apostles 8:1–3.) As he was traveling to the city of Damascus to arrest Christians and bring them back to Jerusalem Saul became a believer in Jesus. (See Acts of the Apostles 9:1–25.) After his conversion Saul began to use his Roman name, Paul. The zeal Paul once used to persecute the followers of Christ he now used to baptize, preach, and teach about Jesus, and make disciples of all nations.

### The Council of Jerusalem

Saint Paul's mission to the Gentiles proved to be both successful and controversial. The Apostles Peter and James the Greater, and other leaders of the Church in Jerusalem, objected to Saint Paul's inclusion of Gentiles among the followers of Jesus without their first becoming Jews. They gathered with Saint Paul at the **Council of Jerusalem** (ca. 51), the first council of the Church, to discuss and settle the controversy over the Gentiles. (See Acts of the Apostles 15:1–21.)

The Council of Jerusalem was a turning point for the Church. The Council's decision to allow Gentile converts into the Church without their first becoming Jews opened the door to the vast growth of the Church in the years to come. Eventually the Church would become predominantly Gentile in makeup and become totally distinct from Judaism.

The Council of Jerusalem is one example of how leaders of the Church struggled to settle their differences and understand the mission Christ gave the Apostles. This council and other historical events testify that the earliest leadership of the Church clearly rested on the shoulders of the Apostles and the **presbyters.** Presbyters were early Church leaders chosen by the Apostles to be their co-workers who governed the Church with them.

***Why was the Council in Jerusalem a turning point in the life of the Church?***

Time LINE

ca. 30–33 Death, Resurrection, Ascension of Jesus
ca. 40–60 Missionary journeys of Saint Paul the Apostle
ca. 51 Council of Jerusalem
64 Persecution of Emperor Nero
ca. 65 †Martyrdom of Saint Peter and Saint Paul
70 Destruction of Temple in Jerusalem by Romans
98 Persecution of Trajan
ca. 100 †Martyrdom of Saint Clement of Rome
ca. 110 †Saint John the Evangelist
ca. 165 †Martyrdom of Saint Justin

Note: The symbol † on the timeline indicates the year of the death of the person or persons.

FAITH CONNECTION

***Think about the opportunities you have had to pass on the teachings of the Apostles to others. Choose one of those opportunities. How did you respond to that opportunity? How might you respond to that opportunity now?***

21

### Faith Connection

Activities that help young people relate the chapter content to their experience.

OUR CHURCH MAKES A DIFFERENCE

Religious sisters distributing clothing to flood victims in Chandipur, eastern India.

Within a few years after the Council of Jerusalem, local Churches sprang up throughout the lands around the Mediterranean. As the Church grew, some Christians, as early as the second century, joined together and formed communities to support one another in living the Gospel. Among the earliest of these communities were those that formed in Egypt around Saint Anthony of the Desert (c. 251–356). Eventually these communities took on the two basic forms which exist in the Church today, namely, contemplative life and apostolic life.

**Religious Communities**

Today members of religious communities, or the consecrated life, live the Gospel of Jesus Christ according to a rule of life approved by the Church. Members make special promises or vows to follow the example of poverty, obedience, and chastity lived by Jesus Christ.

Contemplative Life

Members of contemplative communities commit themselves primarily to silence and prayer. Centering their day around the prayerful praise of God, they live a solitary life within community. Some contemplatives are cloistered. This means that they never leave the places where they live.

Apostolic Life

Members of apostolic religious communities support one another in the work of proclaiming the Gospel and serving others by living the Works of Mercy. Religious brothers and sisters, priests, and deacons work in hospitals and places that help the sick and elderly. They teach in parishes, schools, and universities. Others are active in social issues, working to build a just society for all. Members of other religious communities proclaim the Gospel as missionaries.

***How is both prayer and service part of the way you live the Gospel? How is your parish a community that lives the Gospel?***

Franciscan friars praying the Liturgy of the Hours.

25

## *Our Church Makes a Difference*

Each chapter examines the difference the Church has made and continues to make in the lives of Christians and in the world. The students' Catholic identity is developed as they learn more about how the Church expresses and lives her faith.

## *What Difference Does Faith Make in My Life?*

These pages help young people apply what they have learned each and every week in order to see that our faith *does* make a difference in our life. This important step helps young people recognize that faith is not meant to be isolated or compartmentalized. Faith is meant to be lived. This section in each chapter also provides the students with a set of life skills that helps them live their faith by integrating it into their daily lives.

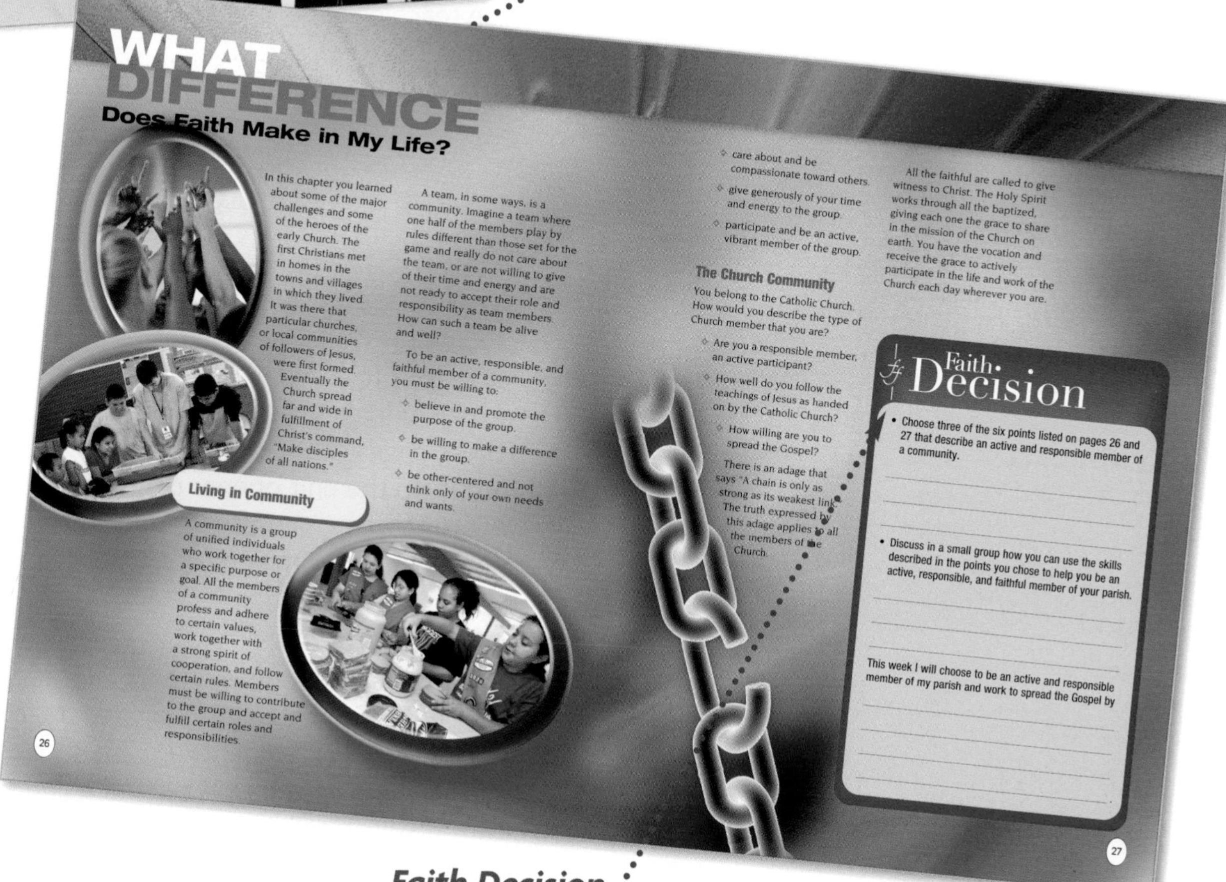

WHAT DIFFERENCE Does Faith Make in My Life?

In this chapter you learned about some of the major challenges and some of the heroes of the early Church. The first Christians met in homes in the towns and villages in which they lived. It was there that particular churches, or local communities of followers of Jesus, were first formed. Eventually the Church spread far and wide in fulfillment of Christ's command, "Make disciples of all nations."

**Living in Community**

A community is a group of unified individuals who work together for a specific purpose or goal. All the members of a community profess and adhere to certain values, work together with a strong spirit of cooperation, and follow certain rules. Members must be willing to contribute to the group and accept and fulfill certain roles and responsibilities.

A team, in some ways, is a community. Imagine a team where one half of the members play by rules different than those set for the game and really do not care about the team, or are not willing to give of their time and energy and are not ready to accept their role and responsibility as team members. How can such a team be alive and well?

To be an active, responsible, and faithful member of a community, you must be willing to:

- believe in and promote the purpose of the group.
- be willing to make a difference in the group.
- be other-centered and not think only of your own needs and wants.
- care about and be compassionate toward others.
- give generously of your time and energy to the group.
- participate and be an active, vibrant member of the group.

**The Church Community**

You belong to the Catholic Church. How would you describe the type of Church member that you are?

- Are you a responsible member, an active participant?
- How well do you follow the teachings of Jesus as handed on by the Catholic Church?
- How willing are you to spread the Gospel?

There is an adage that says "A chain is only as strong as its weakest link." The truth expressed by this adage applies to all the members of the Church.

All the faithful are called to give witness to Christ. The Holy Spirit works through all the baptized, giving each one the grace to share in the mission of the Church on earth. You have the vocation and receive the grace to actively participate in the life and work of the Church each day wherever you are.

Faith Decision

- Choose three of the six points listed on pages 26 and 27 that describe an active and responsible member of a community.
- Discuss in a small group how you can use the skills described in the points you chose to help you be an active, responsible, and faithful member of your parish.

This week I will choose to be an active and responsible member of my parish and work to spread the Gospel by

26

27

## *Faith Decision*

Young people are encouraged to do something intentionally to put into practice what has been learned.

# Building Religious Literacy

*There are many features in* Faith First *that allow and encourage informal assessment of your students. In addition, formal assessment tools are provided for grades 1–8.*

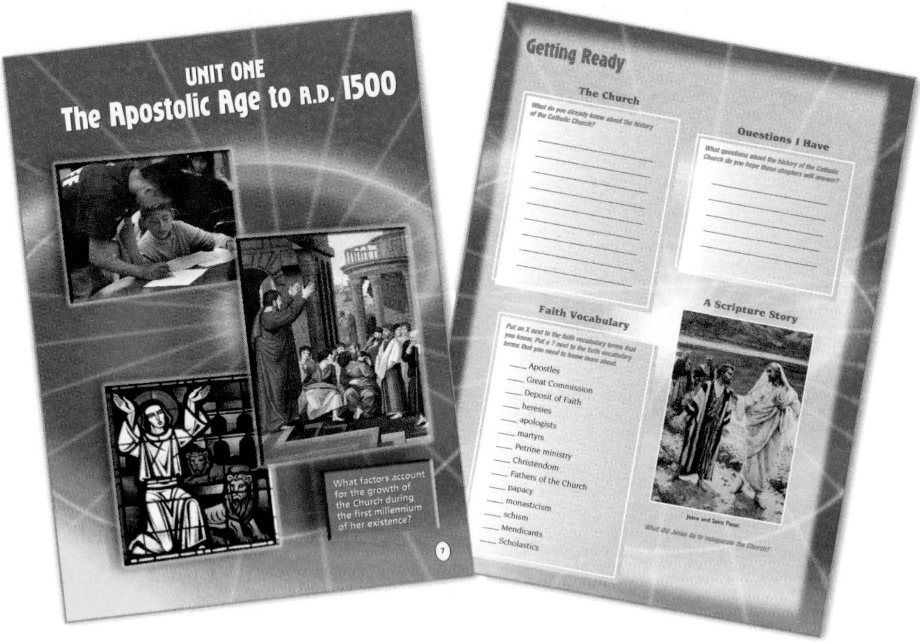

UNIT ONE
The Apostolic Age to A.D. 1500

What factors account for the growth of the Church during the first millennium of her existence?

7

Getting Ready

The Church

What do you already know about the history of the Catholic Church?

Questions I Have

What questions about the history of the Catholic Church do you hope these chapters will answer?

Faith Vocabulary

Put an X next to the faith vocabulary terms that you know. Put a ? next to the faith vocabulary terms that you need to know more about.

___ Apostles
___ Great Commission
___ Deposit of Faith
___ heresies
___ apologists
___ martyrs
___ Petrine ministry
___ Christendom
___ Fathers of the Church
___ papacy
___ monasticism
___ schism
___ Mendicants
___ Scholastics

A Scripture Story

Jesus and Saint Peter.

What did Jesus do to inaugurate the Church?

### *Unit Openers*

*Faith First* unit openers are true teaching tools that

- activate prior knowledge and
- forecast unit faith themes and faith vocabulary.

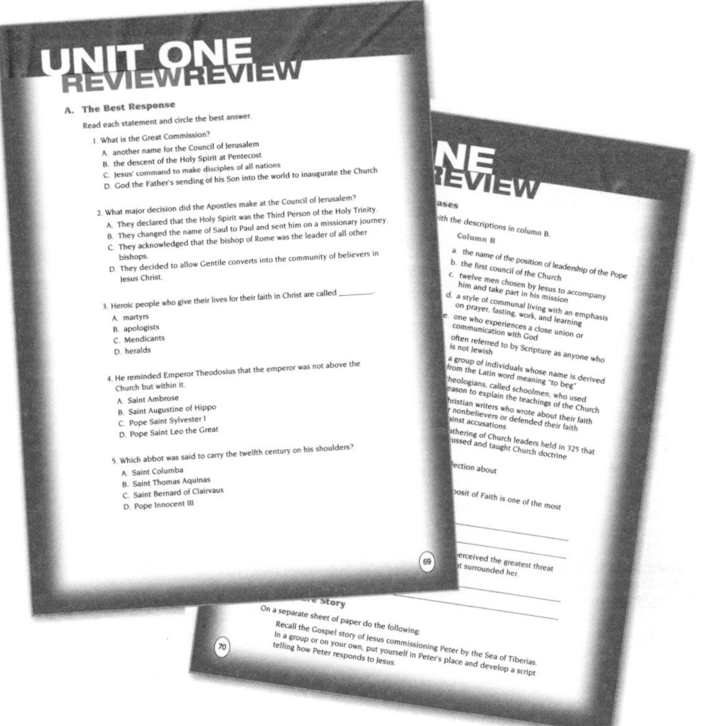

UNIT ONE REVIEW

A. The Best Response

Read each statement and circle the best answer.

1. What is the Great Commission?
   A. another name for the Council of Jerusalem
   B. the descent of the Holy Spirit at Pentecost
   C. Jesus' command to make disciples of all nations
   D. God the Father's sending of his Son into the world to inaugurate the Church
2. What major decision did the Apostles make at the Council of Jerusalem?
   A. They declared that the Holy Spirit was the Third Person of the Holy Trinity.
   B. They changed the name of Saul to Paul and sent him on a missionary journey.
   C. They acknowledged that the bishop of Rome was the leader of all other bishops.
   D. They decided to allow Gentile converts into the community of believers in Jesus Christ.
3. Heroic people who give their lives for their faith in Christ are called ________.
   A. martyrs
   B. apologists
   C. Mendicants
   D. heralds
4. He reminded Emperor Theodosius that the emperor was not above the Church but within it.
   A. Saint Ambrose
   B. Saint Augustine of Hippo
   C. Pope Saint Sylvester I
   D. Pope Saint Leo the Great
5. Which abbot was said to carry the twelfth century on his shoulders?
   A. Saint Columba
   B. Saint Thomas Aquinas
   C. Saint Bernard of Clairvaux
   D. Pope Innocent III

69

...NE
...EVIEW

...ases

...ith the descriptions in column B.

Column B

a. the name of the position of leadership of the Pope
b. the first council of the Church
c. twelve men chosen by Jesus to accompany him and take part in his mission
d. a style of communal living with an emphasis on prayer, fasting, work, and learning
e. one who experiences a close union or communication with God
... often referred to by Scripture as anyone who is not Jewish
... a group of individuals whose name is derived from the Latin word meaning "to beg"
...heologians, called schoolmen, who used ...eason to explain the teachings of the Church
...hristian writers who wrote about their faith ...r nonbelievers or defended their faith ...ainst accusations
...athering of Church leaders held in 325 that ...ussed and taught Church doctrine

...lection about

...posit of Faith is one of the most

...erceived the greatest threat ...t surrounded her.

...e Story

On a separate sheet of paper do the following:

Recall the Gospel story of Jesus commissioning Peter by the Sea of Tiberias. In a group or on your own, put yourself in Peter's place and develop a script telling how Peter responds to Jesus.

70

### *Unit Reviews*

The unit reviews use a variety of strategies to allow teachers to assess what students have accomplished. These pages encourage students to return to the unit opener pages to contrast where they began and what new discoveries they have made.

### *Chapter Reviews*

Every chapter review reinforces core concepts and key terms and encourages critical thinking. Students are asked to reflect on what they have learned and how it will affect their lives.

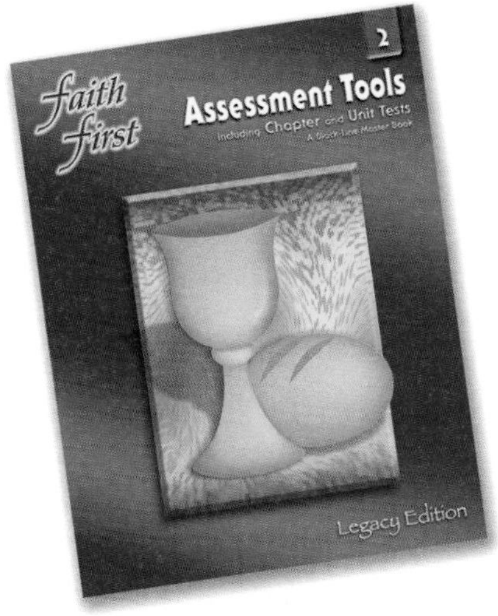


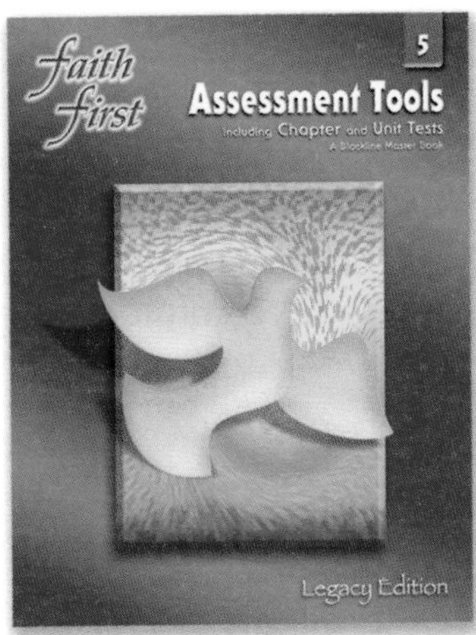

### *Assessment Tools*

A book of reproducible masters helps you create an assessment portfolio for every student with chapter tests, unit tests, and other assessment instruments. In junior high, chapter activities and assessment tools are included in the same booklet.

### *New Test Feature*

The new "Remembering Our Faith" feature uses a multiple-choice testing strategy commonly used in standardized testing instruments, such as A.C.R.E.

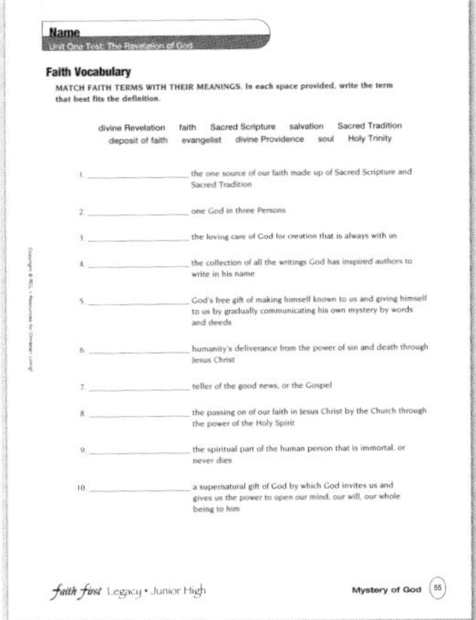

**Name**

Unit One Test: The Revelation of God

**Faith Vocabulary**

**MATCH FAITH TERMS WITH THEIR MEANINGS. In each space provided, write the term that best fits the definition.**

divine Revelation   faith   Sacred Scripture   salvation   Sacred Tradition
deposit of faith   evangelist   divine Providence   soul   Holy Trinity

1. ______ the one source of our faith made up of Sacred Scripture and Sacred Tradition
2. ______ one God in three Persons
3. ______ the loving care of God for creation that is always with us
4. ______ the collection of all the writings God has inspired authors to write in his name
5. ______ God's free gift of making himself known to us and giving himself to us by gradually communicating his own mystery by words and deeds
6. ______ humanity's deliverance from the power of sin and death through Jesus Christ
7. ______ teller of the good news, or the Gospel
8. ______ the passing on of our faith in Jesus Christ by the Church through the power of the Holy Spirit
9. ______ the spiritual part of the human person that is immortal, or never dies
10. ______ a supernatural gift of God by which God invites us and gives us the power to open our mind, our will, our whole being to him

faith first Legacy • Junior High   Mystery of God 55

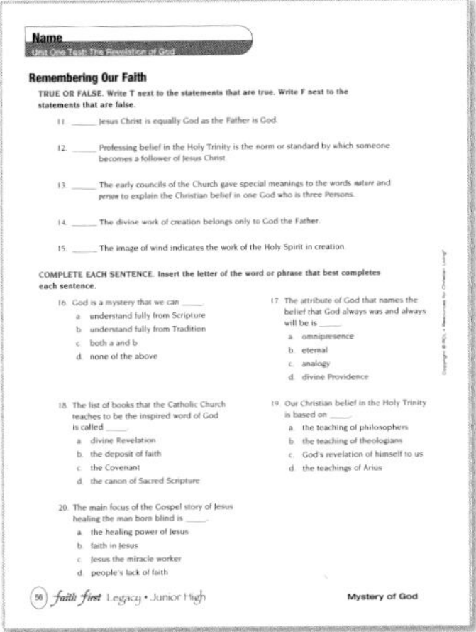

**Name**

Unit One Test: The Revelation of God

**Remembering Our Faith**

**TRUE OR FALSE. Write T next to the statements that are true. Write F next to the statements that are false.**

11. ______ Jesus Christ is equally God as the Father is God.
12. ______ Professing belief in the Holy Trinity is the norm or standard by which someone becomes a follower of Jesus Christ.
13. ______ The early councils of the Church gave special meanings to the words *nature* and *person* to explain the Christian belief in one God who is three Persons.
14. ______ The divine work of creation belongs only to God the Father.
15. ______ The image of wind indicates the work of the Holy Spirit in creation.

**COMPLETE EACH SENTENCE. Insert the letter of the word or phrase that best completes each sentence.**

16. God is a mystery that we can ______.
    a. understand fully from Scripture
    b. understand fully from Tradition
    c. both a and b
    d. none of the above

17. The attribute of God that names the belief that God always was and always will be is ______.
    a. omnipresence
    b. eternal
    c. analogy
    d. divine Providence

18. The list of books that the Catholic Church teaches to be the inspired word of God is called ______.
    a. divine Revelation
    b. the deposit of faith
    c. the Covenant
    d. the canon of Sacred Scripture

19. Our Christian belief in the Holy Trinity is based on ______.
    a. the teaching of philosophers
    b. the teaching of theologians
    c. God's revelation of himself to us
    d. the teachings of Arius

20. The main focus of the Gospel story of Jesus healing the man born blind is ______.
    a. the healing power of Jesus
    b. faith in Jesus
    c. Jesus the miracle worker
    d. people's lack of faith

56 faith first Legacy • Junior High   Mystery of God

### *Online Chapter Reviews at FaithFirst.com*

The students can study and review material from every chapter of every grade level on our Web site. Students can take an interactive test and then e-mail their results to you each week. This is a great way to reinforce learning and to get parents involved at home.

**Church History, Chapter 6**
**Mystics, Mendicants and Scholastics**

**Question 1**

**The followers of Saint Francis of Assisi and Saint Dominic de Guzman are called**

**a. mystics**

**b. scholastics**

**c. mendicants**

**d. disciples**

# Features of the Teacher Guide

*The teacher guide supports you every step of the way. Every lesson provides you with these easy-to-use resources.*

### *Background*

An easy-to-read essay gives you theological background on the content of the chapter. It will help you grow in your adult understanding of the Catholic faith. It concludes with reflection questions that invite you to consider your faith response to the chapter theme.

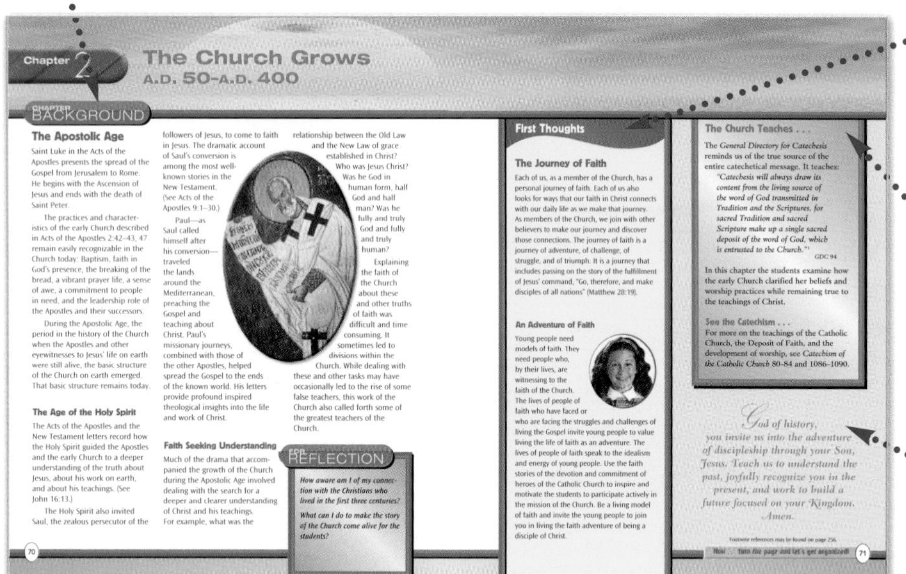

Chapter 2 **The Church Grows** A.D. 50–A.D. 400

CHAPTER BACKGROUND

**The Apostolic Age**

Saint Luke in the Acts of the Apostles presents the spread of the Gospel from Jerusalem to Rome. He begins with the Ascension of Jesus and ends with the death of Saint Peter.

The practices and characteristics of the early Church described in Acts of the Apostles 2:42–43, 47 remain easily recognizable in the Church today: Baptism, faith in God's presence, the breaking of the bread, a vibrant prayer life, a sense of awe, a commitment to people in need, and the leadership role of the Apostles and their successors.

During the Apostolic Age, the period in the history of the Church when the Apostles and other eyewitnesses to Jesus' life on earth were still alive, the basic structure of the Church on earth emerged. That basic structure remains today.

**The Age of the Holy Spirit**

The Acts of the Apostles and the New Testament letters record how the Holy Spirit guided the Apostles and the early Church to a deeper understanding of the truth about Jesus, about his work on earth, and about his teachings. (See John 16:13.)

The Holy Spirit also invited Saul, the zealous persecutor of the followers of Jesus, to come to faith in Jesus. The dramatic account of Saul's conversion is among the most well-known stories in the New Testament. (See Acts of the Apostles 9:1–30.)

Paul—as Saul called himself after his conversion—traveled the lands around the Mediterranean, preaching the Gospel and teaching about Christ. Paul's missionary journeys, combined with those of the other Apostles, helped spread the Gospel to the ends of the known world. His letters provide profound inspired theological insights into the life and work of Christ.

**Faith Seeking Understanding**

Much of the drama that accompanied the growth of the Church during the Apostolic Age involved dealing with the search for a deeper and clearer understanding of Christ and his teachings. For example, what was the relationship between the Old Law and the New Law of grace established in Christ? Who was Jesus Christ? Was he God in human form, half God and half man? Was he fully and truly God and fully and truly human?

Explaining the faith of the Church about these and other truths of faith was difficult and time consuming. It sometimes led to divisions within the Church. While dealing with these and other tasks may have occasionally led to the rise of some false teachers, this work of the Church also called forth some of the greatest teachers of the Church.

FOR REFLECTION

*How aware am I of my connection with the Christians who lived in the first three centuries?*

*What can I do to make the story of the Church come alive for the students?*

70

**First Thoughts**

**The Journey of Faith**

Each of us, as a member of the Church, has a personal journey of faith. Each of us also looks for ways that our faith in Christ connects with our daily life as we make that journey. As members of the Church, we join with other believers to make our journey and discover those connections. The journey of faith is a journey of adventure, of challenge, of struggle, and of triumph. It is a journey that includes passing on the story of the fulfillment of Jesus' command, "Go, therefore, and make disciples of all nations" (Matthew 28:19).

**An Adventure of Faith**

Young people need models of faith. They need people who, by their lives, are witnessing to the faith of the Church. The lives of people of faith who have faced or who are facing the struggles and challenges of living the Gospel invite young people to value living the life of faith as an adventure. The lives of people of faith speak to the idealism and energy of young people. Use the faith stories of the devotion and commitment of heroes of the Catholic Church to inspire and motivate the students to participate actively in the mission of the Church. Be a living model of faith and invite the young people to join you in living the faith adventure of being a disciple of Christ.

**The Church Teaches . . .**

The *General Directory for Catechesis* reminds us of the true source of the entire catechetical message. It teaches:

> *"Catechesis will always draw its content from the living source of the word of God transmitted in Tradition and the Scriptures, for sacred Tradition and sacred Scripture make up a single sacred deposit of the word of God, which is entrusted to the Church."*[1]
> GDC 94

In this chapter the students examine how the early Church clarified her beliefs and worship practices while remaining true to the teachings of Christ.

**See the Catechism . . .**

For more on the teachings of the Catholic Church, the Deposit of Faith, and the development of worship, see *Catechism of the Catholic Church* 80–84 and 1086–1090.

*God of history,*
*you invite us into the adventure*
*of discipleship through your Son,*
*Jesus. Teach us to understand the*
*past, joyfully recognize you in the*
*present, and work to build a*
*future focused on your Kingdom.*
*Amen.*

Footnote references may be found on page 256.

Now . . . turn the page and let's get organized! 71

### *First Thoughts*

These thoughts offer both practical and prayerful ideas to get you started.

### *The Church Teaches*

This feature introduces teachers to important quotes from key Church documents including the *National Directory for Catechesis.*

### *Prayer*

Before you teach, you'll want to center yourself in prayer. Each chapter prayer addresses the heart of your lesson.

The **QuickStart for Religion Teachers** on pages 25–46 and the ***Faith First Legacy Edition*** **In-Service Video** will help you get the year off to a great start. (See page 24 for more details.)

**LESSON PLANNER**

**Chapter Focus**
**To understand how the early Church both struggled to find her identity and proclaimed the Gospel far and wide**

| Focus | Process | Materials and Options |
|---|---|---|
| **DAY 1** **Engage/Teach and Apply** **Pages 19–21** **Focus** To understand the challenges of the early Church to carry Jesus' message to every corner of the Roman Empire | **Opening Prayer** **Discussion** How the Gospel was spread by the people and events of the first three centuries **Presentation** Read, discuss, and summarize content. **Scripture:** Acts of the Apostles 2:47, 6:7, 8:1–3, 15–21; Matthew 28:19 **Activity:** Create news reports based on the people and events in the Church's first century. | **Materials** Bibles; pens or pencils **Options** ***Called to Prayer and Liturgical Lessons*** **booklet:** See options for daily, seasonal, and liturgical prayer and lessons. **Enriching the Lesson (TG page 83)** Writing Job Descriptions for Christians . . . Then and Now |
| **DAY 2** **Teach and Apply** **Pages 22–23** **Focus** To discover how the Gospel was proclaimed in the first centuries of the Church's history | **Prayer** **Presentation** Read, discuss, and summarize content. **Activity:** Discuss leadership in the early Church and in today's Church. **Did you know:** The Apostles' Creed **Faith Connection:** Reflect on how to pass on the teaching of the Apostles. | **Materials** 3" × 5" cards; pens or pencils **Options** **Enriching the Lesson (TG page 83)** Explaining the Faith ***Additional Activities and Assessment Tools*** **booklet** Storyboard: Council of Jerusalem, page 9 |
| **DAY 3** **Teach/Apply and Connect** **Pages 24–25** **Focus** To discover how the practice of Christian worship developed in the early Church | **Prayer** **Presentation** Read, discuss, and summarize content. **Faith Connection:** Consider ways you take part in the liturgical life of the Church. **Our Church Makes a Difference** Learn about the two basic types of religious communities in the Church. | **Materials** pens or pencils **Options** **Enriching the Lesson (TG page 83)** Hearing Guest Speakers from Religious Communities |
| **DAY 4** **Connect and Apply** **Pages 26–27** **Focus** To discover that like our ancestors in faith, we are challenged to be active participants in the life and work of the Church | **Prayer** **What Difference Does Faith Make in My Life?** Understand the value of community and consider how you are a viable member of the Church community. **Faith Decision:** Identify how to be an active and responsible member of the parish and what to do to spread the Gospel. | **Materials** pens or pencils **Options** ***Additional Activities and Assessment Tools*** **booklet** Spiritual Growth Chart, page 10 |
| **DAY 5** **Pray and Review** **Page 28** | **Pray** Pray "Proclaim the Gospel." **Review** **Activities:** Complete the review exercises to reinforce the concepts of the chapter. **Family Discussion:** Encourage the students to share and discuss the question with their family this week. | **Materials** pens and pencils **Options** ***Additional Activities and Assessment Tools*** **booklet** Administer chapter 2 test. **Music Connection** (TG page 83) |

72

**Don't Forget!** You can make lesson planning a breeze—check out the **Online Lesson Planner** at www.FaithFirst.com for additional resources to enhance this chapter.

### *5-Day Lesson Planner*

### *Plan Outline*

Here is the lesson plan for teaching the chapter. The plan includes the lesson focus for each day of the week, objectives, and a list of materials you'll need.

### *Enrichment Activities*

A handy list of all *Faith First* enrichment materials available for this chapter is supplied for you.

### *Online Resources*

And don't forget to visit **www.FaithFirst.com** for additional chapter resources and online lesson-planning tools!

# Teaching Has Never Been Easier

*In* Faith First *you will follow this simple, effective process as you teach each lesson:*

- **Engage**
- **Teach and Apply**
- **Connect**

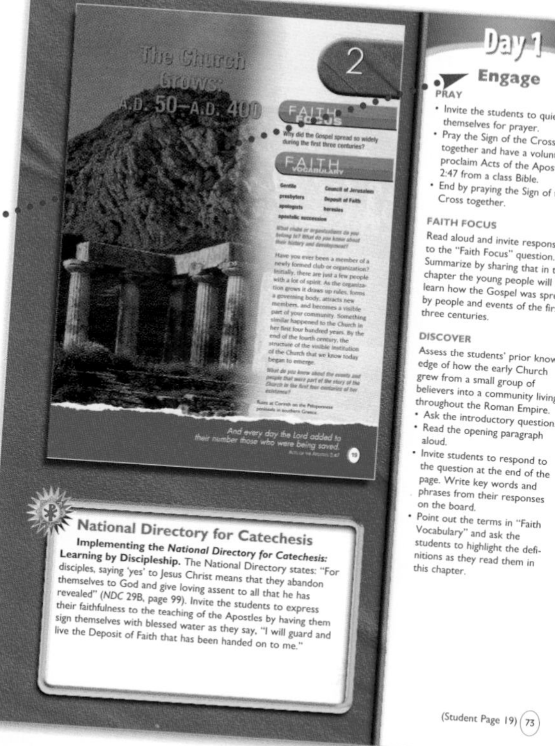

***Engage***

Each chapter begins with prayer and engages the students' interest in what you will be teaching.

***Teach and Apply***

On every two-page spread, first you teach and then you apply.

***Teach***

**Focus**—This simple question brings the students' attention to the core content of each day's lesson.

**Discover**—These are the building blocks of your lesson that will make the core content accessible to the students.

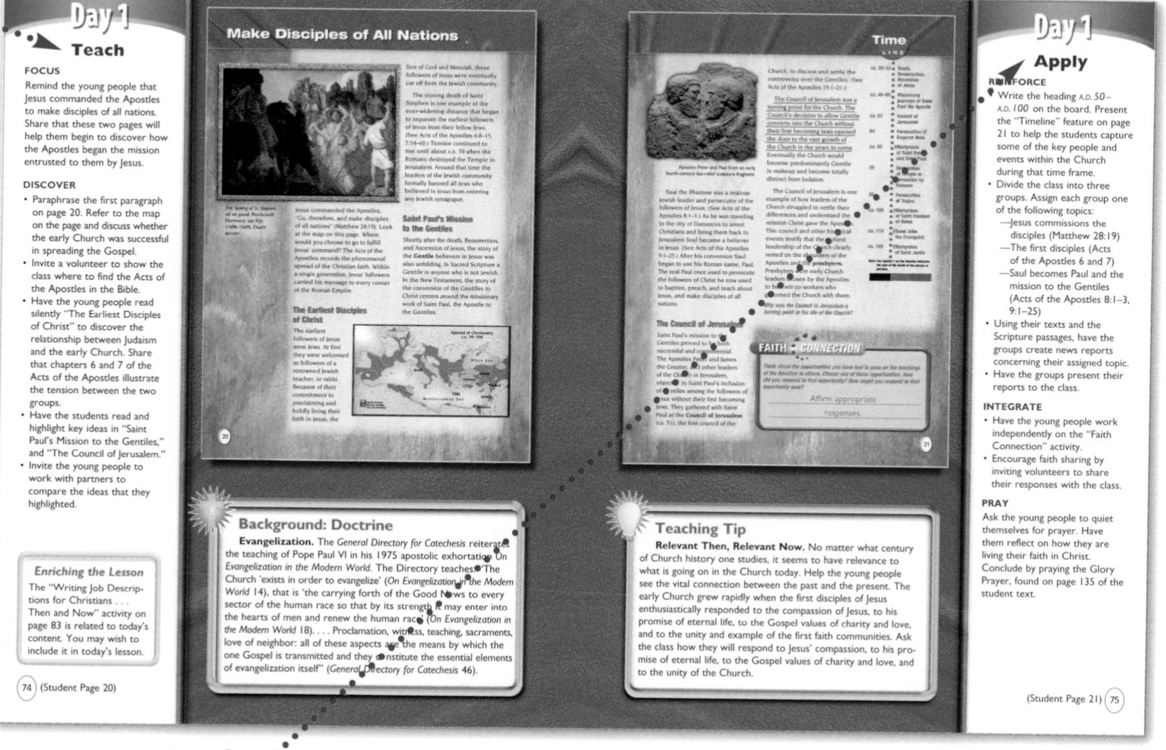

***Apply***

**Reinforce**—An easy way to reinforce learning. Answers to questions are underlined in the teacher guide.

**Integrate**—Using a variety of activities, the students have the opportunity to integrate what they have learned into their daily lives.

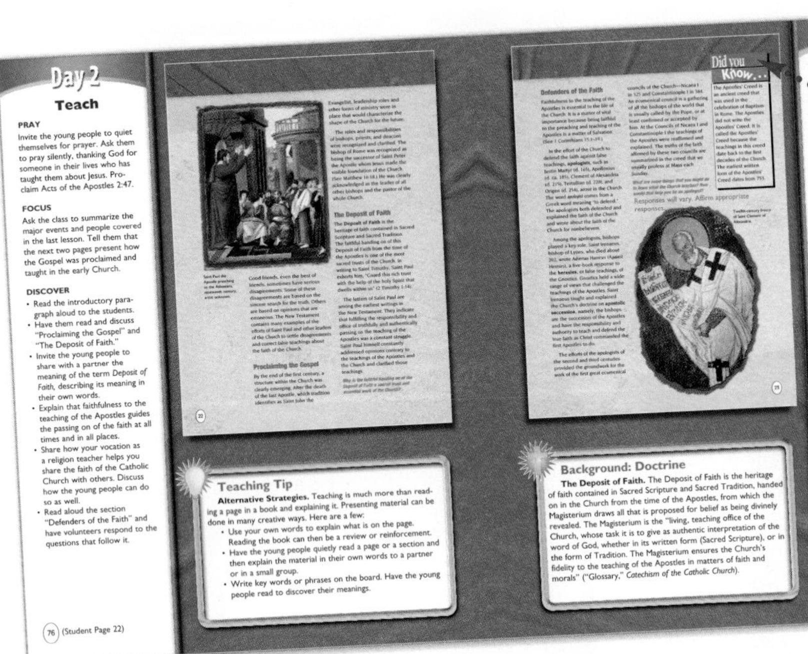

### *Did You Know?*

This feature contains saints and other faith-filled people who serve as role models for youth. It also includes facts about prayer and liturgy, definitions, biblical background, historical events, and other interesting information about the Catholic faith.

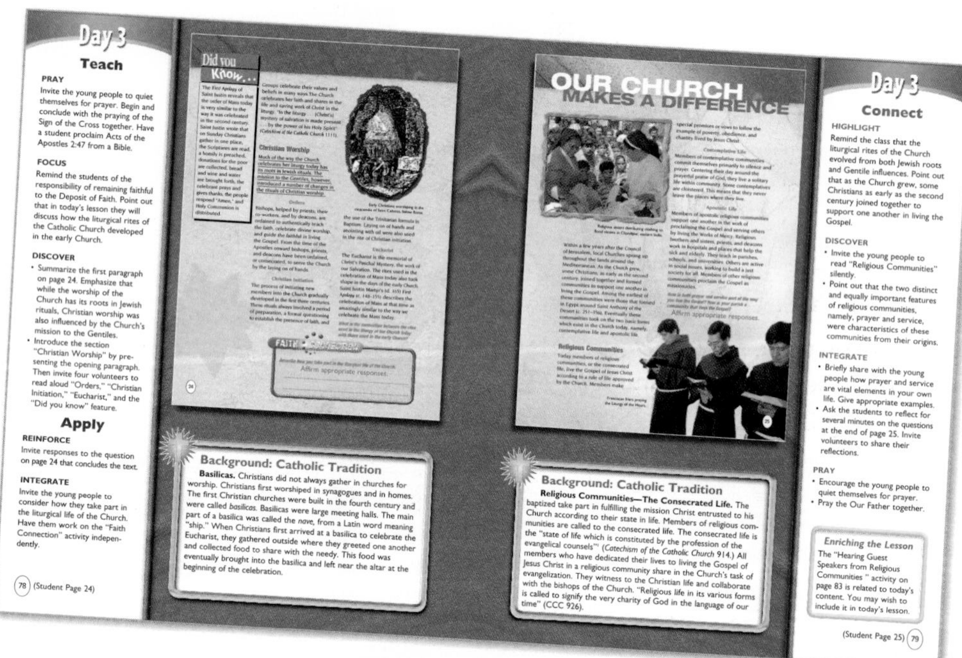

### *Background, Teaching Tips, and More*

Your lessons are filled with ideas, suggestions, and additional background information to help you make your lessons more effective for all the young people. You will find this material in the boxes at the bottom of each page in the teacher guide, including:

- *National Directory for Catechesis*
- Catholic Social Teaching
- Liturgy Tips
- Teaching Tips
- Special Needs
- Background

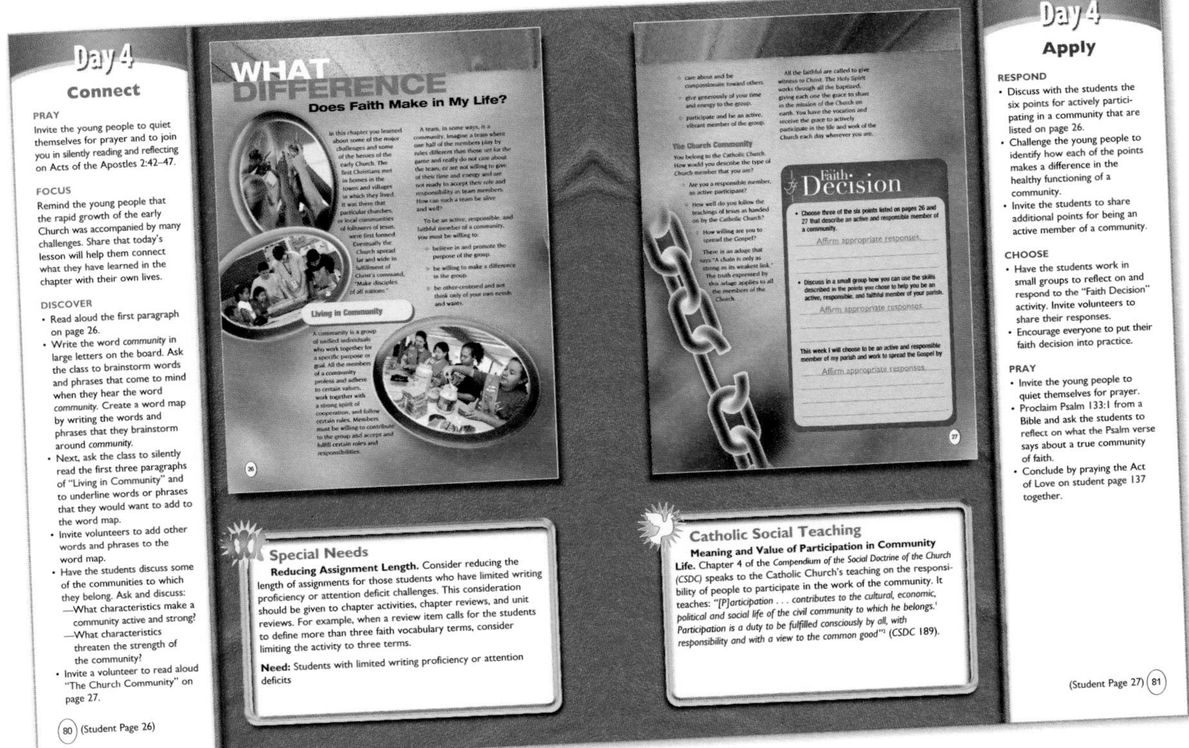

Day 4

**Connect**

PRAY

Invite the young people to quiet themselves for prayer and to join you in silently reading and reflecting on Acts of the Apostles 2:42–47.

FOCUS

Remind the young people that the rapid growth of the early Church was accompanied by many challenges. Share that today's lesson will help them connect what they have learned in the chapter with their own lives.

DISCOVER

- Read aloud the first paragraph on page 26.
- Write the word *community* in large letters on the board. Ask the class to brainstorm words and phrases that come to mind when they hear the word *community*. Create a word map by writing the words and phrases that they brainstorm around *community*.
- Next, ask the class to silently read the first three paragraphs of "Living in Community" and to underline words or phrases that they would want to add to the word map.
- Invite volunteers to add other words and phrases to the word map.
- Have the students discuss some of the communities to which they belong. Ask and discuss:
  —What characteristics make a community active and strong?
  —What characteristics threaten the strength of the community?
- Invite a volunteer to read aloud "The Church Community" on page 27.

80 (Student Page 26)

WHAT DIFFERENCE Does Faith Make in My Life?

Living in Community

26

The Church Community

Faith Decision

Affirm appropriate responses.

Affirm appropriate responses.

Affirm appropriate responses.

27

**Special Needs**

**Reducing Assignment Length.** Consider reducing the length of assignments for those students who have limited writing proficiency or attention deficit challenges. This consideration should be given to chapter activities, chapter reviews, and unit reviews. For example, when a review item calls for the students to define more than three faith vocabulary terms, consider limiting the activity to three terms.

**Need:** Students with limited writing proficiency or attention deficits

**Catholic Social Teaching**

**Meaning and Value of Participation in Community Life.** Chapter 4 of the *Compendium of the Social Doctrine of the Church* (CSDC) speaks to the Catholic Church's teaching on the responsibility of people to participate in the work of the community. It teaches: "[P]*articipation . . . contributes to the cultural, economic, political and social life of the civil community to which he belongs.*' *Participation is a duty to be fulfilled consciously by all, with responsibility and with a view to the common good*"[2] (CSDC 189).

Day 4

**Apply**

RESPOND

- Discuss with the students the six points for actively participating in a community that are listed on page 26.
- Challenge the young people to identify how each of the points makes a difference in the healthy functioning of a community.
- Invite the students to share additional points for being an active member of a community.

CHOOSE

- Have the students work in small groups to reflect on and respond to the "Faith Decision" activity. Invite volunteers to share their responses.
- Encourage everyone to put their faith decision into practice.

PRAY

- Invite the young people to quiet themselves for prayer.
- Proclaim Psalm 133:1 from a Bible and ask the students to reflect on what the Psalm verse says about a true community of faith.
- Conclude by praying the Act of Love on student page 137 together.

(Student Page 27) 81

## Connect

Without a connection to real life, the content remains only head knowledge. This step helps young people understand how they can act on and integrate their faith into their lives. Catholic identity develops by examining Catholic practices and understanding the significant place of the Church in the world.

### Our Church Makes a Difference

Students develop their Catholic identity by examining Catholic practices, important people, and historical events, and by deepening their understanding of the significant place of the Church in the world.

### What Difference Does Faith Make in My Life?

At the heart of each *Faith First* chapter, the young people are asked to apply what they have learned to their lives. In each chapter these pages provide a set of life skills that will help the students connect their faith and life experiences.

### Faith Decision

Young people are encouraged to do something intentionally and concretely each week to put into practice what has been learned. This important step helps young people recognize that faith is not meant to be isolated or compartmentalized. Faith is meant to be lived.

## *Pray and Review*

You began and ended each day with prayer. Now a complete prayer service brings the chapter to a close. Here is a chance to review and celebrate what the students have learned, as well as model the importance of communal prayer in our lives.

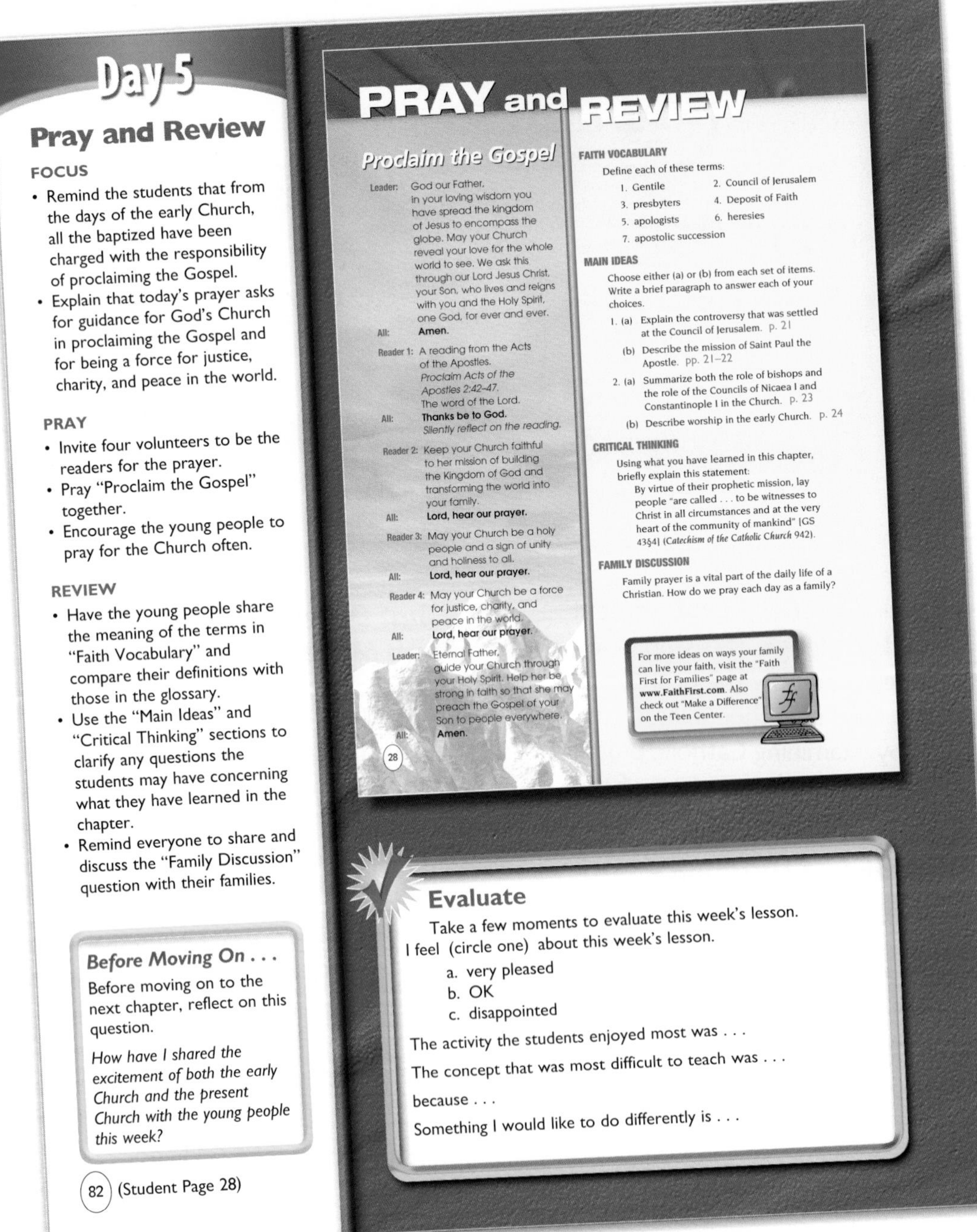

# Day 5

## Pray and Review

**FOCUS**

- Remind the students that from the days of the early Church, all the baptized have been charged with the responsibility of proclaiming the Gospel.
- Explain that today's prayer asks for guidance for God's Church in proclaiming the Gospel and for being a force for justice, charity, and peace in the world.

**PRAY**

- Invite four volunteers to be the readers for the prayer.
- Pray "Proclaim the Gospel" together.
- Encourage the young people to pray for the Church often.

**REVIEW**

- Have the young people share the meaning of the terms in "Faith Vocabulary" and compare their definitions with those in the glossary.
- Use the "Main Ideas" and "Critical Thinking" sections to clarify any questions the students may have concerning what they have learned in the chapter.
- Remind everyone to share and discuss the "Family Discussion" question with their families.

**Before Moving On . . .**

Before moving on to the next chapter, reflect on this question.

*How have I shared the excitement of both the early Church and the present Church with the young people this week?*

82 (Student Page 28)

# PRAY and REVIEW

## *Proclaim the Gospel*

**Leader:** God our Father,
in your loving wisdom you have spread the kingdom of Jesus to encompass the globe. May your Church reveal your love for the whole world to see. We ask this through our Lord Jesus Christ, your Son, who lives and reigns with you and the Holy Spirit, one God, for ever and ever.

**All:** **Amen.**

**Reader 1:** A reading from the Acts of the Apostles.
*Proclaim Acts of the Apostles 2:42–47.*
The word of the Lord.

**All:** **Thanks be to God.**
*Silently reflect on the reading.*

**Reader 2:** Keep your Church faithful to her mission of building the Kingdom of God and transforming the world into your family.

**All:** **Lord, hear our prayer.**

**Reader 3:** May your Church be a holy people and a sign of unity and holiness to all.

**All:** **Lord, hear our prayer.**

**Reader 4:** May your Church be a force for justice, charity, and peace in the world.

**All:** **Lord, hear our prayer.**

**Leader:** Eternal Father,
guide your Church through your Holy Spirit. Help her be strong in faith so that she may preach the Gospel of your Son to people everywhere.

**All:** **Amen.**

28

**FAITH VOCABULARY**

Define each of these terms:

1. Gentile
2. Council of Jerusalem
3. presbyters
4. Deposit of Faith
5. apologists
6. heresies
7. apostolic succession

**MAIN IDEAS**

Choose either (a) or (b) from each set of items. Write a brief paragraph to answer each of your choices.

1. (a) Explain the controversy that was settled at the Council of Jerusalem. p. 21
   (b) Describe the mission of Saint Paul the Apostle. pp. 21–22
2. (a) Summarize both the role of bishops and the role of the Councils of Nicaea I and Constantinople I in the Church. p. 23
   (b) Describe worship in the early Church. p. 24

**CRITICAL THINKING**

Using what you have learned in this chapter, briefly explain this statement:

By virtue of their prophetic mission, lay people "are called . . . to be witnesses to Christ in all circumstances and at the very heart of the community of mankind" [GS 43§4] (*Catechism of the Catholic Church* 942).

**FAMILY DISCUSSION**

Family prayer is a vital part of the daily life of a Christian. How do we pray each day as a family?

For more ideas on ways your family can live your faith, visit the "Faith First for Families" page at **www.FaithFirst.com**. Also check out "Make a Difference" on the Teen Center.

**Evaluate**

Take a few moments to evaluate this week's lesson.

I feel (circle one) about this week's lesson.

a. very pleased
b. OK
c. disappointed

The activity the students enjoyed most was . . .

The concept that was most difficult to teach was . . .

because . . .

Something I would like to do differently is . . .

**_Enriching the Lesson_**
These optional activities in every chapter offer you choices for class activities that include strategies for the many ways that children learn.

**_Music Connection_**
Every chapter is correlated to music that can be easily found in the most widely used Catholic hymnals. Using the hymns that the young people hear and sing at Mass as part of your lessons helps connect the lessons to the liturgical life of the Church.

# ENRICHING THE LESSON

### Writing Job Descriptions for Christians . . . Then and Now

**Purpose**
To reinforce the responsibility of all Christians to spread the Good News of Jesus in the twenty-first century as disciples in the early Church did (taught on pages 20–21)

**Directions**
- Create small study groups.
- Encourage everyone to read and study the Scripture passages referenced in the text on pages 20 and 21.
- Using what they have learned about the disciples of Jesus who lived between A.D. 50 and A.D. 100, have each group prepare a job description for those disciples.
- Next, have the groups create a job description for disciples of Jesus today.
- Allow time for the groups to present their job descriptions.

**Materials**
paper
pens or pencils

### Explaining the Faith

**Purpose**
To reinforce the concept that in every age and in every place Christians are called to explain the faith of the Church (pages 22–23)

**Directions**
- Have the students work in pairs, with one partner assuming the role of teacher and the other partner assuming the role of a non-believing thirteen-year-old.
- Assign each pair of students one of two of the articles of faith named in the Apostles' Creed.
- Have the "teacher" explain one of the articles of faith to the "non-believing thirteen-year-old."
- Then have the partners switch roles, with the new "teacher" explaining a second article of faith.
- Ask volunteers to demonstrate their explanations to the class as time allows.

**Materials**
none

### Hearing Guest Speakers from Religious Communities

**Purpose**
To reinforce that living in a religious community is one of the ways Christians choose to support one another in living the Gospel (taught on page 25)

**Directions**
- Invite two guest speakers who are members of a religious community to visit with your class and participate in a panel discussion on living in religious community. Note: One speaker can be from a contemplative community, the other from a community whose apostolate is service, such as health care, teaching, or serving the poor and vulnerable.
- Have the guests describe how they came to be a part of their community and the ways that being a part of the community helps them live the Gospel in concrete ways.
- Encourage the young people to ask questions.

**Materials**
none

### Music Connection

- "On a Journey Together," J. Angotti. *Gather Comprehensive (GC)* #653.
- "Somos Una Iglesia," E. Cortés. *Flor y Canto* #724.
- "Strength for the Journey," M. J. Poirer. *Voices As One* #87.
- "We Are Marching," (South African). *GC* #516.

83

# Catholic Social Teaching

*This NEW cross-curricular feature places religion at the heart of your entire school curriculum.*

Placed at the end of each unit, this feature invites the students to reflect on a principle of Catholic Social Teaching and apply it to real-life situations. Each feature contains:

- a description of a principle of Catholic Social Teaching,
- a contemporary dilemma related to the principle, and
- a "Making Connections" page, offering three project options related to:
  - —Creative Arts
  - —Math and Science
  - —Language Arts or Social Studies.

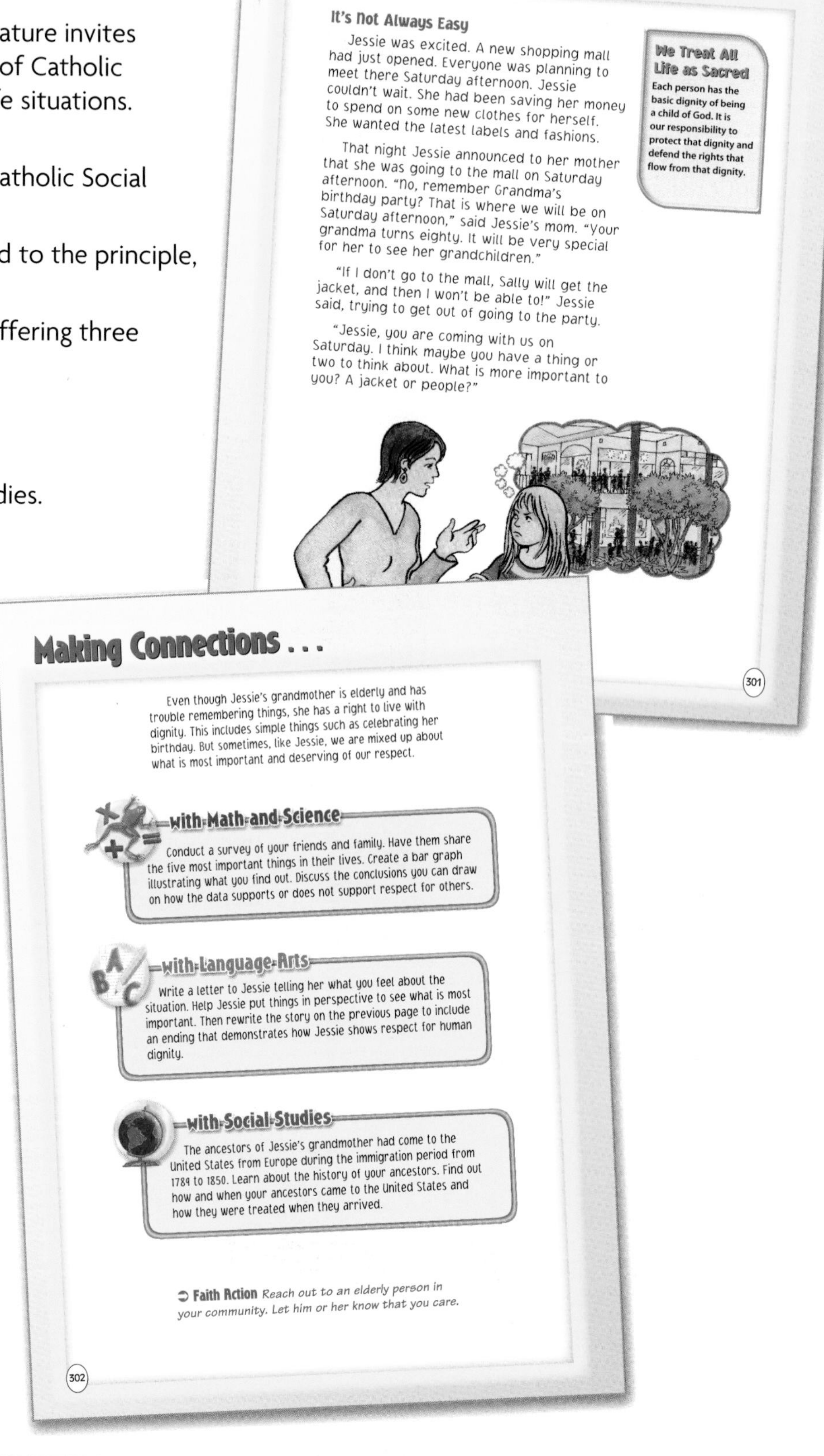

## Catholic Social Teaching

### It's Not Always Easy

Jessie was excited. A new shopping mall had just opened. Everyone was planning to meet there Saturday afternoon. Jessie couldn't wait. She had been saving her money to spend on some new clothes for herself. She wanted the latest labels and fashions.

That night Jessie announced to her mother that she was going to the mall on Saturday afternoon. "No, remember Grandma's birthday party? That is where we will be on Saturday afternoon," said Jessie's mom. "Your grandma turns eighty. It will be very special for her to see her grandchildren."

"If I don't go to the mall, Sally will get the jacket, and then I won't be able to!" Jessie said, trying to get out of going to the party.

"Jessie, you are coming with us on Saturday. I think maybe you have a thing or two to think about. What is more important to you? A jacket or people?"

**We Treat All Life as Sacred**

**Each person has the basic dignity of being a child of God. It is our responsibility to protect that dignity and defend the rights that flow from that dignity.**

301

## Making Connections . . .

Even though Jessie's grandmother is elderly and has trouble remembering things, she has a right to live with dignity. This includes simple things such as celebrating her birthday. But sometimes, like Jessie, we are mixed up about what is most important and deserving of our respect.

**with Math and Science**

Conduct a survey of your friends and family. Have them share the five most important things in their lives. Create a bar graph illustrating what you find out. Discuss the conclusions you can draw on how the data supports or does not support respect for others.

**with Language Arts**

Write a letter to Jessie telling her what you feel about the situation. Help Jessie put things in perspective to see what is most important. Then rewrite the story on the previous page to include an ending that demonstrates how Jessie shows respect for human dignity.

**with Social Studies**

The ancestors of Jessie's grandmother had come to the United States from Europe during the immigration period from 1784 to 1850. Learn about the history of your ancestors. Find out how and when your ancestors came to the United States and how they were treated when they arrived.

**Faith Action** *Reach out to an elderly person in your community. Let him or her know that you care.*

302

In grades 1–6, the two pages of student material appear in the student text. In junior high, the two pages appear as blackline activity masters in the teacher's guide. (See facing page.)

*Full teacher support is provided for this exciting new feature.*

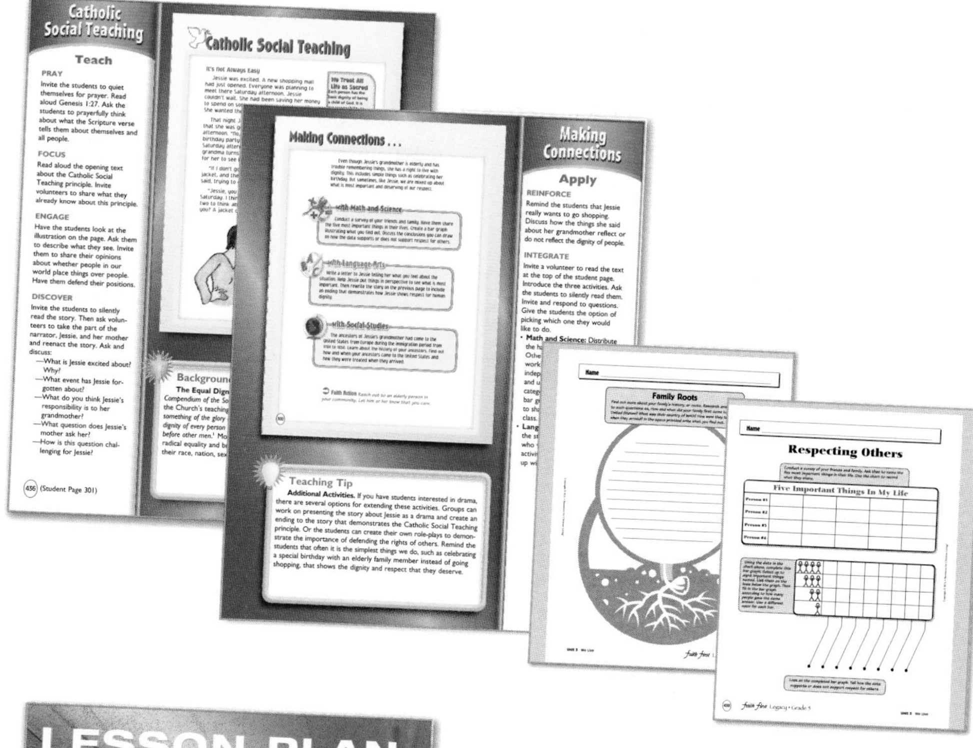


### Grades 1–6

At the end of each unit in the guide, you will find a complete wraparound plan incorporating RCL's popular Teach and Apply methodology, plus two blackline masters accompanying the activities.

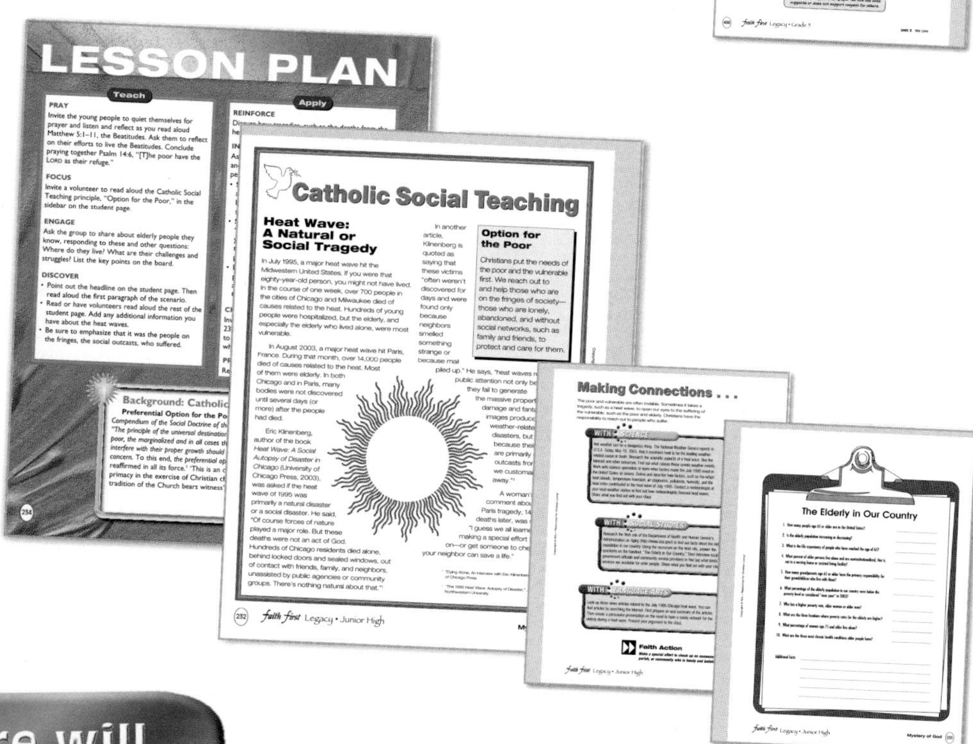


### Junior High

Each cross-curricular feature includes a full teaching plan with three blackline masters containing:

- a presentation of the Catholic Social Teaching principle,
- a dilemma similar to that in the elementary texts, and
- a supporting project blackline master worksheet.

**This feature will help your students make a difference!**

# Faith First Supplements

## Faith First Legacy Edition Junior High Class Kits

Each kit contains:

- ***Activities and Assessment Tools***—These time-saving reproducible blackline masters provide activities that extend learning in class or at home, including chapter reviews, unit tests, and other assessment instruments.
- ***Called to Prayer and Liturgical Lessons***—Touch young people's hearts with a variety of easy-to-use and practical prayer formats, plus twenty-three two-page reproducible lessons for Advent, Christmas, Lent, Easter, and Pentecost. Connect your classes to the liturgical life of the parish community.
- ***Helping Kids Live Their Faith***—Highlighting the seven principles of Catholic Social Teaching, this book helps you encourage and support young people's service and mission to the Church and to the world.

## Faith First Videos

Innovative videos bring your lessons to life with a variety of segments that reinforce and integrate faith formation.

## *Religion Coordinator's Manual*

This manual provides everything the Religion Coordinator needs to implement *Faith First* in your school. It includes ideas for teacher training, for parent meetings, and for using *Faith First* as the foundation for religious education in your whole school community.

## *Keeping Faith First: A Resource Supporting the Whole Community of Faith*

Bring together your whole school community with this unique resource. Help parents and other adults explore the fundamental insights of our tradition. Encourage them to share their stories of faith, and challenge them to be of service in the world. Plus visit **www.WholeCommunityCatechesis.com**.

# FaithFirst.com

**FaithFirst.com** brings living and learning about faith into the twenty-first century. RCL is proud to have been recognized with the Technology Award by the National Conference for Catechetical Leadership.

**FaithFirst.com** enables you to access practical and creative resources for all of your lessons online when and where you need them—twenty-four hours a day, seven days a week.

With **FaithFirst.com** your student books are constantly updated and expanded beyond the printed pages with learning games, chapter reviews, saints, lectionary-based lessons, current events, and so much more!

**FaithFirst.com** encourages parents to spend time online with their children, motivates children to want to learn more about their faith, and empowers you with the latest resources. And remember, every minute a child spends at **FaithFirst.com** brings faith into the home and extends your lessons beyond class time.

**NEW**
**Special Web site for Program Directors & School Religion Coordinators**

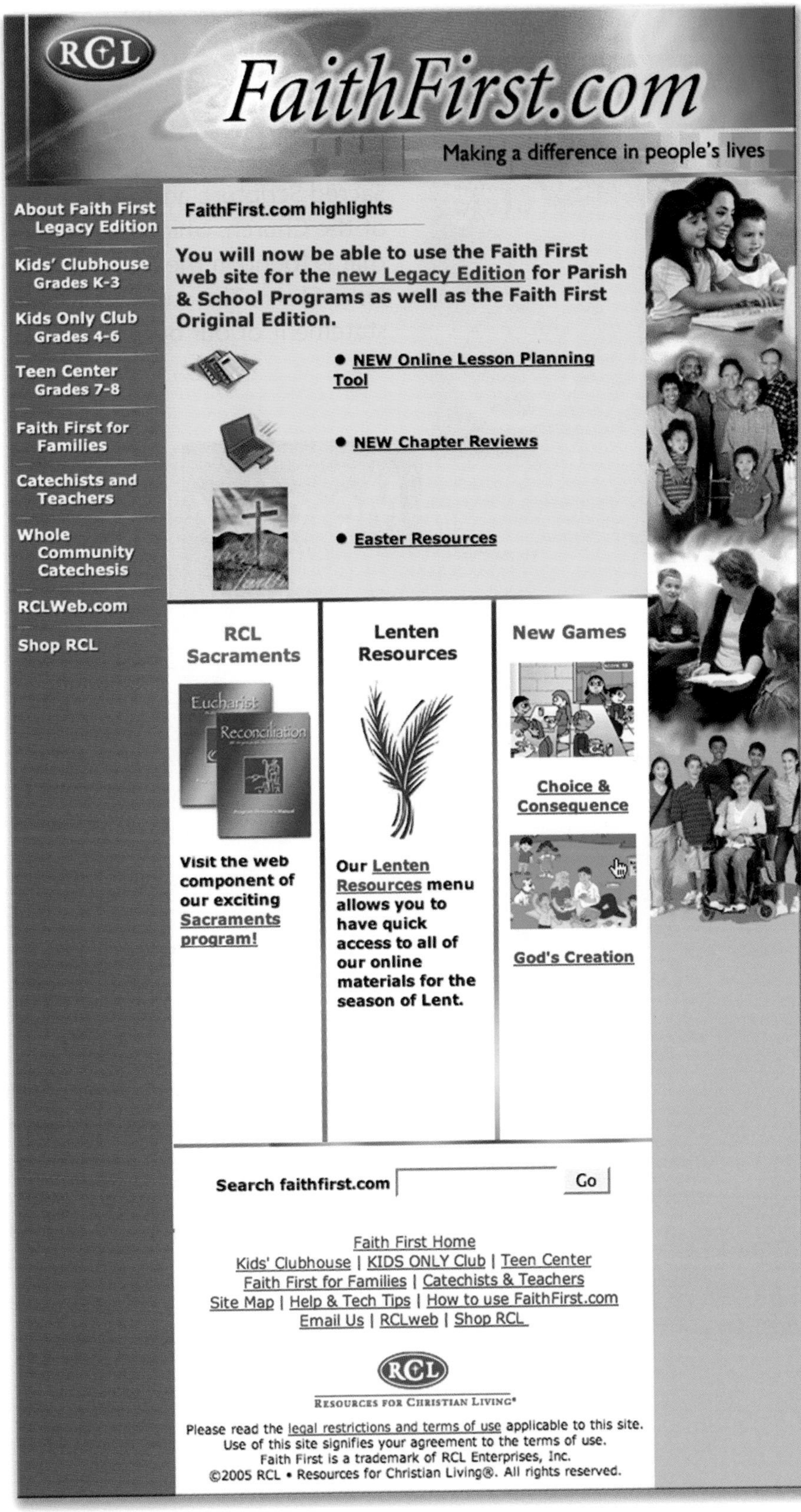

RCL
*FaithFirst.com*
Making a difference in people's lives

About Faith First Legacy Edition
Kids' Clubhouse Grades K-3
Kids Only Club Grades 4-6
Teen Center Grades 7-8
Faith First for Families
Catechists and Teachers
Whole Community Catechesis
RCLWeb.com
Shop RCL

**FaithFirst.com highlights**

**You will now be able to use the Faith First web site for the new Legacy Edition for Parish & School Programs as well as the Faith First Original Edition.**

- NEW Online Lesson Planning Tool
- NEW Chapter Reviews
- Easter Resources

**RCL Sacraments**

Eucharist
Reconciliation

Visit the web component of our exciting Sacraments program!

**Lenten Resources**

Our Lenten Resources menu allows you to have quick access to all of our online materials for the season of Lent.

**New Games**

Choice & Consequence

God's Creation

Search faithfirst.com Go

Faith First Home
Kids' Clubhouse | KIDS ONLY Club | Teen Center
Faith First for Families | Catechists & Teachers
Site Map | Help & Tech Tips | How to use FaithFirst.com
Email Us | RCLweb | Shop RCL

RCL
RESOURCES FOR CHRISTIAN LIVING®

# Junior High

*Five texts, twelve chapters each, can be used interchangeably and enable you to design up to a two-year curriculum for junior high students.*

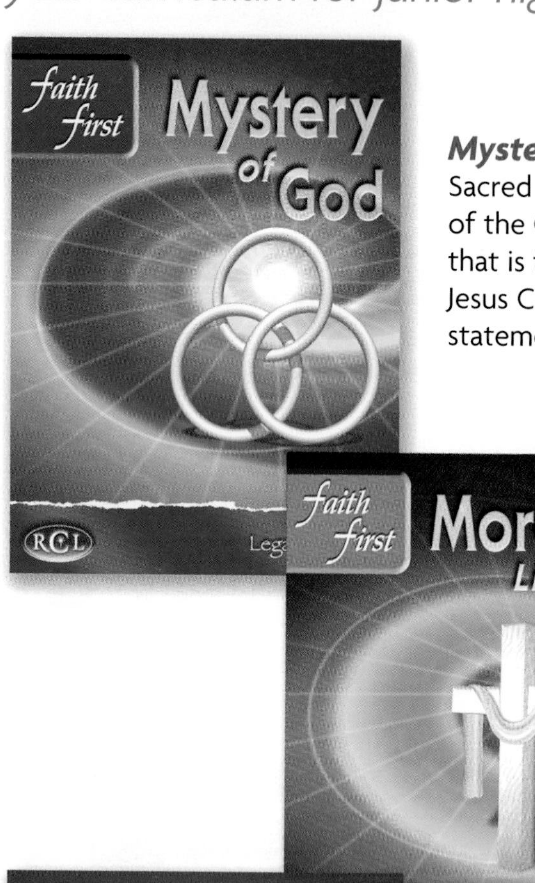


***Mystery of God***
Sacred Scripture and Sacred Tradition are the source of the faith of the Church, which is grounded in the fullness of Revelation that is found in the life, death, Resurrection, and Ascension of Jesus Christ. The students examine the Creed as the summary statement of our beliefs.

***Morality: Life in Christ***
As persons created in God's image, we are guided by the Ten Commandments and the Beatitudes to live a successful moral life. The principles of Catholic morality, including the Social Teachings of the Catholic Church, help young teens make important life choices in their daily lives.

faith first
Church and Sacraments
RCL
Legacy Edition

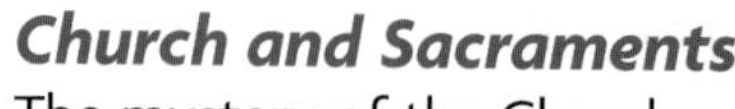

***Church and Sacraments***
The mystery of the Church unfolds as the students discover how believers take on the responsibility of continuing Christ's work on earth. The study of the sacraments centers on how they bind us together as a community of faith.

### *Jesus in the New Testament*

The life and message of Jesus Christ are explored in the four Gospels with emphasis on understanding and praying the Scriptures. The students are also introduced to the writings of Saint Paul, other New Testament letters, and the Book of Revelation.

### *Church History*

Every Christian participates in the journey of faith that begins with Jesus and the Apostles and is guided by the Holy Spirit. By studying the history of the Church, students will be introduced to the major themes, events, and people that have helped build the Church during this ongoing journey.

# In-Service for Teachers

QuickStart for Religion Teachers

*An Interactive Workshop on the Catechetical Ministry*

**Welcome to Faith First!**

As a Catholic School religion teacher, you have agreed to serve this year as a *Faith First* catechist. Faith First invites you, the young people, their families, and the whole faith community to discover the difference that Catholic faith can make.

Faith is rooted in God's call to all people, fully revealed in Jesus Christ, guided by the Holy Spirit. *Faith First* is rooted in five principles:

- **Faith is a gift from God. It is also our free response to all that God has revealed to us.**
- **Faith includes not only an intellectual understanding of doctrine but also a conversion of heart.**
- **Faith grows and develops throughout life.**
- **Faith is lived in community.**
- **Faith-filled people look at their actions and the world differently. All life changes when seen through the eyes of faith.**

As you begin this workshop, take a few moments to reflect on your personal faith.

*In what ways do I live my Catholic faith day by day?*

*Who has been a strong influence in my life of faith?*

25

## *Teacher's Guide*

*Faith First Legacy Edition* provides a "Quickstart for Religion Teachers" in the teacher guide. (See pages 25–45.) This interactive workshop is supported by a video component as well as meeting designs found in the *Religion Coordinator's Manual.*

"Quickstart for Religion Teachers" helps teachers understand:

- the role of the religion teacher,
- the tasks of catechesis as found in the *General Directory for Catechesis,*
- the human methodologies as outlined in the *National Directory for Catechesis,*
- the important task of teaching others to pray,
- the creation of a good environment for catechesis,
- and much more.

## *In-Service Video*

The in-service video is divided into two parts. The first part supports the "Quickstart for Religion Teachers" section of the teacher guide. The second part concentrates on understanding the approach of *Faith First* and teaching your *Faith First* lessons.

## *Religion Coordinator's Manual*

The *Religion Coordinator's Manual* for *Faith First Legacy Edition* is filled with information, professional articles, and reproducible blackline masters for teachers and families to help make your school's faith formation program strong and effective. It includes:

- professional articles,
- models for teacher and parent in-service sessions with handouts,
- practical resources for incorporating prayer and ritual,
- suggestions for using media in teaching,
- *Faith First Legacy* cumulative scope and sequence chart and glossary,
- *Faith First Legacy* calendaring options,
- and much, much more.

# QuickStart for Religion Teachers

## *An Interactive Workshop on the Catechetical Ministry*

### *Welcome to Faith First!*

As a Catholic school religion teacher, you have agreed to serve this year as a *Faith First* catechist. *Faith First* invites you, the young people, their families, and the whole faith community to discover the difference that the Catholic faith can make.

Faith is rooted in God's call to all people, fully revealed in Jesus Christ, guided by the Holy Spirit. *Faith First* is rooted in five principles:

- **Faith is a gift from God. It is also our free response to all that God has revealed to us.**
- **Faith includes not only an intellectual understanding of doctrine but also a conversion of heart.**
- **Faith grows and develops throughout life.**
- **Faith is lived in community.**
- **Faith-filled people look at their actions and the world differently. All life changes when seen through the eyes of faith.**

As you begin this workshop, take a few moments to reflect on your personal faith.

**For REFLECTION**

*In what ways do I live my Catholic faith day by day?*

*Who has been a strong influence in my life of faith?*

# Welcome to Faith First

In choosing to teach a religion class, you are doing more than teaching children concepts about the Catholic faith; you are giving witness to what you believe. In doing these things, you are assisting in the faith formation of the young people in your care. In other words, you are also a catechist. You are joining a long line of dedicated believers stretching back through the ages who have answered God's call to share their faith with others. Like them, you have been touched by your experience of Jesus Christ and are unable to keep the Good News to yourself.

As important as your role is, it is not the most important one in the faith formation of your learners. That role is reserved for their parents; your role is to support them. You assist in their children's faith formation by making more explicit the teachings of the Catholic Church and helping the young people celebrate their faith and apply her teachings to their lives.

Catechists echo the Word of God to deepen understanding in others and to deepen conversion of their minds and hearts to God. You may be a little daunted by this definition, and wonder if it is more than you bargained for when you became a religion teacher. Relax! Your concerns were felt by our ancestors in faith—Moses, Jeremiah, Peter, and Mary. But with God's help they did great things, and you will too!

The *National Directory for Catechesis* published in 2005 reminds us of a number of important qualities of catechists and Catholic school religion teachers. These qualities reflect the mission of the Catholic school, so you have probably developed some of these characteristics already. Others you will develop along the way. As you grow in your commitment to this ministry of the word, you will find that you are doing what all good teachers do well—learning by doing. Some of the qualities of a Catholic school religion teacher are described on the next page.

## Qualities of Religion Teachers

1. **You are responding to a vocational *call*** from the Lord expressed through the Catholic school. You have agreed to catechize others and to continue growing in your own faith and in your knowledge of Sacred Scripture and Tradition.
2. **You are a witness to the Gospel message of Jesus Christ** as taught by his Church. You believe in this message and in its power to change the lives of all who believe in it. You model for your learners what it means to be a follower of Jesus Christ.
3. **You are committed to the Church** and try to express the teachings of the Catholic Church as clearly as you can. You constantly test your own understanding of your faith against the Church's wisdom.
4. **You build a faith community among your learners** because you have experienced the power and importance of faith in your own life, through your participation in your parish and, most especially, through your love of and participation in the Eucharist. You encourage and prepare your learners to gather at the Eucharist, "the source and summit of the Christian life" (*Dogmatic Constitution on the Church [Lumen gentium]* 11), and to live lives of forgiveness, reconciliation, and peacemaking.
5. **You are dedicated to the mission of the Church,** proclaiming the Good News, seeking out and responding to the needs of others, and teaching your learners to do the same.
6. **You are willing to acquire the basic skills and abilities that are needed** to conduct effective catechetical sessions. These skills are explained in the catechist formation guidelines of your diocese.

You can read more about the catechetical ministry in chapters 2 and 8 of the *National Directory for Catechesis.*

**For REFLECTION**

*Place a star next to the qualities that are your greatest strengths. Place a check next to the ones you want to work on this year. Discuss your assessment with another teacher and with your school religion coordinator, who can help you develop a growth plan for the coming year.*

# What Is My Task?

*[T]he definitive aim of catechesis is to put people not only in touch but in communion, in intimacy, with Jesus Christ.*

CATECHESIS IN OUR TIME 5

As a religion teacher in a Catholic school, you do a lot of different things. First and most importantly of all, you are a model for young people of what it means to be a disciple of Jesus Christ. That does not mean that you are perfect. It means that you remember the young people are watching you so that they can learn what it means to be a Catholic. So you try your best to look, act, and sound like one. You are inviting young people to become disciples of Jesus Christ and to commit themselves to the way of life that he teaches. To deliver your message, you will, at various times, make short presentations, tell stories, facilitate dialogue and activities, and lead prayer.

The *General Directory for Catechesis (GDC)* published in 1997 guides the worldwide Church in her catechetical mission. It identifies six important tasks of catechesis (GDC 85–87). Reflect on these tasks that are listed on the next page and assess your abilities in each of these areas before you begin the year.

## Tasks of Catechesis

1. **Promoting knowledge of the faith.** Catechists introduce their learners to all that has been revealed through Jesus Christ by initiating them gradually into the whole truth revealed through Scripture and Tradition. Your *Faith First* student text and teacher guide will show you what to teach this year.
2. **Liturgical education.** As a catechist you help students understand the Church's sacramental life and give them an experience of the signs, symbols, gestures, prayers, and creeds of the Church. The weekly and seasonal *Faith First* prayer experiences will give the young people many opportunities to learn and live the Church's life of prayer.
3. **Moral formation.** Moral catechesis involves both the announcement of the Good News through your proclamation of the Gospel call to moral living and your presentation of what the Church's Tradition teaches about this message. *Faith First* will help you with the best language and strategies to use.
4. **Teaching to pray.** As you teach about the Our Father, the prayer that Jesus taught, you will introduce young people ever more deeply to the forms of prayer that it includes: adoration, praise, thanksgiving, intercession, petition, and expression of sorrow for sins, all expressed with the intimacy that comes from knowing we are children of God. *Faith First* will provide you with a wide variety of prayer experiences.
5. **Education for community life.** You are leading young people into a way of life that you are already experiencing. You invite them to join a loving community of faith, to live simply and humbly, to care for the poor and alienated, to forgive as they wish to be forgiven, and to join in common prayer. Your classroom should be a daily experience of Christian community for your students.
6. **Missionary initiation.** Catechesis prepares young people to live the Gospel in daily life and to work to prepare the way for the coming of the Kingdom of God. *Faith First* is filled with suggestions for outreach activities and service projects to build in students a sense of the Church's mission.

**For REFLECTION**

*For which task of catechesis do I feel most qualified? Which seems most daunting? Share with another religion teacher the strengths and concerns you bring to the catechetical vocation.*

**For FURTHER STUDY**

*See* **Echoes of Faith "Roles of the Catechist"** *module.* **Echoes of Faith** *is a video-assisted resource for the formation and enrichment of catechists in Catholic parishes and schools. It has been developed by the National Conference for Catechetical Leadership and produced by RCL. For more information call 877-275-4725.*

# Teaching Others to Pray

> ***Liturgical formation . . . must explain what the Christian liturgy is, and what the sacraments are. It must also however, offer an experience of the different kinds of celebration and it must make symbols, gestures, etc. known and loved.***
>
> GENERAL DIRECTORY FOR CATECHESIS **87**

You have learned that one of the important tasks of catechesis is teaching others to pray. Prayer is listening with openness to God's word and responding in faith, hope, and love. Our response involves a willingness to spend time with God, to ponder the words of Scripture, to discern his message to us, and to respond with our whole selves—body, mind, and heart.

Worship is simply the prayer of the Church. We gather together to lay our lives before God the Father, to praise him and give thanks for the gift of his love, and to join with his Son in offering our lives for his service. That is why the *Catechism of the Catholic Church* (CCC) refers to liturgy as "the participation of the People of God in 'the work of God'"[1] (CCC 1069). Liturgical celebrations weave together signs and symbols drawn from our human experience—words and actions, singing and music, and sacred images. An artful blending of these elements produces a worship experience that can evoke for us the mystery of God and lead us to a fruitful response.

As young people experience gestures, such as signing, anointing, blessing, and kneeling, within the intimacy of your classroom setting, you will be preparing them to participate more fully in the worship of the whole Church. Just as you have certain ways of praying with which you are most comfortable, you will find that your students have their preferences too. The many approaches to prayer that *Faith First* incorporates will provide a true school of prayer for your students.

## How *Faith First* Will Help You

*Faith First* includes:

- an exposition in the student text of the rich variety of the Church's tradition of prayer, liturgy, and sacraments.
- beginning and closing prayer experiences for each day's lesson.
- a rich variety of weekly prayer experiences using the signs, symbols, and gestures of the Church's liturgy whenever appropriate.
- full instructions on how to lead each prayer experience.

**For REFLECTION**

***How do I create opportunities in my daily life to hear the voice of God speaking to me?***

***What forms of prayer will I most enjoy leading for my learners?***

**For FURTHER STUDY**

*See* **Echoes of Faith "Prayer and Spirituality"** *and* **"Liturgy and Sacraments"** *modules.*

> ***When he saw the crowds, he went up the mountain, and after he had sat down, his disciples came to him. He began to teach them.***
>
> MATTHEW **5:1–2**

Through the centuries, teachers have taught outdoors under trees, in churches, and in public places. Jesus taught while seated on hillsides, walking along roads, and at dinner tables. Twenty-first-century teachers in the United States most often teach in classrooms, in homes, or in school halls or meeting rooms. Your religion class probably takes place within your normal teaching space. However, remember that religion class, even though it relies on sound educational methodology, is concerned with conversion and faith formation. It is a sacred task requiring the creation of a sacred space.

**Your Prayer Center.** Every catechetical space should be centered around an appropriately decorated prayer center. Here are some suggestions:

- Cover the table with an attractive cloth that matches the color of the liturgical season.
- Place a crucifix at the highest point in the prayer center.
- Place a candle on the surface of the table as a sign of the light of faith. Light the candle only during the prayer service. Use an electric candle if school fire regulations require it.
- Enthrone an open Bible on the table. Page 53 of this teacher's guide provides a reproducible prayer service for enthroning the Bible on the first day of class.
- Place a plant or other object(s) in the prayer center to symbolize the lesson theme or the liturgical season.

# The Faith First Approach

*Faith First* lessons are built upon three foundations: the **Word of God** clearly expressed in Scripture and the Church's Tradition, **worship and prayer**, and the **call to service** for the Kingdom of God.

Each *Faith First* chapter teaches as Jesus did:

- **Engage**
  Learners reflect on life experiences and recall prior knowledge about faith concepts.
- **Teach and Apply**
  On each content page, first we teach, then we apply. We teach the story of faith and challenge learners to assimilate concepts and apply them to what they already know.
- **Connect**
  The "Our Church Makes a Difference" page and the two "What Difference Does Faith Make in My Life?" pages help connect chapter concepts to the Church's life and to the lives of the learners.

## A Spiral Approach

*Faith First* uses a spiral approach to curriculum development that incorporates doctrine, Scripture, and liturgy.

**Doctrine**

- Each year in grades 1–6, *Faith First* offers four units correlating to the four pillars, or parts, of the *Catechism of the Catholic Church:*
  —We Believe (Creed),
  —We Worship (Liturgy and Sacraments),
  —We Live (Morality), and
  —We Pray (Prayer and Spirituality).
- We repeat key concepts each year on the Teach and Apply pages. Core content is introduced in primary grades, then developed and reinforced in middle and upper grades.

**Scripture**

Sacred Scripture passages in each lesson and special chapters dedicated to Scripture in each unit deepen the students' understanding and challenge them to live the biblical message.

**Liturgy**

- Weekly prayer experiences introduce the young people to the rich and varied tradition of the Church's prayer and worship.
- Twenty-three special seasonal lessons help the young people and their families explore and celebrate seasonal feasts and seasons of the Church's liturgical year.

On the next five pages, you will see a detailed outline of what you will be teaching this year. Study the outline of the junior high content on the scope and sequence chart, then respond to the reflection questions below.

**For REFLECTION**

***What topics do I feel most comfortable teaching this year?***

***What topics would I like to learn more about?***

**For FURTHER STUDY**

*The five* **Echoes of Faith "Theology"** *modules—***"I Believe/We Believe" (Creed), "Liturgy and Sacraments," "Catholic Morality," "Prayer and Spirituality,"** *and* **"Introduction to the Scriptures"***—will offer you an excellent introduction to the main themes of Catholic teaching.*

# Scope and Sequence

## Mystery of God

## UNIT ONE: The Revelation of God

### CHAPTER 1—WE BELIEVE

**Faith Concepts:** The quest for God; knowledge of God through creation; reason; divine Revelation; faith; Saint Albert the Great
**Sacred Scripture:** Psalm 27:8, 1 Corinthians 13:12
**Faith Vocabulary:** Divine Revelation; faith; mystery
**Did you know . . . :** Saint Augustine; atheism; agnosticism; secularism; secular humanism
**Our Church Makes a Difference:** Catholic education
**Faith-life Skills:** Getting in Touch with God
**Prayer:** An act of faith
***Catechism of the Catholic Church* (*CCC*):** 27, 32–34, 50–53, 153–162

### CHAPTER 2—THE WORD OF GOD

**Faith Concepts:** Inspiration of the Bible; canon of Sacred Scripture; oral tradition; literary genres; Covenants with Noah, Abraham, and Moses; promise of a new Covenant; Sacred Tradition
**Sacred Scripture:** Acts of the Apostles 6:4; Genesis 2:17, 9:8–10; 12–13
**Faith Vocabulary:** Bible, canon of Sacred Scripture, covenant, inspiration, literary genre, oral tradition
**Did you know . . . :** Worldwide use of the Bible; The Home of Abraham and Sarah
**Our Church Makes a Difference:** The Liturgy of the Word
**Faith-life Skills:** Communication Skills
**Prayer:** Praying the Scriptures
***CCC*:** 54–67, 80, 105–108, 110, 120

### CHAPTER 3—THE MAN BORN BLIND: A SCRIPTURE STORY

**Faith Concepts:** The Gospel According to John; faith in Jesus; obstacles to seeing with eyes of faith
**Sacred Scripture:** John 9:2–7, 33–34, 35–38, 20:30–31
**Faith Vocabulary:** Book of Signs; Fourth Gospel; miracle
**Did you know . . . :** Saint John the Apostle and Evangelist
**Our Church Makes a Difference:** Christian Initiation
**Faith-life Skills:** Obstacles to Seeing with Eyes of Faith
**Prayer:** Signing of the Senses
***CCC*:** 124, 514

### CHAPTER 4—THE MYSTERY OF CREATION

**Faith Concepts:** Attributes of God; the biblical accounts of the creation of humans; spiritual soul; original justice; original sin; new creation; Jesus the new Adam
**Sacred Scripture:** Genesis 1:31; Romans 1:20; Deuteronomy 6:4–5; Samuel 7:28; Isaiah 54:10; 1 John 4:8; Genesis 1:26, 27, 2:7
**Faith Vocabulary:** Attribute, eternal, omnipresence, divine Providence, soul
**Did you know . . . :** Saint Teresa of Avila
**Our Church Makes a Difference:** Catholic high school service projects
**Faith-life Skills:** Building Relationships
**Prayer:** Praise God
***CCC*:** 202–221, 302–305, 356–373, 378–379, 385–409

### CHAPTER 5—GOD: FATHER, SON, AND HOLY SPIRIT

**Faith Concepts:** The mystery of God; the Holy Trinity: nature and Persons; the work of the Trinity; creation; salvation
**Sacred Scripture:** Genesis 1:2; John 1:1–3, 14:10, 16–17, 26
**Faith Vocabulary:** Dogma of faith; Holy Trinity
**Did you know . . . :** Saint Athanasius and the first Council of Nicaea; divine mission of the Holy Trinity
**Our Church Makes a Difference:** The Christian family
**Faith-life Skills:** Balancing Relationships
**Prayer:** Apostles' Creed
***CCC*:** 230, 232–249, 257–260

## UNIT TWO: The Gift of Salvation

### CHAPTER 6—JESUS CHRIST, THE SON OF GOD

**Faith Concepts:** Mary: blessed, ever-Virgin, Immaculate Conception, Mother of God; Incarnation; Jesus, true God and true man; infancy narratives; public ministry of Jesus
**Sacred Scripture:** Galatians 4:4; John 1:1, 14; Luke 4:18–19; Philippians 2:11; Mark 1:15
**Faith Vocabulary:** Immaculate Conception; Incarnation; Lord; YHWH
**Did you know . . . :** Ecumenical councils
**Our Church Makes a Difference:** Symbols for Jesus Christ
**Faith-life Skills:** Respecting and Accepting Differences
**Prayer:** Benedictus ***CCC*:** 422–507, 512–560

### CHAPTER 7—THE TRANSFIGURATION OF JESUS: A SCRIPTURE STORY

**Faith Concepts:** Mountains in Sacred Scripture; Jewish feast of Tabernacles; the Transfiguration; Jesus, the fulfillment of the Law and the prophets; the suffering Messiah
**Sacred Scripture:** Psalm 89:9, 13; Matthew 16:15–16, 17:2–13
**Faith Vocabulary:** Messiah; Transfiguration
**Did you know . . . :** Mount Carmel, Mount Tabor, Mount Hermon
**Our Church Makes a Difference:** Blessed Mother Teresa of Calcutta
**Faith-life Skills:** Seeing with the Eyes of Faith
**Prayer:** The Gloria
***CCC*:** 554–556

### CHAPTER 8—THE SUFFERING SERVANT: A SCRIPTURE STORY

**Faith Concepts:** The Book of the Prophet Isaiah: the servant songs, the Servant of YHWH, the suffering Servant; the sinless servant; the suffering Church; Good Friday
**Sacred Scripture:** Hebrews 5:8–9; Isaiah 52:13–15, 53:1–2, 53:3, 7–8, 11–12
**Faith Vocabulary:** Prophets; suffering Servant
**Did you know . . . :** Prophetic books of the Old Testament
**Our Church Makes a Difference:** Archbishop Helder Camara
**Faith-life Skills:** Dealing with Loss
**Prayer:** Veneration of the Cross
***CCC*:** 601

### CHAPTER 9—JESUS' PASSION AND DEATH

**Faith Concepts:** Original justice and original sin; origin and problem of evil; Jesus the New Adam; Jesus' death and descent to the dead
**Sacred Scripture:** John 19:30, Genesis 2:17, 1 Peter 4:6
**Faith Vocabulary:** Expiation; original sin; Paschal Mystery; Redemption
**Did you know . . . :** Moral and physical evil; ancient homily
**Our Church Makes a Difference:** Stations of the Cross
**Faith-life Skills:** From Sadness to Hope
**Prayer:** Litany of the Holy Name of Jesus
***CCC*:** 309–314, 385–390, 396–412, 599–618, 631–635

### CHAPTER 10—JESUS' RESURRECTION AND ASCENSION

**Faith Concepts:** The Resurrection; the Ascension; life after death; particular judgment; Last Judgment; heaven, purgatory, and hell
**Sacred Scripture:** 1 Corinthians 15:3–6, 17; Acts of the Apostles 1:9–11; John 11:25–26
**Faith Vocabulary:** Ascension; heaven; hell; Last Judgment; purgatory; Resurrection
**Did you know . . . :** Development of the structure of the Eucharist
**Our Church Makes a Difference:** Saint Philip Neri
**Faith-life Skills:** Renewed Effort and Perseverance
**Prayer:** Christ, Our Hope
***CCC*:** 639–655, 659–664, 668–679, 988–1014, 1020–1050

### CHAPTER 11—A RESURRECTION STORY: A SCRIPTURE STORY

**Faith Concepts:** Resurrection stories; pattern, audience, and setting; faith testimonies; appearance of the Risen Jesus at the Sea of Tiberias; symbolism of the number seven; light and darkness; the breaking of bread
**Sacred Scripture:** John 21:5–14
**Faith Vocabulary:** Resurrection stories
**Did you know . . . :** Saint Thomas the Apostle
**Our Church Makes a Difference:** Stained-glass windows
**Faith-life Skills:** Faith Sharing
**Prayer:** The Lord Is Risen
***CCC*:** 641–644

### CHAPTER 12—THE HOLY SPIRIT, THE SANCTIFIER

**Faith Concepts:** The Holy Spirit in the Old Covenant, in the Gospels, in the work of Christ, in the life of the Church; the Advocate; charisms and Gifts of the Holy Spirit
**Sacred Scripture:** Acts of the Apostles 2:2–4; Ezekiel 37:1–3, 11, 12, 14; Luke 11:13; Matthew 10:20; 1 Corinthians 3:16; 2 Corinthians 6:16
**Faith Vocabulary:** Advocate; Annunciation; charisms; Holy Spirit
**Did you know . . . :** Ezekiel the Prophet
**Our Church Makes a Difference:** Christian art
**Faith-life Skills:** The Gifts of the Holy Spirit
**Prayer:** Prayer to the Holy Spirit
***CCC*:** 689–690, 692–693, 702–732, 737–741, 797–801

# Scope and Sequence (continued)

## Church and Sacraments

## UNIT ONE: The Church

### CHAPTER 1—THE CHURCH: THE PEOPLE OF GOD

**Faith Concepts:** The Church in God's plan; the new People of God; the Communion of Saints; the vocation of laypeople in the Church; the role of the ordained ministry; the consecrated life
**Sacred Scripture:** Ephesians 1:2, 1 Corinthians 12:4–7
**Faith Vocabulary:** Church, Communion of Saints, consecrated life, laypeople, ordained ministry
**Did you know . . . :** The "new Jerusalem" and the Book of Revelation
**Our Church Makes a Difference:** The Naming of a Pope
**Faith-life Skills:** Vocations in Life
**Prayer:** Prayer for Vocations
***Catechism of the Catholic Church* (*CCC*):** 751, 758–766, 781–786, 874–896, 897–913, 1555–1571

### CHAPTER 2—THE CHURCH: THE BODY OF CHRIST

**Faith Concepts:** Mystery of faith; images of the Church; four Marks of the Church; the Magisterium; infallibility
**Sacred Scripture:** Ephesians 4:5–6; 1 Corinthians 12:27, 14:5; Colossians 1:18; John 14:6, 17:21; Romans 16:26
**Faith Vocabulary:** Apostolic succession, Body of Christ, ecumenism, infallibility, Magisterium, Marks of the Church, Temple of the Holy Spirit
**Did you know . . . :** Saint Thérèse of Lisieux
**Our Church Makes a Difference:** Parish Councils
**Faith-life Skills:** Belonging to Groups
**Prayer:** Psalm 84
***CCC*:** 85–90, 751–757, 787–795, 813–865, 888–892

### CHAPTER 3—PAUL THE APOSTLE: A SCRIPTURE STORY

**Faith Concepts:** Missionary journeys of Paul; shipwreck at sea; Paul's faith; the missionary Church
**Sacred Scripture:** Romans 1:1, 3; Matthew 28:19; Acts of the Apostles 27:22–25, 33–37, 41–44
**Faith Vocabulary:** Missionary, Acts of the Apostles, martyr
**Did you know . . . :** Saint Paul
**Our Church Makes a Difference:** Church Youth on Mission
**Faith-life Skills:** Living with Zeal and Optimism
**Prayer:** An Act of Hope
***CCC*:** 849–856

### CHAPTER 4—THE CHURCH: A PEOPLE OF PRAYER

**Faith Concepts:** A praying community; rhythm of prayer; vocal prayer; meditation; contemplation; sources of prayer
**Sacred Scripture:** Psalm 92:2; Romans 8:14–15, 26; Matthew 26:30
**Faith Vocabulary:** Contemplation, meditation, vocal prayer
**Did you know . . . :** Saint Bernard of Clairvaux, Forty Hours devotion
**Our Church Makes a Difference:** Christian Music
**Faith-life Skills:** Meditation
**Prayer:** Mary's Prayer of Praise
***CCC*:** 1174–1178, 2659–2660, 2652–2658, 2700–2719

### CHAPTER 5—THE PRAYER OF THE CHURCH

**Faith Concepts:** Christian prayer; obstacles to prayer; models of prayer; prayer of Jesus; prayer of the Church; Liturgy of the Church; popular devotions and sacred images
**Sacred Scripture:** Psalm 143:1, 8; Luke 1:38; Matthew 26:39; 1 Thessalonians 5:17–18
**Faith Vocabulary:** Devotions, liturgy, prayer, rites, Covenant, icons
**Did you know . . . :** Liturgy of the Hours, Stations of the Cross
**Our Church Makes a Difference:** Forms of Spirituality
**Faith-life Skills:** Journal Writing
**Prayer:** Prayer for Guidance
***CCC*:** 2623–2625, 2765–2772

## UNIT TWO: Worship and Sacraments

### CHAPTER 6—GIVE THANKS TO THE LORD

**Faith Concepts:** Four ways Christ is always present in the celebration of the liturgy; the work of the Holy Spirit in the liturgy; the sacraments: common elements and rites; liturgical year
**Sacred Scripture:** Psalm 119:105
**Faith Vocabulary:** Grace, liturgical year, Paschal Mystery, sacraments
**Did you know . . . :** The mission of God
**Our Church Makes a Difference:** Professed Religious
**Faith-life Skills:** Recognizing God's Presence
**Prayer:** Te Deum
***CCC*:** 1113–1144, 1153–1155, 1163–1173

### CHAPTER 7—REBORN OF THE SPIRIT: A SCRIPTURE STORY

**Faith Concepts:** Nicodemus; the Sanhedrin; the Scripture story of Jesus and Nicodemus; Jesus' promise of eternal life
**Sacred Scripture:** John 3:1–7, 11–13, 16–18, 21
**Faith Vocabulary:** Eternal life, Pharisee, Sanhedrin, Torah
**Did you know . . . :** Conversation between Jesus and the Samaritan woman at Jacob's well
**Our Church Makes a Difference:** The Re-membering Church Ministry
**Faith-life Skills:** Seeing with the Eyes of Faith
**Prayer:** Prayer of Confidence and Hope
***CCC*:** 1225, 1238, 1257, 1262

### CHAPTER 8—BAPTISM AND CONFIRMATION

**Faith Concepts:** Sacraments of Christian Initiation: new beginning and new birth, rite of Baptism, rite of Confirmation
**Faith Vocabulary:** Baptism, Confirmation, Sacraments of Christian Initiation
**Did you know . . . :** Outward signs of Baptism, Confirmation in the Eastern rite, Catholic Church
**Our Church Makes a Difference:** National Catholic Youth Conference
**Faith-life Skills:** Hospitality
**Prayer:** A Renewal of Baptism Promises
***CCC*:** 1210–1212, 1229–1245, 1262–1270, 1286–1311

### CHAPTER 9—EUCHARIST

**Faith Concepts:** Presence of Jesus in the Eucharist; Eucharist as sacrament, memorial, and sacrifice; celebration of the Eucharist; graces of the Sacrament of the Eucharist
**Sacred Scripture:** Psalm 147:14, Luke 22:19–20, 1 Peter 2:9, John 15:17
**Faith Vocabulary:** Eucharist, memorial, sacrifice
**Did you know . . . :** Names to describe the Eucharist, Christ's presence in the Blessed Sacrament
**Our Church Makes a Difference:** Bread for the World
**Faith-life Skills:** Gratitude
**Prayer:** The Prayer of Saint Patrick
***CCC*:** 1324–1327, 1330–1334, 1337–1340, 1356–1372, 1373–1381, 1390

### CHAPTER 10—JESUS FEEDS FIVE THOUSAND: A SCRIPTURE STORY

**Faith Concepts:** Bread in the Old Testament; Bread in the Gospel; Scripture story of the multiplication of the loaves and fish; connection between Jesus feeding the crowd and the Eucharist
**Sacred Scripture:** Mark 6:9–11, 34–44; John 6:35, 48–51
**Faith Vocabulary:** Exodus, manna, divine Providence
**Did you know . . . :** Breaking bread
**Our Church Makes a Difference:** The H.U.G.S. Truck
**Faith-life Skills:** Sharing Our Blessings
**Prayer:** Eucharistic Prayer III
***CCC*:** 2602

### CHAPTER 11—ANOINTING OF THE SICK AND RECONCILIATION

**Faith Concepts:** Sacraments of Healing; celebrating the sacraments; effects of the sacraments; four essential elements necessary for the celebration of the Sacrament of Reconciliation
**Sacred Scripture:** Luke 5:13
**Faith Vocabulary:** Anointing of the Sick, conversion, Reconciliation, Sacraments of Healing, concupiscence, seal of confession
**Did you know . . . :** Christian Hospitals, Saint Charles Borromeo
**Our Church Makes a Difference:** Ministering with the Sick
**Faith-life Skills:** Forgiveness and Healing
**Prayer:** The Jesus Prayer
***CCC*:** 547–553, 1420–1470, 1499–1525

### CHAPTER 12—MATRIMONY AND HOLY ORDERS

**Faith Concepts:** Sacraments at the Service of Communion; sharers in the Priesthood of Christ; Matrimony: marriage promises, signs of God's Covenant; Holy Orders: ministerial priesthood, rite of ordination
**Sacred Scripture:** John 13:15
**Faith Vocabulary:** Holy Orders, Matrimony, Sacraments at the Service of Communion
**Did you know . . . :** Annulment
**Our Church Makes a Difference:** The Christian Family, the Domestic Church
**Faith-life Skills:** Love Begins at Home
**Prayer:** The Beatitudes
***CCC*:** 1533–1535, 1536–1584, 1544–1547, 1554–1571, 1585–1589

# Morality

## UNIT ONE: Life in Christ

### CHAPTER 1—HUMAN DIGNITY AND HAPPINESS

**Faith Concepts:** Sacredness of human life; intellect and free will; true happiness and holiness; Jesus, our model; the Church; the Beatitudes
**Sacred Scripture:** Isaiah 49:1, 15–16; Matthew 5:3–12, 22:37–40
**Faith Vocabulary:** Actual grace, Beatitudes, free will, holiness, intellect, sanctifying grace, soul
**Did you know . . . :** Pilgrimages
**Our Church Makes a Difference:** Respect Life
**Faith-life Skills:** Choose Life
**Prayer:** The Beatitudes
***Catechism of the Catholic Church* (*CCC*):** 1700–1709, 1716–1724, 1999–2000, 2012–2016

### CHAPTER 2—ONE PERSON'S DECISION: A SCRIPTURE STORY

**Faith Concepts:** The Evangelists; the Gospel according to Mark; the decision to follow Christ; the costs and rewards of discipleship
**Sacred Scripture:** Mark 10:17–31
**Faith Vocabulary:** Evangelists
**Did you know . . . :** Saint Mark the Evangelist; The Twelve
**Our Church Makes a Difference:** Saint Martin de Porres
**Faith-life Skills:** What Is a Simple Life
**Prayer:** Prayer of Thanksgiving
***CCC*:** 514–515

### CHAPTER 3—THE DECISION TO LIVE OUR LIFE IN CHRIST

**Faith Concepts:** Christian morality; freedom of choice; moral decisions; natural law; sin; conscience
**Sacred Scripture:** Matthew 5:16, Romans 6:14, Sirach 15:15
**Faith Vocabulary:** Conscience, morality, mortal sin, natural law, sin, venial sin
**Did you know . . . :** Book of Proverbs; capital sins
**Our Church Makes a Difference:** Retreats and Retreat houses
**Faith-life Skills:** Informed Conscience
**Prayer:** Psalm 139
***CCC*:** 1731–1742, 1749–1756, 1776–1794, 1846–1864, 1954–1960

### CHAPTER 4—HYMN OF LOVE: A SCRIPTURE STORY

**Faith Concepts:** The Church at Corinth; factions; the worshiping community; teachings about love in Paul's first letter to the Corinthians
**Sacred Scripture:** 1 Corinthians 13:1–13, John 13:34–35
**Faith Vocabulary:** Evangelize, love
**Did you know . . . :** The Pauline letters in the New Testament; language of the Pauline letters
**Our Church Makes a Difference:** L'Arche Communities
**Faith-life Skills:** Love Really Is . . .
**Prayer:** Love Never Ends
***CCC*:** 849–856

### CHAPTER 5—THE EXERCISE OF VIRTUE

**Faith Concepts:** Theological and moral virtues; common good; just society; social sin
**Sacred Scripture:** Wisdom 3:15
**Faith Vocabulary:** Common good, moral virtues, social sin, theological virtues, virtues
**Did you know . . . :** Fruits of the Holy Spirit; Corporal and Spiritual Works of Mercy
**Our Church Makes a Difference:** Dorothy Day and Peter Maurin
**Faith-life Skills:** Moral Virtues in Our Lives
**Prayer:** Prayer for the Easter Virtues
***CCC*:** 1803–1809, 1812–1832, 1869, 1890–1896, 1905–1912

### CHAPTER 6—THE GRACE OF THE HOLY SPIRIT

**Faith Concepts:** Grace, parable of the Sower, new life in Christ; sharing in the life of grace
**Sacred Scripture:** Philemon 1:3, Mark 4:3–9
**Faith Vocabulary:** Grace, justification, merit, sanctification, sanctifying grace
**Did you know . . . :** Etymology of the word grace
**Our Church Makes a Difference:** The Parish Community
**Faith-life Skills:** "Response-Ability"
**Prayer:** Prayer to the Holy Spirit
***CCC*:** 1987–1997, 2003

## UNIT TWO: The Ten Commandments

### CHAPTER 7—THE FIRST, SECOND, AND THIRD COMMANDMENTS

**Faith Concepts:** The Decalogue: summary of God's Law; the First Commandment, to put God first; the Second Commandment, the role of reverence; the Third Commandment, the importance of celebrating the Eucharist on Sunday
**Sacred Scripture:** Deuteronomy 30:19, Romans 13:10, Ephesians 3:14–19, Philippians 2:9–11
**Faith Vocabulary:** Decalogue, idols, precepts, reverence
**Did you know . . . :** Statues, icons, and paintings; holy days of obligation
**Our Church Makes a Difference:** Precepts of the Church
**Faith-life Skills:** False Gods
**Prayer:** Let Us Pray
***CCC*:** 2084–2132, 2142–2159, 2168–2188

### CHAPTER 8—MARTHA AND MARY: A SCRIPTURE STORY

**Faith Concepts:** Women disciples of Jesus; qualities of discipleship; gospel account of Jesus' visit to the home of Martha and Mary; two approaches to discipleship
**Sacred Scripture:** Luke 10:38–42
**Faith Vocabulary:** Disciple
**Did you know . . . :** Luke's account of the Gospel
**Our Church Makes a Difference:** The Liturgy of the Hours
**Faith-life Skills:** Balancing Prayer and Action
**Prayer:** The Spirit of Service
***CCC*:** 1174–1178

### CHAPTER 9—THE FOURTH AND FIFTH COMMANDMENTS

**Faith Concepts:** The Fourth Commandment: family life and values, the civic community; the Fifth Commandment: the sacredness of human life; acts of violence against human life: murder, direct abortion, suicide, euthanasia; violent lifestyles
**Sacred Scripture:** Psalm 119:90, Acts of the Apostles 5:29
**Faith Vocabulary:** Direct abortion, euthanasia, obedience
**Did you know . . . :** Pax Christi U.S.A.
**Our Church Makes a Difference:** Choosing Peace
**Faith-life Skills:** Violence Versus Peace
**Prayer:** Prayer for Peace
***CCC*:** 2196–2246, 2258–2317

### CHAPTER 10—THE SIXTH, SEVENTH, AND NINTH COMMANDMENTS

**Faith Concepts:** The Sixth Commandment: using the gift of sexuality wisely according to God's plan; the Seventh Commandment: stewardship, stealing and reparation, concern for the poor, for the common good and for public life
**Sacred Scripture:** Wisdom 1:1
**Faith Vocabulary:** Chastity, reparation, stewardship
**Did you know . . . :** The responsibility of caring for animals
**Our Church Makes a Difference:** Saint Francis of Assisi
**Faith-life Skills:** Mixed Media Messages
**Prayer:** Canticle of Brother Sun
***CCC*:** 2331–2391, 2401–2449, 2514–2527

### CHAPTER 11—THE EIGHTH AND TENTH COMMANDMENTS

**Faith Concepts:** The Eighth Commandment: living as people of truth; responsibility of the media; bearing false witness: lying, perjury, boasting; keeping a confidence; the Tenth Commandment: honoring and respecting the blessings of other people; covetousness, avarice, greed, envy; the virtue of detachment
**Sacred Scripture:** Psalm 25:4, 5; 2 Samuel 7:28; Matthew 6:21
**Faith Vocabulary:** Avarice, covet, greed, lying
**Did you know . . . :** Bearing false witness; St. Francis of Assisi
**Our Church Makes a Difference:** Blessed Josephine Bakhita
**Faith-life Skills:** Peer Pressure
**Prayer:** Prayer for Peace
***CCC*:** 2464–2503, 2534–2550

### CHAPTER 12—THE LORD'S PRAYER

**Faith Concepts:** Summary of the Gospel; the phrases of the Lord's Prayer
**Sacred Scripture:** Matthew 6:9–15; John 17:11; Luke 11:11, 13
**Faith Vocabulary:** Lord's Prayer, temptation
**Did you know . . . :** The Sermon on the Mount; the temptation of Jesus
**Our Church Makes a Difference:** Catholic Relief Services
**Faith-life Skills:** Consumerism
**Prayer:** Prayer for Reconciliation
***CCC*:** 2761–2772, 2777–2796, 2807–2854

# Scope and Sequence (continued)

## Jesus in the New Testament

### UNIT ONE: Introduction to Scripture and the Gospels

#### CHAPTER 1—INTRODUCTION TO SACRED SCRIPTURE

**Faith Concepts:** God's word to us; inspired writers; God's covenant with Moses and the Israelites in the Old Testament and with humankind in the New Testament; living the Covenant
**Sacred Scripture:** 2 Timothy 3:16; Deuteronomy 5:1–7; Acts 2:22–24, 32–33
**Faith Vocabulary:** Covenant, New Testament, Old Testament, Sacred Scripture, canon of Scripture
**Did you know . . . :** Chapters and verses in the Bible; categories of the Old and New Testament writings
**Our Church Makes a Difference:** The Living Word of God
**Faith-life Skills:** Pray the Scriptures Daily
**Prayer:** Prayer to Saint Jerome
***Catechism of the Catholic Church* (*CCC*):** 101–111, 121–133

#### CHAPTER 2—THE GOSPELS

**Faith Concepts:** The Gospels pass on the faith of the Church; the Evangelists; the synoptic Gospels; the Fourth Gospel; comparing the Four Gospels
**Sacred Scripture:** Ephesians 6:19; Matthew 1:1,16; Mark 1:1, 14–15; Luke 1:1–4; John 1:1–5, 20:30–31
**Faith Vocabulary:** Disciples, Evangelists, Fourth Gospel, Gospels, Synoptics
**Did you know . . . :** Symbols of the Evangelists; Titles for Jesus
**Our Church Makes a Difference:** Parish Communities
**Faith-life Skills:** Storytelling
**Prayer:** A Litany of the Holy Name of Jesus
***CCC*:** 75, 124–125, 514–515

#### CHAPTER 3—THE GOSPEL OF MARK

**Faith Concepts:** Literary style, Peter's declaration of Jesus as the Messiah, the ministry of Jesus, the Kingdom of God, the Paschal Mystery
**Sacred Scripture:** Mark 1:29–39, 8:34
**Faith Vocabulary:** Kingdom of God, mission, Paschal Mystery
**Did you know . . . :** Saint Mark the Evangelist; The Sacraments
**Our Church Makes a Difference:** Preparing for the Kingdom of God
**Faith-life Skills:** Discipline Makes Good Disciples
**Prayer:** From the Holy Cross
***CCC*:** 105–107, 515

#### CHAPTER 4—THE GOSPEL OF MATTHEW

**Faith Concepts:** The Torah and its relationship to the five major discourses in Matthew's Gospel; the Sermon on the Mount; the Beatitudes
**Sacred Scripture:** Matthew 5:18–20, 21–22
**Faith Vocabulary:** Beatitudes, discourse, Sermon on the Mount, Torah
**Did you know . . . :** Matthew's Readers
**Our Church Makes a Difference:** Light Among Nations
**Faith-life Skills:** Think and Re-Think
**Prayer:** A Prayer used before each session of the Second Vatican Council
***CCC*:** 105–107, 515

#### CHAPTER 5—THE GOSPEL OF LUKE, THE ACTS OF THE APOSTLES

**Faith Concepts:** Luke as storyteller; Luke's sequence
**Sacred Scripture:** Luke 4:14–22, 28–30, 15:6
**Faith Vocabulary:** Conversion, parables
**Did you know . . . :** Luke the Evangelist
**Our Church Makes a Difference:** The Conversion of Saint Francis of Assisi
**Faith-life Skills:** Apostolic Witnesses
**Prayer:** Prayer of Saint Francis
***CCC*:** 105–107, 515

#### CHAPTER 6—THE GOSPEL OF JOHN

**Faith Concepts:** "I am" sayings; seeing Jesus through the eyes of faith; signs of the Messiah; symbolic language
**Sacred Scripture:** John 1:1, 3:16, 10:6, 11:21–27, 40–44, 20:31; Exodus 3:13–14; 1 Corinthians 12:12–13; Deuteronomy 30:11–14
**Faith Vocabulary:** Book of Glory, Book of Signs, "I am" sayings, symbolic language
**Did you know . . . :** John the Evangelist; two endings to the Gospel of John
**Our Church Makes a Difference:** The Church as Sign of Sacrament
**Faith-life Skills:** Looking Beneath the Surface
**Prayer:** A Gathering Prayer
***CCC*:** 105–107, 515

### UNIT TWO: The Letters and Revelation

#### CHAPTER 7—THE LETTER TO THE ROMANS

**Faith Concepts:** Pauline letters; epistle to the Romans; time and audience, purpose, structure and writing style; new life in Christ; sanctifying, actual and sacramental grace; Paul's comparison of Baptism to the death and Resurrection of Christ
**Sacred Scripture:** Romans 6:3–11, 14–23; 8:14
**Faith Vocabulary:** Epistles, grace, Pauline letters
**Did you know . . . :** Paul of Tarsus; Christian Initiation
**Our Church Makes a Difference:** The Church's Work of Evangelization
**Faith-life Skills:** The Life of Grace
**Prayer:** A Renewal of Baptism Promises
***CCC*:** 105–107, 515

#### CHAPTER 8—THE LETTER TO THE PHILIPPIANS

**Faith Concepts:** Purpose and structure of the letters; Paul's message that faith in Christ involves suffering; a life worthy of the Gospel
**Sacred Scripture:** Philippians 1:12–17, 27–29, 3:1, 20–21, 4:1, 4–9; Matthew 5:11–12
**Faith Vocabulary:** Virtue
**Did you know . . . :** Papyrus; Theological Virtues
**Our Church Makes a Difference:** Letters from the Pope
**Faith-life Skills:** Solving Problems Respectfully
**Prayer:** An Early Christian Hymn
***CCC*:** 105–107, 515

#### CHAPTER 9—THE LETTER TO THE COLOSSIANS

**Faith Concepts:** Purpose and context; Paul's teaching on Christian life; living the way of love
**Sacred Scripture:** Colossians 1:15–20, 2:6–7, 12, 3:1–4, 12–17; Galatians 3:26–27; John 13:34–35, 15:12–13, 17
**Faith Vocabulary:** New commandment
**Did you know . . . :** Colossae; Mercy/Kindness
**Our Church Makes a Difference:** The Standard for Living Our Life in Christ
**Faith-life Skills:** Making Gospel Decisions
**Prayer:** Let All Be Christ
***CCC*:** 105–107, 515

#### CHAPTER 10—THE LETTER OF JAMES

**Faith Concepts:** The Catholic Letters in the New Testament; the Letter of James, put faith in God and express it in good works; doers of the word; social justice
**Sacred Scripture:** James 1:22–27, 2:14–26, 3:13, 17–18; Matthew 23:27, 5:37
**Faith Vocabulary:** Faith, the Catholic Letters, social justice
**Did you know . . . :** The Second Coming of Christ; The Works of Mercy
**Our Church Makes a Difference:** Social Teachings of the Church
**Faith-life Skills:** Working for the Common Good
**Prayer:** A Prayer for Light
***CCC*:** 105–107, 515

#### CHAPTER 11—THE LETTER TO THE HEBREWS

**Faith Concepts:** Connection between the sacrifices of the first covenant and the sacrifice of Christ; our redemption; sharers in the Paschal Mystery
**Sacred Scripture:** Hebrews 8:1–2, 9:1–4, 7, 12–15, 13:23; James 1:22
**Faith Vocabulary:** Apostasy, redemption, sacrifice
**Did you know . . . :** Hebrews; Israelites; Jews
**Our Church Makes a Difference:** Martyrs of the Church
**Faith-life Skills:** Self-Sacrifice
**Prayer:** A Prayer of Faith
***CCC*:** 105–107, 515

#### CHAPTER 12—THE BOOK OF REVELATION

**Faith Concepts:** Apocalyptic writing; the vision of hope; the New Jerusalem and the Second Coming of Christ
**Sacred Scripture:** Revelation 1:1–3, 18:1–2, 4–5, 8, 21:1–6, 22:1–4, 13, 20–21
**Faith Vocabulary:** Temptation, apocalyptic writing, hope, Second Coming of Christ, new Jerusalem
**Did you know . . . :** Apocalyptic writings in Sacred Scripture
**Our Church Makes a Difference:** Joan of Arc
**Faith-life Skills:** Preparing a Way for the Lord
**Prayer:** The Lord's Prayer
***CCC*:** 105–107, 515

# Church History

## UNIT ONE: Apostolic Age to A.D. 1500

### CHAPTER 1—MAKE DISCIPLES OF ALL NATIONS: A SCRIPTURE STORY

**Faith Concepts:** Jesus inaugurated the Church; Jesus crucified; the Resurrection of Jesus; the Great Commission; faith and witness in Church history
**Sacred Scripture:** Matthew 28:2–10, 16–20; Luke 1:68–79
**Faith Vocabulary:** Church, Apostles, Resurrection, Great Commission, Paschal Mystery, Pentecost
**Did you know . . . :** God prepared for the Church in the Old Testament
**Our Church Makes a Difference:** The "catholic" Church
**Faith-life Skills:** How to Follow God's Ways
**Prayer:** The Canticle of Zechariah
***Catechism of the Catholic Church* (*CCC*):** 74–75, 638–640, 761–768, 777

### CHAPTER 2—THE CHURCH GROWS: A.D. 50–A.D. 400

**Faith Concepts:** The first disciples; Paul's mission to the Gentiles; the Council of Jerusalem; proclaiming the Gospel; defenders of the faith; early Christian worship
**Sacred Scripture:** Acts of the Apostles 6, 7, 8:1–3, 9:1–25, 15: 1–21; 2 Timothy 1:12–14
**Faith Vocabulary:** Gentiles, Council of Jerusalem, presbyters, Deposit of Faith, heresies, apologists, apostolic succession
**Did you know . . . :** The Apostles' Creed
**Our Church Makes a Difference:** Religious Communities
**Faith-life Skills:** What Is Community?
**Prayer:** Prayer for the Church
***CCC*:** 80, 84, 97, 1096, 1229

### CHAPTER 3—"BLESSED ARE THE PERSECUTED"

**Faith Concepts:** Persecutions; the culture of paganism; martyrs; Saint Ignatius of Antioch; Saints Agatha, Lucy and Agnes; Emperor Constantine
**Sacred Scripture:** Matthew 28:20
**Faith Vocabulary:** Paganism, martyrs, polytheism
**Did you know . . . :** Time Line
**Our Church Makes a Difference:** Martyrs in El Salvador
**Faith-life Skills:** Change Brings Stress
**Prayer:** The Beatitudes
***CCC*:** 464–465

### CHAPTER 4—JESUS COMMISSIONS PETER: A SCRIPTURE STORY

**Faith Concepts:** Call narratives; New Testament call stories; Jesus calls Peter; the Petrine Ministry
**Sacred Scripture:** John 21:15–19
**Faith Vocabulary:** Call narratives, Petrine ministry
**Did you know . . . :** Miraculous catches of fish
**Our Church Makes a Difference:** Teachings of Pope John Paul II
**Faith-life Skills:** The Corporal Works of Mercy
**Prayer:** Prayer for the Christ in Others
***CCC*:** 880–882

### CHAPTER 5—THE RISE OF CHRISTENDOM

**Faith Concepts:** Christendom; the Fathers of the Church; Saint Ambrose and Saint Augustine of Hippo; the papacy; Pope Saint Sylvester I and Pope Saint Leo the Great; the spread of monasticism
**Sacred Scripture:** Matthew 16:18
**Faith Vocabulary:** Christendom, Fathers of the Church, papacy, monasticism, Edict of Milan
**Did you know . . . :** The monastery of Monte Cassino
**Our Church Makes a Difference:** Saints Monica, Benedict and Scholastica
**Faith-life Skills:** Who Can Be a Leader?
**Prayer:** Praise to the God of All Nations
***CCC*:** 925–927

### CHAPTER 6—MYSTICS, MENDICANTS, AND SCHOLASTICS

**Faith Concepts:** Monasticism during the Dark Ages: Saint Columba and Saint Bernard of Clairvaux; Saint Hildegard of Bingen; Pope Innocent III; the Scholastics; the Mendicants; Saint Francis of Assisi and Saint Dominic
**Sacred Scripture:** Isaiah 62:11–12
**Faith Vocabulary:** Dark Ages, mystics, Scholastics, Mendicants, East-West Schism
**Did you know . . . :** Pope Innocent III and Francis of Assisi; the Great Western Schism
**Our Church Makes a Difference:** Church and Media
**Faith-life Skills:** Herald and Servant
**Prayer:** A Prayer for Heralds of the Gospel
***CCC*:** 2684, 2693

## UNIT TWO: A Call to Renewal: A.D. 1500 to Present

### CHAPTER 7—THE HOLY SPIRIT: A SCRIPTURE STORY

**Faith Concepts:** The role of the Holy Spirit; Mary; Jesus and the Holy Spirit; the promise of the Holy Spirit; Pentecost; The Holy Spirit in Church history
**Sacred Scripture:** Luke 1:32; John 7:38; Luke 11:13; Matthew 10:19–20; John 14:15–16, 26; Acts of the Apostles 1:4–5, 7–8, 2:1–8
**Faith Vocabulary:** Holy Spirit, Incarnation, Advocate, Ascension
**Did you know . . . :** The Holy Trinity
**Our Church Makes a Difference:** Saint Maximilian Kolbe
**Faith-life Skills:** The Fruits of the Holy Spirit
**Prayer:** To the Holy Spirit, Our Advocate
***CCC*:** 685–686, 689, 721–723, 727–729, 731, 737–741, 858

### CHAPTER 8—REFORMATION AND RENEWAL

**Faith Concepts:** Schisms East and West; The Protestant Reformation; Martin Luther; the Catholic Counter-Reformation; Councils of Trent and Vatican I; Saint Charles Borromeo
**Sacred Scripture:** John 17:21
**Faith Vocabulary:** Protestant Reformation, Catholic Reformation, Council of Trent, Vatican Council I
**Did you know . . . :** Decree of Union and the "Uniates"; the Society of Jesus; Time Line
**Our Church Makes a Difference:** The Eastern Rite Catholic Churches
**Faith-life Skills:** Dealing with Conflict
**Prayer:** Prayer for a Pilgrim Church
***CCC*:** 817–819, 855

### CHAPTER 9—EXPLORATION AND EVANGELIZATION

**Faith Concepts:** Missions in an age of exploration and discovery; Saint Francis Xavier; Saint Rose of Lima and Saint Martin de Porres; Saint Juan Diego; African missions
**Sacred Scripture:** Matthew 28:19
**Faith Vocabulary:** Canonize, evangelization, patron saint
**Did you know . . . :** Saint Thérèse of Lisieux; canonization of Juan Diego
**Our Church Makes a Difference:** The missionary travels of Pope Paul VI and Pope John Paul II
**Faith-life Skills:** People with a Mission
**Prayer:** A Prayer for Missionaries
***CCC*:** 828, 849, 854, 905, 957

### CHAPTER 10—THE MISSIONARY CHURCH: A SCRIPTURE STORY

**Faith Concepts:** Divine missions and the prophets; the Book of Jonah; God's persistence; God's Mercy and justice; the missionary, tolerant and repentant Church
**Sacred Scripture:** The Book of Jonah
**Faith Vocabulary:** Salvation History, mission, prophet, exile, parable
**Did you know . . . :** The city of Nineveh
**Our Church Makes a Difference:** Jesuit Volunteer Corps
**Faith-life Skills:** How to Be a Missionary
**Prayer:** The Prayer of Jonah
***CCC*:** 849–856, 863, 913

### CHAPTER 11—THE CHURCH IN THE NEW WORLD

**Faith Concepts:** Cultural heritage of the Church in the United States; Blessed Junipero Serra; Isaac Jogues; the English colonies; Church growth between 1815 and 1965; Saint Elizabeth Ann Seton and Saint John Neumann; the United States Catholic Church in the era of Vatican II
**Sacred Scripture:** Acts of the Apostles 1:8
**Faith Vocabulary:** plenary councils, Third Plenary Council of Baltimore
**Did you know . . . :** Father John Carroll; the legacy of Elizabeth Ann Seton
**Our Church Makes a Difference:** United States Conference of Catholic Bishops
**Faith-life Skills:** Living with Courage
**Prayer:** A Prayer of Praise and Petition
***CCC*:** 2419–2422

### CHAPTER 12—THE SECOND VATICAL COUNCIL . . . AND BEYOND

**Faith Concepts:** The Church between Vatican Councils I and II; the Church as Sacrament; the Second Vatican Council; the documents of the Second Vatican Council; the movement for Christian unity; the Catechism of the Catholic Church
**Sacred Scripture:** Ephesians 1:10, Revelation 7:9
**Faith Vocabulary:** Charisms, aggiornamento, ecumenism, *Catechism of the Catholic Church*
**Did you know . . . :** Aggiornamento; Pope John XXIII and the "prophets of doom"
**Our Church Makes a Difference:** Catholic Social Teachings
**Faith-life Skills:** Virtues
**Prayer:** A New Pentecost
***CCC*:** 10–11, 74, 107, 109–114, 737–738, 748, 771, 775–776, 897–901

# Who Are My Students?

Twelve- to fourteen-year-olds are experiencing rapid and profound physical, emotional, and intellectual growth. While peers are a very strong influence at this age, adults continue to be important in the lives of young teens. This is particularly true when they are troubled, fearful, or unsure of situations in which they find themselves. Because twelve- to fourteen-year-olds are more able to think abstractly than in previous years, they now have the capacity for critical reflection on their faith experiences. Faith tradition and moral guidance of the Church offer this age group the structure and security they need during this turbulent time.

## Growing as Catholics

It is important that young teens be given the opportunity to discover their own unique gifts and the personhood given to them by God. The traditions and beliefs of the Catholic Church can be an anchor in a world that is otherwise changing at a frightening rate of speed. Religion teachers play an important role in the growth of the students as Catholics. Religion teachers can accept the challenging questions students will ask and respond in a positive and affirming manner.

**For REFLECTION**

- *What do I recall about myself as a twelve- to fourteen-year-old? What did I enjoy doing?*
- *What will be the most enjoyable aspects of serving as a religion teacher to twelve- to fourteen-year-olds? What will be most challenging?*

**For FURTHER STUDY**

*See* Echoes of Faith "Introduction to the Learner" *module.*

#### Physical Characteristics

- Young teens are entering or are about to enter puberty.
- Physical growth can vary greatly from student to student.
- Change can seem to happen overnight.

#### Cognitive/Learning Skills

- Abstract reasoning is more developed.
- Capacity for critical reflection is developing.
- Attention span has increased.
- Great diversity of ability in this age group grows as new skills develop.

#### Relationships

- Peer influence is very strong.
- Respect for parents and other adults is still retained.
- Young teens are accepted for the unique persons they are.

#### Religious Growth

Young teens:

- have increased conscience formation.
- seek freedom, but still need structure.
- challenge and question beliefs and norms of the community.
- are able to be more reflective of themselves and their experiences.
- place importance on faith tradition as an anchor and support when everything else is in flux.
- need their questions welcomed and need to be encouraged in their self-expression.

# How Do Children Learn?

## Many Gifts, One Lord

> *There are different kinds of spiritual gifts but the same Spirit; there are different forms of service but the same Lord.*
>
> 1 Corinthians 12:4–5

How do you prefer to learn new things? Do you like to attend a lecture or watch one on TV? Do you like to read novels or see movies and reflect on the life messages they hold? When you cook, do you follow a recipe or learn through trial and error? Do you just want the facts, or do you like open-ended questions with lots of possibilities? The way in which you answer these questions tells a lot about how you prefer to learn and express yourself. You may prefer to learn by listening, by seeing, by imagining, or by doing. Young people, as well, have preferred learning styles.

But there is another way to think about learning. Learning preferences may reflect only our "comfort zones." According to the popular theory of well-known educator Howard Gardner, each of us is born with at least eight different ways of processing and responding to new information that he calls "multiple intelligences." We might think of these "intelligences," as one writer has done, as eight different ways of being smart. We all possess each of these kinds of "smart" in one degree or another. The particular combination of these intelligences that we have is one of the things that makes each of us unique. One or several of these intelligences is probably dominant in each of us.

As you know, some students learn and express their ideas best through words, others by thinking things out or putting them in categories, and still others learn by using their bodies. Some learn and express themselves best when things are presented in a musical or rhythmic way. Some are best at writing and quiet, self-directed activities, others at group activities or sharing. Still others learn best through their contact with nature, through field trips, or by nurturing plants and animals.

In religious formation, as in classroom education, attention to the variety of gifts among the children will help them grow in an understanding of their faith and deepen their relationship with God. *Faith First* offers you many different strategies to honor the gifts that already exist in your learners and to encourage them to express themselves in new ways. Here are some activities related to the eight intelligences that support the different ways children can learn about and express their relationship with God and one another.

### Language- and Music-Related Activities

- Researching word meanings
- Word games and puzzles
- Reading and Bible search activities
- Storytelling and journal writing
- Learning hymns and Mass responses
- Writing prayers or songs
- Using background music for activities

### Object-Related Activities

- Learning "how many?" of different categories: sacraments, Apostles, and so on
- Celebrating the liturgical seasons of the Church
- "You are there" activities placing oneself in the action of a Bible story
- Using maps and models
- Graphic organizers to display information visually
- Posters and "designing" activities
- Crafts and classroom dramas
- Using gestures with songs and prayers
- Expressing response through dance
- Nurturing plants and animals
- Creating gardens or nature areas on school grounds

### Person-Related Activities

- Cooperative group learning activities
- Peer tutoring and sharing
- Teaching other students
- Games and simulations
- Quiet prayer times
- Writing and drawing in journals
- Creating autobiographies
- Self-assessment activities

#### For REFLECTION

***What kinds of activities did I enjoy most as a child?***

***What kinds of activities am I most comfortable leading? What is a new kind of activity I would be willing to try with the young people?***

#### For FURTHER STUDY

***The* Echoes of Faith "Methods for Grades 7 and 8" *module demonstrates a variety of classroom activities that you will enjoy leading.***

# How Do I Teach?

*Under the guidance of the Holy Spirit, catechists powerfully influence those being catechized by their faithful proclamation of the Gospel of Jesus Christ and the transparent example of their Christian lives.*
*NDC* 29E, page 101

The catechetical ministry has been nurtured and renewed in recent years with the publication of three important Church documents: the *Catechism of the Catholic Church,* the *General Directory for Catechesis,* and, most recently, the *National Directory for Catechesis.* You will find references to all three of these core documents in "The Church Teaches" section in the background pages for each chapter in your *Faith First Legacy Edition Teacher Guide.*

The ***Catechism of the Catholic Church (CCC)***, the earliest of these documents, was published in 1993. It provides a systematic presentation of the content of Catholic doctrine based on the four pillars of our faith: Creed, Sacraments, Morality, and Prayer. The ***Faith First Legacy Edition*** for Catholic schools follows the Catechism by addressing the four pillars of our faith every year at every grade level.

The ***General Directory for Catechesis (GDC)***, published in 1997, defines catechesis, its goals, principles, and guidelines. It emphasizes that catechesis is "the process of transmitting the Gospel, as the Christian community has received it, understands it, celebrates it, lives it and communicates it in many ways" (*GDC* 105). The *GDC* presents catechetical guidelines for the worldwide Church.

In May 2005, the ***National Directory for Catechesis (NDC)*** was published to inculturate and apply the principles from the ***General Directory for Catechesis*** to catechesis in the United States. The *NDC* emphasizes the importance of the "new evangelization," focused on "proclaim[ing] Christ to all peoples"[1] (*NDC* 17A page 46), and calls us to discipleship—"making a genuine commitment to [Jesus] and a personal decision to follow him" (*NDC* 17B page 48). The *NDC* also explores the impact that cultural, religious, and regional diversity have on catechesis in the United States.

Chapter 4 of the ***National Directory for Catechesis*** deals with methodology, a topic of interest to every religion teacher. First, the chapter focuses on divine methodology—God's self-Revelation through Jesus and the Holy Spirit. This section reminds us that God has revealed everything we know and believe about our faith. He did so by "[engaging] persons and communities in light of their circumstances and their capacity to accept and interpret Revelation" (*NDC* 28 page 90).

The second part of this chapter of the ***National Directory*** focuses on the elements of human methodology. It emphasizes that, because learning takes place in different ways, we should rely on a variety of methods, as God has done, to pass on our faith to students. The *NDC* lists eight different methods catechists can utilize. (See *NDC,* 29A–H.)

## Eight Human Methodologies

### A. Learning Through Human Experience

We respond to God's invitation through our human experience. Every *Faith First* lesson begins by engaging the young people's interest and imagination and helping them relate the lesson concept to their experience.

### B. Learning by Discipleship

We learn the Way of Jesus Christ by choosing to follow him and do what he asks of us. In *Faith First* we incorporate reflection and activities related to the New Testament to assist in the young people's journey toward discipleship.

### C. Learning Within the Christian Community

The witness of the Church shows children how to believe, worship, and take up the Gospel call to service.

### D. Learning Within the Christian Family

The Christian family is often the first experience a child has of what it means to live in a Christian community. The family offers the first and best environment for growth in faith. *Faith First* engages the family through the "With My Family" take-home pages in grades 1–6, the "Family Discussion" feature in junior high, and through a variety of other projects and activities.

### E. Learning Through the Witness of the Catechist

You will be a powerful influence on your students' faith formation this year, both by the faith knowledge you will share with them and, most importantly, by your witness of your Catholic faith. Your words and actions model for the young people what it means to live a Christian life, and, in some cases, you may be the best model they have.

### F. Learning by Heart

Learning by heart can help us "live by heart," to live a deeply faith-filled response to God's call. Memorization of key definitions, doctrinal formulations, and prayers plays an important role in building religious literacy and identity. *Faith First* highlights faith vocabulary on the teaching pages and reinforces key concepts at the end of every chapter.

### G. Making a Commitment to Live the Christian Life

Our acts of commitment to live the faith made again and again throughout our lives are how we learn what it means to have faith. *Faith First* invites young people to make a faith decision at the end of every chapter so they can live the faith more deeply in the coming week.

### H. Learning by Apprenticeship

Learning by apprenticeship allows us to learn from an experienced Catholic, a mentor, who can give us insight into the Christian life. *Faith First* recognizes this principle by inviting young people to initiate learning activities with younger classes that allow them to hand on their faith knowledge to others.

## Implementing the National Directory for Catechesis

Every chapter of *Faith First Legacy Edition* offers you ideas, tips, and activities that will help you apply the eight human methodology models in your class sessions. You will also find a box on the Engage (opening) page of each chapter's lesson plan to assist you.

# What Is a Good Climate for Catechesis?

**Your Teaching Space.** Just as you carefully prepare your classroom space at the start of a new year, take some time to consider how you will create a distinctive space for catechesis. Here are some questions to help you create an appropriate atmosphere for your religion class.

- Are chairs or desks arranged in such a way that the young people can see one another? If not and it is not practical to arrange your classroom in this way permanently, consider gathering the young people in other ways for cooperative activities and discussions. You might gather students in the prayer center for a more solemn reading of the Bible.
- Can you adjust lighting during reflective activities or prayer services?
- Do you have bulletin board space that you can use exclusively for your religion class throughout the year? You might create a border in the appropriate liturgical color. Display students' activities. Give students the responsibility for decorating the board with your guidance. If a parish catechist uses your classroom space during the week, you might consider setting aside bulletin board space or offering the use of your prayer table or CD/tape player. Occasional joint projects are also a great idea.
- Do you have reflective music CDs or tapes available for use in prayer services and reflective activities? Remember that music can help set the mood appropriately to signal that you are moving into a sacred time.

**Supplies.** Fortunately, you probably have basic materials, such as art supplies, pencils and pens, and paper available to you. You will not have to carry most materials back and forth to your class. Other than the basic materials just named, here are a few items you will want to have available or begin to gather to enhance your religion classes:

- Materials for prayer center
- A class set of Bibles
- Photos and posters that match lesson themes
- Maps of the Bible lands
- *Faith First Legacy Edition* Class Kit
- A CD, DVD, or audiotape player

# Resource Bibliography


## Church Documents

Abbot, Walter M., S.J., gen. ed. *The Documents of Vatican II.* New York: Herder and Herder, 1966.

*Catechism of the Catholic Church.* Washington, D.C.: United States Conference of Catholic Bishops—Libreria Editrice Vaticana, 1997.

*Compendium of the Social Doctrine of the Church.* Washington, D.C.: United States Conference of Catholic Bishops—Libreria Editrice Vaticana, 2005.

Connell, Martin, ed. *The Catechetical Documents: A Parish Resource.* Chicago: Liturgy Training Publications, 1996.

*Family Perspective in Church and Society, A:* Tenth Anniversary Edition. Washington, D.C.: United States Catholic Conference, 1998.

*General Directory for Catechesis.* Congregation for the Clergy. Vatican City: Libreria Editrice Vaticana, 1997.

*Go and Make Disciples: A National Plan and Strategy for Catholic Evangelization in the United States.* Washington, D.C.: National Conference of Catholic Bishops, 1999.

Hoffman, Elizabeth, ed. *The Liturgy Documents,* Volume 1. Chicago: Liturgy Training Publications, 1991.

Lysik, David A., ed. *The Bible Documents.* Chicago: Liturgy Training Publications, 2001.

———. *The Liturgy Documents,* Volume 2. Chicago: Liturgy Training Publications, 1999.

National Conference of Catholic Bishops. *Sharing the Light of Faith: National Catechetical Directory for Catholics of the United States.* Washington, D.C.: USCC, 1979.

*National Directory for Catechesis.* Washington, D.C.: United States Conference of Catholic Bishops, 2005.

*Our Hearts Were Burning Within Us: A Pastoral Plan for Adult Faith Formation in the United States.* Washington, D.C.: United States Catholic Conference, 1999.

Pope John Paul II. *Redemptoris Missio* (The Mission of the Redeemer).

*Sharing Catholic Social Teaching: Challenges and Directions.* Washington, D.C.: United States Catholic Conference, 1998.

Trouvé, Marianne Lorraine, ed. *Mother of the Christ, Mother of the Church: Papal Documents on the Blessed Virgin Mary.* Boston: Pauline Books, 2001.

## Theological Resources

Bokenkotter, Thomas. *A Concise History of the Catholic Church.* New York: Doubleday, 2004.

Cameli, Louis J. *Going to God Together: A Spirituality of Communion.* Notre Dame, IN: Ave Maria Press, 2002.

Groome, Thomas H. *Educating for Life: A Spiritual Vision for Every Teacher and Parent.* San Francisco: HarperSanFrancisco, 1998.

Himes, Michael J. *The Mystery of Faith: An Introduction to Catholicism.* Cincinnati, OH: St. Anthony Messenger Press, 2004.

Huebsch, Bill. *The General Directory for Catechesis in Plain English.* Mystic, CT: Twenty-third Publications, 2001.

McKenzie, John, S.J. *Dictionary of the Bible.* New York: Macmillan, 1965. (Reprint edition: Touchstone Books, 1995.)

## Catechetical Resources

Arbuckle, Gerald A. *Earthing the Gospel: An Inculturation Handbook for the Pastoral Worker.* Maryknoll, NY: Orbis Books, 1990.

Armstrong, Thomas. *Multiple Intelligences in the Classroom.* Virginia: ASCD, 1994.

Cahill, Thomas. *The Gifts of the Jews.* New York: Doubleday, 1998.

Campbell, Anne, Kathryn Waite, and Anne Mikelonis. *Creative Crafts for All Seasons: Projects That Help Kids Learn.* Allen, TX: RCL • Resources for Christian Living, 1999.

Campbell, Anne, et al. *The Faith-Filled Classroom: Top 10 Ideas That Really Work.* Allen, TX: RCL • Resources for Christian Living, 1999.

Coles, Robert, Ph.D. *The Spiritual Life of Children.* Boston: Houghton-Mifflin, 1990.

Costello, Gwen. *School Year Activities for Religion Classes.* Mystic, CT: Twenty-third Publications, 2000.

Dues, Greg. *Catholic Customs & Traditions: A Popular Guide.* Mystic, CT: Twenty-third Publications, 1990.

Duggan, Robert. *Teaching Kids the Basics of Liturgy: Making Rituals More Meaningful.* Allen, TX: RCL • Resources for Christian Living, 1999.

Dulles, Avery Robert Cardinal. *A History of Apologetics.* Second Edition. Chicago: Ignatius Press, 2005.

———. *Models of the Church.* Expanded edition. New York: Image Books, 1987.

Florian, Amy. *Sign & Symbol, Word and Song.* Notre Dame, IN: Ave Maria Press, 2001.

Gallagher, Maureen. *The Art of Catechesis: What You Need to Be, Know, and Do.* Mahwah, NJ: Paulist Press, 1998.

Gardner, Howard. *Intelligence Reframed: Multiple Intelligences for the 21st Century.* New York: Basic Books, 2000.

Gargiulo, Barbara. *How Do I Talk to God? Prayers for the School Year.* Allen, TX: RCL • Resources for Christian Living, 1999.

Huebsch, Bill. *A Handbook for Success in Whole Community Catechesis.* Mystic, CT: Twenty-third Publications, 2004.

———. *Whole Community Catechesis in Plain English.* Mystic, CT: Twenty-third Publications, 2002.

Jambor, Mary Beth. *Helping Kids Live Their Faith: Service Projects That Make a Difference.* Allen, TX: RCL • Resources for Christian Living, 1999.

Kelly, John F. The Collegeville Church History Time-Line. Collegeville, Minnesota: Liturgical Press, 2005.

MacDonald, Margaret Read. *The Storyteller's Start-up Book.* Little Rock, AR: August House Publishers, 1993.

Mazer, Peter. *School Year, Church Year: Activities and Decorations for the Classroom.* Chicago: Liturgy Training Publications, 2001.

McGrath, Eileen, Ph.D. *Kids Get Stressed Too: Understanding What's Going On and How to Help.* Allen, TX: RCL • Resources for Christian Living, 1999.

McManners, John, ed. *The Oxford Illustrated History of Christianity.* Oxford: Oxford University Press, 1990.

Mongoven, Anne Marie. *The Prophetic Voice in Catechesis.* Mahwah, NJ: Paulist Press, 2000.

Palomares, Susanna. *Lessons in Tolerance and Diversity.* Jalmar Press. (Available through Pro-Ed, Inc., Austin, TX)

Rotunno, Jo McClure. *Heritage of Faith: A Framework for Whole Community Catechesis.* Mystic, CT: Twenty-third Publications, 2004.

Vasiloff, Barbara C. *Teaching Self-Discipline to Children: 15 Essential Skills.* Mystic, CT: Twenty-third Publications, 2003.

# *A Teacher's Prayer*

*Gracious God, I ask for your blessing as I begin this year as a teacher. I wonder if I am up to the task. Yet I am inspired by my ancestors in faith who also were surprised by God.*

*Give me the* **courage** *of Abraham and Sarah, who did not hesitate when God called them to a new land. With them as my models, surely I can face a class of energetic students.*

*Let me be a* **liberator** *like Moses, setting students free from their fears and giving them the hope that comes from believing in you, a Provident God.*

*Give me the* **wisdom** *of Samuel to listen more than I speak. Remind me to allow the moments of silence that permit young people to reflect on you.*

*Give me the* **patience** *of Job, so that when the students get beyond me, or my best-laid plans fall flat, I can believe that the next time we gather will be better.*

*Give me the* **justice** *of Amos, so that I will challenge the young people to take up the work of building your kingdom of justice and peace here on earth.*

*Give me the* **faith** *of Joseph, so that I can be a model of faith to the young people in my care. Let the students learn what faith is, not only from the definitions that I teach them, but from the witness of my life.*

*Give me the* **humility** *of Mary, so that I will remember that you are the source of all good I do. Help me create a loving, fair, and secure environment for the sharing of faith, as Mary and Joseph did for the child Jesus.*

*Give me the* **hospitality** *of Martha and Mary, as I joyfully welcome the students each time we gather. Help me remember to be, like Mary, a prayerful person who listens to your will for me. But like Martha, help me also do the practical work that ensures a successful session.*

*Give me the* **enthusiasm** *of Mary Magdalene, the first witness to the Resurrection. Help me enter my classroom each day with the same passion to share the Good News of the Risen Lord.*

*Above all, let me never waver in my* **respect** *for the dignity of each student whom you have entrusted to my care. Let me teach, as your Son did, listening to them and allowing them to grow in the ways that are best for them.*

*With your* **love**, *the example of your Son, and the power of the Holy Spirit, I think I am ready to begin!*

*Amen.*

# Church History

*faith first*

Legacy Edition

RESOURCES FOR CHRISTIAN LIVING®

www.FaithFirst.com

"The Ad Hoc Committee to Oversee the Use of the Catechism, United States Conference of Catholic Bishops, has found this catechetical series, copyright 2007, to be in conformity with the *Catechism of the Catholic Church.*"

**NIHIL OBSTAT**
Rev. Msgr. Robert M. Coerver
Censor Librorum

**IMPRIMATUR**
† Most Rev. Charles V. Grahmann
Bishop of Dallas

June 20, 2006

The Nihil Obstat and Imprimatur are official declarations that the material reviewed is free of doctrinal or moral error. No implication is contained therein that those granting the Nihil Obstat and Imprimatur agree with the contents, opinions, or statements expressed.



Send all inquiries to:
RCL • Resources for Christian Living
200 East Bethany Drive
Allen, Texas 75002-3804

Toll Free 877-275-4725
Fax 800-688-8356

Visit us at **www.RCLweb.com**
**www.FaithFirst.com**

Printed in the United States of America

**20547** ISBN 0-7829-1128-5 (Student Book)

**20550** ISBN 0-7829-1131-5 (Teacher Guide)

1 2 3 4 5 6 7 8 9 10
06 07 08 09 10 11 12

**ACKNOWLEDGMENTS**

Scripture excerpts are taken or adapted from the *New American Bible with Revised New Testament and Psalms* Copyright © 1991, 1986, 1970, Confraternity of Christian Doctrine, Inc., Washington, DC. Used with permission. All rights reserved. No part of the *New American Bible* may be reprinted without permission in writing from the copyright owner.

Excerpts from the English translation of the *Catechism of the Catholic Church* for the United States of America © 1994, United States Catholic Conference, Inc.—Libreria Editrice Vaticana. English translation of the: *Catechism of the Catholic Church Modifications from the Editio Typica* Copyright © 1997, United States Catholic Conference, Inc.—Libreria Editrice Vaticana. Used with permission.

Excerpts are taken or adapted from the English translation of *A Book of Prayers* © 1982, International Committee on English in the Liturgy, Inc. (ICEL). All rights reserved.

English translation of "The Nicene Creed," "The Apostles' Creed," "Gloria Patri," and "Magnificat" by the International Consultation on English Texts (ICET).

Excerpts from *Evangelii Nuntiandi: On Evangelization in the Modern World* © 1975, Daughters of St. Paul, Boston, MA.

Excerpts from the *Dogmatic Constitution on the Church* (Lumen gentium); *Decree on Pastoral Office of the Bishops in the Church* (Christus Dominus); *Dogmatic Constitution on Divine Revelation* (Dei Verbum) from *Vatican Council II: The Conciliar and Post Conciliar Documents,* New Revised Edition, Austin Flannery, O.P., Gen. Ed., Copyright © 1975, 1986, 1992, 1996 by Costello Publishing Company, Inc. Used with Permission.

Excerpt from Pope Paul VI, *Credo of the People of God* 1968.

Excerpt from Pope John Paul II, homily, World Youth Day, Paris, 1997.

Excerpts from Pope Benedict XVI, encyclical *God is Love;* address at Youth Vigil, World Youth Day, Cologne, 2005.

Footnotes may be found on page 152.

# Faith First Legacy Edition Development Team

Developing a religion program requires the gifts and talents of many individuals working together as a team. RCL is proud to acknowledge the contributions of these dedicated people.

*Program Theology Consultants*
Reverend Louis J. Cameli, S.T.D.
Reverend Robert D. Duggan, S.T.D.

*Advisory Board*
Judith Deckers, M.Ed.
Marina Herrera, Ph.D.
Elaine McCarron, SCN, M.Div.
Reverend Frank McNulty, S.T.D.
Reverend Ronald J. Nuzzi, Ph.D.

*Contributing Writers*
*Student Book and Teacher Guide*
Christina DeCamp
Judith Deckers
Reverend Robert D. Duggan, S.T.D.
Mary Beth Jambor
Reverend Steven M. Lanza, S.T.L.
Eileen A. McGrath
Susan Stark

*Director of Creative Development*
Jo Rotunno

*National Catechetical Consultant*
Kate Sweeney Ristow

*Managing Editor*
Susan Smith

*Art & Design Director*
Lisa Brent

*Electronic Page Makeup*
Laura Fremder, *Manager*

*Production Director*
Jenna Nelson

*Designer*
Tricia Legault

*Project Editors*
Patricia A. Classick
Steven M. Ellair
Craig W. O'Neill

*Web Site Producers*
Joseph Crisalli
A. C. Ware

*General Editor*
Ed DeStefano

*President/Publisher*
Maryann Nead

# Contents

# Welcome to Faith First

Welcome to ***Faith First: Church History.*** This book invites you to explore the journey of the new People of God, the Church. You will learn how the journey began with Jesus and the Apostles and how it has continued up to the present day. You will meet many interesting people who have helped shape the life and work of the Church. You will gain deeper insight into the way events, both within and outside the Church, have affected her and contributed to making her the community and institution that you know today.

It is vital for citizens of a country to know the important people and events that helped shape their nation. In the same way it is vital for you, a member of the Church, to know the roots and understand the history of the Church. Just as your nation has grown and changed over time and renewed its commitment to the values upon which it was founded, so has the Church. Under the guidance of the Holy Spirit, the Church continually renews herself, seeking to respond to the needs of people in a way that is faithful to Christ and his Gospel.

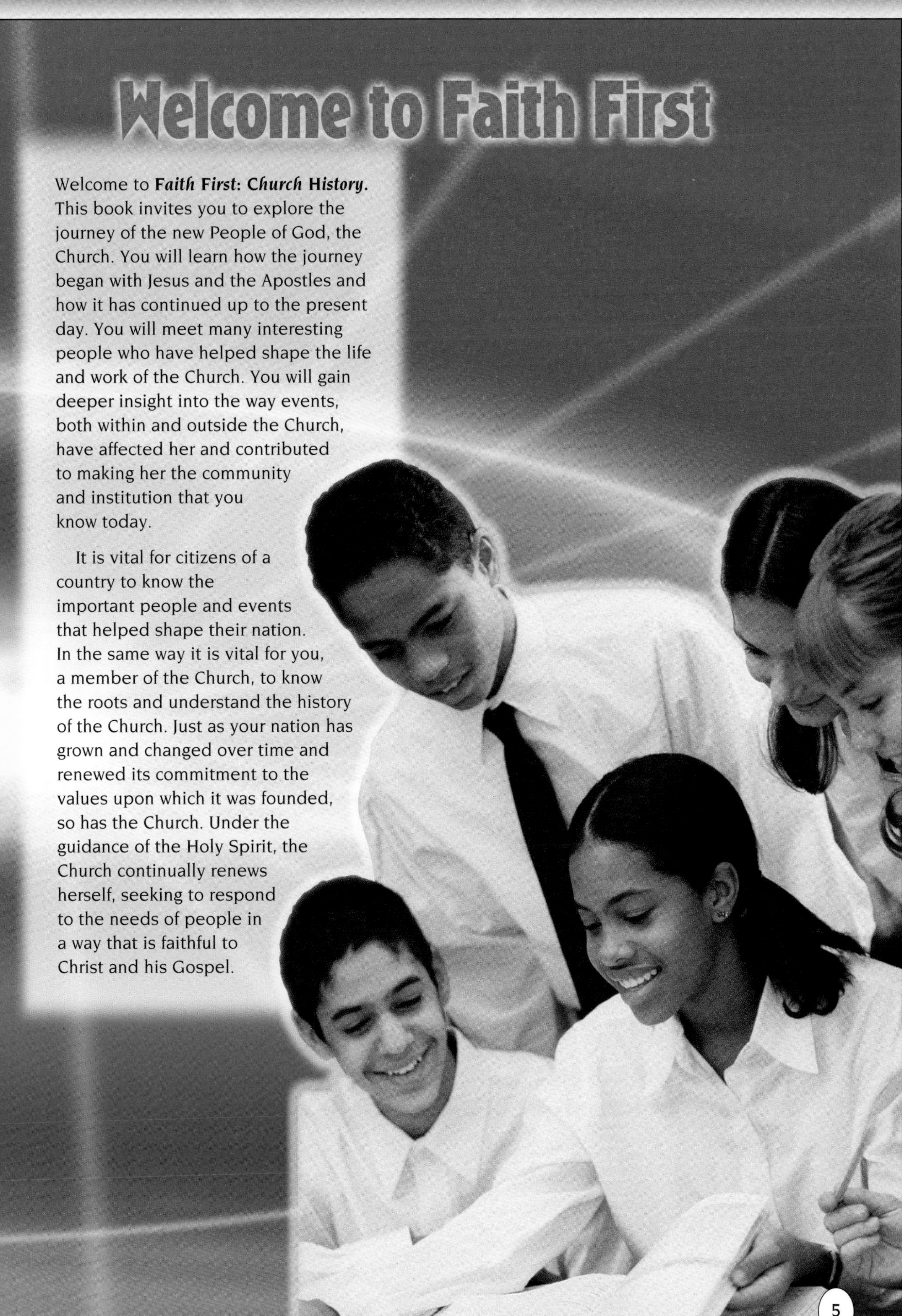

5

# Church History

## Beginning Reflections

The Church grew from a small group of disciples into a worldwide community of believers. She experienced times of joyful triumph and suffered during times of trial and distress. Central to the story of the Church are the many heroes of the faith. Among the people you will learn about are Saint Ignatius of Antioch and other early martyrs; Saints Augustine of Hippo and Bernard of Clairvaux; Saints Hildegard of Bingen, Thomas Aquinas, and Francis of Assisi; Saints Charles Borromeo, Rose of Lima, and Elizabeth Ann Seton. You will meet important political leaders such as the Emperors Constantine and Charlemagne, and Church leaders such as Pope Saint Leo the Great, Blessed Pope John XXIII, Pope John Paul II, and Pope Benedict XVI.

You are the Church. Through Baptism and your celebration of the other Sacraments of Christian Initiation—Confirmation and Eucharist—you have become a member of the Church. Therefore, the story of the Church is also your story. Your participation in her life and work contributes to the ongoing history of the Church.

**Jesus is the Head of the Church. You became a member of the Body of Christ by being baptized.**

**I will show I am a member of the Body of Christ by**

______________________________

______________________________

______________________________

______________________________.

**Baptism has made you a participant in Church history.**

**I will participate in the life of the Church by**

______________________________

______________________________

______________________________

______________________________.

**Remember that the story of the establishing of the Church is found in the New Testament.**

**I will prepare to understand these days of early Church history by reading from the following books in the New Testament:**

______________________________

______________________________

______________________________

______________________________.

**The history of the Church covers more than two thousand years. There is much to learn and much that will fascinate and inspire you.**

**I will begin to learn and prepare for this history now. One specific way I can do this is by**

______________________________

______________________________

______________________________

______________________________.

6

# *Go to All Peoples*

*Use this prayer service after the students complete "Beginning Reflections" on page 6 of the student book. The leader walks in procession to the prayer area, holding the Bible high for all to see. The leader opens the Bible and places it on a table in the prayer area.*

**All:** **In the name of the Father, and of the Son, and of the Holy Spirit. Amen.**

**Leader:** God our Father, / you will all people to be saved / and come to the knowledge of your truth. / Send workers into your great harvest / that the gospel may be preached to every creature. We ask this in the name of Jesus Christ, your Son.

**All:** **Amen.**

From Opening Prayer, Mass for the Spread of the Gospel, *Roman Missal*

**Reader:** A reading from the holy gospel according to Matthew.

**All:** **Glory to you, Lord.**

**Reader:** *Proclaim Luke 10:1–9.*
The gospel of the Lord.

**All:** **Praise to you, Lord Jesus Christ.**

**Leader:** Let us ask the Spirit to send forth laborers to proclaim the Gospel to all peoples.

Come, Holy Spirit, fill the hearts of all the baptized with the gifts of your wisdom and understanding and send them forth to proclaim the good news of Jesus Christ.

**All:** **Come, Holy Spirit.**

**Leader:** Come, Holy Spirit, fill the hearts of all the baptized with your gifts of knowledge and reverence and send them forth to invite all peoples to live in communion with you, Jesus, and the Father.

**All:** **Come, Holy Spirit.**

**Leader:** Come, Holy Spirit, fill the hearts of all the baptized with your gifts of right judgment and courage and send them forth to build the kingdom of justice, peace, and love proclaimed by Jesus.

**All:** **Come, Holy Spirit.**

**Leader:** Come, Holy Spirit, fill the hearts of all the baptized with your gift of wonder and awe and send them forth to renew the face of the earth with your love.

**All:** **Come, Holy Spirit.**

**Leader:** Lord God, Father of all, / look upon the face of Christ your Son / who gave up his life to set all [people] free. / Through him may your name be praised / among all peoples from East to West. We ask this through Christ our Lord.

**All:** **Amen.**

From Prayer Over the Gifts, Mass for the Spread of the Gospel, *Roman Missal*

*Come forward and reverence the Bible.*

# Unit 1 Opener

The opener pages are designed to assess, through a variety of questioning techniques, the students' prior knowledge and understanding of key faith concepts presented in each unit of the student book. Processing these pages should not take more than ten or fifteen minutes.

**USING ILLUSTRATIONS**

Pictures help stimulate the religious imagination. The first opener page contains three pictures that illustrate key concepts presented in this unit of the text.

- Have the young people look at and think about the pictures to gain insight into the mysteries of faith and the events in the history of the Church portrayed by the pictures.
- Invite volunteers to describe what each picture says to them about the Catholic Church.
- Ask several volunteers to share a response to the question at the bottom of the page.

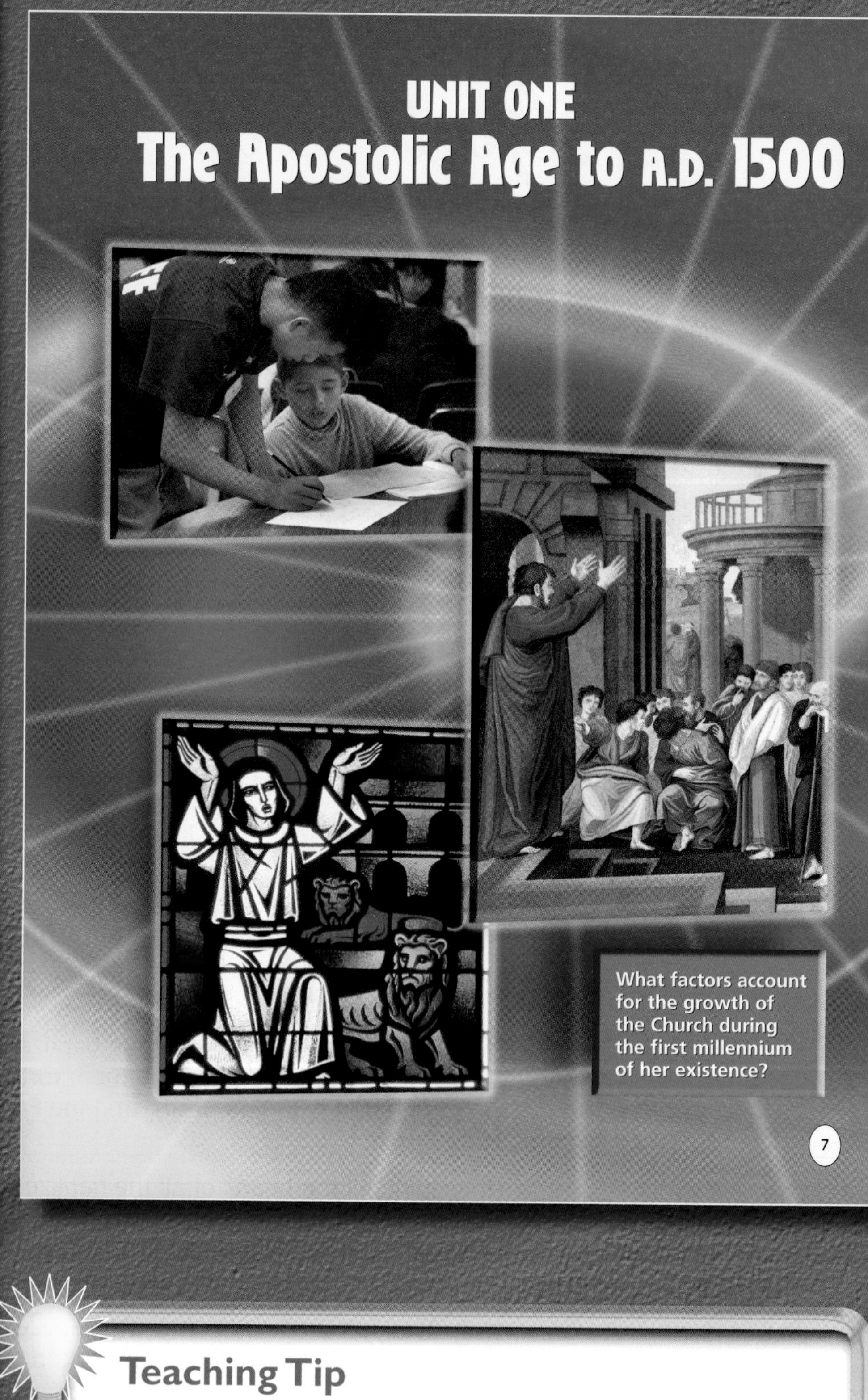


## Teaching Tip

**Importance of Prior Knowledge.** The members of the group come with varying degrees of prior faith knowledge and faith experiences. You will want to draw upon this knowledge and these experiences to help the students build a deeper understanding of the faith and history of the Catholic Church. By starting with each person's knowledge and experiences you show them that you respect and value their thinking. There are many techniques to assess prior knowledge. Pictures, questions, vocabulary, and Scripture stories have been incorporated into these pages to encourage the young people to share what they already know about the faith and history of the Catholic Church.

# Getting Ready

### The Church

*What do you already know about the history of the Catholic Church?*

### Questions I Have

*What questions about the history of the Catholic Church do you hope these chapters will answer?*

### Faith Vocabulary

*Put an X next to the faith vocabulary terms that you know. Put a ? next to the faith vocabulary terms that you need to know more about.*

____ Apostles
____ Great Commission
____ Deposit of Faith
____ heresies
____ apologists
____ martyrs
____ Petrine ministry
____ Christendom
____ Fathers of the Church
____ papacy
____ monasticism
____ schism
____ Mendicants
____ Scholastics

### A Scripture Story

Jesus and Saint Peter.

*What did Jesus do to inaugurate the Church?*

8

## Teaching Tip

**Ready, Set, Go.** The opener pages provide you with insights into how to plan your lessons. As you observe the students at work, make notes to yourself identifying the differences in their prior knowledge of the faith. Building upon their prior knowledge will increase their interest in the faith concepts presented in each session. Feel confident that the Holy Spirit is at work in these sessions as you help the young people grow in faith and love of God.

## GETTING READY

The second opener page invites the young people to reflect on key concepts presented in this unit of the text and to identify questions that they wish to have answered.

### *The Church*

Brainstorm brief answers to the question in the box. List the responses on the board.

### *Faith Vocabulary*

This section is a quick assessment of the young people's familiarity with some of the key terms used in unit 1 of the text. During the review at the end of this unit, the young people will be asked to return to this page and once again share their understanding of the terms.

### *Questions I Have*

This section encourages the students to reflect on the many ways they have come to know and believe in God and his love for them. Have the students list their questions privately and then invite volunteers to share their questions and list them on a chart. As you work through the text, always refer back to the chart and integrate the responses to the questions into your lessons.

### *A Scripture Story*

This section invites the students to reflect on the Scripture story. Invite the students to share their responses to the question.

Chapter 1

# Make Disciples of All Nations A Scripture Story

## CHAPTER BACKGROUND

### Proclaiming Christ

The Church's life depends entirely upon the life of Jesus Christ. He is the light of the Church, and aside from him she has no other light. According to the Church Fathers, "the Church is like the moon, all its light reflected from the sun" (CCC 748). That sun is Jesus Christ, the Son of God.

It is through Jesus and the power of the Holy Spirit that God the Father, in his loving kindness, chose to call all humanity to share in the life of the Holy Trinity. It was into a holy Church that the Father determined from the beginning of time to gather together all those who would come to believe in his Son. Church history, then, is the story of this gathering of believers in Christ.

#### The Resurrection

The crowning truth of the Church's belief in Christ is his Resurrection. Saint Paul writes: "For I handed on to you as of first importance what I also received: that Christ died for our sins in accordance with the scriptures; that he was buried; that he was raised on the third day in accordance with the scriptures" (1 Corinthians 15:3–4).

There are many reasons why Jesus' Resurrection is both the foundational event of Jesus' life and the central truth of the Church's life.

- Saint Paul uses the phrase "in accordance with the scriptures." This is an acknowledgement that Jesus' Resurrection fulfills both the promises of Jesus during his ministry and those of the Old Testament.
- The Resurrection verifies Christ's divinity. Jesus himself said, "When you lift up the Son of Man, then you will realize that I AM" (John 8:28).
- By his death Jesus "gave himself for us to deliver us from all lawlessness and to cleanse for himself a people as his own" (Titus 2:14). By his Resurrection, he opens for us a new life, reinstating us into God's grace and making us adopted children of the Father.
- Jesus' Resurrection is "the principle and source of our future resurrection" (CCC 655). "For since death came through a human being, the resurrection of the dead came also through a human being. For just as in Adam all die, so too in Christ shall all be brought to life" (1 Corinthians 15:21–22).

In his parting words to his Apostles, Jesus commissioned them to make disciples of all nations. Church history tells how men and women from the time of Jesus onward have fulfilled this command proclaiming the Resurrection and the hope of eternal life.

## FOR REFLECTION

***How does my belief in the Resurrection influence my life?***

***What are some ways I can help the students come to know the presence of the Risen Lord with them?***

## First Thoughts

### Birth Stories

How many times have you sat with family members and friends and talked about your own (or their) birth stories? Most of us want to know, "What was it like when I was born?" Our histories—our stories—are central to our identities as human persons. The Church's history, starting with her birth story, is central to our identity as Catholics. This rich history of faith reaches from the past to inform and form us to live out the mission of Jesus with zeal today.

### Young Adolescents and Their Stories

As you explore the beginnings of the Church, help history come alive for the young people by making connections between what they are learning and their participation in the developing story of the Church. For example, have the students reflect on how they are living as disciples of Jesus at home, at school, and in their parish. Discuss how they can see their own stories as a part of the bigger story of the Church. Remember that young adolescents long to belong. Look for opportunities in the parish where they can truly participate in the mission of the Church. They need the support and influence of significant adults other than their parents on their faith journey. Share your own faith story with them. Welcome them to share their own stories too.

## The Church Teaches . . .

The *National Directory for Catechesis* (NDC) teaches:

> Christ is the center of salvation history and the end toward which human history is being drawn. The apostles are to announce the salvation won by Christ to all the world and are to gather the many nations into communion with him.
>
> *NDC* 1, page 5

This chapter examines the origins and mission of the Church, founded by Jesus Christ and guided by the Holy Spirit.

### See the Catechism . . .

For more on the teachings of the Catholic Church regarding the Resurrection, the birth of the Church, and the Church's mission, see *Catechism of the Catholic Church* 638–655, 766–767, and 830–831.

*Lord of history,*
*may the insight we gain*
*from the past help us live our*
*faith more fully in the present.*
*Inspire us with the zeal*
*of the first disciples*
*to participate in the*
*Church's mission of hope.*
*Amen.*

Footnote references may be found on page 256.

Now . . . turn the page and let's get organized!

# LESSON PLANNER

**Chapter Focus**
**To learn about the origin, foundation, and mission of the Church**

| Focus | Process | Materials and Options |
|---|---|---|
| **DAY 1**<br>**Engage/Teach and Apply**<br>**Pages 9–11**<br>**Focus**<br>To understand that Jesus Christ inaugurated the Church | **Opening Prayer**<br>**Discussion**<br>How the Church came to be<br>**Presentation**<br>Read, discuss, and summarize content.<br>**Scripture:** 1 Corinthians 3:11<br>**Did you know:** The Covenant<br>**Faith Connection:** Imagine being a witness of Jesus' Crucifixion. | **Materials**<br>paper, tape<br>pens, markers<br>**Options**<br>***Called to Prayer and Liturgical Lessons* booklet:** See options for daily, seasonal, and liturgical prayer and lessons.<br>***Additional Activities and Assessment Tools* booklet**<br>News Report: The Origins of the Church, page 7 |
| **DAY 2**<br>**Teach and Apply**<br>**Pages 12–13**<br>**Focus**<br>To discover the role of the Resurrection in the mission of Christ and the role of the Great Commission in the mission of the Church | **Prayer**<br>**Presentation**<br>Read, discuss, and summarize content.<br>**Scripture:** Matthew 28:1–10, 16–20<br>**Activity:**<br>• Create a timeline that illustrates the birth of the Church.<br>• Develop two-minute presentations on how Christ is the Church's foundation. | **Materials**<br>paper<br>pens or pencils<br>**Options**<br>**Enriching the Lesson (TG page 69)**<br>Creating Personal Faith Timelines<br>***Additional Activities and Assessment Tools* booklet**<br>Bible Search: The Early Church, page 8 |
| **DAY 3**<br>**Teach/Apply and Connect**<br>**Pages 14–15**<br>**Focus**<br>To understand that Jesus commissioned his disciples to keep alive his mission in the world | **Prayer**<br>**Presentation**<br>Read, discuss, and summarize content.<br>**Faith Connection:** Create symbols for the Resurrection and the Great Commission.<br>**Our Church Makes a Difference**<br>Discuss World Mission Sunday and how the mission of the Church is a mission of hope. | **Materials**<br>3" x 5" cards<br>tape, scissors<br>markers, pens or pencils<br>**Options**<br>**Enriching the Lesson (TG page 69)**<br>Exploring the Nicene Creed |
| **DAY 4**<br>**Connect and Apply**<br>**Pages 16–17**<br>**Focus**<br>To discover how to follow the way of Christ | **Prayer**<br>**What Difference Does Faith Make in My Life?**<br>Learn how to follow the way of Christ<br>**Activity:** Create action plans for how to follow the way of Christ.<br>**Faith Decision:** Identify how you can take part in the mission of the Church at school, at home, and in your community. | **Materials**<br>newsprint, tape<br>markers<br>**Options**<br>**Enriching the Lesson (TG page 69)**<br>Living the Mission |
| **DAY 5**<br>**Pray and Review**<br>**Page 18** | **Pray**<br>Pray the Canticle of Zechariah in alternating groups.<br>**Review**<br>**Activities:** Complete the review exercises to reinforce the concepts of the chapter.<br>**Family Discussion:** Encourage the students to share and discuss the question with their family this week. | **Materials**<br>pens or pencils<br>**Options**<br>***Additional Activities and Assessment Tools* booklet**<br>Administer chapter 1 test.<br>**Music Connection** (TG page 69) |

**Don't Forget!** You can make lesson planning a breeze—check out the **Online Lesson Planner** at www.FaithFirst.com for additional resources to enhance this chapter.

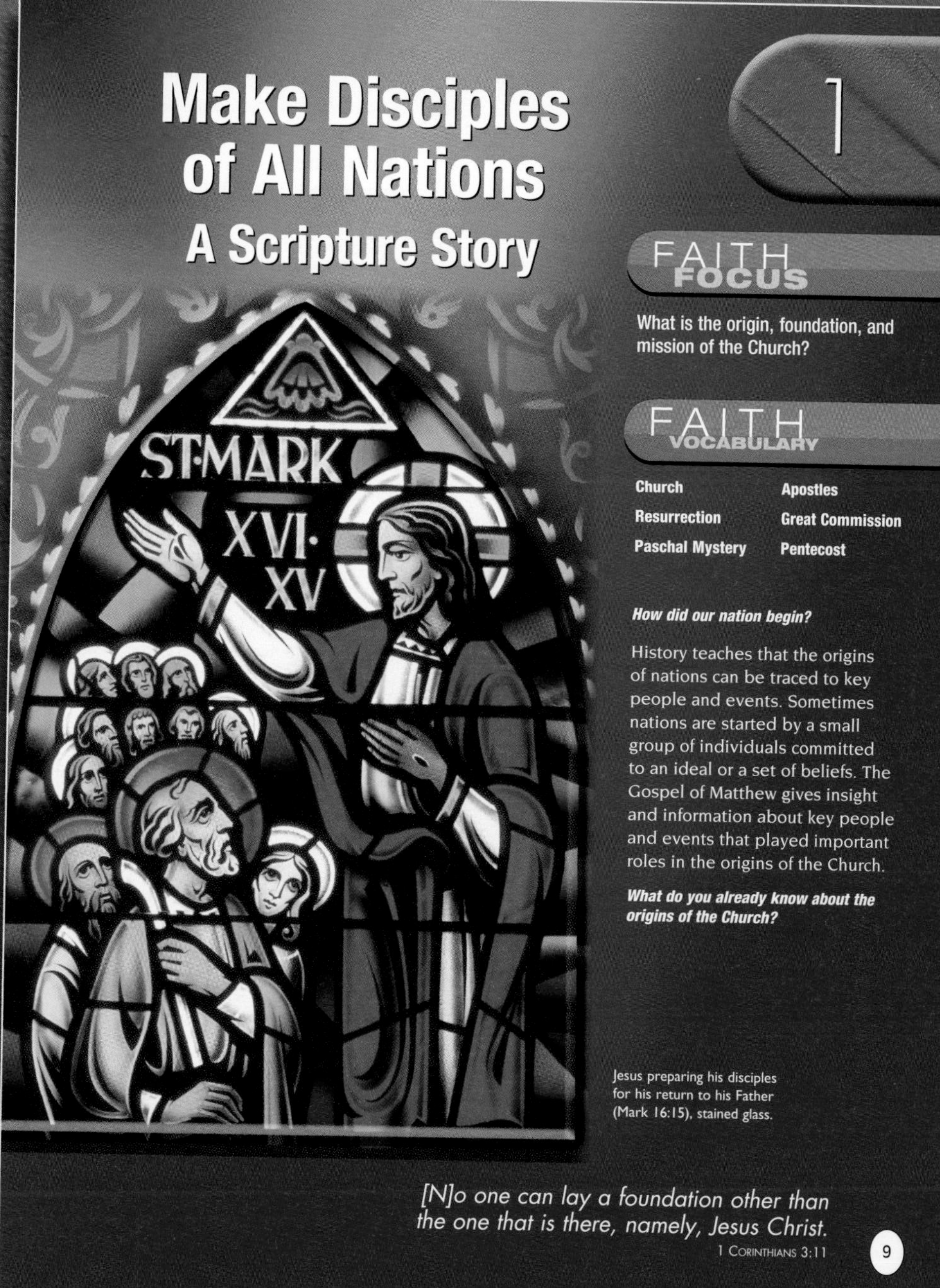

# Make Disciples of All Nations

## A Scripture Story

1

**FAITH FOCUS**

What is the origin, foundation, and mission of the Church?

**FAITH VOCABULARY**

| | |
|---|---|
| Church | Apostles |
| Resurrection | Great Commission |
| Paschal Mystery | Pentecost |

***How did our nation begin?***

History teaches that the origins of nations can be traced to key people and events. Sometimes nations are started by a small group of individuals committed to an ideal or a set of beliefs. The Gospel of Matthew gives insight and information about key people and events that played important roles in the origins of the Church.

***What do you already know about the origins of the Church?***



Jesus preparing his disciples for his return to his Father (Mark 16:15), stained glass.

*[N]o one can lay a foundation other than the one that is there, namely, Jesus Christ.*
1 CORINTHIANS 3:11

9

# Day 1

## Engage

### PRAY

- Gather the class for prayer.
- Invite them to think about their first memory of the Church. Lead the group in praying the Sign of the Cross.
- Pray, Lord, help us learn more about our Church and our faith. / May we follow Jesus more closely today and in the days to come. / Amen.
- Proclaim 1 Corinthians 3:11 together.

### FAITH FOCUS

Share one of your first memories of the Church. Then suggest that our own personal histories are joined to the histories of others throughout the centuries. Read the "Faith Focus" question aloud. Share with the students that in this chapter they will explore the beginnings of the Church and the mission Jesus entrusted to her.

### DISCOVER

Assess the young people's prior knowledge of the key people and events that were a part of the origin of the Church.

- Pose the opening question. Ask several volunteers to answer it briefly. Read aloud the first paragraph. Suggest that knowing our origins as a nation helps us understand the freedoms we enjoy.
- Invite a volunteer to read the second paragraph while you write the "Faith Vocabulary" words on the board.
- Invite the the young people to use the faith vocabulary words to answer the closing question on the page. Affirm appropriate responses.

## National Directory for Catechesis

**Implementing the *National Directory for Catechesis:* Learning Within the Christian Community.** The National Directory teaches that "the effectiveness of catechesis depends to a great extent on the vitality of the Christian community in which it is given" (*NDC* 29C, page 100). As you discuss the early Church and the Great Commission, have the students name specific ways in which your parish community responds to Christ's call to share the Gospel with others. Emphasize the responsibility of all the baptized to take part in the work of the Church.

# Day 1

## Teach

### FOCUS

Point out to the young people that these two pages will both tell about how the Church has been a part of God's plan since the beginning of time and explore the role of the Church in the divine plan of Salvation.

### DISCOVER

- Ask the students to read the first paragraph silently. Invite volunteers to summarize their understanding or ask clarifying questions. Discuss how original sin destroyed our communion with God and one another and how Christ restored that communion.
- Invite volunteers to read aloud "The Church—Instituted by Christ" to discover that the Church is both a visible and spiritual society. Write the terms *Jesus Christ, People of God, New Covenant, Church, seed,* and *Kingdom of God* on the board. Discuss with the group how the terms are related to one another based on what the students have just read.
- Draw the young people's attention to the "Did you know" feature on page 11 to help them understand more about the Apostles.
- Add the word *Apostles* to the board.

## Bible Background

The Church has always been a part of God's plan. He created all people to know and love him and to share in his divine life. The Church teaches:

> The gathering together of the People of God began at the moment when sin destroyed the communion of men with God, and that of men among themselves.
>
> Catechism of the Catholic Church 761

This communion is restored by the "convocation," or "calling together," of humanity in Christ. The name of this "convocation" is the **Church.**

10

### The Church—Instituted by Christ

Jesus Christ is the Incarnate Son of God who freely offered himself for our Salvation. He is true God and true man. Sent by the Father out of love, Jesus freely accepted and fulfilled his mission to be the expiation for our sins and to accomplish the divine plan of Salvation.

The divine plan of Salvation included the inauguration of the Church. The Church is both the means and goal of the divine plan. She is both visible and spiritual. She is both a hierarchical society and the Mystical Body of Christ. She lives from him, in him, and for him. He lives with her and in her. She is formed of both a human and a divine component. The Church, like a seed planted in a garden, is the beginning of the Kingdom of God that will be fully realized when Christ comes again in glory at the end of time.

### The Birth of the Church

Jesus accomplished the divine plan of Salvation by freely sacrificing his life on the cross. Through the sacrifice of Christ the Church was born.

*The Eucharist.* Julie Lonneman, contemporary American illustrator.

## Background: Doctrine

**Images for the Church.** Because the Church is a mystery, the Church uses a variety of images to help us grasp the meaning of this mystery. We can capture only part of the meaning of the mystery of the Church in any one given image. One image, the new People of God, helps us begin to partially understand that the Church is the people gathered together (the word *church* means "convocation") by God the Father in Christ, the new and everlasting Covenant. (See *Catechism of the Catholic Church* 751–757, 770–776, and 781–786.)

*In His Hands.* Lars Justinen, contemporary American artist.

At the Last Supper Jesus told his disciples, "And when I am lifted up from the earth, I will draw everyone to myself" (John 12:32). The Apostles at first did not grasp what Jesus meant. This is evidenced by the fact that after the arrest of Jesus, the Apostles, with the exception of Saint John, fled and abandoned Jesus, leaving him to the cruelty of the crowd and Roman soldiers. Far from their seeing his Passion and death as an event that would draw everyone to Jesus, the Apostles saw his arrest, trial, and execution on the cross as a reason to hide. Fearing for their lives, the Apostles cowered behind locked doors. (See John 20:19.)

What the disciples of Jesus had not yet come to believe at the time of these saving events was that a new day was dawning. They did not yet see that Jesus' death and burial was the beginning of a new and glorified life—the beginning of the new creation of the world in Christ.

***How did Jesus inaugurate the Church?***

### Did you Know...

**The Apostles**

Jesus would build his Church on the Twelve, or the **Apostles**, and entrust it to them. The word *apostle* means "one who is sent" or "messenger." "The names of the twelve apostles are these: first, Simon called Peter, and his brother Andrew; James, the son of Zebedee, and his brother John; Philip and Bartholomew, Thomas and Matthew the tax collector; James, the son of Alphaeus, and Thaddeus; Simon the Cananean, and Judas Iscariot who betrayed him" (Matthew 10:2–4). After the Ascension of Jesus, Matthias and Paul became Apostles. (See Acts of the Apostles 1:26, 9:15, and Romans 1:1.)

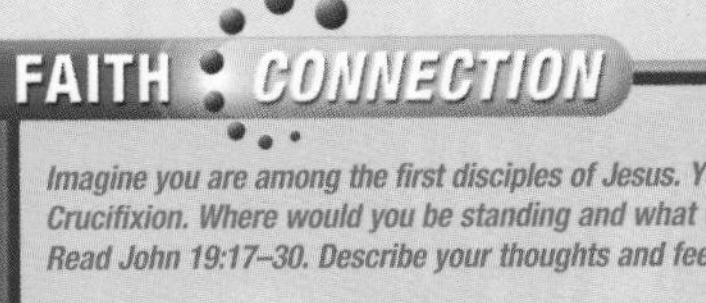

### FAITH CONNECTION

***Imagine you are among the first disciples of Jesus. You are witnessing the Crucifixion. Where would you be standing and what would you be doing? Read John 19:17–30. Describe your thoughts and feelings.***

Affirm appropriate responses.

11

## Teaching Tip

**Using Visuals to Teach.** The visuals in this textbook are meant to draw the students into the heart and soul of the text's presentation of the faith. Discussing the illustrations and the photos is an excellent teaching opportunity that appeals to the more visual learners. As you progress through the book, you might consider having the young people look back through the text and note the different artwork used. Have them try to identify what each is presenting about the faith. This will add to the learning that has already taken place throughout these chapters.

# Apply

### REINFORCE

Ask the young people to join with a partner and write one or two sentences that highlight a key point about the Church that they have learned thus far. Then have the partners read "The Birth of the Church" on pages 10 and 11 and, in one or two sentences, describe how Jesus inaugurated the Church. Invite the pairs to share their work with the large group.

### INTEGRATE

- Add the word *cross* to the board and ask the group to tell why the cross is so important both to the life of Christ and the life of Christians. Without Jesus' free sacrifice of his life on the cross, there would be no Church today. Emphasize that the Church was born from Jesus' total self-giving on the cross.
- Give the young people a few minutes to silently respond to the "Faith Connection" activity. Invite volunteers to share their responses with the class.
- Keep the responses on the board for use in the next session.

### PRAY

Invite the young people to reflect for a moment on how Jesus reconciled us to God and to one another by offering his life on the cross. Then pray, Jesus, by your Cross and Resurrection / you have set us free. / You are the Savior of the world. / Amen.

# Day 2

## Teach

**PRAY**

Invite the young people to quiet themselves for prayer. Remind them of the presence of our all-loving God. Ask everyone to rest in and reflect on that presence for a moment.

**FOCUS**

- Write the word *Church* on the board. Then write the words *origin, foundation,* and *mission* under it and invite volunteers to tell what they know about each of the words as they relate to the Church.
- Tell the students that these two pages will help them learn about the centrality of the Resurrection in the life and mission of the Church.

**DISCOVER**

- Read aloud the opening paragraph to the students.
- Have them listen attentively to discover the centrality of the Resurrection for the Christian faith as you present "The Resurrection: The First Day of the New Creation."
- Add the word *Resurrection* to the board.
- Invite the young people to dramatically read Matthew 28:1–7. Assign volunteers to be narrator, Mary Magdalene, the angel, and Jesus.
- Ask the group to respond to the question at the end of page 12. The Resurrection ushers in the new creation. Add the phrase *new creation* to the board.
- Have volunteers read aloud "The Great Commission" on page 13 to discover its importance for the Church.

## Reading the Word of God

After Jesus died on the cross, one of his disciples, Joseph of Arimathea, went to the authorities and asked for Jesus' body. Joseph wrapped his body in clean linen, placed it in a tomb hewn out of rock, and rolled a huge stone to seal the entrance. What may have appeared to be the dramatic end of Jesus' life and ministry was in truth a new beginning.

### The Resurrection: The First Day of the New Creation

The Gospel of Matthew, as do all four Gospels, announces the astounding news of the **Resurrection.** It is the news that changed the course of human history:

After the sabbath, as the first day of the week was dawning, Mary Magdalene and the other Mary came to see the tomb. And behold, there was a great earthquake; for an angel of the Lord descended from heaven, approached, rolled back the stone, and sat upon it. . . . Then the angel said to the women in reply, "Do not be afraid! I know that you are seeking Jesus the crucified. He is not here, for he has been raised just as he said. . . . [G]o quickly and tell his disciples, 'He has been raised from the dead, and he is going before you to Galilee; there you will see him.' " MATTHEW 28:1–2, 5–7

"The Resurrection of Jesus is the crowning truth of our faith in Christ" (*Catechism of the Catholic Church* 638). The Resurrection of Jesus is the bodily raising of Jesus from the dead on the third day after his death on the cross and burial in the tomb. The centrality of this saving event for the faith of the Church is proclaimed by Saint Paul, who wrote, "And if Christ has not been raised, then empty [too] is our preaching; empty, too, your faith" (1 Corinthians 15:14). The Church passes on this same message to all people today and will do so until Christ comes again in glory.

***What is the role of the Resurrection in the mission of Christ on earth?***

*Women at the Tomb,* contemporary stained glass.

12

### Special Needs

**Provide Options for Assignments.** Strive to meet the needs of all your learners. Assignments that give young people some power over the outcome can be highly motivating. Provide activities for the young people that give them options. For example, on this page, instead of having them read the Scripture story directly from the page, have them role-play or do a dramatic presentation of the content. Assign narrators and characters. Encourage movement of the young people in your teaching strategies. You will be supporting a developmental need of young adolescents.

**Need:** Students with limited reading proficiency

### The Great Commission

For forty days the Risen Jesus appeared on numerous occasions to the Apostles and other disciples. He ate and drank with them and continued to teach them about the Kingdom of God.

When the time came for his Ascension, or return in glory to his Father, Jesus gathered the Eleven (Judas who betrayed him had hung himself on a tree) in Galilee. Matthew tells us what happened:

> Jesus approached and said to them, "All power in heaven and on earth has been given to me. Go, therefore, and make disciples of all nations, baptizing them in the name of the Father, and of the Son, and of the holy Spirit, teaching them to observe all that I have commanded you. And behold, I am with you always, until the end of the age." MATTHEW 28:18–20

*Ascension of Our Lord,* sixteenth-century Russian icon, Pskov school.

The sending of the Apostles on this mission is known as the **Great Commission.** The Risen Christ shared his mission with the Apostles and commissioned them to make disciples of all nations, to baptize them, and to teach them until the end of time.

The Church is in the world as the sign and instrument of Salvation, of communion with God, and of unity of all humanity. She is the sign and instrument of the Kingdom of God announced by Christ which will come about when Christ returns in glory.

***What is the importance of the Great Commission for the Church?***

13

## Liturgy Tip

**Prayerful Reflection.** Consider interspersing opportunities for quiet prayer into the week's lessons. Choose a focus from the day's lesson, lead the students in praying the Sign of the Cross, and then ask them to spend several minutes reflecting on the focus you have chosen. Help them become comfortable with silence and let them know that prayers do not always have to be spoken aloud. You can end the moments of silent prayer with a short vocal prayer asking for God's blessing and by praying the Sign of the Cross together.

# Day 2

## Apply

### REINFORCE

- Add the phrase *Great Commission* to the board.
- Ask the class what they now know about the origins of the Church. Highlight key events and people.
- Have the students work together using their responses to create a timeline on the board that illustrates the origin of the Church. Label the timeline with the key events and people. Save this material on the board for the next lesson.

### INTEGRATE

- Have the class work in small groups. Based on what they have learned from the chapter so far, ask the groups to come up with a two-minute presentation that explains or illustrates 1 Corinthians 3:11, namely, Jesus Christ is the foundation of the Church.
- Encourage the young people to use the terms in "Faith Vocabulary" and the other terms on the board as aids in developing their presentations.
- Have the groups make their presentations to the class.

### PRAY

Invite the young people to prayerfully reflect on the Gospel passage about the Great Commission and what it means for them personally. End by praying the Sign of the Cross together.

### *Enriching the Lesson*

The "Creating our Personal Faith Timelines" activity on page 69 is related to today's content. You may wish to include it in today's lesson.

# Day 3

## Teach

**PRAY**

Invite the young people to quiet themselves for prayer. Pray 1 Corinthians 3:11 together.

**FOCUS**

- Read the "Faith Focus" question on page 9 to the students. Ask them to think about how they might now answer it.
- Point out that on page 14 they will learn why Pentecost is another key event in the origin of the Church and in the fulfillment of the mission given to her by Christ.

**DISCOVER**

- Explain the concept of "a turning point in history." Ask the young people about historical events that are such turning points. Share that the Paschal Mystery of Christ is the most important turning point in all of history.
- Write the phrase *Paschal Mystery* on the timeline on the board, and have the students read the first paragraph on page 14 and underline the meaning of Paschal Mystery.
- Invite volunteers to read aloud "Pentecost" to discover the role of Pentecost in the history of the Church.

## Apply

**REINFORCE**

Discuss the importance of the Pentecost event in the mission of the Church.

**INTEGRATE**

Have the students create symbols for the Resurrection and the Great Commission. Create a collage of their work and display it.

## Understanding the Word of God

Historical turning points so deeply impact history that they shape the course of future human decisions and events. The **Paschal Mystery** of Christ—the redemptive work of his Passion, death, Resurrection, and glorious Ascension—is the greatest of all turning points in human history. It is the mission of the Church to invite all people to become disciples of Jesus and to share in the saving power of his Paschal Mystery.

### Pentecost

Luke tells us in his Acts of the Apostles that after Jesus' Ascension, the Eleven, accompanied by Mary, returned to Jerusalem where they chose Matthias as Judas' successor. Then when "the time came for the feast of **Pentecost** to be fulfilled," the Holy Spirit came to them. Filled with the gift of the Holy Spirit, Saint Peter and the other Apostles left the upper room and entered the marketplace. Peter proclaimed:

> "You who are Israelites, hear these words. Jesus the Nazorean was a man commended to you by God. . . . God raised this Jesus; of this we are all witnesses. . . . Therefore let the whole house of Israel know for certain that God has made him both Lord and Messiah." . . . Those who accepted his message were baptized, and about three thousand persons were added that day.
>
> Acts of the Apostles 2:22, 32, 36, 41

On the day of Pentecost, Jesus' mission on earth was fulfilled and the work of the Holy Spirit, in a sense, took center stage. The Holy Spirit constantly builds up, inspires, animates, and blesses the Church. From the age of the Apostles to the present, the Church, under the guidance of the Holy Spirit, has grown into a visible sign and instrument of the mystery of God's saving love at work in the world.

***Design a symbol that incorporates both the Resurrection and the Great Commission. Write your ideas for your symbol in this space.***

Affirm appropriate responses.

14

### Background: Doctrine

**Paschal Mystery.** The Paschal Mystery is the Passion, death, Resurrection, and glorious Ascension of Jesus Christ. This mystery "stands at the center of the Good News that the apostles and the Church following them, are to proclaim to the world." Through Jesus' Paschal Mystery, God accomplished his plan for Salvation. The Paschal Mystery, which is both a historical fact and a transcendent reality, is faithfully recounted and handed down to us in the Gospels. Through reading the New Testament writings and other historical sources we can better understand the meaning of Redemption and its history-changing impact on the world. (See *Catechism of the Catholic Church* 571 and 572.)

# OUR CHURCH MAKES A DIFFERENCE

In the Nicene Creed we profess that the Church is "one holy catholic and apostolic." These are the four Marks, or the essential attributes, of the Church founded by Jesus Christ. The third Mark of the Church named in the Nicene Creed is "catholic." The Church is "catholic" because she has been sent by Christ on a mission to the whole world, to all people of all time. The Church is the Body of Christ and is always joined to Christ, the Head of the Church, the Savior of the world. She is the sign and instrument of Salvation for the whole world. In her is found the fullness of the means of Salvation.

### World Mission Sunday

Each year on the next to the last Sunday in October, the Church celebrates World Mission Sunday. World Mission Sunday is organized by the Society for the Propagation of the Faith. Offerings collected on that Sunday are distributed in the Pope's name by the Society for the Propagation of the Faith to the missions and missionaries of the world.

The Propagation of the Faith provides ongoing support for the pastoral and evangelizing programs of the Catholic Church in Africa, Asia, the islands of the Pacific and remote regions of Latin America. This includes aid for the education of seminarians, Religious novices and lay catechists, for the work of religious communities for education, health care and social services, and for communication and transportation needs.

On World Mission Sunday, Catholics around the world are given the opportunity to take part in this missionary work of the Church through prayer and sacrifice. Through their prayers, sacrifices, and generosity Catholics make a difference. For example: $25 supports a catechist, $75 provides for the work of Sisters, $100 helps a mission parish. As always, your prayers are your most treasured gift to this missionary work.

***Why is the mission of the Church a mission of hope for all people of all times?***

Parade of Nations Procession celebrating World Mission Sunday, Diocese of Scranton, Pennsylvania.

15

## Teaching Tip

**An Important Page.** The "Our Church Makes a Difference" page in each chapter highlights how the teachings of the Catholic Church presented in the chapter have made and continue to make a difference in the Church and in the lives of Catholics today. This page helps the young people make that important connection between what they have learned and how those teachings are being lived in the life of the Church. The concepts presented on this page will help the young people discover and value the difference living the faith of the Church makes.

# Day 3

## Connect

### HIGHLIGHT

Remind the class that all the baptized are called to participate in the mission of the Church. Emphasize that Jesus commissions each of us, as his disciples, to keep alive the mission of the Church in the world. Point out that this is work we do together.

### DISCOVER

- Write the word *catholic* on the board. Ask the students to name the prayer in which we use the word *catholic.* The Nicene Creed. Paraphrase the first paragraph on page 15.
- Circle the word *catholic* on the board and ask a volunteer to tell what it means.
- Invite the young people to read "World Mission Sunday" silently to discover one way the Catholic Church fulfills the mission Christ gave to her.

### INTEGRATE

Have the young people discuss why the mission of the Church is a mission of hope. Encourage them to give specific examples.

### PRAY

Invite the class to join you in praying a prayer of petition for people who need hope today.

### *Enriching the Lesson*

The "Exploring the Nicene Creed" activity on page 69 is related to today's content. You may wish to include it in today's lesson.

# Day 4

## Connect

### PRAY

Have the young people quiet themselves and ask the Holy Spirit to help them discover ways to fulfill the mission of the Church to spread hope in the world.

### FOCUS

- Ask the "Faith Focus" question on page 9 and invite the young people to use what they have learned in this chapter to answer it. List key words and phrases from their responses on the board.
- Point out that pages 16 and 17 will help them make the connection between what they have learned about the earliest days of the Church and the way the Church challenges them today to take part in the mission of the Church.

### DISCOVER

- Paraphrase the first paragraph on page 16, emphasizing the guiding role of the Pope and bishops. Tell the young people that Pope Benedict XVI joins the timeline of the Church's history as the 265th successor to Saint Peter.
- Divide the class into five groups. Have each group silently read "Following the Way of Christ" to consider concrete ways to participate in the mission of the Church.
- Distribute newsprint and markers.
- Assign one of the five points of Pope Benedict to each group. Have the groups create an action plan to implement the point assigned to it.
- Invite the groups to present their plans to the class.

# WHAT DIFFERENCE

## Does Faith Make in My Life?

World Youth Day, Pope Benedict XVI celebrating prayer vigil with youth at Marienfeld near Cologne, Germany, August 20, 2005.

Pope Benedict XVI is the 265th successor of Saint Peter the Apostle. Guided by the same Holy Spirit who guided Saint Peter and the other Apostles, Pope Benedict XVI and the other bishops guide the Church in living in communion with God and in unity with all people as Christ taught.

### Following the Way of Christ

In August 2005 Pope Benedict XVI traveled to Cologne, Germany. There he celebrated World Youth Day with youth from around the globe. In speaking at the Youth Vigil Service on August 20, 2005, Pope Benedict said to the youth:

> The Church is like a human family, but at the same time it is the great family of God, through which he establishes an overarching communion and unity that embraces every continent, culture and nation.

In his talk that day Pope Benedict XVI gave the youth of this world valuable advice on how to follow God's ways and live as members of his family.

- **Discover the true face of God.** Youth search for God in many ways. Pope Benedict guided the youth in their search for God by telling them, "In Jesus Christ, who allowed his heart to be pierced for us, the true face of God is seen."

16

## Teaching Tip

**Integrating Faith into Daily Life.** Give the young people time to process the "What Difference Does Faith Make in My Life?" pages. Processing these two pages is an integral part of the students' discovering the connection between the teachings of the Catholic Church and their personal lives. These pages provide the young people the opportunity to move from the knowledge of the faith that they have learned to applying and integrating the faith into their daily lives.

- **Learn God's ways.** Youth also search for happiness and success in many ways. The Pope reminded the youth that many people would have them believe that success and happiness are achieved only by gaining power over others, being beautiful or popular, or attaining extraordinary wealth. Pope Benedict reminded the young people that in contrast to the showy way of the world, Jesus, through his life and death, revealed that the "defenseless power of love is the true path to success and happiness."
- **Study the lives of the saints.** Pope Benedict urged youth to look to "the saints—both known and unknown—in whose lives the Lord has opened up the Gospel." The saints "show you how to be Christian; how to live life as it should be lived—according to God's way."
- **Give of yourself to others.** The saints consistently teach the lesson of self-giving. "The saints and the blessed did not doggedly seek their own happiness, but simply wanted to give themselves, because the light of Christ had shone upon them. They show us the way to attain happiness, they show us how to be truly human."
- **Remind yourself that you are a work in progress and to be patient with your faults and weaknesses.** Do not let your faults and failings disqualify you from taking your place in God's family. He has not given up on you. Pope Benedict encouraged the youth: "Despite all our defects, we can still hope to be counted among the disciples of Jesus, who came to call sinners."

### Faith Decision

- Brainstorm in a small group a list of words and phrases that express your image of a disciple of Christ who is committed to sharing the Gospel with other people.
- Discuss ways that young people can take part in the mission of the Church in school, at home, and in their civic community.

This week I will take part in the mission of the Church by

Affirm appropriate responses.

17

## Liturgy Tip

**Preparing for Prayer.** Set aside time to prepare for the prayer that ends each chapter. Involve the young people as readers and leaders. Other volunteers can arrange the class prayer space and incorporate symbols from the week's work as a part of the environment for prayer. Help the young people discover how they, as a group, are able to pray best. Create an atmosphere of openness by encouraging them to pray about what is in their hearts. Pray for the young people and their families when they have special needs or issues, or on special occasions, such as birthdays. Ask the students to keep you in their prayers. Help them pray for themselves, for those they love, and for the poor and sick. Remind and encourage them to pray for one another.

# Day 4

## Apply

### RESPOND

- After the groups have presented their plans, invite the students to review the ideas independently.
- Have the students rejoin their groups and brainstorm words and phrases that express their image of what it means to be a disciple of Christ and write their ideas on newsprint.
- Display their responses and have the young people circle the room, reviewing the other groups' lists of words and phrases.
- As a class, talk about concrete ways young people can take part in the mission of the Church in school, at home, and in the community.

### CHOOSE

- Invite the young people to reflect on what they have learned about the mission that Christ entrusted to his Church.
- Invite them to privately make and write their faith decision.
- Encourage everyone to put their faith decision into practice.

### PRAY

Invite the students to quiet themselves for prayer. Pray 1 Corinthians 3:11 together.

### *Enriching the Lesson*

The "Living the Mission" activity on page 69 is related to today's content. You may wish to include it in today's lesson.

# Day 5

## Pray and Review

### FOCUS

Introduce Zechariah, the father of Saint John the Baptist and the husband of Saint Elizabeth. Point out that after his vision about the forthcoming birth of his son, Zechariah was made speechless because he did not believe the angel's words that Elizabeth would bear a child. After he regained his speech, Zechariah praised God for sending the Savior. Explain that Zechariah's prayer of praise is also known as the Benedictus and is recited daily as a part of the Morning Prayer of the Church.

### PRAY

- Identify the two groups who will pray their part together.
- Pray "The Canticle of Zechariah."

### REVIEW

- Have the young people share the meaning of the terms in "Faith Vocabulary" and compare their definitions with those in the glossary.
- Use the "Main Ideas" and "Critical Thinking" sections to clarify any questions the students may have concerning what they have learned in the chapter.
- Remind everyone to share and discuss the "Family Discussion" question with their family.

### *Before Moving On . . .*

Before moving on to the next chapter, reflect on this question.

*How well have I made connections for the young people between what they are learning and their lives?*

# PRAY and REVIEW

## The Canticle of Zechariah

**Leader:** Living God, our Savior, you are ever present among us, working the wonder of our Salvation. Let us lift up our hearts in thanksgiving and praise of you for your wonderful deeds.

**Group 1:** "Blessed be the Lord, the God of Israel, / for he has visited and brought redemption to his people. /

**Group 2:** He has raised up a horn for our salvation / within the house of David his servant, / even as he promised through the mouth of his holy prophets from of old: /

**Group 1:** salvation from our enemies and from the hand of all who hate us, / to show mercy to our fathers / and to be mindful of his holy covenant /

**Group 2:** and of the oath he swore to Abraham our father, / and to grant us that, rescued from the hand of enemies, / without fear we might worship him in holiness and righteousness / before him all our days."

Luke 1:68–75

**All:** **Glory to the Father, and to the Son, and to the Holy Spirit: / as it was in the beginning, is now, and will be for ever. Amen.**

### FAITH VOCABULARY

Define each of these terms.

1. Church
2. Apostles
3. Resurrection
4. Great Commission
5. Paschal Mystery
6. Pentecost

### MAIN IDEAS

Choose either (a) or (b) from each set of items. Write a brief paragraph to answer each of your choices.

1. (a) Describe the origins of the Church. pp. 10–11
   (b) Explain the importance of Jesus' Resurrection. p. 12
2. (a) Explain the work of the Holy Spirit in the Church. p. 14
   (b) Compare the work of the Apostles with the work of the Church on earth today. pp. 13–15

### CRITICAL THINKING

Using what you have learned in this chapter, reflect on and explain the meaning of this teaching of the Church:

"The Church in this world is the sacrament of salvation, the sign and the instrument of the communion of God and men" (*Catechism of the Catholic Church* 780).

### FAMILY DISCUSSION

What can your family do to participate more fully in the work of the Church?

For more ideas on ways your family can live your faith, visit the "Faith First for Families" page at **www.FaithFirst.com**. Read the Bible story on the Teen Center this week.

18

## Evaluate

Take a few moments to evaluate this week's lesson.

I feel (circle one) about this week's lesson.

a. very pleased
b. OK
c. disappointed

The activity the students enjoyed most was . . .

The concept that was most difficult to teach was . . .

because . . .

Something I would like to do differently is . . .

# ENRICHING THE LESSON

## Creating Personal Faith Timelines

### Purpose

To reinforce that as members of the Church we each have our own personal histories of faith as we strive to follow Christ's way (taught on page 13)

### Directions

- Distribute construction paper and markers to the young people.
- Invite the students to create personal timelines beginning with their births.
- Create your own timeline in advance to share with the young people as an example.
- Invite them to use different colored markers to add key people and key events to their timelines.
- Display the timelines and invite volunteers to share their timelines with the class.

### Materials

construction paper and markers

## Exploring the Nicene Creed

### Purpose

To reinforce that the core beliefs of the Church stated in the Nicene Creed unite all faithful believers in Christ (taught on page 15)

### Directions

- Invite the young people to read the Nicene Creed on page 136.
- Ask the students to write down one belief stated in the Nicene Creed that they would like to learn more about.
- Have them research the meaning of that belief and give a one-paragraph report the next time the class meets.
- Gather the reports and create a booklet to display as a reminder of the faith tradition of the Catholic Church.

### Materials

paper, pens, construction paper for booklets

## Living the Mission

### Purpose

To reinforce the many ways that young people can actively participate in the mission of the Church (taught on page 17)

### Directions

- Invite a panel of guests to meet with your class. Invite parish and school leaders and others who witness to their faith in the community.
- Ask the guests to share their faith stories, focusing on key events and key people who have been a part of their faith "history." Be sure that each guest tells how they are participating in the mission of the Church. Note: When selecting your guests, include someone who will share specifically about the opportunities young people have to be disciples in their school, parish, and community.
- Allow time for questions and discussion.
- Invite the students to write thank-you notes to send to the guests after their visit.

### Materials

paper and markers for student-made thank-you notes

## Music Connection

- "Amor de Dios/O Love of God," B. Hurd. *Flor y Canto* #656.
- "City of God," D. Shutte. *Gather Comprehensive (GC)* #663.
- "Sing a New Church" (Traditional). *GC* #644.
- "We Are One Body," D. Scallon. *Voices As One* #98.

* Music in *Gather Comprehensive* comes from the second edition.

# Chapter 2 The Church Grows
## A.D. 50–A.D. 400

## CHAPTER BACKGROUND

### The Apostolic Age

Saint Luke in the Acts of the Apostles presents the spread of the Gospel from Jerusalem to Rome. He begins with the Ascension of Jesus and ends with the death of Saint Peter.

The practices and characteristics of the early Church described in Acts of the Apostles 2:42–43, 47 remain easily recognizable in the Church today: Baptism, faith in God's presence, the breaking of the bread, a vibrant prayer life, a sense of awe, a commitment to people in need, and the leadership role of the Apostles and their successors.

During the Apostolic Age, the period in the history of the Church when the Apostles and other eyewitnesses to Jesus' life on earth were still alive, the basic structure of the Church on earth emerged. That basic structure remains today.

### The Age of the Holy Spirit

The Acts of the Apostles and the New Testament letters record how the Holy Spirit guided the Apostles and the early Church to a deeper understanding of the truth about Jesus, about his work on earth, and about his teachings. (See John 16:13.)

The Holy Spirit also invited Saul, the zealous persecutor of the followers of Jesus, to come to faith in Jesus. The dramatic account of Saul's conversion is among the most well-known stories in the New Testament. (See Acts of the Apostles 9:1–30.)

Paul—as Saul called himself after his conversion—traveled the lands around the Mediterranean, preaching the Gospel and teaching about Christ. Paul's missionary journeys, combined with those of the other Apostles, helped spread the Gospel to the ends of the known world. His letters provide profound inspired theological insights into the life and work of Christ.

### Faith Seeking Understanding

Much of the drama that accompanied the growth of the Church during the Apostolic Age involved dealing with the search for a deeper and clearer understanding of Christ and his teachings. For example, what was the relationship between the Old Law and the New Law of grace established in Christ? Who was Jesus Christ? Was he God in human form, half God and half man? Was he fully and truly God and fully and truly human?

Explaining the faith of the Church about these and other truths of faith was difficult and time consuming. It sometimes led to divisions within the Church. While dealing with these and other tasks may have occasionally led to the rise of some false teachers, this work of the Church also called forth some of the greatest teachers of the Church.

## FOR REFLECTION

***How aware am I of my connection with the Christians who lived in the first three centuries?***

***What can I do to make the story of the Church come alive for the students?***

## First Thoughts

### The Journey of Faith

Each of us, as a member of the Church, has a personal journey of faith. Each of us also looks for ways that our faith in Christ connects with our daily life as we make that journey. As members of the Church, we join with other believers to make our journey and discover those connections. The journey of faith is a journey of adventure, of challenge, of struggle, and of triumph. It is a journey that includes passing on the story of the fulfillment of Jesus' command, "Go, therefore, and make disciples of all nations" (Matthew 28:19).

#### An Adventure of Faith

Young people need models of faith. They need people who, by their lives, are witnessing to the faith of the Church. The lives of people of faith who have faced or who are facing the struggles and challenges of living the Gospel invite young people to value living the life of faith as an adventure. The lives of people of faith speak to the idealism and energy of young people. Use the faith stories of the devotion and commitment of heroes of the Catholic Church to inspire and motivate the students to participate actively in the mission of the Church. Be a living model of faith and invite the young people to join you in living the faith adventure of being a disciple of Christ.

### The Church Teaches . . .

The *General Directory for Catechesis* reminds us of the true source of the entire catechetical message. It teaches:

> *"Catechesis will always draw its content from the living source of the word of God transmitted in Tradition and the Scriptures, for sacred Tradition and sacred Scripture make up a single sacred deposit of the word of God, which is entrusted to the Church."*[1]
>
> *GDC* 94

In this chapter the students examine how the early Church clarified her beliefs and worship practices while remaining true to the teachings of Christ.

#### See the Catechism . . .

For more on the teachings of the Catholic Church, the Deposit of Faith, and the development of worship, see *Catechism of the Catholic Church* 80–84 and 1086–1090.

*God of history,
you invite us into the adventure
of discipleship through your Son,
Jesus. Teach us to understand the
past, joyfully recognize you in the
present, and work to build a
future focused on your Kingdom.
Amen.*

Footnote references may be found on page 256.

Now . . . turn the page and let's get organized!

# LESSON PLANNER

**Chapter Focus**
**To understand how the early Church both struggled to find her identity and proclaimed the Gospel far and wide**

| Focus | Process | Materials and Options |
|---|---|---|
| **DAY 1**<br>**Engage/Teach and Apply**<br>**Pages 19–21**<br>**Focus**<br>To understand the challenges of the early Church to carry Jesus' message to every corner of the Roman Empire | **Opening Prayer**<br>**Discussion**<br>How the Gospel was spread by the people and events of the first three centuries<br>**Presentation**<br>Read, discuss, and summarize content.<br>**Scripture:** Acts of the Apostles 2:47, 6:7, 8:1–3, 15–21; Matthew 28:19<br>**Activity:** Create news reports based on the people and events in the Church's first century. | **Materials**<br>Bibles<br>pens or pencils<br>**Options**<br>***Called to Prayer and Liturgical Lessons* booklet:** See options for daily, seasonal, and liturgical prayer and lessons.<br>**Enriching the Lesson (TG page 83)**<br>Writing Job Descriptions for Christians . . . Then and Now |
| **DAY 2**<br>**Teach and Apply**<br>**Pages 22–23**<br>**Focus**<br>To discover how the Gospel was proclaimed in the first centuries of the Church's history | **Prayer**<br>**Presentation**<br>Read, discuss, and summarize content.<br>**Activity:** Discuss leadership in the early Church and in today's Church.<br>**Did you know:** The Apostles' Creed<br>**Faith Connection:** Reflect on how to pass on the teaching of the Apostles. | **Materials**<br>3" x 5" cards<br>pens or pencils<br>**Options**<br>**Enriching the Lesson (TG page 83)**<br>Explaining the Faith<br>***Additional Activities and Assessment Tools* booklet**<br>Storyboard: Council of Jerusalem, page 9 |
| **DAY 3**<br>**Teach/Apply and Connect**<br>**Pages 24–25**<br>**Focus**<br>To discover how the practice of Christian worship developed in the early Church | **Prayer**<br>**Presentation**<br>Read, discuss, and summarize content.<br>**Faith Connection:** Consider ways you take part in the liturgical life of the Church.<br>**Our Church Makes a Difference**<br>Learn about the two basic types of religious communities in the Church. | **Materials**<br>pens or pencils<br>**Options**<br>**Enriching the Lesson (TG page 83)**<br>Hearing Guest Speakers from Religious Communities |
| **DAY 4**<br>**Connect and Apply**<br>**Pages 26–27**<br>**Focus**<br>To discover that like our ancestors in faith, we are challenged to be active participants in the life and work of the Church | **Prayer**<br>**What Difference Does Faith Make in My Life?**<br>Understand the value of community and consider how you are a viable member of the Church community.<br>**Faith Decision:** Identify how to be an active and responsible member of the parish and what to do to spread the Gospel. | **Materials**<br>pens or pencils<br>**Options**<br>***Additional Activities and Assessment Tools* booklet**<br>Spiritual Growth Chart, page 10 |
| **DAY 5**<br>**Pray and Review**<br>**Page 28** | **Pray**<br>Pray "Proclaim the Gospel."<br>**Review**<br>**Activities:** Complete the review exercises to reinforce the concepts of the chapter.<br>**Family Discussion:** Encourage the students to share and discuss the question with their family this week. | **Materials**<br>pens and pencils<br>**Options**<br>***Additional Activities and Assessment Tools* booklet**<br>Administer chapter 2 test.<br>**Music Connection** (TG page 83) |

**Don't Forget!** You can make lesson planning a breeze—check out the **Online Lesson Planner** at www.FaithFirst.com for additional resources to enhance this chapter.

# The Church Grows: A.D. 50–A.D. 400

2

FAITH FOCUS

Why did the Gospel spread so widely during the first three centuries?

FAITH VOCABULARY

| | |
|---|---|
| Gentile | Council of Jerusalem |
| presbyters | Deposit of Faith |
| apologists | heresies |
| apostolic succession | |

***What clubs or organizations do you belong to? What do you know about their history and development?***

Have you ever been a member of a newly formed club or organization? Initially, there are just a few people with a lot of spirit. As the organization grows it draws up rules, forms a governing body, attracts new members, and becomes a visible part of your community. Something similar happened to the Church in her first four hundred years. By the end of the fourth century, the structure of the visible institution of the Church that we know today began to emerge.

***What do you know about the events and people that were part of the story of the Church in the first four centuries of her existence?***

Ruins at Corinth on the Peloponnese peninsula in southern Greece.

*And every day the Lord added to their number those who were being saved.*
Acts of the Apostles 2:47

19

## National Directory for Catechesis

**Implementing the *National Directory for Catechesis:* Learning by Discipleship.** The National Directory states: "For disciples, saying 'yes' to Jesus Christ means that they abandon themselves to God and give loving assent to all that he has revealed" (*NDC* 29B, page 99). Invite the students to express their faithfulness to the teaching of the Apostles by having them sign themselves with blessed water as they say, "I will guard and live the Deposit of Faith that has been handed on to me."

# Day 1

## Engage

### PRAY

- Invite the students to quiet themselves for prayer.
- Pray the Sign of the Cross together and have a volunteer proclaim Acts of the Apostles 2:47 from a class Bible.
- End by praying the Sign of the Cross together.

### FAITH FOCUS

Read aloud and invite responses to the "Faith Focus" question. Summarize by sharing that in this chapter the young people will learn how the Gospel was spread by people and events of the first three centuries.

### DISCOVER

Assess the students' prior knowledge of how the early Church grew from a small group of believers into a community living throughout the Roman Empire.

- Ask the introductory question.
- Read the opening paragraph aloud.
- Invite students to respond to the question at the end of the page. Write key words and phrases from their responses on the board.
- Point out the terms in "Faith Vocabulary" and ask the students to highlight the definitions as they read them in this chapter.

# Day 1

## Teach

**FOCUS**

Remind the young people that Jesus commanded the Apostles to make disciples of all nations. Share that these two pages will help them begin to discover how the Apostles began the mission entrusted to them by Jesus.

**DISCOVER**

- Paraphrase the first paragraph on page 20. Refer to the map on the page and discuss whether the early Church was successful in spreading the Gospel.
- Invite a volunteer to show the class where to find the Acts of the Apostles in the Bible.
- Have the young people read silently "The Earliest Disciples of Christ" to discover the relationship between Judaism and the early Church. Share that chapters 6 and 7 of the Acts of the Apostles illustrate the tension between the two groups.
- Have the students read and highlight key ideas in "Saint Paul's Mission to the Gentiles," and "The Council of Jerusalem."
- Invite the young people to work with partners to compare the ideas that they highlighted.

### Enriching the Lesson

The "Writing Job Descriptions for Christians . . . Then and Now" activity on page 83 is related to today's content. You may wish to include it in today's lesson.

## Make Disciples of All Nations

*The Stoning of St. Stephen*, oil on panel. Rembrandt Harmensz van Rijn (1606–1669), Dutch painter.

Jesus commanded the Apostles, "Go, therefore, and make disciples of all nations" (Matthew 28:19). Look at the map on this page. Where would you choose to go to fulfill Jesus' command? The Acts of the Apostles records the phenomenal spread of the Christian faith. Within a single generation, Jesus' followers carried his message to every corner of the Roman Empire.

### The Earliest Disciples of Christ

The earliest followers of Jesus were Jews. At first they were welcomed as followers of a renowned Jewish teacher, or rabbi. Because of their commitment to proclaiming and boldly living their faith in Jesus, the Son of God and Messiah, these followers of Jesus were eventually cut off from the Jewish community.

The stoning death of Saint Stephen is one example of the ever-widening distance that began to separate the earliest followers of Jesus from their fellow Jews. (See Acts of the Apostles 6:8–15, 7:54–60.) Tension continued to rise until about A.D. 70 when the Romans destroyed the Temple in Jerusalem. Around that time the leaders of the Jewish community formally banned all Jews who believed in Jesus from entering any Jewish synagogue.

### Saint Paul's Mission to the Gentiles

Shortly after the death, Resurrection, and Ascension of Jesus, the story of the **Gentile** believers in Jesus was also unfolding. In Sacred Scripture a Gentile is anyone who is not Jewish. In the New Testament, the story of the conversion of the Gentiles to Christ centers around the missionary work of Saint Paul, the Apostle to the Gentiles.

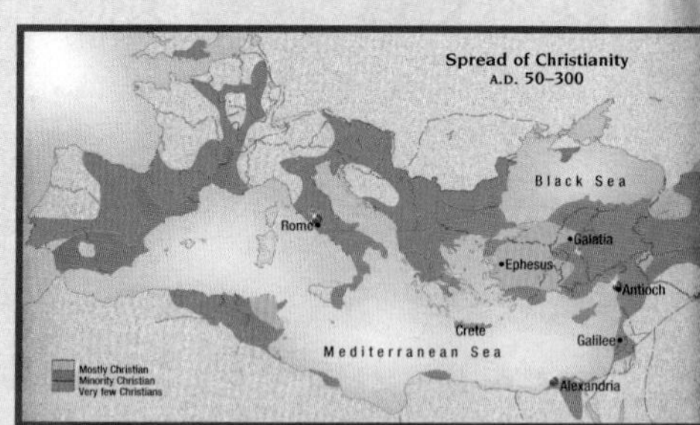


20

### Background: Doctrine

**Evangelization.** The *General Directory for Catechesis* reiterates the teaching of Pope Paul VI in his 1975 apostolic exhortation *On Evangelization in the Modern World*. The Directory teaches: "The Church 'exists in order to evangelize' (*On Evangelization in the Modern World* 14), that is 'the carrying forth of the Good News to every sector of the human race so that by its strength it may enter into the hearts of men and renew the human race' (*On Evangelization in the Modern World* 18). . . . Proclamation, witness, teaching, sacraments, love of neighbor: all of these aspects are the means by which the one Gospel is transmitted and they constitute the essential elements of evangelization itself" (*General Directory for Catechesis* 46).

Apostles Peter and Paul from an early fourth-century bas-relief sculpture fragment.

Saul the Pharisee was a zealous Jewish leader and persecutor of the followers of Jesus. (See Acts of the Apostles 8:1–3.) As he was traveling to the city of Damascus to arrest Christians and bring them back to Jerusalem Saul became a believer in Jesus. (See Acts of the Apostles 9:1–25.) After his conversion Saul began to use his Roman name, Paul. The zeal Paul once used to persecute the followers of Christ he now used to baptize, preach, and teach about Jesus, and make disciples of all nations.

### The Council of Jerusalem

Saint Paul's mission to the Gentiles proved to be both successful and controversial. The Apostles Peter and James the Greater, and other leaders of the Church in Jerusalem, objected to Saint Paul's inclusion of Gentiles among the followers of Jesus without their first becoming Jews. They gathered with Saint Paul at the **Council of Jerusalem** (ca. 51), the first council of the Church, to discuss and settle the controversy over the Gentiles. (See Acts of the Apostles 15:1–21.)

The Council of Jerusalem was a turning point for the Church. The Council's decision to allow Gentile converts into the Church without their first becoming Jews opened the door to the vast growth of the Church in the years to come. Eventually the Church would become predominantly Gentile in makeup and become totally distinct from Judaism.

The Council of Jerusalem is one example of how leaders of the Church struggled to settle their differences and understand the mission Christ gave the Apostles. This council and other historical events testify that the earliest leadership of the Church clearly rested on the shoulders of the Apostles and the **presbyters.** Presbyters were early Church leaders chosen by the Apostles to be their co-workers who governed the Church with them.

***Why was the Council in Jerusalem a turning point in the life of the Church?***

### Time LINE

| | |
|---|---|
| ca. 30–33 | Death, Resurrection, Ascension of Jesus |
| ca. 40–60 | Missionary journeys of Saint Paul the Apostle |
| ca. 51 | Council of Jerusalem |
| 64 | Persecution of Emperor Nero |
| ca. 65 | †Martyrdom of Saint Peter and Saint Paul |
| 70 | Destruction of Temple in Jerusalem by Romans |
| 98 | Persecution of Trajan |
| ca. 100 | †Martyrdom of Saint Clement of Rome |
| ca. 110 | †Saint John the Evangelist |
| ca. 165 | †Martyrdom of Saint Justin |

Note: The symbol † on the timeline indicates the year of the death of the person or persons.

### FAITH CONNECTION

*Think about the opportunities you have had to pass on the teachings of the Apostles to others. Choose one of those opportunities. How did you respond to that opportunity? How might you respond to that opportunity now?*

Affirm appropriate responses.

21

## Teaching Tip

**Relevant Then, Relevant Now.** No matter what century of Church history one studies, it seems to have relevance to what is going on in the Church today. Help the young people see the vital connection between the past and the present. The early Church grew rapidly when the first disciples of Jesus enthusiastically responded to the compassion of Jesus, to his promise of eternal life, to the Gospel values of charity and love, and to the unity and example of the first faith communities. Ask the class how they will respond to Jesus' compassion, to his promise of eternal life, to the Gospel values of charity and love, and to the unity of the Church.

# Day 1

## Apply

**REINFORCE**

- Write the heading A.D. *50*–A.D. *100* on the board. Present the "Timeline" feature on page 21 to help the students capture some of the key people and events within the Church during that time frame.
- Divide the class into three groups. Assign each group one of the following topics:
  —Jesus commissions the disciples (Matthew 28:19)
  —The first disciples (Acts of the Apostles 6 and 7)
  —Saul becomes Paul and the mission to the Gentiles (Acts of the Apostles 8:1–3, 9:1–25)
- Using their texts and the Scripture passages, have the groups create news reports concerning their assigned topic.
- Have the groups present their reports to the class.

**INTEGRATE**

- Have the young people work independently on the "Faith Connection" activity.
- Encourage faith sharing by inviting volunteers to share their responses with the class.

**PRAY**

Ask the young people to quiet themselves for prayer. Have them reflect on how they are living their faith in Christ. Conclude by praying the Glory Prayer, found on page 135 of the student text.

# Day 2

## Teach

### PRAY

Invite the young people to quiet themselves for prayer. Ask them to pray silently, thanking God for someone in their lives who has taught them about Jesus. Proclaim Acts of the Apostles 2:47.

### FOCUS

Ask the class to summarize the major events and people covered in the last lesson. Tell them that the next two pages present how the Gospel was proclaimed and taught in the early Church.

### DISCOVER

- Read the introductory paragraph aloud to the students.
- Have them read and discuss "Proclaiming the Gospel" and "The Deposit of Faith."
- Invite the young people to share with a partner the meaning of the term *Deposit of Faith,* describing its meaning in their own words.
- Explain that faithfulness to the teaching of the Apostles guides the passing on of the faith at all times and in all places.
- Share how your vocation as a religion teacher helps you share the faith of the Catholic Church with others. Discuss how the young people can do so as well.
- Read aloud the section "Defenders of the Faith" and have volunteers respond to the questions that follow it.

Saint Paul the Apostle preaching to the Athenians, nineteenth century, artist unknown.

Good friends, even the best of friends, sometimes have serious disagreements. Some of these disagreements are based on the sincere search for the truth. Others are based on opinions that are erroneous. The New Testament contains many examples of the efforts of Saint Paul and other leaders of the Church to settle disagreements and correct false teachings about the faith of the Church.

#### Proclaiming the Gospel

By the end of the first century, a structure within the Church was clearly emerging. After the death of the last Apostle, which tradition identifies as Saint John the Evangelist, leadership roles and other forms of ministry were in place that would characterize the shape of the Church for the future.

The roles and responsibilities of bishops, priests, and deacons were recognized and clarified. The bishop of Rome was recognized as being the successor of Saint Peter the Apostle whom Jesus made the visible foundation of the Church. (See Matthew 16:18.) He was clearly acknowledged as the leader of all other bishops and the pastor of the whole Church.

#### The Deposit of Faith

The **Deposit of Faith** is the heritage of faith contained in Sacred Scripture and Sacred Tradition. The faithful handing on of this Deposit of Faith from the time of the Apostles is one of the most sacred trusts of the Church. In writing to Saint Timothy, Saint Paul exhorts him, "Guard this rich trust with the help of the holy Spirit that dwells within us" (2 Timothy 1:14).

The letters of Saint Paul are among the earliest writings in the New Testament. They indicate that fulfilling the responsibility and office of truthfully and authentically passing on the teaching of the Apostles was a constant struggle. Saint Paul himself constantly addressed opinions contrary to the teachings of the Apostles and the Church and clarified those teachings.

***Why is the faithful handing on of the Deposit of Faith a sacred trust and essential work of the Church?***

22

### Teaching Tip

**Alternative Strategies.** Teaching is much more than reading a page in a book and explaining it. Presenting material can be done in many creative ways. Here are a few:

- Use your own words to explain what is on the page. Reading the book can then be a review or reinforcement.
- Have the young people quietly read a page or a section and then explain the material in their own words to a partner or in a small group.
- Write key words or phrases on the board. Have the young people read to discover their meanings.

## Defenders of the Faith

Faithfulness to the teaching of the Apostles is essential to the life of the Church. It is a matter of vital importance because being faithful to the preaching and teaching of the Apostles is a matter of Salvation. (See 1 Corinthians 15:1–19.)

In the effort of the Church to defend the faith against false teachings, **apologists**, such as Justin Martyr (d. 165), Apollonius (d. ca. 185), Clement of Alexandria (d. 215), Tertullian (d. 228), and Origen (d. 254), arose in the Church. The word *apologist* comes from a Greek word meaning "to defend." The apologists both defended and explained the faith of the Church and wrote about the faith of the Church for nonbelievers.

Among the apologists, bishops played a key role. Saint Irenaeus, bishop of Lyons, who died about 202, wrote *Adversus Haereses* (*Against Heresies*), a five-book response to the **heresies**, or false teachings, of the Gnostics. Gnostics held a wide range of views that challenged the teachings of the Apostles. Saint Irenaeus taught and explained the Church's doctrine on **apostolic succession**, namely, the bishops are the successors of the Apostles and have the responsibility and authority to teach and defend the true faith as Christ commanded the first Apostles to do.

The efforts of the apologists of the second and third centuries provided the groundwork for the work of the first great ecumenical councils of the Church—Nicaea I in 325 and Constantinople I in 384. An ecumenical council is a gathering of all the bishops of the world that is usually called by the Pope, or at least confirmed or accepted by him. At the Councils of Nicaea I and Constantinople I the teachings of the Apostles were reaffirmed and explained. The truths of the faith affirmed by these two councils are summarized in the creed that we usually profess at Mass each Sunday.

***What are some things that you might do to learn what the Church teaches? How would that help you be an apologist?***

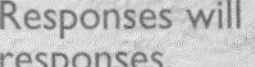

Responses will vary. Affirm appropriate responses.

### Did you Know...

The Apostles' Creed is an ancient creed that was used in the celebration of Baptism in Rome. The Apostles did not write the Apostles' Creed. It is called the Apostles' Creed because the teachings in this creed date back to the first decades of the Church. The earliest written form of the Apostles' Creed dates from 753.

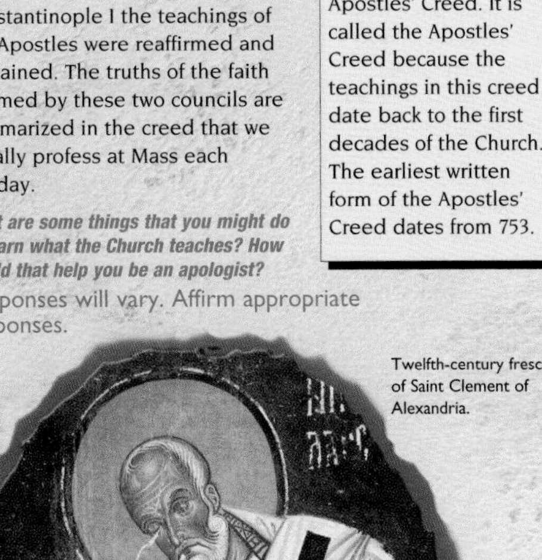

Twelfth-century fresco of Saint Clement of Alexandria.

23

# Day 2

## Apply

### REINFORCE

- Point out that while the term *apologists* is not commonly used today, the job of explaining the faith is a necessary task in every period of the Church's history.
- Invite a volunteer to read aloud the "Did you know" feature to learn more about the Apostles' Creed.

### INTEGRATE

- Distribute 3" x 5" cards to the group. Have the young people write a short description of someone they know or have read about who explains the Catholic faith today by leading others to a correct understanding of the faith of the Catholic Church.
- Have the students read aloud their finished index cards.

### PRAY

- Ask the students to quiet themselves. Then ask them to spend several minutes reflecting on how they respond to opportunities they have to pass on the teaching of the Apostles to others.
- Conclude by proclaiming Matthew 28:19 together.

## Background: Doctrine

**The Deposit of Faith.** The Deposit of Faith is the heritage of faith contained in Sacred Scripture and Sacred Tradition, handed on in the Church from the time of the Apostles, from which the Magisterium draws all that is proposed for belief as being divinely revealed. The Magisterium is the "living, teaching office of the Church, whose task it is to give as authentic interpretation of the word of God, whether in its written form (Sacred Scripture), or in the form of Tradition. The Magisterium ensures the Church's fidelity to the teaching of the Apostles in matters of faith and morals" ("Glossary," *Catechism of the Catholic Church*).

### *Enriching the Lesson*

The "Explaining the Faith" activity on page 83 is related to today's content. You may wish to include it in today's lesson.

# Day 3

## Teach

**PRAY**

Invite the young people to quiet themselves for prayer. Begin and conclude with the praying of the Sign of the Cross together. Have a student proclaim Acts of the Apostles 2:47 from a Bible.

**FOCUS**

Remind the students of the responsibility of remaining faithful to the Deposit of Faith. Point out that in today's lesson they will discuss how the liturgical rites of the Catholic Church developed in the early Church.

**DISCOVER**

- Summarize the first paragraph on page 24. Emphasize that while the worship of the Church has its roots in Jewish rituals, Christian worship was also influenced by the Church's mission to the Gentiles.
- Introduce the section "Christian Worship" by presenting the opening paragraph. Then invite four volunteers to read aloud "Orders," "Christian Initiation," "Eucharist," and the "Did you know" feature.

## Apply

**REINFORCE**

Invite responses to the question on page 24 that concludes the text.

**INTEGRATE**

Invite the young people to consider how they take part in the liturgical life of the Church. Have them work on the "Faith Connection" activity independently.

### Did you Know...

The *First Apology* of Saint Justin reveals that the order of Mass today is very similar to the way it was celebrated in the second century. Saint Justin wrote that on Sunday Christians gather in one place, the Scriptures are read, a homily is preached, donations for the poor are collected, bread and wine and water are brought forth, the celebrant prays and gives thanks, the people respond "Amen," and Holy Communion is distributed.

Groups celebrate their values and beliefs in many ways.The Church celebrates her faith and shares in the life and saving work of Christ in the liturgy. "In the liturgy . . . [Christ's] mystery of salvation is made present . . . by the power of his Holy Spirit" (*Catechism of the Catholic Church* 1111).

Early Christians worshiping in the catacombs of Saint Calixtus, below Rome.

### Christian Worship

Much of the way the Church celebrates her liturgy today has its roots in Jewish rituals. The mission to the Gentiles, however, introduced a number of changes in the rituals of Christian worship.

#### Orders

Bishops, helped by priests, their co-workers, and by deacons, are ordained to authentically teach the faith, celebrate divine worship, and guide the faithful in living the Gospel. From the time of the Apostles onward bishops, priests, and deacons have been ordained, or consecrated, to serve the Church by the laying on of hands.

#### Christian Initiation

The process of initiating new members into the Church gradually developed in the first three centuries. These rituals always involved a period of preparation, a formal questioning to establish the presence of faith, and the use of the Trinitarian formula in Baptism. Laying on of hands and anointing with oil were also used in the rite of Christian initiation.

#### Eucharist

The Eucharist is the memorial of Christ's Paschal Mystery, the work of our Salvation. The rites used in the celebration of Mass today also took shape in the days of the early Church. Saint Justin Martyr's (d. 165) *First Apology* (c. 148–155) describes the celebration of Mass at that time as amazingly similar to the way we celebrate the Mass today.

***What is the connection between the rites used in the liturgy of the Church today with those used in the early Church?***

**FAITH CONNECTION**

*Describe how you take part in the liturgical life of the Church.*

Affirm appropriate responses.

24

### Background: Catholic Tradition

**Basilicas.** Christians did not always gather in churches for worship. Christians first worshiped in synagogues and in homes. The first Christian churches were built in the fourth century and were called *basilicas.* Basilicas were large meeting halls. The main part of a basilica was called the *nave,* from a Latin word meaning "ship." When Christians first arrived at a basilica to celebrate the Eucharist, they gathered outside where they greeted one another and collected food to share with the needy. This food was eventually brought into the basilica and left near the altar at the beginning of the celebration.

# OUR CHURCH MAKES A DIFFERENCE

Religious sisters distributing clothing to flood victims in Chandipur, eastern India.

Within a few years after the Council of Jerusalem, local Churches sprang up throughout the lands around the Mediterranean. As the Church grew, some Christians, as early as the second century, joined together and formed communities to support one another in living the Gospel. Among the earliest of these communities were those that formed in Egypt around Saint Anthony of the Desert (c. 251–356). Eventually these communities took on the two basic forms which exist in the Church today, namely, contemplative life and apostolic life.

### Religious Communities

Today members of religious communities, or the consecrated life, live the Gospel of Jesus Christ according to a rule of life approved by the Church. Members make special promises or vows to follow the example of poverty, obedience, and chastity lived by Jesus Christ.

#### Contemplative Life

Members of contemplative communities commit themselves primarily to silence and prayer. Centering their day around the prayerful praise of God, they live a solitary life within community. Some contemplatives are cloistered. This means that they never leave the places where they live.

#### Apostolic Life

Members of apostolic religious communities support one another in the work of proclaiming the Gospel and serving others by living the Works of Mercy. Religious brothers and sisters, priests, and deacons work in hospitals and places that help the sick and elderly. They teach in parishes, schools, and universities. Others are active in social issues, working to build a just society for all. Members of other religious communities proclaim the Gospel as missionaries.

***How is both prayer and service part of the way you live the Gospel? How is your parish a community that lives the Gospel?***

Affirm appropriate responses.

Franciscan friars praying the Liturgy of the Hours.

25

## Background: Catholic Tradition

**Religious Communities—The Consecrated Life.** The baptized take part in fulfilling the mission Christ entrusted to his Church according to their state in life. Members of religious communities are called to the consecrated life. The consecrated life is the "state of life which is constituted by the profession of the evangelical counsels"[1] (*Catechism of the Catholic Church* 914.) All members who have dedicated their lives to living the Gospel of Jesus Christ in a religious community share in the Church's task of evangelization. They witness to the Christian life and collaborate with the bishops of the Church. "Religious life in its various forms is called to signify the very charity of God in the language of our time" (CCC 926).

# Day 3

## Connect

### HIGHLIGHT

Remind the class that the liturgical rites of the Church evolved from both Jewish roots and Gentile influences. Point out that as the Church grew, some Christians as early as the second century joined together to support one another in living the Gospel.

### DISCOVER

- Invite the young people to read "Religious Communities" silently.
- Point out that the two distinct and equally important features of religious communities, namely, prayer and service, were characteristics of these communities from their origins.

### INTEGRATE

- Briefly share with the young people how prayer and service are vital elements in your own life. Give appropriate examples.
- Ask the students to reflect for several minutes on the questions at the end of page 25. Invite volunteers to share their reflections.

### PRAY

- Encourage the young people to quiet themselves for prayer.
- Pray the Our Father together.

### *Enriching the Lesson*

The "Hearing Guest Speakers from Religious Communities " activity on page 83 is related to today's content. You may wish to include it in today's lesson.

# Day 4

## Connect

### PRAY

Invite the young people to quiet themselves for prayer and to join you in silently reading and reflecting on Acts of the Apostles 2:42–47.

### FOCUS

Remind the young people that the rapid growth of the early Church was accompanied by many challenges. Share that today's lesson will help them connect what they have learned in the chapter with their own lives.

### DISCOVER

- Read aloud the first paragraph on page 26.
- Write the word *community* in large letters on the board. Ask the class to brainstorm words and phrases that come to mind when they hear the word *community*. Create a word map by writing the words and phrases that they brainstorm around *community*.
- Next, ask the class to silently read the first three paragraphs of "Living in Community" and to underline words or phrases that they would want to add to the word map.
- Invite volunteers to add other words and phrases to the word map.
- Have the students discuss some of the communities to which they belong. Ask and discuss:
  —What characteristics make a community active and strong?
  —What characteristics threaten the strength of the community?
- Invite a volunteer to read aloud "The Church Community" on page 27.

# WHAT DIFFERENCE Does Faith Make in My Life?

In this chapter you learned about some of the major challenges and some of the heroes of the early Church. The first Christians met in homes in the towns and villages in which they lived. It was there that particular churches, or local communities of followers of Jesus, were first formed. Eventually the Church spread far and wide in fulfillment of Christ's command, "Make disciples of all nations."

## Living in Community

A community is a group of unified individuals who work together for a specific purpose or goal. All the members of a community profess and adhere to certain values, work together with a strong spirit of cooperation, and follow certain rules. Members must be willing to contribute to the group and accept and fulfill certain roles and responsibilities.

A team, in some ways, is a community. Imagine a team where one half of the members play by rules different than those set for the game and really do not care about the team, or are not willing to give of their time and energy and are not ready to accept their role and responsibility as team members. How can such a team be alive and well?

To be an active, responsible, and faithful member of a community, you must be willing to:

- believe in and promote the purpose of the group.
- be willing to make a difference in the group.
- be other-centered and not think only of your own needs and wants.

26

## Special Needs

**Reducing Assignment Length.** Consider reducing the length of assignments for those students who have limited writing proficiency or attention deficit challenges. This consideration should be given to chapter activities, chapter reviews, and unit reviews. For example, when a review item calls for the students to define more than three faith vocabulary terms, consider limiting the activity to three terms.

**Need:** Students with limited writing proficiency or attention deficits

✧ care about and be compassionate toward others.

✧ give generously of your time and energy to the group.

✧ participate and be an active, vibrant member of the group.

### The Church Community

You belong to the Catholic Church. How would you describe the type of Church member that you are?

✧ Are you a responsible member, an active participant?

✧ How well do you follow the teachings of Jesus as handed on by the Catholic Church?

✧ How willing are you to spread the Gospel?

There is an adage that says "A chain is only as strong as its weakest link." The truth expressed by this adage applies to all the members of the Church.

All the faithful are called to give witness to Christ. The Holy Spirit works through all the baptized, giving each one the grace to share in the mission of the Church on earth. You have the vocation and receive the grace to actively participate in the life and work of the Church each day wherever you are.

## Faith Decision

- Choose three of the six points listed on pages 26 and 27 that describe an active and responsible member of a community.

Affirm appropriate responses.

- Discuss in a small group how you can use the skills described in the points you chose to help you be an active, responsible, and faithful member of your parish.

Affirm appropriate responses.

This week I will choose to be an active and responsible member of my parish and work to spread the Gospel by

Affirm appropriate responses.

27

## Catholic Social Teaching

**Meaning and Value of Participation in Community Life.** Chapter 4 of the *Compendium of the Social Doctrine of the Church (CSDC)* speaks to the Catholic Church's teaching on the responsibility of people to participate in the work of the community. It teaches: *"[P]articipation . . . contributes to the cultural, economic, political and social life of the civil community to which he belongs.*[1] *Participation is a duty to be fulfilled consciously by all, with responsibility and with a view to the common good"*[2] (CSDC 189).

# Day 4

## Apply

### RESPOND

- Discuss with the students the six points for actively participating in a community that are listed on page 26.
- Challenge the young people to identify how each of the points makes a difference in the healthy functioning of a community.
- Invite the students to share additional points for being an active member of a community.

### CHOOSE

- Have the students work in small groups to reflect on and respond to the "Faith Decision" activity. Invite volunteers to share their responses.
- Encourage everyone to put their faith decision into practice.

### PRAY

- Invite the young people to quiet themselves for prayer.
- Proclaim Psalm 133:1 from a Bible and ask the students to reflect on what the Psalm verse says about a true community of faith.
- Conclude by praying the Act of Love on student page 137 together.

# Day 5

## Pray and Review

### FOCUS

- Remind the students that from the days of the early Church, all the baptized have been charged with the responsibility of proclaiming the Gospel.
- Explain that today's prayer asks for guidance for God's Church in proclaiming the Gospel and for being a force for justice, charity, and peace in the world.

### PRAY

- Invite four volunteers to be the readers for the prayer.
- Pray "Proclaim the Gospel" together.
- Encourage the young people to pray for the Church often.

### REVIEW

- Have the young people share the meaning of the terms in "Faith Vocabulary" and compare their definitions with those in the glossary.
- Use the "Main Ideas" and "Critical Thinking" sections to clarify any questions the students may have concerning what they have learned in the chapter.
- Remind everyone to share and discuss the "Family Discussion" question with their families.

**Before Moving On . . .**

Before moving on to the next chapter, reflect on this question.

*How have I shared the excitement of both the early Church and the present Church with the young people this week?*

# PRAY and REVIEW

## Proclaim the Gospel

**Leader:** God our Father, in your loving wisdom you have spread the kingdom of Jesus to encompass the globe. May your Church reveal your love for the whole world to see. We ask this through our Lord Jesus Christ, your Son, who lives and reigns with you and the Holy Spirit, one God, for ever and ever.

**All:** **Amen.**

**Reader 1:** A reading from the Acts of the Apostles.
*Proclaim Acts of the Apostles 2:42–47.*
The word of the Lord.

**All:** **Thanks be to God.**
*Silently reflect on the reading.*

**Reader 2:** Keep your Church faithful to her mission of building the Kingdom of God and transforming the world into your family.

**All:** **Lord, hear our prayer.**

**Reader 3:** May your Church be a holy people and a sign of unity and holiness to all.

**All:** **Lord, hear our prayer.**

**Reader 4:** May your Church be a force for justice, charity, and peace in the world.

**All:** **Lord, hear our prayer.**

**Leader:** Eternal Father, guide your Church through your Holy Spirit. Help her be strong in faith so that she may preach the Gospel of your Son to people everywhere.

**All:** **Amen.**

28

### FAITH VOCABULARY

Define each of these terms:

1. Gentile
2. Council of Jerusalem
3. presbyters
4. Deposit of Faith
5. apologists
6. heresies
7. apostolic succession

### MAIN IDEAS

Choose either (a) or (b) from each set of items. Write a brief paragraph to answer each of your choices.

1. (a) Explain the controversy that was settled at the Council of Jerusalem. p. 21
   (b) Describe the mission of Saint Paul the Apostle. pp. 21–22
2. (a) Summarize both the role of bishops and the role of the Councils of Nicaea I and Constantinople I in the Church. p. 23
   (b) Describe worship in the early Church. p. 24

### CRITICAL THINKING

Using what you have learned in this chapter, briefly explain this statement:

By virtue of their prophetic mission, lay people "are called . . . to be witnesses to Christ in all circumstances and at the very heart of the community of mankind" [GS 43§4] (*Catechism of the Catholic Church* 942).

### FAMILY DISCUSSION

Family prayer is a vital part of the daily life of a Christian. How do we pray each day as a family?

For more ideas on ways your family can live your faith, visit the "Faith First for Families" page at **www.FaithFirst.com**. Also check out "Make a Difference" on the Teen Center.

## Evaluate

Take a few moments to evaluate this week's lesson.

I feel (circle one) about this week's lesson.

a. very pleased
b. OK
c. disappointed

The activity the students enjoyed most was . . .

The concept that was most difficult to teach was . . .

because . . .

Something I would like to do differently is . . .

# ENRICHING THE LESSON

## Writing Job Descriptions for Christians . . . Then and Now

**Purpose**

To reinforce the responsibility of all Christians to spread the Good News of Jesus in the twenty-first century as disciples in the early Church did (taught on pages 20–21)

**Directions**

- Create small study groups.
- Encourage everyone to read and study the Scripture passages referenced in the text on pages 20 and 21.
- Using what they have learned about the disciples of Jesus who lived between A.D. 50 and A.D. 100, have each group prepare a job description for those disciples.
- Next, have the groups create a job description for disciples of Jesus today.
- Allow time for the groups to present their job descriptions.

**Materials**

paper
pens or pencils

## Explaining the Faith

**Purpose**

To reinforce the concept that in every age and in every place Christians are called to explain the faith of the Church (pages 22–23)

**Directions**

- Have the students work in pairs, with one partner assuming the role of teacher and the other partner assuming the role of a non-believing thirteen-year-old.
- Assign each pair of students one or two of the articles of faith named in the Apostles' Creed.
- Have the "teacher" explain one of the articles of faith to the "non-believing thirteen-year-old."
- Then have the partners switch roles, with the new "teacher" explaining a second article of faith.
- Ask volunteers to demonstrate their explanations to the class as time allows.

**Materials**

none

## Hearing Guest Speakers from Religious Communities

**Purpose**

To reinforce that living in a religious community is one of the ways Christians choose to support one another in living the Gospel (taught on page 25)

**Directions**

- Invite two guest speakers who are members of a religious community to visit with your class and participate in a panel discussion on living in religious community. Note: One speaker can be from a contemplative community, the other from a community whose apostolate is service, such as health care, teaching, or serving the poor and vulnerable.
- Have the guests describe how they came to be a part of their community and the ways that being a part of the community helps them live the Gospel in concrete ways.
- Encourage the young people to ask questions.

**Materials**

none

### Music Connection

- "On a Journey Together," J. Angotti. *Gather Comprehensive (GC)* #653.
- "Somos Una Iglesia," E. Cortés. *Flor y Canto* #724.
- "Strength for the Journey," M. J. Poirer. *Voices As One* #87.
- "We Are Marching," (South African). *GC* #516.

Chapter 3

# "Blessed Are the Persecuted"

## CHAPTER BACKGROUND

### The Age of Martyrs

History can be perceived in many ways. It may be seen as an endless cycle that constantly repeats itself, a lemming-like march toward annihilation, or a fitful but continuous journey with Christ toward unity and peace. Christ came to bring the world the oneness and peace that it so desperately seeks and for which God created it. The Church is the Holy Spirit's instrument to establish that oneness and peace.

With the outpouring of the Holy Spirit at Pentecost, the Church began that mission. The Church started small, in a remote and unruly outpost of the Roman Empire. The world in which the Church took her first bold steps can be described as "senseless, faithless, heartless, ruthless" (Romans 1:31). These harsh circumstances soon took their toll on the fledgling Church as she attracted the attention of heartless and ruthless civil authorities.

### The Missionary Church

From the small community of Apostles and other disciples in Jerusalem, a missionary outreach first began among Greeks, Romans, Africans, and the peoples at the perimeters of the Roman Empire. This missionary work was conducted by such early heroes as Saints Peter, Paul of Tarsus, Bartholomew, James, and the other Apostles. The Roman authorities soon realized that there was a movement across its lands that recognized an authority other than its emperor.

An age of persecution was initiated. Christians were sporadically hunted down, imprisoned, and sometimes put to death by Roman authorities for nearly three hundred years. Although there were occasional intervals of peace, the first centuries of the Church had become an age filled with both senseless cruelty and heroic fidelity. The martyrs of the early Church have come to be revered not just as figures of the past but as living intercessors for those living during dangerous times.

### The Teaching Church

Dangers, however, existed not only outside the Church but also within the Church. Saint Paul addressed this fact when he warned: "Keep watch over yourselves and over the whole flock. . . . [F]rom your own group, men will come forward perverting the truth to draw the disciples away after them" (Acts of the Apostles 20:28, 30). Indeed, many threatened the Gospel with a variety of false teachings, or heresies. The early Church countered by developing structures that met the challenge and preserved the purity of the Gospel with a unity centered on the Eucharist.

## FOR REFLECTION

***What sacrifices am I willing to make to be faithful to the Gospel?***

***How can I help the young people identify and face contemporary challenges to their living the Gospel?***

## First Thoughts

### Giving It Their All

Junior high adolescents are very familiar with making sacrifices. The aspiring dancers and skaters, football players and swimmers, musicians and actors among you sacrifice much, at even this young age, to reach goals they have judged to be worth pursuing. In an analogous sense, they are willing to be "martyrs," willing to give it their all, sometimes no matter what the cost, to achieve their goals. Use this connection to help your students begin to appreciate the depth of faith and commitment of the martyrs of the Church.

### Really Real

The life stories of the martyrs of the early Church can have an immense impact on your students. The young people will be amazed as you read and share with them the courage of these faith-filled people. Young adolescents grasp the reality of martyrdom—that these are real stories about real people and that they really did live and die for their faith. Remind them that Christians today are willing to die for their faith.

## The Church Teaches . . .

In his homily at the Shrine of Namugongo, Uganda, Pope Paul VI explained why martyrs should be honored. He said:

> It is because they have performed the most heroic, and therefore the greatest and most beautiful of all actions, they have, as I said, laid down their lives for their Faith, that is, for their religion and for the freedom of their conscience. Therefore they are our champions, our heroes, our teachers (August, 1969).

This chapter explores how martyrs throughout the history of the Church have strengthened the faith of the baptized and inspired nonbelievers to become followers of Christ.

### See the Catechism . . .

For more on the teachings of the Catholic Church on martyrs, see *Catechism of the Catholic Church* 957, 1173, 2473, and 2474.

*Faithful God,
the example of the
Church's martyrs shows
us how to live our
faith with conviction.
Strengthen us to stand
up for our faith in you.
Amen.*

Now . . . turn the page and let's get organized!

# LESSON PLANNER

**Chapter Focus**
**To discover how the martyrs in the early Church influenced the faith of the Church**

| Focus | Process | Materials and Options |
|---|---|---|
| **DAY 1**<br>**Engage/Teach and Apply**<br>**Pages 29–31**<br>**Focus**<br>To understand why the blood of the martyrs was called the seed of the Church | **Opening Prayer**<br>**Discussion**<br>How the faith of the martyrs influenced other believers<br>**Presentation**<br>Read, discuss, and summarize content.<br>**Scripture:** Matthew 5:11<br>**Activity:** Compare the martyrs and the Church's growth.<br>**Did you know:** Persecutions of the early Church<br>**Faith Connection:** Identify Gospel values. | **Materials**<br>pens or pencils<br>**Options**<br>***Called to Prayer and Liturgical Lessons* booklet:** See options for daily, seasonal, and liturgical prayer and lessons.<br>***Additional Activities and Assessment Tools* booklet**<br>Haiku: Martyrs of the Church, page 11 |
| **DAY 2**<br>**Teach and Apply**<br>**Pages 32–33**<br>**Focus**<br>To explore the causes behind the martyrdom that occurred in the early Church | **Prayer**<br>**Presentation**<br>Read, discuss, and summarize content.<br>**Activity:** Discuss Judaism and Christianity in the Roman Empire.<br>**Did you know:** The letters of Saint Ignatius of Antioch<br>**Faith Connection:** Describe the sacrifices of martyrs. | **Materials**<br>3" x 5" cards or slips of paper<br>pens or pencils<br>**Options**<br>**Enriching the Lesson (TG page 97)**<br>Reporting on Contemporary Christian Persecutions<br>Writing Prayers of Thanksgiving |
| **DAY 3**<br>**Teach/Apply and Connect**<br>**Pages 34–35**<br>**Focus**<br>To identify and learn about contemporary martyrs | **Prayer**<br>**Presentation**<br>Read, discuss, and summarize the content.<br>**Activity:** Identify the difference between Roman and Christian values and beliefs.<br>**Faith Connection:** Reflect on your freedom to worship.<br>**Our Church Makes a Difference**<br>Read and discuss the Martyrs of El Salvador. | **Materials**<br>newsprint<br>markers<br>pens or pencils<br>**Options**<br>***Additional Activities and Assessment Tools* booklet**<br>Facing Faith Challenges with Hope and Joy, page 12 |
| **DAY 4**<br>**Connect and Apply**<br>**Pages 36–37**<br>**Focus**<br>To identify and learn skills to cope with change and stress | **Prayer**<br>**What Difference Does Faith Make in My Life?**<br>Identify steps to handle stress.<br>**Activity:** Discuss how to handle stressful situations common to junior high students.<br>**Faith Decision:** Choose to deal with challenges to live your faith this week. | **Materials**<br>pens or pencils<br>**Options**<br>**Faith First *Liturgy and Morality* video**<br>Segment 4: "Story of Faith"<br>**Enriching the Lesson (TG page 97)**<br>Creating Review Games |
| **DAY 5**<br>**Pray and Review**<br>**Page 38** | **Pray**<br>Pray "Blessed by God" together.<br>**Review**<br>**Activities:** Complete the review exercises to reinforce the concepts of the chapter.<br>**Family Discussion:** Encourage the students to share and discuss the question with their family this week. | **Materials**<br>pens or pencils<br>**Options**<br>***Additional Activities and Assessment Tools* booklet**<br>Administer chapter 3 test.<br>**Music Connection** (TG page 97) |

**Don't Forget!** You can make lesson planning a breeze—check out the **Online Lesson Planner** at www.FaithFirst.com for additional resources to enhance this chapter.

# "Blessed Are the Persecuted"

How did Christians' suffering for the faith influence the early Church?

FAITH VOCABULARY

martyrs
paganism
polytheism

***When have you been ridiculed or hurt for living your faith in Jesus Christ?***

Imagine a situation during which an individual or a group of people might be persecuted for zealously living out their beliefs and values in a society which rejected those beliefs and values. That is what happened to the early Church—and continues to happen today.

***How do you think the persecution of the early Church helped strengthen the Church?***

*Saint Lawrence receiving the treasures of the Church,* fresco. Fra Angelico, Friar Giovanni da Fiesole, (c. 1395–1455), Dominican priest, early Italian renaissance painter.

*"Blessed are you when they . . . persecute you . . . because of me."*
MATTHEW 5:11



## National Directory for Catechesis

**Implementing the *National Directory for Catechesis:* Making a Commitment to Live the Christian Life.** The National Directory emphasizes that the "active participation of all the catechized in their Christian formation fosters learning by doing" (*NDC* 29G, page 104). As you discuss how the faith of the martyrs inspires us to live our faith, ask the students to consider how their own personal example and witness can be a source of inspiration for others. Invite the students to prayerfully reflect and identify one particular way that they might inspire others to live their faith in Jesus.

# Day 1

## Engage

### PRAY

Ask the young people to quiet themselves for prayer. Remind them of God's faithful presence. Pray the Sign of the Cross and proclaim Matthew 5:11 together.

### FAITH FOCUS

Read or paraphrase the "Faith Focus" question about how the suffering of the early Church for the faith influenced the growth of the Church. Share that in this chapter the young people will learn about the persecution of the early Church.

### DISCOVER

Assess the students' prior knowledge of persecution and martyrdom in the early Church.

- Ask the opening question. Invite volunteers to share their responses. Share appropriate examples of your own experiences of being ridiculed or hurt because of your faith.
- Read or paraphrase the paragraph.
- Have partners discuss the question at the end of the page.
- Gather the students in one large group. Then ask, Why do you think Jesus called those who are persecuted because of him blessed?

# Day 1

## Teach

**FOCUS**

- Remind the class that over the centuries, Christians have stood up for their faith in Jesus.
- Explain that these pages introduce them to persecution and martyrdom in the early Church.

**DISCOVER**

- Ask the students to respond "true" or "false" to this statement: The Church today suffers and is persecuted as she proclaims the Gospel.
- Invite volunteers to give examples to support their response. Then ask volunteers to share times when they have experienced suffering for living their faith in Jesus Christ.
- Suggest that the seed is often used as an image or symbol for growth. Write the phrase *Seed of the Church* on the board. Invite volunteers to read aloud "The Seed of the Church."
- Discuss Tertullian's statement that "The blood of the martyrs was the seed of the Church."
- Introduce the section "Persecutions" and have the class silently read it and underline two key points presented in the section.
- Have volunteers share the points that they underlined with the class.

## Witnessing to the Faith

*Public Life in the Forum in Rome*, third century, artist unknown.

The Church today, as she has in the past, suffers and is persecuted as she proclaims the Gospel. This happens in both dramatic and in silent, less dramatic ways.

### "The Seed of the Church"

The tradition of the Church recounts that all the Apostles, with the exception of Saint John the Evangelist, were **martyrs** of the Church. The word *martyr* comes from a Greek word meaning "witness." The martyrs of the Church are those who witness to their faith in Christ by suffering death.

After the death of the last Apostle, countless other Christians followed their example and gave heroic witness to their faith in Christ. They courageously responded to the demands of discipleship described by Jesus:

> "Whoever wishes to come after me must deny himself, take up his cross, and follow me. For whoever wishes to save his life will lose it, but whoever loses his life for my sake will find it." Matthew 16:24–25

The courage and heroism of the martyrs testified to their faith in the Paschal Mystery, to their hope in the eternal life promised by Christ, and to their love for Christ. The North African theologian Tertullian of Carthage (160–d. ca. 215) described the vital role that martyrs played in the growth of the Church. He

Defeat of Roman Emperor Valerian by Shapur I of Persia at Edessa in 260. Persian bas-relief.

30

### Teaching Tip

**Work on Concentration Skills.** Some learners have disabilities that affect their ability to concentrate. Here are a few suggestions to consider in working with these learners:

- Give the young people very clear and specific tasks.
- Provide them with opportunities to choose activities that interest them.
- Be very clear when giving directions.
- Rephrase the directions and invite questions to assure everyone understands them.

Roman Emperor Diocletian.

expressed it this way, "The blood of the martyrs was the seed of the Church."

Take a moment to name the religions whose members freely worship in your town or city. While religious freedom is a right we take for granted in our country, the Church was not always free to worship publicly and still is not free to do so in some countries today.

### Persecutions

While Christians in the second and third centuries often faced the reality of martyrdom, the ancient Roman Empire was, for the most part, characterized by a high degree of religious tolerance. The Romans had a live-and-let-live approach to the people living in the territories they had conquered. As long as people observed Roman rule, offered sacrifice to the Roman deities, paid taxes, and did not engage in any rebellious activity, they were allowed to conduct their religious practices unhampered.

Luke's Gospel describes an incident that reflects this working relationship that existed between the Jews and the Romans. Luke tells us about a time when the scribes and chief priests, in an attempt to trap Jesus and get him to speak out against the Romans, questioned Jesus:

> "Is it lawful for us to pay tribute to Caesar or not?" Recognizing their craftiness he said to them, "Show me a denarius; whose image and name does it bear?" They replied, "Caesar's." So he said to them, "Then repay to Caesar what belongs to Caesar and to God what belongs to God." LUKE 20:22–25

Initially, the Roman authorities perceived the followers of Jesus as a Jewish sect. The Church was tolerated and left undisturbed to practice her faith in Christ. But as Christians refused to offer sacrifice to the Roman gods, they aroused the anger of the emperor and other local officials. This "rebellious" activity led to periodic persecutions.

***Why did so many Christians continue to live and give witness to their faith, even in the face of death?***

### Did you Know...

Most of the persecutions suffered by the early Church were localized and relatively short-lived. However, under several of the Roman emperors there were extensive persecutions throughout the Empire. The most notable of these occurred during the reigns of the emperors Trajan (d. 117), Decius (d. 251), Valerian (d. 260), and Diocletian (d. 316).

### FAITH CONNECTION

***Work with a partner. Identify Gospel values and teachings of the Church that are contrary to or rejected by contemporary society. Discuss how living these values might cause you to be ridiculed by your peers.***

Responses will vary.

Affirm appropriate responses.

31

# Day 1

## Apply

### REINFORCE

- Present the "Did you know" feature to clarify the students' understanding of the persecutions of the early Church.
- Call for responses to the question on page 31.
- Highlight the faith vocabulary word *martyr* and have the young people define the term as a large group, then check their answers using the glossary.

### INTEGRATE

- Invite the young people to complete the "Faith Connection" activity with a partner. Have them imagine knowing a martyr of the early Church and consider how witnessing the martyrdom would impact their faith.
- Ask them to imagine a contemporary martyr, such as Archbishop Oscar Romero. Discuss how witnessing or knowing about someone's martyrdom in today's world would impact their faith.

### PRAY

Ask the young people to quiet themselves for prayer. Pray together the Prayer to the Holy Spirit on page 137.

## Teaching Tip

**Brainstorming.** Brainstorming is a good technique for assessing learning and student understanding of the material. Today, assess how well the young people are connecting the past history of people in the Church with their own present experiences as young Catholics. Brainstorm a list of things in the world today that make it difficult for Christians to live the Gospel. Challenge them to name things that make it difficult for young Catholics to live the Gospel today. Encourage every student to contribute. Point out that the early Church was challenged by aspects of Roman society that made it difficult to live the Gospel.

# Day 2

## Teach

### PRAY

Remind the young people of God's loving presence and call them to prayer. Pray the Sign of the Cross together. Ask a student to proclaim the Scripture passage on page 29. After a moment of silent reflection, conclude by praying the Sign of the Cross together.

### FOCUS

Ask several volunteers to tell about one way that a martyr would have a positive influence on someone's faith. Tell them that in the next two pages they will learn about several martyrs of the early Church.

### DISCOVER

- Have the class recall Tertullian's statement about the role that martyrs played in the growth of the Church, "The blood of martyrs was the seed of the Church."
- Brainstorm ways that Catholics in the United States might suffer for their faith today.
- Have the students silently read the introductory paragraph.
- Ask the class to divide into three groups. Assign one of the three sections presented on pages 32 and 33 to each group. Have each group read about the martyr or martyrs who are portrayed in the section assigned to it. Make sure that the group assigned Saint Ignatius of Antioch includes the "Did you know" feature in their reading.
- Have a volunteer from each group present the key points from its reading to the whole class.

### Did you Know...

Saint Ignatius of Antioch wrote many letters while the Roman authorities transported him from Antioch to Rome to face death. He wrote letters to the Church at Ephesus, Magnesia, Tralles, Rome, Philadelphia, Smyrna, and to Saint Polycarp (ca. 69–ca.156), the bishop of Smyrna who would also suffer martyrdom. In his letters Saint Ignatius urged Christians to live a life of love as Christ commanded in the hope of eternal life promised by Christ.

Saint Ignatius of Antioch, stained glass.

Many of the martyrs in the early Church died during times of persecution such as the persecution under Trajan, who was the Roman emperor from 98 to 117. Trajan permitted the death penalty for Christians who refused to worship the gods of Rome. His edict warned the Roman authorities, however, that Christians were not to be arrested and put to death on anonymous tips.

#### Saint Ignatius of Antioch

Saint Ignatius of Antioch (d. ca. 110), the second or third bishop of Antioch, was among the martyrs who were put to death as a result of Trajan's policy. When the civil authorities demanded that he comply with Trajan's order to worship the gods of Rome, Ignatius refused to comply. He was arrested, placed in prison, and condemned to death. By arresting Ignatius and condemning him to death, the imperial authorities hoped that the faith of the Church in Antioch would be weakened and that Christians would comply with Trajan's order. For the most part, however, the opposite happened.

During the trip from Antioch to Rome, which lasted several months, Ignatius was greeted by his supporters in cities along the way. He responded to his well-wishers by writing letters encouraging them to remain strong in their faith and to preserve the unity of the Church. When his friends in Rome offered to intercede on his behalf with the Roman authorities, Ignatius declined, writing to the Church at Rome, "I am God's wheat and bread. Pray to Christ for me that the animals will be the means of making me a sacrificial victim for God." Tradition has it that Ignatius was eaten by lions in Rome's amphitheater.

32

### Background: Catholic Tradition

**Saint Ignatius of Antioch, Bishop and Martyr.** Much of what we know about the first-century Church comes from the writings of Saint Ignatius of Antioch who died around A.D. 107. He tells us he was the bishop of the local church, and was assisted by priests and deacons. Saint Ignatius taught that the Eucharist was a sign of oneness of the Church; Sunday, the first day of the week, was the Lord's Day. When we read the writings of Saint Ignatius of Antioch, we see the close connection of the Church today with the apostolic Church.

## Saints Agatha, Lucy, and Agnes

Saint Agatha (d. ca. 251), Saint Agnes (d. ca. 258), and Saint Lucy (d. ca. 304) lived and were martyred during the rule of Emperor Diocletian. Saints Agatha and Lucy are associated with the island of Sicily, and Saint Agnes lived in or near the city of Rome.

While little historical detail is known about the lives and deaths of these third- and fourth-century martyrs of the Church, tradition says that they were sent to their death for refusing to surrender their virginity and for their faithfulness to Christ. Christians found the faith of these women a source of courage and fidelity to the Lord in times of their own persecution.

## Saint Lawrence the Deacon

Saint Lawrence the Deacon (d. 258), along with Pope Sixtus II and six other deacons, suffered martyrdom during the persecution of Valerian, who was the Roman emperor from 253 to 260. As one of the deacons of Pope Sixtus II, Lawrence was responsible for the care and use of the property of the Church in Rome. Among these responsibilities was caring for the poor.

Tradition passes on to us this remarkable story about Saint Lawrence. When the prefect of the city of Rome demanded that Lawrence turn over the gold of the Church to Rome, Lawrence gathered the poor of the city. Pointing to them he declared, "Here are the true treasures of the Church." Enraged by Lawrence's actions, the emperor had him killed.

***How do the faith stories of the early martyrs of the Church help you give witness to your faith in Christ?***

Responses will vary.
Affirm appropriate responses.

*Trial of Saint Lucy*, fresco. Altichiero da Zevio (1320–1385), Italian painter.

### Time LINE

- 215 †Tertullian of Carthage
- 229–250 Persecution under Emperor Decius
- 251 †Saint Agatha
- 258 Persecution under Emperor Valerian
- †Saint Agnes
- †Saint Lawrence the Deacon
- 303–305 Persecution under Emperor Diocletian
- 304 †Saint Lucy

33

## Teaching Tip

**Guidelines for Personal Sharing.** Here are a few guidelines for inviting the young people to share ideas during the sessions:

- Explain the importance of privacy and confidentiality.
- Do not force sharing.
- Talk privately with any member of the class who shares a serious problem or issue. Refer the situation to the proper staff members or professionals approved by the school when necessary.

# Day 2

## Apply

### REINFORCE

- Draw the students' attention to the timeline on the page, which illustrates the persecutions they have just learned about.
- Discuss with the students their responses to the question that concludes the text on page 33.

### INTEGRATE

- Distribute 3" x 5" cards or slips of paper to the young people.
- Ask the students to work independently and write down the sacrifices that people make today to give witness to their faith in Christ.
- Collect the cards to use in the closing prayer.
- As a group, work on the "Faith Connection" activity.

### PRAY

- Tell the students they will pray a prayer of thanksgiving for people who make sacrifices to follow the Gospel today.
- Read the sacrifices from the cards or slips of paper. After each is read, have the young people respond, "For giving witness to the Gospel, we thank you."
- Conclude by leading the class in praying the Glory Prayer.

### *Enriching the Lesson*

The "Reporting on Contemporary Christian Persecutions" and "Writing Prayers of Thanksgiving" activities on page 97 are related to today's content. You may wish to include them in today's lesson.

# Day 3

## Teach

### PRAY

Lead the students in praying the Act of Faith on page 137.

### FOCUS

Remind the students that Christians have always faced and met challenges to living their faith. Share that in today's lesson they will learn about the challenges the Church has faced and continues to face to live her faith.

### DISCOVER

- Point out that living in a pagan society was one of the challenges the early Church faced. Ask the students to silently read "Paganism."
- Have volunteers describe why paganism and polytheism were serious threats to the spiritual welfare of the Church.

## Apply

### REINFORCE

- Create small groups.
- Distribute newsprint and markers and have each group create a two-column chart, using the headings "Romans" and "Christians."
- Have each group list the key differences between the Romans and the Christians.
- Invite each group to share its work with the class.

### INTEGRATE

- Invite responses to discuss how different it would be in our country if people were not allowed the freedom to worship.
- Have the youth complete the "Faith Connection" activity independently. Ask volunteers to share their responses.



---

***Paganism*** is the term used in the early Church to designate a religion other than Christianity or Judaism whose values are contrary to the teachings of Sacred Scriptures. Pagan values, customs, and practices permeated the societies during the first centuries of the Church's existence. The conflict between paganism and Christianity was often at the root of the persecution of the Church.

### Paganism

Pagan religions practiced **polytheism**, or the belief in many gods. Romans offered sacrifices and practiced other rituals to placate their gods, who they believed had great influence over their daily lives.

Other pagan values were strongly opposed to the faith of the Church. For example, concern for the poor was not considered a virtue; undisciplined and immoral behavior was the norm of the day; minimal value was placed on human life. This was attested to by the widespread practice of infanticide, or the killing of infants. These values and practices posed serious threats to the spiritual welfare of the Church and the faith of Christians. The refusal of Christians to live by these values and practices placed the Church in direct conflict with Roman authorities.

***Why were pagan societies a threat to the spiritual life of the Christians?***

Saint Cecilia, mosaic. Martyred during persecution of Emperor Decius in 230.

S^T VINCENT, PATRON DES VIGNERON.

Saint Vincent of Saragossa, Spain. Martyred during persecution of Emperor Diocletian c. 304.

**FAITH CONNECTION**

***The right to worship is a basic human right. Describe how being free to worship God contributes toward your living the Catholic faith.***

Responses will vary.

Affirm appropriate responses.



---

## Teaching Tip

**Challenges to Living One's Faith in Christ.** It is highly unlikely that the young people you are working with will ever experience anything like the persecution suffered by the early Church. They may not be able to see themselves in a position of needing to aspire to martyrdom. Emphasize that while they may never literally give their lives for the faith, they can in fact give their lives for the faith every day through their attitudes and actions, their moral choices, and their efforts to be just and peaceful people. Help them see Christian discipleship as an adventure to be lived today.

# OUR CHURCH MAKES A DIFFERENCE

Clockwise from top: Fr. Ignacio Martin-Baró, Fr. Amando López, Julia Elba Ramos (housekeeper), Fr. Ignacio Ellacuria, Fr. Segundo Montes, Fr. Juan Ramón Mareno, Celina Mariset Ramos (housekeeper's daughter), Fr. Joaquin López y López.

Heroes who give their lives for their faith in Christ are still a part of Church history today.

## Martyrs in El Salvador

On March 24, 1980, Oscar Romero, Archbishop of San Salvador in El Salvador and advocate for the repressed and brutalized poor in his country, was assassinated while he was celebrating Mass. As he was about to elevate the bread and wine for the sacrifice, he was shot through the heart.

On December 2, 1980, Sisters Maura Clarke, Ita Ford, and Dorothy Kazel, and lay worker Jean Donovan met at the San Salvador airport and proceeded toward their next destination. Their bodies were later found mutilated and buried in shallow graves. They were martyred because their work of educating and serving the poor in El Salvador was considered by some to be a threat to people in authority.

On November 16, 1989, members of the El Salvador army invaded the campus of the University of Central America in San Salvador, where faculty members had often spoken out against human rights violations by the government and military. The gunmen murdered a housekeeper and her daughter and six Jesuit priests.

***What are some of the ways you see others making sacrifices to live their faith in Christ?***

Responses will vary. Affirm appropriate responses.

Archbishop Oscar Romero.

Left to right: Jean Donovan; Sr. Ita Ford, M.M.; Sr. Maura Clarke, M.M.; Sr. Dorothy Kazel, O.S.U.

35

## Teaching Tip

**Valuing Faith as a Treasure.** The lives and deaths of the martyrs of the Church profoundly illustrate the value of faithfully and courageously living the faith. Share with the young people that faith in Jesus is a treasure that it is worth losing one's life over. Faith is worth living for . . . and dying for. Share the statement, "The tyrant dies and his rule is over, the martyr dies and his rule begins," with the class to help the young people value the tremendous influence the martyrs have made on the life of the Church long after their deaths.

# Connect

### HIGHLIGHT

Recall with the students that the suffering of martyrs strengthened the Church. Emphasize that the witness of martyrs gave others who were undergoing suffering and persecution hope and inspiration. Point out that since the inauguration of the Church, members have experienced times of trial and persecution for the faith.

### DISCOVER

- Ask the students to describe the qualities of a hero. Then read aloud "Martyrs in El Salvador." Ask if the martyrs of El Salvador should be considered heroes based on the class's definitions. Ask and discuss why martyrs are honored as heroes of the Church.

### INTEGRATE

- Hold a class conversation based on these questions:
  —Why do other people's lives of faith inspire us?
  —How do the lives of people of faith inspire you to live your faith in God?
- Summarize by sharing with the class that Christians who inspire us by living their faith also strengthen us to live our faith.

### PRAY

Ask the young people to quiet themselves. After a moment of quiet reflection pray the Apostles' Creed together.

# Day 4

## Connect

### PRAY

Ask the young people to quiet themselves. Have a volunteer pray aloud Matthew 5:11. Ask everyone to reflect on the meaning of the Gospel passage for their own life.

### FOCUS

- Recall the "Faith Focus" question on page 29. Ask volunteers to answer it, using what they have learned in this chapter. List responses on the board.
- Present the introductory paragraph and point out that throughout the Church's history, the faithful have sacrificed much, including their lives, to follow Christ.

### DISCOVER

- Read aloud the two sections "Stress" and "Distress" under "Dealing with Change and Stress." Help the young people relate change to their own lives by asking them about some of the major (and minor) changes in their personal lives. Share a few of the changes you have experienced.
- List some common reasons that people in society get distressed as well as what people do to relieve distress.
- Have the young people silently read "Attitude Is Your Paintbrush" on pages 36 and 37.
- Discuss the section as a class.
- Lead the students through the "Steps to Handle Stress." Use real-life examples. Emphasize how healthy it is for a person to handle stress in the manner outlined.

# WHAT DIFFERENCE

## Does Faith Make in My Life?

The early years of the Church were times of great transition. But the attitude and commitment of the early Church toward Christ was firm. The disciples, under the guidance of the Holy Spirit, spread the Gospel far and wide.

### Dealing with Change and Stress

Any change or transition brings with it a time of distress. It is an uncomfortable time because it stirs up uneasy feelings, and it is new and unknown. Many people do not like change, yet it is one of the certainties of life. We are ever growing and constantly changing throughout our lives.

#### Stress

Many researchers claim that stress is neutral, neither negative nor positive. Stress is needed in our lives. It stimulates the athlete into motion and is the thing that gets us moving to do what we need to do. It is the way our body automatically responds to whatever happens. For example, you hear a loud bang overhead. You are startled, your body responds, your heart rate quickens, and your blood pressure rises. This is stress. Or, it is your birthday and people say "surprise" and sing to you. This is also stress and your body will respond in the same way. Hopefully one situation is more pleasant than the other. Your body responds the same way whether the situation is pleasant or not.

#### Distress

A negative response is called distress. A research doctor found that prolonged distress can make you sick. Distress is the negative stress that we cause within ourselves. It is caused by tension that results from the way we are handling a situation. We may overreact, get angry, and lash out at times. Most doctors agree that it is our attitude, our reaction, and our response to something that causes this distress.

### Attitude Is Your Paintbrush

There is a poster that states "Your attitude is your paintbrush that colors every situation." When unpleasant things happen or things do not go your way, you have a choice about the way you handle them. That choice is often influenced by your attitude.

Think about the following situations and your attitude toward each. How would you respond? Could you respond differently?

- Someone bumps into you in the movie line. Your popcorn and soda spill all over you.

36

## Teaching Tip

**Affirming All Young People.** Make a special effort to help the students strengthen their sense of self-esteem. Issues of self-esteem are common in the personal and social development of young teenagers. While peer influence is strong during these years, young teens look to trusted adults, especially when they are troubled or unsure of situations in which they find themselves. Give all the members of the group opportunities to share their gifts during the sessions.

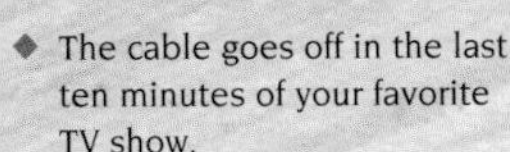

- ◆ The cable goes off in the last ten minutes of your favorite TV show.
- ◆ You are ready to go out with your friends when your mom calls and says she has to work late, so you will have to stay home and babysit your younger brother.

It is usually the little everyday stuff that gets us so upset. You can choose to act or react to what happened. This does not mean to push down your feelings or pretend that what happened did not bother you. How we choose to respond to these everyday situations will have an influence on how we respond to the more serious tragedies that are sometimes part of our personal life.

**Steps to Handle Stress**

It is your attitude, your choice that determines whether it is stress or distress. Here are a few steps to combine with a positive attitude to deal with situations effectively.

- ◆ State what just happened.
- ◆ Take a look at your attitude—Did you rant and rave, or stay calm?
- ◆ Express your feelings—"I feel mad or upset."
- ◆ Ask the Holy Spirit to help you stop and calm down.
- ◆ Strive for positive self-talk and self-control.

You cannot always control what happens. But you can control your attitude toward both the expected and unexpected in your life. Change your attitude when little annoying things happen. You will be a better person, a better Christian, and your body will thank you.

## Faith Decision

- Discuss with a partner a stressful situation in your life. Share how you could choose to handle the situation.
- Think about a time that you were challenged to live your faith. How stressful was that situation for you? In a journal write about how you handled the situation.

This week I will live my faith in Christ by looking at my attitude and choosing to deal with situations by

Responses will vary.

Affirm appropriate responses.

37

## Catholic Social Teaching

**Life and Dignity of the Human Person.** All human life is sacred, and every person demands our respect because every person has been created in the image and likeness of God. The social teachings of the Catholic Church call us to treat all people accordingly. (See *Catechism of the Catholic Church* 2258–2317.)

**Tip:** Remind the students that God dwells within each person. Invite the class to find and discuss Gospel stories that demonstrate Jesus' respect for the dignity of others, especially people who were cast out or marginalized by society in his time. Encourage the young people to examine their own attitudes toward others, including those marginalized in our society.

# Day 4

## Apply

### RESPOND

- Ask the students how they would respond to the three situations named in the text on pages 36 an 37.
- Read aloud the directions for the "Faith Decision" activity.
- Invite the youth to work with partners and talk about how they might handle a stressful situation they are presently experiencing.
- Allow the partners to share their ideas with the class and receive feedback. Clarify responses as necessary.

### CHOOSE

- Give the young people a few moments to quietly reflect on how they have met challenges to living their faith as well as the stress they felt in doing so.
- Have the students make and write their faith decision.
- Encourage everyone to put their faith decision into practice.

### PRAY

- Have the young people quiet themselves for prayer.
- Have them sit in silence in God's presence. End with this or a similar prayer: "Help us, Lord, to slow down. / Help us to remember that our attitudes are our paintbrushes, / and that we can paint beautiful colors in our day with positive attitudes. / Amen."

### *Enriching the Lesson*

The "Creating Review Games" activity on page 97 is related to today's content. You may wish to include it in today's lesson.

# Day 5

## Pray and Review

### FOCUS

- Recall the opening Scripture passage for this chapter, Matthew 5:11. Tell the students that the verse concludes the Beatitudes in Matthew's Gospel. Remind the class that the Beatitudes describe the vocation of the faithful.
- Share that the closing prayer will be the Beatitudes.

### PRAY

- Divide the class into Group 1 and Group 2.
- Lead the class in praying "Blessed by God."

### REVIEW

- Have the young people share the meaning of the terms in "Faith Vocabulary" and compare their definitions with those in the glossary.
- Use the "Main Ideas" and "Critical Thinking" sections to clarify any questions the students may have concerning what they have learned in the chapter.
- Remind everyone to share and discuss the "Family Discussion" question with their family.

### *Before Moving On . . .*

Reflect on this question before moving on to the next chapter.

*How have I shared my own faith this week, particularly the sacrifices it takes in today's world to live as a disciple of Jesus?*

# PRAY and REVIEW

## *Blessed by God*

Leader: The Beatitudes set before us the values and vision that are at the heart of the Gospel. By the witness of their deaths, Christian martyrs are models of the Beatitudes.

Group 1: "Blessed are the poor in spirit, /
All: **for theirs is the kingdom of heaven.**

Group 2: Blessed are they who mourn, /
All: **for they will be comforted.**

Group 1: Blessed are the meek, /
All: **for they will inherit the land.**

Group 2: Blessed are they who hunger and thirst for righteousness, /
All: **for they will be satisfied.**

Group 1: Blessed are the merciful, /
All: **for they will be shown mercy.**

Group 2: Blessed are the clean of heart, /
All: **for they will see God.**

Group 1: Blessed are the peacemakers, /
All: **for they will be called children of God.**

Group 2: Blessed are they who are persecuted for the sake of righteousness, /
All: **for theirs is the kingdom of heaven."** MATTHEW 5:3–10

38

**FAITH VOCABULARY**

Define each of these terms:

1. martyr
2. paganism
3. polytheism

**MAIN IDEAS**

Choose either (a) or (b) from each set of items. Write a brief paragraph to answer each of your choices.

1. (a) Explain the effect of the lives of martyrs on the growth of the Church. pp. 30–31
   (b) Describe the contribution of Saint Ignatius of Antioch to the growth of the Church. p. 32
2. (a) Describe the role of persecutions in the growth of the Church. p. 31
   (b) How did pagan values affect the lives of Christians in the first three centuries? p. 34

**CRITICAL THINKING**

Using what you have learned in this chapter, briefly explain this statement:
The blood of martyrs is the seed of faith.

**FAMILY DISCUSSION**

What attitudes and beliefs in our society support Catholics in living our faith as a family? What attitudes and beliefs make it more difficult to live our faith?

For more ideas on ways your family can live your faith, visit the "Faith First for Families" page at **www.FaithFirst.com**. Also check out the Teen Center and read this week's interactive story.

## Evaluate

Take a few moments to evaluate this week's lesson.
I feel (circle one) about this week's lesson.

a. very pleased
b. OK
c. disappointed

The activity the students enjoyed most was . . .

The concept that was most difficult to teach was . . .

because . . .

Something I would like to do differently is . . .

# ENRICHING THE LESSON

## Reporting on Contemporary Christian Persecutions

**Purpose**

To reinforce that the persecution of the Church is not only a history lesson but happens today as well (taught on page 32)

**Directions**

- Share these headlines with the class:
  —"Police Raid Christian Worship Service"
  —"Bishop Accuses Troops of Plot Against Church"
  —"Security Forces Close Down Church"
- Suggest that these headlines describe the persecution of the Church today.
- Have the students research news reports about the persecution of the Church throughout the world today. Tell them that they can work independently, in pairs, or in small groups of three to four students.
- Have the young people give an oral report on their research in future sessions.

**Materials**

newspapers
*Maryknoll* and other Catholic magazines
Web references
paper, pens or pencils

## Writing Prayers of Thanksgiving

**Purpose**

To reinforce that the Church is filled with gratitude for the witness of her martyrs (taught on page 33)

**Directions**

- Have the students work in small groups to create prayers of thanksgiving.
- Each prayer should include: (1) a statement of gratitude for what the martyrs have sacrificed, (2) a statement of compassion for their suffering, and (3) a statement identifying what faith qualities the martyrs have passed along to the Church.
- Invite a sharing of the prayers. If possible, incorporate them into the closing prayer for the day's lesson and future lessons.

**Materials**

paper, pens or pencils

## Creating Review Games

**Purpose**

To reinforce the chapter content in an interactive way (taught on page 38)

**Directions**

Use this activity as a way to hold a creative review session of the chapter.

- Divide the class into small groups.
- Each group has the assignment to create a game that the class can use to review the content of the chapter. For example, they can create a Jeopardy®-style game whose subject is martyrs. Or they can create a "Name that Church History" fact game. Or they can choose to play charades or do pantomimes of certain events and people. Point out that their game must cover two or three concepts or facts from each page of the chapter.
- After they have developed their games, play them.

**Materials**

3" x 5" cards
paper, pens or pencils

## Music Connection

- "Bread of Life," M. J. Poirer. *Voices As One (VAO)* #11.
- "Here I Am, Lord," D. Shutte. *Gather Comprehensive (GC)* #671.
- "Nada Te Turbe/Nothing Can Trouble," J. Berthier. *GC* #626.
- "Show Us the Way," D. Light and P. Tate. *VAO* #87.

Chapter 4

# Jesus Commissions Peter A Scripture Story

## CHAPTER BACKGROUND

### Vicar of Christ Shepherd of the Church

One of the most remarkable features of the Second Vatican Council was the humility with which it approached its task of renewing the Church. The humility of the Council was characteristic of Pope John Paul II, who took the occasion at the turn of the new millennium to acknowledge the many mistakes and failings that members of the Church had made over the centuries. With his acknowledgement and apologies for past failings of the Church, the Pope embodied the story in John's Gospel where Saint Peter repents of his threefold denial of Jesus by making his threefold affirmation of love.

### "Feed My Sheep"

Jesus responded to Saint Peter's repentance by calling him to lead the disciples and by entrusting him with the ministry of shepherding the Church. This ministry has continued to the present in the abiding presence of the Holy Spirit who guides the successors of Saint Peter.

History testifies to the amazing number of Popes who were extraordinarily wise, holy, and courageous leaders of Christ's flock. The ministry of the bishop of Rome, the Petrine ministry as it is called, has played a pivotal role in the story of the human race since the time of Jesus. Whether one chronicles a spiritual history of the world or takes a more secular perspective, the men called to succeed Saint Peter have been key players in events that have shaped human history.

### Pope John Paul II Pope Benedict XVI

We have been privileged in our own lifetime to witness the ministry of a succession of Popes whose influence on events inside and outside the Church has been decisive.

Called from a humble Polish family to lead the flock of Christ, Pope John Paul II was clearly an instrument of the Holy Spirit. He served as a catalyst in the collapse of totalitarian communism. He called on the nations of the developed world to reorder their moral priorities and to do a better job of addressing the pressing social issues of our time. He worked for forgiveness and reconciliation with the Jewish people and inspired young Christians to meet the challenges of leading lives of faith and self-sacrificing love of neighbor. He criss-crossed the globe to bring the Gospel to peoples everywhere.

Pope Benedict XVI was elected the 265th successor of Saint Peter in 2005. He continues the mission the Risen Jesus gave to Saint Peter. His first encyclical, *God Is Love,* gives us a glimpse of the focus of his papacy and his response to Jesus' command "Feed my sheep."

## FOR REFLECTION

***What has led me to a deeper holiness when I acknowledged failure and started over?***

***What can I do to help the young people deepen their commitment to live a holy life?***

## First Thoughts

### God Calls

God takes the first step. He already has with you and me. He has called us. And if we are not listening, he waits and persistently calls us again, and again, and again. God is patient. He has something in mind for each of us, so he will not give up. When we hear his call, we might be surprised or scared, saying, "No, not me, God." Eventually we accept his call, because that is what people of faith do.

### Who, Me?

The young people you teach might say, "Me do that Gospel stuff? Why would God expect that of me? I don't have anything special to offer." Be patient with your students. Affirm them. Encourage them. Invite them again and again to live the Gospel. Help them discover the wondrous adventure of finding out what God is calling them to do and what gifts he has given them to use in service to the world. Help the young people see how the men and women of the early Church entered this adventure too. The lives of the faithful who have walked the journey of faith ahead of them are their guides and inspiration.

## The Church Teaches . . .

The bishops gathered at the Second Vatican Council were fulfilling Christ's command to feed his flock, the Church. They taught:

> It is through the faithful preaching of the Gospel by the Apostles and their successors—the bishops with Peter's successor as their head—through their administering the sacraments, and through their governing in love, that Jesus Christ wishes his people to increase.
>
> *Decree on Ecumenism* 2

In this chapter the students are invited to discover that not only the shepherds of the Church but also all the baptized are called to live the Gospel message passed down from the Apostles.

### See the Catechism . . .

For more on the teachings of the Catholic Church on the ministry of Saint Peter and the call of all the baptized to holiness, see *Catechism of the Catholic Church* 880–882 and 1273.

*Wondrous God, Father of all,
you have called all the baptized,
young and old, throughout the ages
to follow your Son, Jesus Christ.
Send the Holy Spirit to help me
listen to your call, inviting me to
serve you and my students. Amen.*

Now . . . turn the page and let's get organized!

# LESSON PLANNER

## Chapter Focus

**To learn about the role of Saint Peter and his successors, the Popes, and of all the baptized in putting the Gospel into action**

| Focus | Process | Materials and Options |
|---|---|---|
| **DAY 1**<br>**Engage/Teach and Apply**<br>**Pages 39–41**<br>**Focus**<br>To discover that God calls all the baptized to participate in the mission of the Church | **Opening Prayer**<br>**Discussion**<br>The call narratives in the Scriptures<br>**Presentation**<br>Read, discuss, and summarize content.<br>**Scripture:** John 21:17<br>**Faith Connection:** Compare call narratives in the Gospels. | **Materials**<br>pens or pencils<br>**Options**<br>***Called to Prayer and Liturgical Lessons* booklet:** See options for daily and seasonal prayers and liturgical prayers and lessons.<br>**Enriching the Lesson (TG page 111)**<br>Analyzing Call Narratives |
| **DAY 2**<br>**Teach and Apply**<br>**Pages 42–43**<br>**Focus**<br>To learn about Jesus' call to Saint Peter | **Prayer**<br>**Presentation**<br>Read, discuss, and summarize content.<br>**Scripture:** John 20:3–8, 21:15–17, 18–19<br>**Activity:** Identify the key points in the call of Peter. | **Materials**<br>newsprint, pens or pencils<br>**Options**<br>**Enriching the Lesson (TG page 111)**<br>Doing a Group Scripture Search |
| **DAY 3**<br>**Teach/Apply and Connect**<br>**Pages 44–45**<br>**Focus**<br>To discover that the ministry given to Saint Peter is carried out by the Church today | **Prayer**<br>**Presentation**<br>Read, discuss, and summarize content.<br>**Did you know:** Pope Benedict XVI<br>**Faith Connection:** Identify and describe your role in your parish Church.<br>**Our Church Makes a Difference**<br>Discover the teachings of Pope John Paul II and Pope Benedict XVI. | **Materials**<br>pens or pencils<br>**Options**<br>**Enriching the Lesson (TG page 111)**<br>Preparing a Social Concerns Budget<br>***Additional Activities and Assessment Tools* booklet**<br>Screenplay: Saint Peter's Commissioning, page 13 |
| **DAY 4**<br>**Connect and Apply**<br>**Pages 46–47**<br>**Focus**<br>Identify ways to live the Corporal Works of Mercy | **Prayer**<br>**What Difference Does Faith Make in My Life?**<br>Learn about the Corporal Works of Mercy.<br>**Activity:** Develop a class plan for putting the Corporal Works of Mercy into action.<br>**Faith Decision:** Choose and live out one of the Corporal Works of Mercy this week. | **Materials**<br>sticky notes<br>seven sheets of newsprint<br>pens or pencils, markers<br>**Options**<br>**Enriching the Lesson (TG page 111)**<br>Putting the Spiritual Works of Mercy into Action |
| **DAY 5**<br>**Pray and Review**<br>**Page 48** | **Pray**<br>Pray "Lord, When Did We See You?" together.<br>**Review**<br>**Activities:** Complete the review exercises to reinforce the concepts of the chapter.<br>**Family Discussion:** Encourage the students to share and discuss the question with their family this week. | **Materials**<br>pens or pencils<br>**Options**<br>***Additional Activities and Assessment Tools* booklet**<br>Administer the chapter 4 test.<br>**Music Connection** (TG page 111) |

**Don't Forget!** You can make lesson planning a breeze—check out the **Online Lesson Planner** at **www.FaithFirst.com** for additional resources to enhance this chapter.

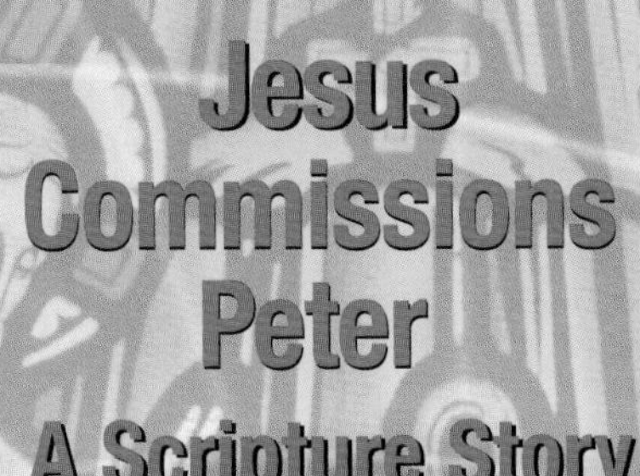

# Jesus Commissions Peter

## A Scripture Story

4

FAITH FOCUS

What does the story of the appearance of the Risen Jesus to his disciples by the lake teach us about the ministry of Saint Peter and his successors, the Popes?

FAITH VOCABULARY

**call narrative**

**Petrine ministry**

***When has someone given you a task that affected others?***

Some people, such as teachers, coaches, and civic officials, receive the responsibility of making decisions that can have serious affects on the lives of other people. Such trust and responsibility change us—sometimes for the rest of our lives. In this chapter we listen to the Gospel account of Jesus commissioning Saint Peter, giving him the authority to shepherd the flock of Christ in his name.

***What do you know about the work that Jesus called Saint Peter the Apostle to do?***

"[Y]ou are Peter, and upon this rock I will build my church" (Matthew 16:18), stained glass.

*[Jesus] said to [Simon Peter], "Feed my sheep."*
JOHN 21:17

39

# Day 1

## Engage

### PRAY

- Call the students to prayer.
- Pray the Sign of the Cross together.
- Ask a volunteer to proclaim John 21:17.
- Invite the young people to reflect on what Jesus might be asking of them today.
- Conclude by praying the Sign of the Cross together.

### FAITH FOCUS

Read aloud and invite responses to the "Faith Focus" question. Summarize by sharing that in this chapter they will discover and discuss how Jesus called Saint Peter the Apostle to shepherd his Church.

### DISCOVER

Assess the young people's prior knowledge of Jesus' calling of Saint Peter to shepherd his Church.

- Write the faith vocabulary terms on the board. Ask the young people to share what they know about these terms. Write their responses next to the terms.
- Have the students silently reflect on the opening question. Then engage in an interactive discussion that covers the content in the paragraph.
- Using the various elements depicted in the stained glass on page 39, have volunteers share what they know about the work Jesus called Saint Peter to do.

## National Catechetical Directory

**Implementing the *National Directory for Catechesis*: Learning Through the Witness of the Catechist.** The National Directory teaches that "catechists powerfully influence those being catechized by their faithful proclamation of the Gospel of Jesus Christ and the transparent example of their Christian lives" (*NDC* 29E, page 101). This chapter provides you with the opportunity to look for occasions to "call" your students to bear witness to their faith in Jesus. Always affirm their Christian words and actions toward classmates and younger students. Your recognition and affirmation of their living the Gospel will reinforce their efforts to live the teachings you share with them.

# Day 1

## Teach

**FOCUS**

- Share a time when someone has given you a responsibility to do something that impacted the lives of other people.
- Remind the young people that they and all the baptized are called to bring Jesus' mission of hope to the world. Call their attention to the illustrations of Abraham and Moses, and explain that these two pages will help them understand how God has called people throughout history to help him bring about the divine plan of Salvation.

**DISCOVER**

- Read the opening paragraph and discuss the question it poses.
- Invite volunteers to read aloud "Old Testament Call Narratives" to discover the pattern used by the biblical writers to pass on God's calling of people to take part in his work in the world.
- Summarize by outlining the five elements of the "core narrative" on the board.
- Have the students read silently "New Testament Call Narratives" to discover the similarity between the Old Testament and the New Testament call narratives.
- Summarize by emphasizing that the call narratives involving Jesus highlight his divinity.

## Bible Background

The Old Testament contains accounts of God calling individuals to help him bring about the divine plan of Salvation. Who are some of the people whom you recall from your study of the Old Testament who were called for this special work?

Call of Abraham (Genesis 12:1–3), stained glass.

### Old Testament Call Narratives

The biblical writers carefully recorded how God called Abraham, Moses, the prophets, and others and entrusted to each of them a special work, or mission. Over a period of time, these written accounts took a certain literary form and became known as **call narratives.**

While some of the details in these narratives vary with the individual person and the circumstances of their particular call into God's service, certain elements appear regularly. A kind of "core narrative," whose outline became quite familiar, began to emerge in the narrative. These reappearing elements are:

- It is always God who takes the initiative.
- The person being called at first expresses surprise, reluctance, fear, or some similar emotion.
- God persists—sometimes by reassuring and sometimes by commanding—in calling the individual.
- God entrusts a mission to the person and promises blessings and help so the person can fulfill that mission.
- The individual accepts God's call, and the person's destiny—sometimes even their name—is changed forever.

Call of Moses (Exodus 3:1–17), stained glass.

40

## Background: Catholic Tradition

**States of Life.** God calls each of the baptized to a "state of life," or way of living out the Christian life.

- *Ordained life:* Men serve as bishops, priests, or deacons.
- *Religious life:* Men or women live in a community that follows a spirituality approved by the Church and modeled after the example and teaching of its founder.
- *Married life:* Men and women answer God's call to holiness by making a lifetime commitment to a spouse and by being open to the gift of children.
- *Single life:* Men or women serve the community directly as single persons.

Sea of Tiberias, also called Sea of Galilee, in modern-day Israel.

**New Testament Call Narratives**

The New Testament writers were intimately familiar with the Old Testament call narratives. They used this literary device to describe Jesus calling his disciples.

We find most of the elements of a classic call narrative in the Risen Jesus' conversation with Saint Peter by the Sea of Tiberias. This encounter takes place after the Resurrection, following a meal that points to the Eucharist.

The fact that this scene follows a miraculous catch of fish further heightens the reader's awareness of Jesus' divinity. Clearly, the author of this passage wants us to be aware that it is God who is calling Saint Peter to a special mission of caring for the flock of Jesus.

In a subtle way, the fact that in the New Testament it is Jesus who is doing the calling reveals to the perceptive reader that Jesus is doing something ordinarily reserved for God alone. Without directly saying that Jesus is divine, the Gospel writer is making this declaration clear by reporting the incident the way he does.

***What is the focus or purpose of call narratives in the Bible?***

Fishermen, ancient Palestine, hand-colored woodcut.

**FAITH CONNECTION**

***How do you respond to your baptismal call to love God, your neighbors, and yourself as Jesus taught?***

Responses will vary

Affirm appropriate responses.

41

# Day 1

## Apply

**REINFORCE**

- Write the faith vocabulary term *call narrative* on the board. Invite volunteers to create a word map to describe it, using key points presented on these two pages.
- Have the students share with a partner their responses to the question at the end of page 41. Discuss responses as a large group.

**INTEGRATE**

- Give the young people time to complete the "Faith Connection" activity independently.
- Discuss responses to the activity as a class.
- Allow time for volunteers to share their stories with the class, if they feel comfortable doing so. You may wish to share about a time when you had a sense that God was calling you.

**PRAY**

Ask the young people to remember God's presence with them, gently calling them to follow him. After a moment of prayerful reflection proclaim John 21:17 together.

### Background: Scripture

**Fishermen in the New Testament.** Jesus' disciples were professional fishermen. Fishermen in Jesus' time were not solitary anglers who went out on their own to catch a fish or two. Fishing was a cooperative effort. It took more than one person to put down the net and to bring in the heavy nets full of fish. Emphasize to your students that the members of the Church are called to work together to do the work of the Church.

### *Enriching the Lesson*

The "Analyzing Call Narratives" activity on page 111 is related to today's content. You may wish to include it in today's lesson.

# Day 2

## Teach

**PRAY**

Invite the students to quiet themselves for prayer. Ask them to reflect on how God might be calling them to participate in Jesus' mission today. Proclaim John 21:17 together.

**FOCUS**

Invite a volunteer to summarize the elements of the call narratives in Sacred Scripture. Discuss Tissot's paintings on page 42 and 43. Then share that today the class will focus more closely on Jesus' call to Saint Peter the Apostle.

**DISCOVER**

- Present the opening paragraph and discuss the questions in it. Encourage the young people to give specific examples and challenge them to think about how they felt when asked to perform an important task.
- Ask the class to share what they remember about Saint Peter the Apostle from the Gospels. Be sure that they include what he did on the day prior to Jesus' Crucifixion. Peter denied Jesus three times.
- Invite the students to read "Feed My Sheep" and underline the key points.
- Ask volunteers to respond to the question on page 43.

### Enriching the Lesson

The "Doing a Group Scripture Search" activity on page 111 is related to today's content. You may wish to include it in today's lesson.

## Reading the Word of God

*The Charge of Peter.* James J. Tissot (1836–1902), French painter.

When has a teacher, coach, or someone in authority called you to lead others in performing an important task? How did you respond? Imagine what it was like for Saint Peter when Jesus called him to lead the Church in his name.

### "Feed My Sheep"

In chapter 18 of John's Gospel we read the account of Saint Peter's three-fold denial of Jesus. In the midst of Jesus' darkest hour, Saint Peter stands in the courtyard. Three times he denies that he is a disciple of Jesus, asserting that he did not even know Jesus. We do not meet Saint Peter again in John's Gospel until chapter 20. There Mary Magdalene announces the news of Jesus' Resurrection. Saint Peter and "the other disciple" rush to the empty tomb. John's Gospel reports what happened. We read:

> Peter and the other disciple went out and came to the tomb. They both ran, but the other disciple ran faster than Peter and arrived at the tomb first; he bent down and saw the burial cloths there, but did not go in. When Simon Peter arrived after him, he went into the tomb and saw the burial cloths there, and the cloth that had covered his head, not with the burial cloths but rolled up in a separate place. Then the other disciple also went in, the one who had arrived at the tomb first, and he saw and believed.
>
> John 20:3–8

Finally, in chapter 21, the last chapter of his Gospel, John again brings Saint Peter to center stage. There John gives this account of Saint Peter's encounter with the Risen Jesus on the shore of the Sea of Tiberias:

> When they had finished breakfast, Jesus said to Simon Peter, "Simon, son of John, do you love me more than these?" He said to him, "Yes, Lord, you know that I love you." He said to him, "Feed my lambs." He then said to him a second time,

42

### Background: Scripture

**Shepherds and Sheep.** In the Old Testament, God is portrayed as a shepherd. For example, see Psalm 23 or Ezekiel 24. In the New Testament, Jesus compared himself to a shepherd in John 10:1–8. The image of the shepherd conveys God's compassion, love, and care for his sheep—that is, his people and, by extension, all people. Sheep have an unconditional trust in their shepherd who will protect them to the point of defending them with his life. This trust is so deep that sheep respond only to the voice of their shepherd.

"Simon, son of John, do you love me?" He said to him, "Yes, Lord, you know that I love you." He said to him, "Tend my sheep." He said to him the third time, "Simon, son of John, do you love me?" Peter was distressed that he had said to him a third time, "Do you love me?" and he said to him, "Lord, you know everything; you know that I love you." [Jesus] said to him, "Feed my sheep." John 21:15–17

Jesus gives Saint Peter the opportunity to redeem his three-fold betrayal by a three-fold affirmation of love. Each time, Jesus responds by entrusting Saint Peter with a unique pastoral role—to tend the flock of Jesus. This solemn calling reflects the awareness in the early Church that Saint Peter had received a divine mandate to shepherd and lead the Church.

Jesus goes on to point to Saint Peter's destiny—his martyrdom. Saint Peter will bear witness in an ultimate way to his faith and love for Jesus:

[Jesus said to Peter], "Amen, amen, I say to you, when you were younger, you used to dress yourself and go where you wanted; but when you grow old, you will stretch out your hands, and someone else will dress you and lead you where you do not want to go." He said this signifying by what kind of death he would glorify God. And when he had said this, he said to him, "Follow me." John 21:18–19

This wonderful call narrative helps us understand more deeply the role of Saint Peter and his successors, the Popes, in the Church. Saint Peter, and after him the Popes, are to shepherd the flock of Jesus in his name and in his place. Saint Peter was called to shepherd the Church by bearing witness to the faith, even to the point of witnessing in his blood.

Saint Peter the Apostle was first and foremost a disciple of Jesus—one who followed the Master. His ministry as shepherd of the whole Church is a ministry of love. This is what later generations of theologians were to call a primacy of love and self-sacrifice.

***What does this call of Saint Peter teach you about the Church?***

*Feed My Lambs.*
James J. Tissot.

43

## Teaching Tip

**Making a Real Life Connection.** There is subtext in today's lesson with which you can make an important connection for your students. Remind them that even though Saint Peter the Apostle denied Jesus, not just once but three times, Jesus reached out to him, and Peter reaffirmed his love for Jesus. It is vital that young people know this wondrous love of Jesus—a love that never rejects anyone who turns away from it. His is the love of the Good Shepherd who searches for us when we wander away from him. Look for ways to make this and other real connections as you share the faith of the Church with your students.

# Day 2

## Apply

### REINFORCE

- Invite the students to work in small groups to share the key points they underlined from the reading.
- Ask them to list their group's responses on newsprint to share with the class.

### INTEGRATE

- As a class, listen to each group's list and write the key points on the board.
- Facilitate a large group discussion on the importance of this call narrative for their own life of faith and the life of the Church today.

### PRAY

- Include a choral or antiphonal reading of John 21:15–19. Have volunteers take the roles of narrator, Jesus, and Saint Peter.
- Have the class quiet themselves for prayer.
- Lead them in this or another appropriate closing prayer.

Lord,
give to your shepherd
(name of Pope),
a spirit of courage and
right judgment,
a spirit of knowledge
and love.
May he, as successor
to Saint Peter,
build your Church into a
sacrament of unity, love,
and peace for all the
world.

Based on Roman Missal, "Votive Mass for the Pope"

# Day 3

## Teach

**PRAY**

Invite the young people to prayer. Begin and conclude by praying the Sign of the Cross together. Ask the students to turn to page 137 and silently pray the Act of Love.

**FOCUS**

- Remind the young people that Jesus gave Saint Peter the opportunity to repent for his threefold betrayal by inviting him to affirm his love for Jesus three times.
- Point out that on page 44 they will learn about the unique ministry that Jesus gave to Saint Peter and his successors, the Popes.

**DISCOVER**

Invite the young people to silently read "The Petrine Ministry."

## Apply

**REINFORCE**

Write the faith vocabulary term *Petrine ministry* on the board and ask volunteers to describe it using what they have learned from reading the text. Summarize by having the students turn to the glossary and read the definition of *Petrine ministry*.

**INTEGRATE**

- Have the young people complete the "Faith Connection" reflection on their own.
- Invite volunteers to share their responses with the class.

## Understanding the Word of God

### Did you Know...

Pope Benedict XVI, at the age of seventy-eight, was elected the 265th successor of Saint Peter the Apostle on April 19, 2005. He was born in Germany on April 16, 1927, and named Joseph Alois. He was ordained a priest on June 29, 1951, and became a professor of theology and philosophy. He was ordained a bishop in 1977 and named a cardinal by Pope Paul VI the same year. In 1981 he was named Prefect of the Congregation for the Doctrine of the Faith. In 2002 he became dean of the college of cardinals.

Pope Benedict XVI. Annual meeting with young Catholics, Saint Peter's Square, Vatican City.

### The Petrine Ministry

The Gospels clearly identify Saint Peter as the leader of the Twelve. He is the one who has privileged access to the Lord in key moments of his life. He is the spokesperson for the others. Saint Peter is also the disciple who is corrected by the Lord and always set again on the straight path.

Guided by the Holy Spirit the Church has reflected on the words and stories in the Gospel. Over many centuries of prayer and reflection, she has come to understand the **Petrine ministry**—the ministry of Saint Peter and his successors, the Popes—to be a ministry of service and unity of faith and self-sacrificial love for the whole flock of Christ. The *Catechism of the Catholic Church* teaches:

> The Lord made Simon alone, whom he named Peter, the "rock" of his Church. He gave him the keys of his Church and instituted him shepherd of the whole flock.[1] . . . The *Pope*, Bishop of Rome and Peter's successor, "is the perpetual and visible source and foundation of the unity both of the bishops and of the whole company of the faithful."[2]
>
> CATECHISM OF THE CATHOLIC CHURCH 881 AND 882

### FAITH CONNECTION

*What roles do you play in the life of your parish church? Choose one of those roles and describe how it serves the people of your parish.*

Responses will vary.

Affirm appropriate responses.

44

### Special Needs

**Using a Variety of Visuals.** Visuals are an integral part of the design of *Faith First*. The *Faith First* student texts provide the students with the experience of a wide variety of visuals, such as contemporary poster art, classic masterpiece art, contemporary art, and photographic imagery. These visuals have been carefully chosen to speak to today's visual generation to facilitate the young people's discovery of the deeper meaning of the faith of the Church in a way that words alone cannot achieve. Integrate these visuals into your presentation. Allow time for the students to reflect on and discuss them.

**Need:** Young people with limited reading proficiency

# OUR CHURCH MAKES A DIFFERENCE

For hundreds of years after the death of Jesus, his disciples lived in a pagan culture whose values and behaviors were often at odds with the values and principles he taught and passed on to the Church in the New Testament. As in those early centuries of her existence, the Church today often finds herself at odds with contemporary culture. The followers of Jesus today find themselves being called by the shepherds of the Church to stand up for the teachings of Christ in our own time.

### The Voice of Two Popes

Down through the centuries the Popes have fulfilled the mission given to Saint Peter, "Feed my sheep." One way that they have done this is by writing letters to the faithful. In these letters the Popes often call the faithful to live the Gospel as Jesus taught.

Pope John Paul II

In his 1987 encyclical, *On the Social Concerns of the Church*, Pope John Paul II guided the faithful in living the Gospel of love proclaimed by Jesus. Like a loving father, he pointed to his poor children and declared that the goods of the world are intended for all. He reminded wealthy nations and people blessed with abundance that they have the responsibility to make impoverished people and nations their top priority. He called this the "preferential option for the poor," which was one of the themes he most frequently taught throughout his papacy.

Pope Benedict XVI

The first encyclical of Pope Benedict XVI, *God Is Love*, calls all the faithful to reflect on and live a life of love as Christ did and taught. Pope Benedict XVI begins his encyclical with the words "'God is love, and he who abides in love abides in God, and God abides in him' (1 John 4:16). These words from the *First Letter of John* express with remarkable clarity the heart of the Christian faith: the Christian image of God and the resulting image of mankind and its destiny." He concludes his encyclical, "Love is possible, and we are able to practise it because we are created in the image of God . . . and in this way to cause the light of God to enter into the world—this is the invitation I would like to extend with the present Encyclical." (*God Is Love* 1, 39.)

***How can you make the teachings of Pope John Paul II and Pope Benedict XVI part of your life?***

Responses will vary.
Affirm appropriate responses.

45

## Catholic Social Teaching

**Option for the Poor and Vulnerable.** We cry out to God in prayer and give witness to our communion with God by responding in faith to those who cry out in need to us. We are to reach out to those who are poor and vulnerable in society and work to eliminate the sinful inequalities that exist between people. Doing these works gives glory to God. (See *Compendium of the Social Doctrine of the Church* 182 and 449.)

**Tip:** Invite a representative of a Catholic social outreach organization to come share with the young people facts and stories about the local community's poor and vulnerable. Brainstorm ways the class might provide assistance to this organization.

# Day 3

## Connect

### HIGHLIGHT

- Remind the class that the early Church faced the challenges of living in a pagan culture.
- Point out that today, just as in the time of the early Church, the Church is challenged to stand up for the teachings of Christ in a culture that sometimes has values that do not support or may be contrary to the Gospel.

### DISCOVER

Ask volunteers to read aloud "Our Church Makes a Difference" to discover teachings of Pope John Paul II and Pope Benedict XVI that help us live the Gospel in our time.

### INTEGRATE

- Write the sentence "The Gospel is above all else a basis for motivation for action" on the board.
- Discuss the statement with the class and ask how they can make the teachings of Pope John Paul II and Pope Benedict XVI part of their lives.

### PRAY

Invite the young people to remember God's presence. Pray together, "Lord, help us recognize the dignity in each person. Amen."

### *Enriching the Lesson*

The "Preparing a Social Concerns Budget" activity on page 111 is related to today's content. You may wish to include it in today's lesson.

# Day 4

## Connect

**PRAY**

Invite the students to quiet themselves for prayer and place themselves in God's presence. Ask them to reflect on how God might be calling them to live as disciples of Jesus.

**FOCUS**

Recall the "Faith Focus" question on page 39. Ask volunteers to answer it, using what they have learned in this chapter. Present the introductory paragraph and point out that Jesus calls not only the Pope, but all the baptized to proclaim the Gospel by the way they live.

**DISCOVER**

- Recall the discussion of the statement you wrote on the board in the previous lesson about the Gospel being a motivation for action. Ask the young people to describe actions that reflect living the Gospel. List their ideas on the board.
- Read aloud the first two paragraphs of "Living the Corporal Works of Mercy."
- Divide the class into seven small groups. Have them read together the seven Corporal Works of Mercy and brainstorm ideas for ways they might live each Work of Mercy.

# WHAT DIFFERENCE Does Faith Make in My Life?

Jesus proclaimed, "Blessed are the merciful, for they will be shown mercy" (Matthew 5:7). When we show mercy to others as God shows us his mercy, we are living as followers of Jesus. We show our love for one another as Jesus commanded us to do. (See Matthew 25:31–40 and John 13:34–35.) We are putting the Gospel into action.



### The Corporal Works of Mercy

The Corporal and Spiritual Works of Mercy guide us in living as a "merciful" people. One of the chief witnesses to our love for another is the giving of alms to the poor, or sharing our material and spiritual blessings with others. (See *Catechism of the Catholic Church* 2447.)

The Corporal Works of Mercy guide us in helping people meet their bodily needs. After each of the Corporal Works of Mercy you will find a fact about a real need in today's world for putting this work of mercy into action. Next, you will find a suggestion for living the work of mercy. Finally, a blank space has been left for you to write another way that you think someone your age might respond to Jesus' call for love of neighbor.

**Feed people who are hungry**

**Fact:** The world produces enough food to feed each person between 3,000 to 4,000 calories per day. Hunger is a symptom of poverty and inequality and not simply of food scarcity.

**Suggestion:** Organize a church or school program providing food for a shelter that serves people in need.

**Your Idea:**________________

**Give drink to people who are thirsty**

**Fact:** Worldwide, 2.3 billion people suffer from water-related diseases. Unclean water and poor sanitation kill 12 million people each year, mostly in developing countries.

**Suggestion:** Conserve water. Never take this life-sustaining resource for granted and never contribute to water pollution in any way.

**Your Idea:**________________

**Clothe people who need clothes**

**Fact:** Countless children and adults in the world would walk barefooted and have little to wear, except for donations of usable clothing.

**Suggestion:** Collect clothes for the needy and donate to charitable organizations that serve people in need.

**Your Idea:**________________

Ashokan Reservoir, part of New York City water supply system.

46

## Background: Doctrine

**The Works of Mercy.** God has revealed himself to be a God of mercy. The People of God are called to be a people of mercy. The Gospel mandate requires that disciples of Jesus come to the aid of their neighbors and care for their spiritual and bodily needs. The Spiritual Works of Mercy include instructing, advising, consoling, comforting, forgiving, and bearing wrongs patiently. The Corporal Works of Mercy listed in today's lesson meet the physical needs of people. Among all the Works of Mercy, "giving alms to the poor is one of the chief witnesses to fraternal charity; it is also a work of justice pleasing to God." (See *Catechism of the Catholic Church* 2447, Matthew 25:31–46, Luke 3:11, and Luke 11:41.)

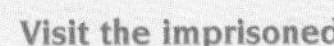

**Visit the imprisoned**

**Fact:** Some people in prison today are there simply because of their inability to secure adequate legal assistance to defend themselves in court.

**Suggestion:** Support (or begin) a parish or other program sponsored by the Church to provide gifts for prisoners and their children at Christmas time.

Your Idea:____________________

**Shelter people who are homeless**

**Fact:** There are an estimated two million people living on the streets in the United States on any given day.

**Suggestion:** Write a letter to the appropriate person in your parish or civic community advocating that they work to assist the homeless.

Your Idea:____________________

**Visit people who are sick**

**Fact:** In virtually every community there are people who are isolated by illness, injury, or old age because they have no family living nearby.

**Suggestion:** Organize a class "get-well-soon" project that sends get-well cards to elderly people who are ill and who live alone.

Your Idea:____________________

**Bury people who have died**

**Fact:** Countless people still die alone and without adequate assistance.

**Suggestion:** Support religious and other organizations, such as the hospice movement, dedicated to care for the terminally ill.

Your Idea:____________________

Pass Christian, Mississippi, tent center day care center for homeless Katrina hurricane victims.

## Faith Decision

- Brainstorm as a class and decide on one of the Corporal Works of Mercy that your class will put into action.
- Work in small groups. Research information on the Internet and in the school or parish library about people who may be affected by the Work of Mercy the class has chosen. Come up with a plan to put the Work of Mercy into action.

This week I will practice the Corporal Works of Mercy by:

Responses will vary.

Affirm appropriate responses.

47

### Teaching Tip

**Guidelines for Service Projects.** Here are a few tips to keep in mind as your class selects a service project.

- Make sure the project is "youth friendly" and that it provides opportunities for all the youth to be involved.
- Consider the commitment of time, energy, and resources required.
- Select a project that matches the abilities, interests, needs, time, and responsibilities of the young people.
- Integrate fun with service whenever possible.
- Consider projects that allow young adolescents and their families to participate together.

# Day 4

## Apply

### RESPOND

- Create seven columns on the board, labeling each with one of the Corporal Works of Mercy.
- Have a member of each of the small groups write their brainstorming results for the Work of Mercy in the appropriate column.
- Use these ideas to facilitate the "Faith Decision" activity to determine a Work of Mercy that the class can put into action.

### CHOOSE

- Invite everyone to prayerfully reflect on how they might live the Corporal Works of Mercy and write their faith decision.
- Tell the young people to choose something concrete that they can do on their own.
- Encourage everyone to put their faith decision into practice this week.

### PRAY

- Ask the young people to pause for prayer. Invite volunteers to read the Corporal Works of Mercy. After each Work of Mercy is proclaimed, invite everyone to pray: "Lord, make me an instrument of your work in the world."
- Conclude by praying the Our Father together.

### *Enriching the Lesson*

The "Putting the Spiritual Works of Mercy into Action" activity on page 111 is related to today's content. You may wish to include it in today's lesson.

# Day 5

## Pray and Review

### FOCUS

- Remind the class that the early Church reached out to the poor and vulnerable as Jesus commanded in Matthew 25:31–46.
- Point out that today's closing prayer is based on that teaching.
- Prepare for the prayer by selecting a leader and readers.

### PRAY

Gather for prayer and lead the class in praying "Lord, When Did We See You?"

### REVIEW

- Have the young people share the meaning of the terms in "Faith Vocabulary" and compare their definitions with those in the glossary.
- Use the "Main Ideas" and "Critical Thinking" sections to clarify any questions the students may have concerning what they have learned in the chapter.
- Remind everyone to share and discuss the "Family Discussion" question with their family.

## PRAY and REVIEW

### "Lord When Did We See You?"

**Leader:** Lord God our loving Father, your Son told us that whatever we do for a sister or brother in need we do for him. Send the Holy Spirit to guide us in loving you and our neighbor.

Let us remember all who suffer.

**Reader 1:** Lord Jesus, you said, "I was hungry and you gave me food."

**All:** **Lord, when did we give you food?**

**Reader 2:** "I was thirsty and you gave me drink."

**All:** **Lord, when did we give you drink?**

**Reader 3:** "I was a stranger and you welcomed me."

**All:** **Lord, when did we welcome you?**

**Reader 4:** "I was naked and you clothed me."

**All:** **Lord, when did we clothe you?**

**Reader 5:** "I was ill and you cared for me."

**All:** **Lord, when did we care for you?**

**Reader 6:** "I was in prison and you visited me."

**All:** **Lord, when did we visit with you?**

BASED ON MATTHEW 25:35–36

**Leader:** Let us pray.
Lord Jesus, we ask you to watch over all who suffer. Give us eyes to see you in all who are in need and to comfort the sorrowing. Give us compassionate hearts like your own.

**All:** **Amen.**

48

#### FAITH VOCABULARY

Define each of these faith terms:

1. call narrative  2. Petrine ministry

#### MAIN IDEAS

Choose either (a) or (b) from each set of items. Write a brief paragraph to answer each of your choices.

1. (a) Explain the role of the call narratives found in the Bible. pp. 40–41
   (b) Name the core elements found in the biblical call narratives. p. 41
2. (a) Describe Jesus' calling of Saint Peter by the Sea of Tiberias to shepherd the flock of Christ. pp. 42–43
   (b) Compare the ministry of Saint Peter with the ministry of his successors, the Popes. p. 44

#### CRITICAL THINKING

Using what you have learned in this chapter, briefly explain these words:

The Pope is the shepherd of the whole Church.

#### FAMILY DISCUSSION

What are some of the ways the members of your family live out their baptismal call to live as Jesus taught?

For more ideas on ways your family can live your faith, visit the "Faith First for Families" page at **www.FaithFirst.com**. Also check out "Life Timelines" on the Teen Center.

### Before Moving On . . .

Reflect on these questions before moving on to the next chapter.

*How do I see my students reaching out with love and compassion to one another? How do I affirm the young people when I see them putting the Gospel into action?*

### Evaluate

Take a few moments to evaluate this week's lesson.

I feel (circle one) about this week's lesson.

a. very pleased
b. OK
c. disappointed

The activity the students enjoyed most was . . .

The concept that was most difficult to teach was . . .

because . . .

Something I would like to do differently is . . .

# ENRICHING THE LESSON

## Analyzing Call Narratives

### Purpose

To reinforce the core elements of a call narrative (taught on page 40)

### Directions

- Divide the class into small groups.
- Assign each group one of the following call narratives from the Old Testament: The Call of Noah (Genesis 6, 7:1–5), The Call of Abraham (Genesis 12:1–9),The Call of Moses (Exodus 3:4-4:1–9).
- Have each group read the narrative assigned to it and, using the elements of a call narrative, outline on newsprint each of the core elements found in the narrative.
- Invite the groups to present to the class how their Scripture passage reflects the core elements of a call narrative.

### Materials

Bibles, newsprint
pens or pencils and markers

## Doing a Group Scripture Search

### Purpose

To reinforce the concept of the call narratives found in Scripture (taught on pages 42 and 43)

### Directions

- Create small groups.
- Distribute Bibles to each person.
- Ask each small group to do a Scripture search of the Gospels and look for examples of call narratives.
- Have them note the Gospel citations and write a brief summary of two of the narratives they find.
- Invite the groups to present their research to the class.

### Materials

Bibles
paper, pens or pencils

## Putting the Spiritual Works of Mercy Into Action

### Purpose

To reinforce the concept that the Works of Mercy include both the Corporal Works of Mercy and the Spiritual Works of Mercy (taught on 46)

### Directions

- Using seven 3" by 5" cards, write one of the Spiritual Works of Mercy on each card.
- Create seven groups of students. Ask the members of each group to read and reflect on the Spiritual Works of Mercy on page 142 of their text.
- Invite a member from each group to come forward and pick one of the "Spiritual Works of Mercy" cards you have prepared.
- Have each group prepare and present, without naming it, a pantomime, role-play, or charade of the Work of Mercy described on the card they have picked.
- Ask the class to name each Work of Mercy after it has been presented.
- Encourage the young people to choose one of the Spiritual Works of Mercy and put it into action this week.

### Materials

3" by 5" cards

## Music Connection

- "God Has Chosen Me," B. Farrell. *Gather Comprehensive (GC)* #669.
- "Quiero Decirte que Sí," C. Gabaráin. *Flor y Canto* #496.
- "We Are Called," D. Haas. *GC* #710.
- "We Gather As One," C. Dinise and C. Howard. *Voices As One (VAO)* #100.

Chapter 5

# The Rise of Christendom

## CHAPTER BACKGROUND

### The Church Emerges both Free and Privileged

As the Church endured the persecutions of the first three centuries, she grew stronger, both in numbers and in faith. Many nonbelievers witnessing the courage of the martyrs and the commitment of other Christians to Christ and to living the Gospel became believers. Constantine the Great and Theodosius I were among the Roman emperors who became believers. Constantine gave the Church the freedom to worship publicly, and Theodosius recognized the Church as the official religion of the Roman Empire.

As a result of this new freedom and privileged status, Christians were free to preach the Gospel with the blessing of the emperor and the state. With that blessing the Church would one day emerge, not only as a spiritual authority, but also as a dominant world power.

### New Challenges

As the Church entered the second millennium, she suffered from a number of challenges both internally and externally. Many of these were met successfully and others not so successfully. In 1054 the Church in the East separated itself from the Church in the West. That separation, or schism, remains a source of disunity within the Church today.

In 1096 the first of the Crusades initiated an age of bloodshed and destruction into the Church's spiritual quest to reopen the Holy Land to Christian pilgrims. In the 1200s the Inquisition utilized cruel measures against those who were considered heretics and infidels.

In the late 1300s and early 1500s the interference of civil authorities with the life of the Church led to the Pope fleeing Rome. This eventually led to several candidates who were simultaneously supported and recognized as "Popes."

### New Lights

Throughout all this history of the Church, laypeople, religious sisters and brothers, and the ordained performed acts of charity too numerous to count, leaving a legacy of kindness, reverence, and fidelity. Both their recorded and unrecorded testimony bears witness to the undying power of the Holy Spirit in the Church.

Led by the Holy Spirit, women and men provided dazzling examples of Christ living in our midst. Saint Ambrose, Saint Augustine, and other Fathers of the Church provided the Church with an authentic understanding of the mysteries of the Christian faith. Popes, such as Saint Sylvester I and Saint Leo the Great, strengthened the papacy by the example of their courage and holiness. Saint Benedict of Nursia and Saint Scholastica established monasticism in the West, and the *Rule of Saint Benedict* is still as fresh now as it was in the fifth century.

Throughout these times missionaries traveled to England, Ireland, parts of Spain, Germany, and Russia to preach the Gospel. Compelling tales of their heroism and fidelity unfold as each page is turned in the story of the Church.

## FOR REFLECTION

***How is the Holy Spirit leading me to live the Gospel?***

***What highlights from my faith story can I appropriately share with the young people?***

## First Thoughts

### Guided by the Holy Spirit

History is full of good times and not-so-good times. History is a lot like our own personal lives. There are ups and downs, joys and sorrows, struggles and victories. The history of the Church provides a rich story of men and women at their best, and sometimes at their worst. Nevertheless the Holy Spirit is always present, through dark times and bright times in the Church's past and present, guiding her and inspiring the faithful to deepen the communion with Christ and live as clear signs and effective instruments of Salvation in the world.

#### What's the Point?

If your students ask, "What's the point about learning all this Church history?" share that just as it is vital for citizens to know the important events and people that brought us to our country's position today, it is vital for us, the People of God, to know where we come from—our roots and our history. To be an active and faithful member of the Church, we need to understand her mission and ministry. Explain to the students that history opens the window to that understanding.

## The Church Teaches . . .

*Sharing the Light of Faith: National Catechetical Directory for Catholics of the United States* © 1979 *(NCD)* teaches:

> Like Christ, who came into the world "not to be served by others but to serve" (Matthew 20:28), the Church seeks to minister to all peoples. It has a mission to heal and reconcile as its founder did. (Cf. 2 Corinthians 5, 18f) . . . The good and faithful servant acts out of concern and love, not for personal gain or glory. (Cf. Luke 22, 27) *NCD 66*

This chapter helps students recognize that they are called to be heralds of God's word and to put themselves at the service of others in God's name.

### See the Catechism . . .

For more on the teachings of the Catholic Church on announcing the good news of Jesus, the monastic life, and serving the Church, see *Catechism of the Catholic Church* 739, 904–913, and 925–927.

*Lord of history,
help us understand your
amazing actions among us
throughout the ages. Show
us your everlasting love and
bring us ever closer to you.
Amen.*

Now . . . turn the page and let's get organized!

# LESSON PLANNER

**Chapter Focus**

**To understand how the mission of being both a herald and servant of the Gospel characterized the rise of Christendom**

| Focus | Process | Materials and Options |
|---|---|---|
| **DAY 1**<br>**Engage/Teach and Apply**<br>**Pages 49–51**<br>**Focus**<br>To discover the growth of the Church in the fourth century | **Opening Prayer**<br>**Discussion**<br>How the Church serves the world as a herald and servant<br>**Presentation**<br>Read, discuss, and summarize content.<br>**Scripture:** Acts of the Apostles 28:28<br>**Faith Connection:** Make a coat or crest of arms for a herald of the Gospel. | **Materials**<br>pens or pencils<br>**Options**<br>**Enriching the Lesson (TG page 125)**<br>Writing an Edict<br>***Called to Prayer and Liturgical Lessons* booklet:** See options for daily and seasonal prayers and liturgical prayers and lessons. |
| **DAY 2**<br>**Teach and Apply**<br>**Pages 52–53**<br>**Focus**<br>To explore how the authority of the papacy grew | **Prayer**<br>**Presentation**<br>Read, discuss, and summarize content.<br>**Activity:** Create five-question quizzes on the work of the papacy.<br>**Did you know:** Ecumenical councils | **Materials**<br>paper<br>pens or pencils<br>**Options**<br>***Additional Activities and Assessment Tools* booklet**<br>Question and Answer Challenge: Christendom, page 15 |
| **DAY 3**<br>**Teach/Apply and Connect**<br>**Pages 54–55**<br>**Focus**<br>To discover how monasticism affected the spiritual growth of the Church | **Prayer**<br>**Presentation**<br>Read, discuss, and summarize content.<br>**Faith Connection:** Name one thing you can do to live a simple life.<br>**Our Church Makes a Difference**<br>Discover the contribution of the renewal of monasticism to the life of the Church. | **Materials**<br>markers<br>pens or pencils<br>**Options**<br>**Enriching the Lesson (TG page 125)**<br>Creating a Timeline |
| **DAY 4**<br>**Connect and Apply**<br>**Pages 56–57**<br>**Focus**<br>To explore the concept of leadership as it applies to the Church and her members | **Prayer**<br>**What Difference Does Faith Make in My Life?**<br>Learn to recognize and build good leadership skills for serving the Church.<br>**Activity:** Brainstorm qualities of effective spiritual leaders.<br>**Faith Decision:** Evaluate yourself as a spiritual leader and decide how you will be a better leader this week. | **Materials**<br>paper<br>pens or pencils<br>**Options**<br>**Enriching the Lesson (TG page 125)**<br>Researching Profiles of Contemporary Heralds of the Gospel<br>***Additional Activities and Assessment Tools* booklet**<br>Cinquain: Christian Leaders, page 16 |
| **DAY 5**<br>**Pray and Review**<br>**Page 58** | **Pray**<br>Pray "Praise to the God of All Nations!"<br>**Review**<br>**Activities:** Complete the review exercises to reinforce the concepts of the chapter.<br>**Family Discussion:** Encourage the students to share and discuss the question with their family this week. | **Materials**<br>pens or pencils<br>**Options**<br>***Additional Activities and Assessment Tools* booklet**<br>Administer the chapter 5 test.<br>**Music Connection** (TG page 125) |

**Don't Forget!** You can make lesson planning a breeze—check out the **Online Lesson Planner** at www.FaithFirst.com for additional resources to enhance this chapter.

# 5

# The Rise of Christendom

## FAITH FOCUS

In what ways did the Church grow in the 1,200 years after Constantine?

## FAITH VOCABULARY

Edict of Milan
Fathers of the Church
papacy
Christendom
monasticism

***Heralds announce important news. When have you acted as a herald? What news did you share?***

The press secretary for the president of the United States often serves as a herald. In the name of the president, the U.S. press secretary announces news that is important and vital to citizens. Saint John the Baptist was a herald who announced the important news of the coming of Jesus, the Lamb of God and Savior of the world. The Church is the herald and servant of the Gospel. She is called by God to announce the Good News of Salvation in Jesus Christ.

***What have you learned about how the Church serves the world as a herald?***

*Baptism of Constantine I*, oil on canvas. Pierre Puget (1620–1694), French painter.

*"Let it be known to you that this salvation of God has been sent to the Gentiles; they will listen."*
Acts of the Apostles 28:28

49

## National Directory for Catechesis

**Implementing the *National Directory for Catechesis:* Learning by Apprenticeship.** The National Directory teaches that learning by apprenticeship "links an experienced Christian believer, or mentor, with one who seeks a deeper relationship with Christ and the Church" (*NDC* 29H, page 104). Talk with the class about how your school leaders are living examples for them. Invite the students to write letters to the principal and other parish leaders, such as the pastor, DRE, or the head of a specific ministry group, thanking them for their leadership and influence in the parish and school community. Arrange for the completed letters to be delivered to the recipients.

# Day 1

## Engage

### PRAY

- Invite the young people to recall how Jesus commissioned the Apostles to bring the Gospel to the world.
- Gather the class and proclaim Acts of the Apostles 28:28 together.

### FAITH FOCUS

Read aloud and invite brief responses to the "Faith Focus" question. Summarize by pointing out to the students that in this chapter they will discover ways the Church grew during the fourth through the twelfth centuries.

### DISCOVER

Assess the students' prior knowledge and understanding of Church history from the fourth to the twelfth century.

- Write the faith vocabulary terms on the board. Ask the young people to share what they already know about the meanings of the faith terms. Write their responses next to the appropriate terms on the board.
- Pose the opening question and share a time when you have acted as a herald. Then invite volunteers to respond to the question.
- Ask a volunteer to read the opening paragraph aloud.
- Encourage the students to tell what they know about how the Church serves the world as a herald.
- Discuss the image of the Baptism of Constantine as a preparation for presenting pages 50 and 51.

# Day 1

## Teach

**FOCUS**

Invite volunteers to share what a herald does. Remind the students that the Church serves the world as a herald. Point out the images on pages 50 and 51 and explain that in the next two pages, they will learn about several of the heralds who faithfully proclaimed the Gospel.

**DISCOVER**

- Read the opening paragraph to the students.
- Invite the students to silently read "The Emperor Constantine" and "The Fathers of the Church."
- Have the students work in three groups. Assign one group "The Emperor Constantine," one group "Saint Ambrose of Milan," and the third group "Saint Augustine of Hippo."
- Have each group summarize what they have learned about how the person assigned to them contributed to the growth of the Church. Tell them that they may choose any form they wish to present their summary to the class.
- Allow each group to present to the class.

## Roman Empire to Christendom

Constantine I, statue in York, England, where he was proclaimed Roman Emperor in 306.

This chapter and chapter 6 will focus on the history of the Church from the Edict of Milan (313) to the period of the Reformation in the sixteenth century. Examining the work of the Church's heralds and servants during this 1,200-year period will help us discover how the Church carried out the commission that the Risen Jesus first gave to the Apostles.

### Emperor Constantine

We begin this period of the story of the Church with the Emperor Constantine the Great (ca. 288–337). Constantine became co-ruler of the Roman Empire in 306 with Licinius Augustus, his brother-in-law and rival Emperor in the East. While Constantine delayed his Baptism until just before he died, he declared himself to be a Christian in 312.

The Church's privileged status began under Constantine in the **Edict of Milan** in 313. In the Edict of Milan Constantine declared with Licinius:

> [I]t has pleased us to remove all conditions whatsoever, which were in the rescripts formerly given to you officially, concerning the Christians and now any one of these who wishes to observe Christian religion may do so freely and openly, without molestation. . . . Let this be done so that . . . Divine favor towards us . . . may, for all time, preserve and prosper our successes together with the good of the state.
>
> EDICT OF MILAN

This was confirmed by Emperor Theodosius I (346–395), who outlawed paganism and declared Christianity as the official religion of the Roman Empire. From that time on the Church continued to grow even as Rome fell to the Alaric and the Visigoth army in 410 and the power of the Roman Empire declined.

As the Church emerged from a time of external persecutions, new threats and challenges came from within the Church. Meeting these challenges was undertaken, for the most part, by the Fathers of the Church and the councils of the Church.

***What role did Constantine and the Edict of Milan play in the history of the Church?***

50

### Background: Catholic Tradition

**Edict of Milan.** As Constantine I prepared for battle against Maxentius at the Milvian Bridge, which crosses the Tiber River, he had a vision of a cross and the words "in this sign you shall conquer." Emperor Constantine attributed his miraculous victory at the battle of the Milvian Bridge to the God of the Christians. Tradition tells us that this experience moved Constantine to declare he was a Christian, though he delayed his Baptism until he became seriously ill, as he prepared for battle in 337, shortly before he died.

### The Fathers of the Church

The **Fathers of the Church** were theologians and writers of the first eight centuries of the Church. The Fathers of the Church are classified into two groups, namely, the Latin Fathers of the Church and the Greek Fathers of the Church. Saint Ambrose of Milan and Saint Augustine of Hippo were among the Latin Fathers of the Church in the West. Saint John Damascene (c. 675–c. 749), one of the Greek Fathers of the Church, is considered the last of the Fathers of the Church.

#### Saint Ambrose of Milan

Saint Ambrose was the archbishop of Milan in what is now Italy. While he was serving as a governor of a northern province of Italy, Ambrose (339–397) was elected bishop of Milan in 374, even though he was not baptized. In 385 he confronted the Empress-mother Justina's attempt to take over the basilica in Milan. In two face-to-face confrontations with the Emperor Theodosius, Saint Ambrose admonished Theodosius, reminding him that the emperor was not above the Church but within it. Saint Ambrose also called for reform within the Church. In his treatise, *On the Duties of the Clergy*, he called the members of the clergy to live lives of spiritual discipline.

#### Saint Augustine of Hippo

After listening to Saint Ambrose preach and then meeting with him, Augustine (354–430) was baptized by Saint Ambrose in 387. Four years later he was ordained as a priest. Four years after that he was consecrated bishop of Hippo in northern Africa. The brilliance of Saint Augustine's writings and the energy he brought to the care of the faithful in his diocese have earned Saint Augustine the title Doctor of the Church.

***How did Saint Ambrose and Saint Augustine influence the Church?***

*The Emperor Theodosius and Saint Ambrose.*
Peter Paul Rubens (1577–1640), Flemish painter.

**FAITH CONNECTION**

***Create a coat of arms or crest for yourself, symbolizing your calling to be a herald of the Gospel. In this space write the motto that will appear on the crest.***

Responses will vary

Affirm appropriate responses.

51

# Day 1

## Apply

### REINFORCE

After the presentations, have the class discuss the boldfaced questions at the end of each section. Clarify the responses as necessary.

### INTEGRATE

- Write the faith vocabulary terms *Edict of Milan* and *Fathers of the Church* on the board.
- Invite the young people to create a word map for the terms by adding new words and phrases to the terms on the board.
- Introduce the "Faith Connection" activity and have the students work on it independently. Invite volunteers to present their coat of arms or crests to the class.

### PRAY

Invite the students to quiet themselves for prayer. After a moment of prayerful reflection on the call of all the baptized to be heralds of the Gospel, lead the class in praying the Prayer to the Holy Spirit on page 137 in the student text.

## Background: Catholic Tradition

**Spiritual Legacy of the Church Fathers.** The Church Fathers continue to have a significant influence on the spiritual life of the Church. The writings of the Church Fathers give authentic witness to the life and teachings of Jesus. The wisdom of the Church Fathers will continue to influence the spiritual formation and growth of Christians and inspire those who follow Jesus to give authentic witness to the Gospel. In their spiritual writings the Church Fathers remind us that the spiritual substance of life and true happiness come only from God. They invite us to pass that legacy on to future generations.

### *Enriching the Lesson*

The "Writing an Edict" activity on page 125 is related to today's content. You may wish to include it in today's lesson.

# Day 2

## Teach

**PRAY**

- Invite the students to quiet themselves for prayer. Proclaim Acts of the Apostles 28:28 together.
- Pray together, "Lord, we are thankful for your heralds and servants, / in the past and in the present. / May we too / serve your Church well. / Amen."

**FOCUS**

Share with the students that in the fourth century a new age was dawning for the Church. The days of persecution were ending. Point out that on the next two pages they will learn more about the emergence of Christianity as an established religion in the Roman Empire.

**DISCOVER**

- Read aloud or paraphrase the opening paragraph.
- Invite the students to silently examine the art on pages 52 and 53 and read "Christendom" and "The Papacy" to discover how the Church fulfilled her mission to be a herald of the Gospel in the first millennium of her existence.
- Share the "Did you know" feature to make the students aware that there have been twenty-one ecumenical councils of the Church.

### Did you Know...

There have been twenty-one ecumenical councils of the Church. They are:

- Nicaea I (325)
- Constantinople I (381)
- Ephesus (431)
- Chalcedon (451)
- Constantinople II (553)
- Constantinople III (680–681)
- Nicaea II (787)
- Constantinople IV (869–870)
- Lateran I (1123)
- Lateran II (1139)
- Lateran III (1179)
- Lateran IV (1215)
- Lyons I (1245)
- Lyons II (1274)
- Vienne (1311–1312)
- Constance (1414–1418)
- Florence (1431–c. 1445)
- Lateran V (1512–1517)
- Trent (1545–1563)
- Vatican I (1869–1870)
- Vatican II (1962–1965)

*Council of Nicaea, 325.* Cesare Nebbia (1534–1614), Italian painter.

After Emperor Theodosius I declared Christianity the official religion of the empire, the Church gained an even greater influence in society. The Church grew and lived in freedom. Elaborate basilicas were constructed throughout the Roman Empire. The Popes took on a role of leadership, not only within the Church, but also in society.

### Christendom

Beginning in the fourth through sixth centuries, Christianity became thoroughly established throughout the Roman Empire. From the Council of Nicaea (325) through the **papacy** of Gregory the Great (d. 604), the role of the Pope grew stronger. The papacy is the name of the position of leadership, the office and authority, of the Pope. The Pope enjoys by divine institution "supreme, full, immediate, and universal power in the care of souls" [CD2] (*Catechism of the Catholic Church* 937).

By the twelfth century the papacy became the dominant force that helped shape the West. The twelfth- and thirteenth-century councils at the Lateran in Rome (1123, 1139, 1179, and 1215) are the most visible signs of the resurgence of the papacy during this period. By the turn of the first millennium, the Gospel had been preached virtually throughout all of Western Europe. The term **Christendom** refers to the eventual outcome of that process.

While the term *christendom* has many meanings, it usually refers to the growth of Christianity both in territory populated by Christians and in political and spiritual power. The role of the Pope and bishops continued to develop during this period as the authority of the emperor, and eventually that of kings, diminished. The result was that the Pope's authority in the West surpassed that of the emperors.

52

### Teaching Tip

**Checking Our Attitude Toward Content.** Every once in a while it is good for teachers to pause and check their own attitudes toward the subject matter. Our attitudes can have tremendous impact on the way we present the content of a lesson. For example, if your attitude toward Church history is one of bored indifference, your students may easily adopt a similar attitude. On the other hand, your interest and excitement about the process of discovering new things about the Church and her history can motivate and inspire your class.

### Pope Saint Sylvester I

At the time of the First Council of Nicaea, Constantine was the Roman emperor and Sylvester I was the first bishop of Rome to call himself Pope. The word *Pope* means "father." In the early Church, it was sometimes used to refer to any influential and respected bishop. Only later was the name *Pope* used only for the bishop of Rome.

Pope Saint Sylvester I, who was Pope from 314 to 335, is a symbol of the Church living in her new-found freedom. Now that Christians could worship openly without fear of persecution, he oversaw the beginning of the building of two important churches, Basilica of Saint Peter and Saint John Lateran Basilica in Rome.

### Pope Saint Leo the Great

Saint Leo the Great, who became Pope in 440, was a great preacher and defender of the Church's teaching. Focusing on Jesus' words "[Y]ou are Peter, and upon this rock I will build my church" (Matthew 16:18), Leo affirmed that his own authority as Pope was the same authority that Jesus gave to Saint Peter the Apostle. He was also the first Pope to effectively use his authority in civil matters.

In 452 Pope Saint Leo the Great met with Attila the Hun on the road to Rome, persuading Attila to turn north and not to attack the city. There is a legend that claims Attila gave in to Leo's demands because he saw Saint Peter and Saint Paul marching with the Pope. In 455 Pope Leo again saved Rome from being burned to the ground, this time by meeting with Genseric, the leader of the Vandals who had sacked the great city.

***What role did the papacy play in the life of the Church and in the life of society in the fourth and fifth centuries?***

*Saint Gregory.* Titian, Tiziano Vecellio, (ca. 1477–1576), Italian painter, chief master of the Venetian school.

53

## Background: Catholic Tradition

**Vatican Diplomatic Corps.** Today the Roman Catholic Church has diplomatic relations with the governments of more than 160 nations through the Vatican Diplomatic Corps. On January 10, 1984, President Ronald Reagan established full diplomatic relations with the Vatican after a 116-year hiatus. Today the U.S. Ambassador to the Vatican works on a wide range of international issues including world peace, protection of human rights, and promotion of religious tolerance and freedom.

# Day 2

## Apply

### REINFORCE

- Divide the class into three groups. Assign one of the following sections from the reading to each small group: "Christendom," "Pope Saint Sylvester I," and "Pope Saint Leo the Great."
- Each group's task is to create a five-question fill-in-the-blank, matching, or true/false quiz based on the content of their section.
- Ask everyone to close their textbooks. Then invite the groups to quiz their classmates.
- If they need to, allow the class to quickly open their books to pages 52 and 53 and review the content to retake the quizzes.

### INTEGRATE

- Give the young people time to complete closing questions independently.
- Invite volunteers to share what they might advise the Pope about serving the Church today.

### PRAY

Have the students quiet themselves for prayer. Lead the class in praying the Nicene Creed on page 136 in the student text.

# Day 3

## Teach

### PRAY

Have the students quiet themselves for prayer and proclaim Acts of the Apostles 28:28 together.

### FOCUS

Remind the class that the term *Christendom* refers to the growth of Christianity geographically, as well as in political and spiritual authority. Point out to the students that in today's lesson they will discover the vital role that monasticism plays in the life of the Church.

### DISCOVER

- Paraphrase the introductory paragraph and write on the board the key phrases that describe the Church as a society. Structured hierarchy, mystical, visible, spiritual, earthly, and heavenly.
- Invite volunteers to read aloud "Monasticism" to discover the contributions of Saint Martin of Tours, Saint Benedict of Nursia, and Saint Scholastica to the development of monasticism in the Church in the West.
- Have the young people discuss the question at the end of the page with a partner.

## Apply

### REINFORCE

Highlight the meaning of the word *monasticism* and ask the students to define it in their own words.

### INTEGRATE

Have the students complete the "Faith Connection" activity independently and make a decision to live a simple lifestyle.

**Time LINE**

| | |
|---|---|
| 407 | †Saint John (of Constantinople) Chrysostom |
| 410 | Fall of Rome |
| 417 | †Pope Innocent |
| 420 | †Saint Jerome |
| 430 | Saint Augustine of Hippo |
| 431 | Council of Ephesus |
| 444 | †Saint Cyril of Alexandria |
| 451 | Council of Chalcedon |
| 452 | Attila the Hun invades Italy |
| 453 | †Saint Benedict of Nursia |
| | †Saint Scholastica |
| 455 | Vandals sack Rome |
| 461 | †Pope Saint Leo the Great |
| 476 | Western empire ends |

The Church is both visible and spiritual. One of her essential characteristics, or Marks, is that she is "holy." God the Father is her author, Christ is her bridegroom, and she is the Temple of the Holy Spirit. She is the sacrament of the Holy Trinity's communion with humanity.

### Monasticism

The spiritual growth of the Church during this period of her history was centered in **monasticism.** Monasticism is a lifestyle of communal living. It is dedicated to guiding its members to live out the Gospel counsels of obedience, poverty, and chastity in simplicity and is centered on prayer, fasting, work, and learning. Saint Martin of Tours and Saint Benedict of Nursia and his twin sister, Saint Scholastica, helped spread monasticism in the West.

#### Saint Martin of Tours

The monastic movement spread to the West when Saint Martin of Tours founded a monastery near Poitiers in 362. After Martin, "the dirty, disheveled man, dressed in rags," was elected bishop, he built a small room next to the cathedral where he spent his free time living the monastic life.

#### Saint Benedict of Nursia<br>Saint Scholastica

Saint Benedict of Nursia (ca. 480–ca. 543) is the founder of monasticism in the Church in the West. The *Rule of Saint Benedict,* which became a model for future ages, guided the lives of the monks in the monasteries founded by Saint Benedict and the lives of the nuns in the convents founded by Saint Scholastica (ca. 480–ca. 543). The great monastery founded by Saint Benedict around 529 at Monte Cassino about forty miles south of Rome was badly damaged during the Second World War. Later rebuilt according to its original plan and reconsecrated in 1964, it stands today as a symbol of the spiritual life of the Church.

***Who were some of the leaders of the monastic movement? How were they heralds of the Gospel and servants of the Church?***

*Saint Benedict Among Benedictine Monks,* fresco. Il Sodoma (ca. 1477–1549), Italian painter.

**FAITH CONNECTION**

***Simplicity** is a term that is often used to characterize the monastic lifestyle. What are some things you can do to live a simple life?*

Responses will vary

Affirm appropriate responses.

54

### Background: Catholic Tradition

***The Rule of Saint Benedict.*** The monks and nuns who follow the *Rule of Saint Benedict* today are called to live a life of prayer and works. Their motto is "Ora et Labora," which means "Pray and Work." The *Rule of Saint Benedict* defines the three solemn promises Benedictine monks and nuns formally profess: (1) stability—both to the monastery and to the heart; (2) fidelity—to the monastic life and to a conversion of one's own life; and (3) obedience.

# OUR CHURCH MAKES A DIFFERENCE

Trappists at prayer, Chapel at Abbey of Gethsemani, Trappist, Kentucky.

When have you heard the word *renewal* used? It is sometimes used by people within an organization who are dedicated to making sure that an organization is living by its values and achieving the goals for which it was founded.

### Renewal of Monasticism

The renewal of monasticism throughout the history of the Church has contributed significantly to helping people deepen their spiritual life. In the tenth and eleventh centuries the monasteries at Cluny and Clairvaux became focal points for the renewal of monasticism, particularly for living the *Rule of Saint Benedict*.

#### Cistercians/Trappists

Bernard of Fontaines, later known as Saint Bernard of Clairvaux, began the renewal of monasticism at Citeaux in 1112. Before he died in 1153 Bernard and his followers founded about 300 other monasteries dedicated to strictly living the *Rule of Saint Benedict*. His work was so important in his own time that it was said that Bernard carried the twelfth century on his shoulders.

The Order of Cistercians (named after the site of their origin, Citeaux), continued to grow to 742 monasteries by the time of the Reformation. It, too, underwent renewal in the seventeenth century. This renewal of Cistercians, whom we know today as Trappists, began under the leadership of Armand Jean de Rancé, who established the Abbey of Notre Dame de la Grande Trappe as the site of the renewal. The work of the quiet, shy Bernard of Clairvaux still renews the Church in the twenty-first century.

#### Oblates of Saint Benedict

The Oblates of Saint Benedict are married or single laypeople living in the world. They are dedicated to living the *Rule of Saint Benedict*, including the evangelical counsels of obedience, poverty, and chastity according to their state of life.

Oblates of Saint Benedict cleaning home, New Orleans, after Hurricane Katrina.

***If you were to draw up a plan for the renewal of your spiritual life, what would that plan contain?***

Responses will vary. Affirm appropriate responses.

55

## Teaching Tip

**Partner Work.** The young people should regularly work with partners or in small groups. For example, have partners or groups create the interview questions that they would like to ask their pastor. Then have partners or groups role-play their interviews before the entire class, with one partner or group member being the interviewer and the other partner or another group member taking on the role of the pastor. Clarify the answers to questions the respondents in each group give.

# Day 3

## Connect

### HIGHLIGHT

Remind the students that the Church has continued to grow visibly and spiritually over the centuries. Point out that this page will help them further appreciate the importance of the monastic tradition for the life of the Church.

### DISCOVER

- Write the word *renewal* on the board and paraphrase the first paragraph on page 55. Stress that renewal of all organizations is vital to their life. Ask the students to explain why this is so.
- Invite the young people to silently read "Renewal of Monasticism" to discover the continuing role that the *Rule of Saint Benedict* plays in helping the faithful grow spiritually.

### INTEGRATE

- Invite the students to join with a partner and discuss the question at the end of the page.
- Share appropriate ideas about your own spiritual renewal plan.
- Ask volunteers to share elements that would be a part of their spiritual renewal plans.

### PRAY

Ask the students to pause for prayer. End by praying the Act of Love on page 137 in the student text.

### *Enriching the Lesson*

The "Creating a Timeline" activity on page 125 is related to today's content. You may wish to include it in today's lesson.

# Day 4

## Connect

### PRAY

- Invite the young people to quiet themselves for prayer.
- Proclaim Acts of the Apostles 28:28 together. Then lead the class in praying the Prayer to the Holy Spirit on page 137 of the student book.

### FOCUS

Recall the "Faith Focus" question on page 49. Ask volunteers to answer it, using what they have learned in this chapter. Explain that throughout the centuries, faithful men and women of the Church have been heralds of Jesus' mission. Tell the class that these pages will help them explore the concept of leadership as it applies to their serving the Church as a herald of the Gospel.

### DISCOVER

- Create a virtual continuum in the classroom by naming one end of the room "Highly Agree" and the other "Highly Disagree."
- Have the young people get up and align themselves along the continuum based on their opinions of these statements:
  —A leader is someone who influences the behavior of others.
  —Leaders are born, not made.
- Read aloud the introductory paragraph to the class.
- Have the students silently read "Serving the Church" to discover skills that will enable them to responsibly participate in the work of the Church.

# WHAT DIFFERENCE Does Faith Make in My Life?

The Church is the Body of Christ. He lives with her and in her. The Church is the Temple of the Holy Spirit who dwells within the Church, working in the world to build up the Church on earth and make disciples of all nations. The work of Christ and the Holy Spirit is inseparable. Christ and the Holy Spirit always work together to bring about the divine plan for the world.

### Serving the Church

While churches, cathedrals, and other places of worship have been built over the centuries, we must always remember that the Church is not simply a building. The Church is the new People of God, the Body of Christ, and the Temple of the Holy Spirit. You are a member of the Church. You are called to be a herald of the Gospel. The Holy Spirit is always giving the members of the Church the charisms, or special graces, to live as vibrant, active members of the Church.

#### Who Can Be a Leader?

There are many different ways you can offer yourself to serve the Church. Some people are said to be born leaders. Others are recognized for their charisma and learn how to become leaders. With sufficient motivation and a certain amount of work, you can develop the qualities needed to be a good leader in the Church by living as a vibrant, active member of the Church.

56

## Teaching Tip

**Discerning One's Vocation.** Each of the baptized receives a special call, or vocation, from God to serve him and the Church. John Henry Cardinal Newman (1801–1890) described his vocation this way: "God has created me to do some definite service; he has committed some work to me which he has not committed to another. I have my mission." Share a story about your own call to serve the Church. Then encourage the students to think about their gifts and talents and to ask the Holy Spirit to guide them in using their gifts and talents to serve the Gospel. Point out that this is an important step in discerning their vocation.

## Leadership Qualities

One broad definition of a leader is one who influences the behavior of others. Here are a few qualities that characterize good and effective leaders.

Good and effective leaders:

- encourage people to use their gifts and reach their potential; they have a positive influence on people.
- express their ideas and listen as other people express their opinions; they use effective communication skills.
- are patient and persistent; they know that it takes time and energy to get the job done well.
- are compassionate and respectful; they are concerned for the welfare of others.
- are people of integrity; they are honest, genuine, dependable, and trustworthy; they lead others in the right direction, even when it is unpopular.
- have a sense of humor and recognize their own limitations.
- view potential and real problems as opportunities and challenges.

Every day you are influenced by others and at the same time you are an influence on others—more than you may even know. Recognizing and building good leadership qualities is important for all of the members of the Church.

## Faith Decision

- Brainstorm in small groups the qualities of an effective spiritual leader who builds up the Church. List those qualities here:

  Responses will vary
  Affirm appropriate responses.

- Now work independently to evaluate yourself as a spiritual leader.
  - —What leadership qualities do you already have?
  - —What qualities would you like to enhance?
  - —In what situations at home and in school have you been called upon to be a leader?

This week I will be a better spiritual leader by

Responses will vary
Affirm appropriate responses.

57

# Day 4
## Apply

### INTEGRATE

- Have the students work in small groups to complete the steps in the "Faith Decision" brainstorming activity.
- Summarize their brainstorming with the class, then direct them to independently evaluate themselves as leaders.
- Ask volunteers to share their evaluation with the class.

### CHOOSE

- Invite the young people to prayerfully reflect on how they will be better spiritual leaders. Then have them make and write their faith decision.
- Encourage them to put their faith decision into practice this week.

### PRAY

Ask the students to end the lesson by praying the Our Father together.

## Teaching Tip

**Identifying Local Church Leaders.** Help the students refresh their memory of the names of the pastoral leaders of the parish and diocese. Have them work in small groups to gather the names or provide them with the following names. **Parish pastoral leaders:** pastor, associate pastors, deacons, school principal, director of religious education, parish council president, and names of the appointed coordinators of parish ministries. **Diocesan pastoral leaders:** Local ordinary and auxiliary bishop(s), vicar general, chancellor, and appointed heads of diocesan ministerial commissions. If possible, have the students report on or provide the class with a description of the primary responsibilities of these pastoral leaders.

### *Enriching the Lesson*

The "Researching Profiles of Contemporary Heralds of the Gospel" activity on page 125 is related to today's content. You may wish to include it in today's lesson.

# Day 5

## Pray and Review

**FOCUS**

Remind the young people of the tremendous growth of the Church, visibly and spiritually, during the time period they have just studied.

**PRAY**

- Divide the class into two groups, and assign a leader for the prayer.
- Ask each group to silently prepare the part of the prayer assigned to it.
- Have the class stand and pray "Praise to the God of All Nations!" together.

**REVIEW**

- Have the young people share the meaning of the terms in "Faith Vocabulary" and compare their definitions with those in the glossary.
- Use the "Main Ideas" and "Critical Thinking" sections to clarify any questions the students may have concerning what they have learned in the chapter.
- Remind everyone to share and discuss the "Family Discussion" question with their family.

### *Before Moving On . . .*

Reflect on this question before moving on to the next chapter.

*In what ways have I demonstrated a positive attitude toward learning more about the Church's history through my teaching?*

# PRAY and REVIEW

## *Praise to the God of All Nations!*

**Leader:** God, Father of all nations, we lift up our hearts to you. We praise you. We thank you for calling us to be your Church.

**Reader:** A reading from the holy gospel according to Matthew.

**All:** **Glory to you, O Lord.**

**Reader:** *Read Matthew 5:13–16.* The gospel of the Lord.

**All:** **Praise to you, Lord Jesus Christ. Shout joyfully to God, all you on earth; / sing of his glorious name; / give him glorious praise.**

**Group 1:** Come and see the works of God, / awesome in the deeds done for us.

**Group 2:** Bless our God, you peoples; / loudly sound his praise.

**Group 1:** Come and hear, all you who fear God, / while I recount what has been done for me.

**Group 2:** I called to the Lord with my mouth; / praise was upon my tongue.

**All:** **Shout joyfully to God, all you on earth, / sing of his glorious name; / give him glorious praise.**

BASED ON PSALM 66:1, 2, 5, 8, 16, 17

58

**FAITH VOCABULARY**

Define each of these faith vocabulary terms:

1. Edict of Milan
2. Fathers of the Church
3. papacy
4. Christendom
5. monasticism

**MAIN IDEAS**

Choose either (a) or (b) from each set of items. Write a brief paragraph to answer each of your choices.

1. (a) Discuss the influence of the Fathers of the Church on the life of the Church. p. 51
   (b) Describe the contributions Saint Ambrose and Saint Augustine made to the Church. p. 51
2. (a) Explain the role of the papacy during the fourth through fourteenth centuries. pp. 52–53
   (b) Describe the contributions of the monastic movement to the life of the Church. p. 54

**CRITICAL THINKING**

Using what you have learned in this chapter, briefly explain this statement:

> The mission of the Church "is to be salt of the earth and light of the world,' . . . [the] 'seed of unity, hope, and salvation for the whole human race.' "
>
> CATECHISM OF THE CATHOLIC CHURCH 782

**FAMILY DISCUSSION**

How can we as a family be a herald of the Gospel and a servant of the Church in the world today?

For more ideas on ways your family can live your faith, visit the "Faith First for Families" page at **www.FaithFirst.com**. Also check out "Bible Zone" on the Teen Center.

## Evaluate

Take a few moments to evaluate this week's lesson.

I feel (circle one) about this week's lesson.

a. very pleased
b. OK
c. disappointed

The activity the students enjoyed most was . . .

The concept that was most difficult to teach was . . .

because . . .

Something I would like to do differently is . . .

# ENRICHING THE LESSON

## Writing an Edict

### Purpose

To reinforce the concept of the nature and purpose of an edict (taught on page 51)

### Directions

- Recall with the students the Edict of Milan. Then explain to them the nature and purpose of an edict, namely, "a decree of proclamation issued by an authority and having the force of law" (*The American Heritage Dictionary® of the English Language,* Fourth Edition. Copyright 2002, 2000).
- Create small groups of three or four students.
- Have each group write an edict that will proclaim a rule for the class.
- Have each group present their edict to the entire group.

### Materials

paper, pens or pencils

## Creating a Timeline

### Purpose

To further explore the key people and events in the history of the Church from 400 to 1000 (taught on page 54)

### Directions

- Invite the students to work with a partner. Assign each pair one of the people or events on the timeline on page 54 and have them create a brief two-minute report that tells about their assigned person or event.
- Encourage each pair of students to be as creative as they wish in deciding how they will present to the class.
- Have the pairs create a living timeline by lining up around the classroom in chronological order according to the timeline.
- Have each pair of students make a presentation about the person or event assigned to it.

### Materials

pens or pencils

## Researching Profiles of Contemporary Heralds of the Gospel

### Purpose

To reinforce the concept that heralds have been in the past and are in the present important to the life of the Church (taught on page 57)

### Directions

- Ask the students to list on the board recent people that have made a contribution to the work of the Church.
- Assist the students in identifying people by allowing them to look in the texts that they have used this year.
- Have the students work in small groups to create a list of the heralds of the Gospel.
- Distribute art paper and markers. Instruct the groups to design a panel portraying several of the heralds they have identified by writing the name of the person, the date, and a summary of how the person was a herald of the Church.
- Combine the panels and put the combined panels on display.

### Materials

art paper, tape, markers
pens or pencils

## Music Connection

- "The Church of Christ," J. Bell. *Gather Comprehensive (GC)* #665.
- "Envía Tu Espíritu," B. Hurd. *Flor y Canto* #516.
- "For All the Saints," (Traditional). *GC* #791.
- "Shine on Us, Lord," J. Mattingly. *Voices As One* #82.

# Chapter 6 Mystics, Mendicants, and Scholastics

## CHAPTER BACKGROUND

### "Teach All I Commanded You"

Following the conversion of the Roman Emperor Constantine in 312, the Church was no longer impeded by the state. The Church could freely and without fear of persecution carry out the mission given to her by Christ.

Despite the period of cultural decline in the West, known as the Dark Ages, the Church experienced growth in many ways. The monastic movement in the West, inspired by figures such as Saint Benedict of Nursia and Saint Scholastica, offered stability and growth in the midst of cultural decay. Missionaries traveled throughout Europe, converting whole populations to Christ and uniting them under the leadership of the Church.

### Challenges to Society and the Church

The freedom and acceptance that the Church enjoyed also led the Church to assume temporal power. The bishop of Rome gained control of the city of Rome and gradually acquired vast land holdings throughout the Italian peninsula, becoming both a political and a spiritual leader. Charlemagne aimed to establish an unbreakable link between the Church and the

emerging Holy Roman Empire.

There were moments of confusion within the Church and external pressures challenging the Church to remain faithful to her identity and mission. These included heretical movements, invasions of barbarian hordes, and the collapse of civic structures.

During the century before the turn of the second millennium society was fragmented by the assaults of Asiatic warriors, Norsemen, and Saracen pirates. The papacy fell into decline as it became too controlled by contentious ducal clans. With the Church of the West, which was experiencing such confusion, many people expected the year 1000 to be the time of Christ's return. This, of course, did not happen.

### Renewal

In the midst of these dark times the Holy Spirit was working to bring about a renewal within the Church. As the second millennium opened, majestic cathedrals were built, monastic foundations prospered, and saints walked upon the land.

Saint Bernard of Clairvaux became a recognized leader of the renewal of the monastic movement, and the mystic Saint Hildegard of Bingen was acknowledged as a woman of uncommon vision.

Foundations were laid for such religious orders as the Dominicans and the Franciscans. Theological thought, stimulated by newly discovered texts by ancient Greek scholars, experienced new vigor and found its crown in the works of such Scholastics as Saint Bonaventure, Saint Thomas Aquinas, and Blessed John Duns Scotus.

## FOR REFLECTION

***How have I met the challenges to my faith as opportunities for spiritual growth?***

***What can I do to encourage the students to grow in their spiritual life?***

## First Thoughts

### Great Teachers

The names of great teachers fill the history of the Church. From the days of the early Church to the present, the Holy Spirit has called and empowered men and women of the Church to fulfill Jesus' command, "Go, therefore, and make disciples of all nations, . . . teaching them to observe all that I have commanded you" (Matthew 28:19–20). The dynamic lives of these holy and wise men and women have been lights guiding the flock of Christ on its pilgrimage to the Kingdom of God. You are a part of this great heritage.

### Much to Aspire To

The faith development of young adolescents involves the task of seeking and growing in their identity as Catholics. You are a vital member of the team of family, school, and parish guiding the young people in this task. The young people you teach are working to establish a firm set of beliefs, attitudes, and values to help guide them on their life's journey. The people and events who make up the Church's history provide them with much to aspire to as they grow in faith and develop a deeper personal relationship with God.

### The Church Teaches . . .

The Second Vatican Council spoke to the challenges of the Church to fulfill her mission. It taught:

> [T]he Church . . . is given strength to overcome, in patience and in love, her sorrows and difficulties, both those that are from within and those that are from without.
>
> *Dogmatic Constitution of the Church [Lumen Gentium]* 8

In this chapter the students will learn how the Church kept the light of faith and learning alive during the Middle Ages.

### See the Catechism . . .

For more on the teachings of the Catholic Church on the light of faith, schism, renewal, and the media, see *Catechism of the Catholic Church* 26, 298, 817–822, and 2493–2498.

*Gracious God,*
*through the grace of your*
*Holy Spirit, men and*
*women throughout the*
*ages have led inspired*
*lives in our Church.*
*We thank you for their*
*wisdom, teaching, and*
*leadership. Help us*
*emulate them.*
*Amen.*

Now . . . turn the page and let's get organized!

# LESSON PLANNER

**Chapter Focus**

**To understand how the light of faith was ignited during the Middle Ages and beyond**

| Focus | Process | Materials and Options |
|---|---|---|
| **DAY 1**<br>**Engage/Teach and Apply**<br>**Pages 59–61**<br>**Focus**<br>To understand how the Church has the guarantee of development | **Opening Prayer**<br>**Discussion**<br>What it means to say that the Church has the guarantee of development<br>**Presentation**<br>Read, discuss, and summarize content.<br>**Scripture:** Isaiah 62:12, Matthew 28:20<br>**Activity:** Discuss the Dark Ages.<br>**Faith Connection:** Decide how you can grow in your understanding of the faith of the Church. | **Materials**<br>miscellaneous materials students need to present their "lessons," pens or pencils<br>**Options**<br>***Called to Prayer and Liturgical Lessons* booklet:** See options for daily and seasonal prayers and liturgical prayers and lessons.<br>**Enriching the Lesson (TG page 139)**<br>Creating Quizzes |
| **DAY 2**<br>**Teach and Apply**<br>**Pages 62–63**<br>**Focus**<br>To discover the people and events that called the Church to renewal | **Prayer**<br>**Presentation**<br>Read, discuss, and summarize content.<br>**Scripture:** John 14:25–26<br>**Did you know:** Doctors of the Church<br>**Activity:** Hold a news conference interviewing Saint Francis of Assisi and Saint Dominic. | **Options**<br>**Enriching the Lesson (TG page 139)**<br>Discovering the Doctors of the Church<br>***Additional Activities and Assessment Tools* booklet**<br>Lights of Faith, page 17 |
| **DAY 3**<br>**Teach/Apply and Connect**<br>**Pages 64–65**<br>**Focus**<br>To discover how the Church fulfills her commission to preach the Gospel | **Prayer**<br>**Presentation**<br>Read, discuss, and summarize content.<br>**Scripture:** Matthew 5:14–16<br>**Faith Connection:** Decide how you can use your gifts and talents to live the Gospel.<br>**Our Church Makes a Difference**<br>Discover how the Church uses the media to spread the Gospel. | **Materials**<br>Bibles, pens or pencils<br>**Options**<br>**Enriching the Lesson (TG page 139)**<br>Creating a Good News Web Page |
| **DAY 4**<br>**Connect and Apply**<br>**Pages 66–67**<br>**Focus**<br>To explore how to be heralds and servants as members of the Church today | **Prayer**<br>**What Difference Does Faith Make in My Life?**<br>Explore how to be a herald and servant of the Gospel.<br>**Activity:** Develop an action plan to be heralds and servants of the Gospel.<br>**Faith Decision:** Decide how you will be a herald and servant of the Church this week. | **Materials**<br>markers, pens or pencils<br>**Options**<br>***Additional Activities and Assessment Tools* booklet**<br>Help Wanted Ad: Youth Minister Needed, page 18 |
| **DAY 5**<br>**Pray and Review**<br>**Page 68** | **Pray**<br>Pray "A Prayer for Today's Heralds and Servants of the Gospel."<br>**Review**<br>**Activities:** Complete the review exercises to reinforce the concepts of the chapter.<br>**Family Discussion:** Encourage the students to share and discuss the question with their family this week. | **Materials**<br>pens or pencils<br>**Options**<br>***Additional Activities and Assessment Tools* booklet**<br>Administer the chapter 6 test.<br>Plan for the unit one test.<br>**Music Connection** (TG page 139) |

**Don't Forget!** You can make lesson planning a breeze—check out the **Online Lesson Planner** at www.FaithFirst.com for additional resources to enhance this chapter.

6

# Mystics, Mendicants, and Scholastics

**FAITH FOCUS**

Who were some of the men and women who ignited the light of faith throughout the Dark Ages and beyond?

**FAITH VOCABULARY**

| | |
|---|---|
| **Dark Ages** | **East-West Schism** |
| **mystics** | **Mendicants** |
| **Scholastics** | **Crusades** |

***Describe the ups and downs of some organization you are familiar with, for example, a sports team, a business, or even a country.***

We often observe the paradox that both decline and development, reform and renewal, go hand in hand. This dual pattern can also be used to describe periods of history in the Church.

***What does it mean when we say that the Church has the guarantee of development and renewal?***

*Saint Francis Preaching to the Birds,* fresco. Giotto di Bondone (ca. 1266–1337), Italian painter, architect, and sculptor.

*They shall be called the holy people, / the redeemed of the LORD.*
ISAIAH 62:12

59

# Day 1

## Engage

### PRAY

Begin by asking the young people to quiet themselves for prayer. After a moment of silence pray the Sign of the Cross. Then proclaim Isaiah 62:12 together.

### FAITH FOCUS

Read aloud and invite brief responses to the "Faith Focus" question. Point out to the students that in this chapter they will further their exploration and discovery of the Church as herald and servant by looking at the period of the Middle Ages. Explain that the Middle Ages cover the period A.D. 500 to A.D. 1500.

### DISCOVER

Assess the students' prior knowledge of this period of Church history.

- Write the terms in "Faith Vocabulary" on the board. Ask volunteers what they already know about the meanings of the faith terms. Write their responses next to the appropriate terms on the board.
- Read aloud the bold text that begins the paragraph. Invite responses and share your own.
- Have the students silently read the opening paragraph.
- Discuss their responses to the concluding question.
- Summarize by discussing the art "Saint Francis Preaching to the Birds." Emphasize that Saint Francis of Assisi responded to God's call to renew the Church.

## National Directory for Catechesis

**Implementing the *National Directory for Catechesis:* Learning Through Human Experience.** The National Directory teaches: "Human experiences provide the sensible signs that lead the person, by the grace of the Holy Spirit, to a better understanding of the truths of the faith" (*NDC* 29A, page 97). Following the students' study of the Church and the media in the "What Difference Does Faith Make in My Life?" section of the chapter, ask them to use the Internet at home to find Catholic Web sites that serve the People of God. Have them bring to class printouts from the sites they selected.

# Day 1

## Teach

**FOCUS**

Remind the students that the Holy Spirit is always present with the Church, guiding her to fulfill her mission of renewing her life by observing everything Jesus commanded. Explain that these two pages will help them learn more about how the Church fulfilled this mission.

**DISCOVER**

- Read aloud the first paragraph on page 60.
- Have volunteers describe in their own words why the Church has a guarantee of development. The Holy Spirit is the Church's divine guide and teacher.
- Inform the class that they will teach each other the content on the next two pages.
- Divide the class into six groups. Assign each group one of the headings: "Dark Ages," "Charlemagne," "East-West Schism," "The Lamp of Learning," "Saint Columba," and "Saint Hildegard of Bingen."
- Have each group read the section assigned to it and decide on a way to teach the rest of the class about it.
- Invite the groups to make their presentations. Clarify as necessary.
- Summarize by using the images on pages 60 and 61.

## Decline and Development

*Coronation of Charlemagne by Pope Leo III*, miniature from *History of the Emperors*, artist unknown.

The Church has the guarantee of development and renewal because she has a divine guide, the Holy Spirit. The Holy Spirit is always at work in the Church, leading her to a renewed and deeper faith and vision. The Holy Spirit, in each age of the history of the Church, calls heroes of faith to show the Church the way to announce the Gospel to all nations, teaching them to observe all that Jesus commanded (see Matthew 28:20) until Christ comes again in glory at the end of time.

*The Monk Copyist.* Edward Laning (1906–1981), American painter.

### Dark Ages

The Church continued to grow and develop even as the Roman Empire in the West began to decline. In 476 the Vandals, who had aligned themselves with the emperor in the East, deposed the last Roman emperor in the West. This event marked a decline in the West for many centuries to come.

The resulting period, the early Middle Ages (476 to about 1100), has also been called the **Dark Ages** of Europe. In part, this period of history was a time of violence and of the decline of many institutions of culture and learning. Nonetheless the truth is that many lights were burning during this same period, leading both the Church and society in general toward many positive developments.

#### Charlemagne

Out of the ruins and the chaos of the old Roman Empire, Charlemagne (742–814) emerged. Charlemagne, whose name means "Charles the Great," was the most influential ruler in the West during the early Middle Ages. On Christmas night in the year 800, Pope Leo III (750–816) crowned him as the Holy Roman Emperor. This symbolized the dawn and development of a new era in the relationship of the Church with the world. Pope Leo III and Emperor Charlemagne became partners. Together they forged an alliance that reestablished stability and unity throughout the lands ruled by Charlemagne.

#### East–West Schism

As the papacy in the West became more closely linked to the Holy Roman Empire, the gap between the Churches of the West and East widened. In 1054 this temporal alliance, as well as controversies over Church doctrine, eventually resulted in the **East-West Schism,** or division. This division between the Churches under the leadership of the patriarch of Constantinople and the Churches under the leadership of the bishop of Rome, the Pope, still exists today.

60

FAITH WORDS

### Faith Vocabulary

**Dark Ages.** The term *Dark Ages* is attributed to Petrarch (1304–1374), the father of Italian Renaissance humanism in the 1330s. Christian writers had long used the metaphors of light and darkness to describe good versus evil. Petrarch applied the metaphor to the secular culture, suggesting that the period from A.D. 476 to 1000 lacked the cultural achievements of classical antiquity. Most contemporary historians refer to this time period as the Early Middle Ages and dismiss the notion that the period was "dark." They point out that the idea was based on ignorance and stereotypes about that era of history.

# Day 1

## Apply

**REINFORCE**

- Invite responses to the concluding question by asking the students what kept the lamp of learning burning during this period of the Church's history. Affirm appropriate responses.
- Have the students silently examine the "Timeline" feature for an overview of key events and people of this period.

**INTEGRATE**

- Ask the young people to complete the "Faith Connection" activity independently.
- Invite volunteers to share their responses with the class.

**PRAY**

Invite the students to silently pray the Apostles' Creed, which they can find on page 136 of their books.

Island of Iona, Scotland.

### The Lamp of Learning

The lamp of learning that burned so brightly during the era of the Fathers of the Church continued to burn, if not as brightly, during the Dark Ages. As in the era of the Fathers of the Church, the development and renewal of monasticism kept the lamp of learning aglow in the West during this period of European history.

**Saint Columba**

Saint Columba (521–597) spent fifteen years traveling about Ireland, preaching Christ and establishing monasteries. In 563 he embarked in a wicker boat for the island of Iona, off the west coast of Scotland. Iona soon became the center of Irish missionary activity in Scotland and northern England. During the time of emerging darkness and decline on the European continent, Saint Columba and his monks created a haven of culture and learning that continues to influence us today.

**Saint Hildegard of Bingen**

Saint Hildegard (1098–1174) lived her life according to the *Rule of Saint Benedict*. She was a woman of remarkable intelligence and dazzling spiritual gifts. The first of many renowned German **mystics,** Saint Hildegard was also a poet, physician, and composer. A mystic is one who experiences a close union or communication with God. Many people today continue to seek out her writings to enrich their lives with her spiritual wisdom.

***How are the Dark Ages a time of development and growth for the Church?***

**Time LINE**

- 597 †Saint Columba
- 800 Charlemagne crowned Holy Roman Emperor by Pope Leo III
- 814 †Charlemagne
- 816 Pope Leo III
- 1054 East-West Schism; †Anselm of Canterbury; †Pope Saint Leo IX
- 1085 †Pope Saint Gregory VII
- 1095 First Crusade
- 1099 Crusaders take Jerusalem
- 1153 †Saint Bernard of Clairvaux
- 1174 †Saint Hildegard of Bingen
- 1215 Fourth Lateran Council
- 1216 †Pope Innocent III
- 1221 †Saint Dominic
- 1226 †Saint Francis of Assisi; †Saint Clare of Assisi
- 1274 †Saint Thomas Aquinas; †Saint Bonaventure
- 1272 Last Crusade ends

**FAITH CONNECTION**

*Describe ways you can grow in your understanding of the faith of the Church.*

Responses will vary.

Affirm appropriate responses.

61

## Catholic Social Teaching

**Rights and Responsibilities of the Human Person.** Every human has fundamental human rights—a right to life, to the necessities required to live a decent and healthy life, to meaningful work, and to freedom. Corresponding to these rights, of course, are responsibilities to one another, to our families, and to our community.

**Tip:** Have the class create a list and retell stories of faith-filled people who lived Christian lives of responsibility by dedicating their lives to the education of people.

### Enriching the Lesson

The "Creating Quizzes" activity on page 139 is related to today's content. You may wish to include it in today's lesson.

# Day 2

## Teach

### PRAY

Invite the young people to quiet themselves for prayer. Have a volunteer proclaim John 14:25–26 from the class Bible.

### FOCUS

Remind the class that the Holy Spirit is always with the Church. Tell them that the next two pages will help them come to know four people whom the Holy Spirit called to renew the Church in the thirteenth century.

### DISCOVER

- Present the opening paragraph on page 62. Then have the students silently read the first paragraph of "Spiritual Development: The Mendicants."
- Next, divide the class into four groups. Assign two groups "Saint Francis of Assisi" and two groups "Saint Dominic."
- Have one of the groups for each saint play the role of team reporters and develop a list of questions to ask the other group. Have the other group play the role of press agents for their saint and respond to the questions.
- Hold a news conference about Saint Francis of Assisi and Saint Dominic.
- After the news conference, have the young people silently read page 63 and highlight key words and ideas about Saint Thomas Aquinas and Saint Bonaventure. Ask volunteers to share what they learned.

*Saint Francis Praying in San Damiano,* Giotto di Bondone.

**Saint Francis of Assisi**

Saint Francis of Assisi (ca. 1181–1226) was the son of a wealthy cloth merchant. While at prayer in the Church of San Damiano, which was near the city of Assisi, Francis received the call to "rebuild my Church." Responding to that call, Francis traveled to Rome and returned to Assisi with permission to undertake that work. The followers of Saint Francis became known as the Order of Friars Minor, or Lesser Brothers. Today they are called Franciscans.

**Saint Dominic de Guzman**

While visiting Rome with his bishop in 1203 and 1205, Saint Dominic (ca. 1170–1221) was inspired to become a mendicant preacher. In 1216 he founded the Order of Preachers

Beginning with Pope Saint Leo IX (1002–1054) and Pope Saint Gregory VII (ca. 1020–1085), the next several centuries were filled with events and people calling the Church to renewal. Among the most famous of the reformers of the thirteenth century were Saint Francis of Assisi and Saint Dominic.

### Spiritual Development: The Mendicants

The followers of Saint Francis and Saint Dominic became known as **Mendicants.** The word *mendicant* comes from a Latin word meaning "to beg." The followers of Saint Francis and Saint Dominic traveled about preaching the Gospel. As they traveled they begged for food and lodging.

Saint Dominic, bronze sculpture. Artist unknown.

62

## Background: Catholic Tradition

**The Franciscans.** The followers of Saint Francis of Assisi identify themselves by writing the initials OFM after their name. Explain that OFM stands for "Order of Friars Minor." The title "Friar" comes from the Latin word *frater,* which means "brother." When Francis lived in Assisi, there was a class distinction in society. The nobles were the "majores" and the merchants were the "minores." Francis's father was a wealthy cloth merchant. Born into the "minores," Francis came to understand that the real "minores" were not the merchants but the outcasts of society. He called his "brothers," or "friars," the Order of Friars Minor. They were to live as true "minores," as Christ did.

*Welcoming St. Bonaventure into the Franciscan Order*, oil on canvas. Francisco Herrera the Elder (1576–1656), Spanish painter, founder of Seville school.

whose mission was to preach the Gospel and teach the Catholic faith. Today the followers of Saint Dominic are known as Dominicans.

### Intellectual Development: The Scholastics

In the twelfth and thirteenth centuries, social stability was returning to Europe, commerce and urban centers were reviving, and learning was once again possible outside the monasteries. Schools grew up where theologians, called schoolmen, or **Scholastics**, used human reason to explain the teachings of the Church. Among the most famous of the Scholastics was Thomas Aquinas (ca. 1225–1274), a Dominican, and Saint Bonaventure (1221–1274), a Franciscan.

#### Saint Thomas Aquinas

Thomas was educated at the Benedictine monastery at Monte Cassino in Italy, where he studied the writings of the Greek philosopher Aristotle. In 1244 he became a member of the Order of Preachers and studied in Paris and Cologne until 1252 when he was ordained a priest.

Thomas returned to Paris where he became a master teacher of theology. He commented on Sacred Scripture, answered questions about the faith, and preached. It was in Paris from 1268 to 1272 that Thomas wrote a major part of his most famous work, *Summa Theologica*. The Summa is a summary, or synthesis, of theology.

#### Saint Bonaventure

Saint Bonaventure was a friend of Saint Thomas Aquinas and the official biographer of Saint Francis of Assisi. Bonaventure briefly taught theology before becoming the minister general, or leader, of the Franciscans. Much of Bonaventure's writing centered on the spirituality of the mendicant way of life, and his *Journal of the Soul into God* is a spiritual classic.

***What was the contribution of the Mendicants and Scholastics to the development of the Church?***

Affirm appropriate responses.

Saint Thomas Aquinas with Aristotle (left) and Plato (right), oil on panel. Benozzo Gozzoli (1420–1497), Italian Early Renaissance painter.

### Did you Know...

The Catholic Church has honored thirty-three saints with the title Doctor of the Church. The Doctors of the Church who lived during this period of the history of the Church are:

- St. Peter Damian (1007–1072)
- St. Anselm (1033–1109)
- St. Bernard of Clairvaux (ca. 1090–1153)
- St. Anthony of Padua (1195–1231)
- St. Albert the Great (1206–1280)
- St. Bonaventure (1221–1274)
- St. Thomas Aquinas (1225–1274)
- St. Catherine of Siena (1347–1380)

63

# Day 2

## Apply

### REINFORCE

- Invite responses to the question on page 63.
- Have the students review the "Did you know" feature on page 63 to discover the names of some of the great teachers, or Doctors, of the Church of the eleventh through fourteenth centuries.

### INTEGRATE

Invite each student to write one question about the teaching of the Catholic Church that they would like to learn more about. Collect the questions and provide answers in future classes.

### PRAY

End the lesson by praying the Glory Prayer together.

## Background: Doctrine

**Parents as Teachers.** Parents have the primary responsibility to educate their children in the faith. This parental responsibility has been affirmed time and time again by the Church. The *General Directory for Catechesis* (*GDC*) teaches:

> Parents receive in the sacrament of Matrimony "the grace and the ministry of the Christian education of their children,"[1] to whom they transmit and bear witness to human and religious values. *GDC* 227

The work of catechists and religion teachers supports parents and families so that they might fulfill this responsibility.

### *Enriching the Lesson*

The "Discovering the Doctors of the Church" activity on page 139 is related to today's content. You may wish to include it in today's lesson.

# Day 3

## Teach

### PRAY

Invite the students to quiet themselves and acknowledge God's presence. Then proclaim Matthew 5:14–16 together.

### FOCUS

Recall with the students the contribution of the Mendicants and Scholastics to the spiritual and intellectual life of the Church in the thirteenth century. Point out that in today's lesson they will learn more about the papacy during this same period of Church history.

### DISCOVER

- Have the students silently read page 64 and underline key points about Pope Innocent III and the Crusades.
- Review the content on the page by discussing the image on page 64 and using this or similar questions, What kind of leadership did Innocent III hold? He was involved in both the spiritual and temporal dimensions of society.

## Apply

### REINFORCE

Discuss as a class the question at the end of the section.

### INTEGRATE

Introduce the "Faith Connection" activity. Have the students read Matthew 5:14–16 from their Bibles and consider how they can use the gifts God has given them to live the Gospel at school.

**Did you Know...**

The shrines in the Holy Land marking the sites of the major events in the life of Christ have been the destination of Christian pilgrimages since the fourth century. In the thirteen century the Pope entrusted the care of the shrines in the Holy Land to the Franciscans. Today this work includes the support of schools and missions as well as care for refugees and other needy people throughout the Holy Land.

During the Middle Ages the papacy continued to play a role in the society. For example, in the papacy of Innocent III, who was Pope from 1198 to 1216, we see how the spiritual and secular dimensions of human life were joined.

Pope Urban II preaching the First Crusade at Council of Clermont in France in 1095, fourteenth-century illuminated manuscript.

#### Pope Innocent III and the Crusades

Innocent III was intensely involved not only in the reform of the Church but also in world affairs. In 1215 he presided over the Fourth Lateran Council and laid the groundwork for the Fifth Crusade (1217–1221).

The era of the **Crusades** (1096–1272) illustrates how the temporal and spiritual leadership of the people merged in the Pope. The aim of the Crusades was to bring Jerusalem and the Holy Land under Christian control and to open them to Christian pilgrims. This quest began under Pope Urban II in 1099 and ended in failure in 1291 as the last of the Crusaders left Jerusalem.

As Vicar of Christ, Innocent III asserted that he had been given the whole world to govern. He claimed the right to intervene in affairs between secular rulers. His time in office marks the climax of the temporal power of the Pope during the medieval period of Western history.

***How did the leadership of the Pope during this period of Church history affect both the decline and the development of the Church?***

**FAITH CONNECTION**

***Read Matthew 5:14–16. How can you be a light in the world? Describe the difference you can make in your school by using your gifts and talents to live the Gospel.*** Responses will vary. Affirm appropriate responses.

| TALENT | DIFFERENCE I CAN MAKE |
| --- | --- |
| | |
| | |
| | |

64

### Background: Catholic Tradition

**The Crusades.** During the eleventh through the thirteenth centuries, beginning in 1096 and ending in 1272, there were eight crusades to the Holy Land. They were the First Crusade (1096–1099), the Second Crusade (1147–1149), the Third Crusade (1188–1192), the Fourth Crusade (1202–1204), the Fifth Crusade (1217–1221), the Sixth Crusade (1228–1229), the Seventh Crusade (1248–1254), and the Eighth Crusade (1270–1272).

# OUR CHURCH MAKES A DIFFERENCE

Down through the ages, the Church has fulfilled her commission of preaching the Gospel and inviting all peoples to become disciples of Jesus Christ. In one way, fulfilling this command is easier today than it was in the past. We live in a time when we can communicate almost instantly with people around the world. Pope John Paul II, on World Communications Day in 1999, challenged us to answer two questions about the media:

- How might the media work with God rather than against him?
- How might the media be a friendly companion to those searching for God's loving presence in their lives?

### Church and Media

Remember that the first book to roll off Gutenberg's printing press was a Bible. Today the Church continues to use technology to spread the message of Jesus.

#### Radio and Television

Weekly radio broadcasts of Mass are heard in almost every city. Many dioceses televise the celebration of Mass for those people who are unable to participate in celebrating the Mass in their parish church.

#### The Web

Cyberspace is filled with the message of Jesus. At any hour of the day or night, one can log on to the Internet and learn about Jesus and his Church. Many parish churches have their own Web site to proclaim the Gospel and to show the ways they serve the People of God. The Web site of the National Conference of Catholic Bishops at www.usccb.org features the work of the bishops of the Church in the United States of America. The Pope also has a Web site. The Vatican homepage at www.vatican.va is a source for all kinds of information about the Catholic Church. More than 1,000 documents of the Catholic Church and the speeches of the Pope are available on this site.

In every place and time the Church has been a light for the world. She has been and is a light both for Christians and for all people as they journey to live in peace and unity with the Holy Trinity and with one another. The media can be a great friend on this journey.

***In what ways does your school and parish use technology to share the faith of the Church with others? How can you use modern technology to both learn about and share the faith of the Church?***

Affirm appropriate responses.

65

## Teaching Tip

**Becoming Familiar with Catholic Newspapers.** If your diocese publishes a newspaper, bring several copies to class. Share the copies with the young people after they complete the activity on this page. Point out the various kinds of articles and features addressed. Then have the young people talk about the different ways people their age can contribute to diocesan newspapers, for example, by writing a letter to the editor.

# Day 3

## Connect

### HIGHLIGHT

Recall with the class that throughout the ages the Church has fulfilled her commission to preach the Gospel and to invite others to become disciples of Jesus Christ. Point out that today the media serves as a powerful tool for spreading the Gospel.

### DISCOVER

- Read or paraphrase the introductory paragraph on page 65. Pose the questions of Pope John Paul II and invite and discuss responses.
- Have the students silently read "Church and Media."

### INTEGRATE

Invite the students to work in small groups to discuss how their school can use technology to share the faith of the Catholic Church with others.

### PRAY

- Invite the students to open their Bibles to Matthew 5:14–16 and to quiet themselves for prayer.
- Have them prayerfully read and reflect on the passage.
- Conclude the meditation by praying the Prayer to the Holy Spirit on page 137 of their text.

### *Enriching the Lesson*

The "Creating a Good News Web Page" activity on page 139 is related to today's content. You may wish to include it in today's lesson.

# Day 4

## Connect

**PRAY**

Invite the students to quiet themselves for prayer. Pray the Sign of the Cross together.

**FOCUS**

Recall the "Faith Focus" question from page 59. Ask volunteers to answer it using what they learned in this chapter. List responses on the board. Point out that on the next two pages they will further explore how they can be heralds and servants as members of the Church today.

**DISCOVER**

- Read aloud the introductory paragraph and ask the young people to name some of the Church's heralds and servants they have learned about.
- Ask a volunteer to read aloud the first paragraph of "Proclaiming the Gospel as Heralds and Servants."
- Have volunteers elaborate on the meaning of *herald* and *servant* in their own words.
- Have the young people work in small groups and list the ways to be a herald of the Gospel, using examples of people whom they know, have read or heard about, or who are described in the text.
- Have the students process the list of ways to be a servant in the same way as they did for heralds above.
- Invite each group to share its lists with the class, naming specific ways they see the people on their lists being heralds or servants.

# WHAT DIFFERENCE

## Does Faith Make in My Life?

Two models we use to describe the Church are those of herald and servant. In this chapter you learned about some of the Catholic Church's key heralds and servants during a time of both decline and development.

### Proclaiming the Gospel as Heralds and Servants

As a member of the Church, you are called to join with all the baptized and be a herald and a servant of the Gospel. What does that mean? A Christian herald proclaims and invites others to accept the good news of God's love revealed in Jesus Christ. A Christian servant serves and helps others as Christ did.

**Herald**

There are many ways that you can fulfill your responsibility to be a herald of the Gospel. Here are a few suggestions.

- Speak kindly to and about others and show by your words and actions that you believe in the message of Jesus.
- Share with others the teachings of the Catholic Church and demonstrate that the Catholic faith makes a difference for you and for others.
- Share your faith with your classmates and help them grow in faith by participating in religion class discussions.
- Support a missionary or a missionary community, such as Maryknoll, by writing letters, collecting money, or giving food and clothing.
- Help a younger person learn about their faith.
- Volunteer to be a reader at Mass.
- If you believe something is wrong or believe that people are being mistreated, do not be afraid to voice your beliefs.

List other ways that you can be a herald of the Gospel.

Responses will vary.

___

___

66

## Background: Catholic Tradition

**Word, Worship, and Service.** Taking part in the mission of the Church includes taking part in the Church's threefold work, or ministry, of word, worship, and service. "Faith is expressed in words and deeds. . . . As the community of believers grows in understanding, its faith is expressed in creeds, dogmas, and moral principles and teachings. . . . What we believe is also expressed in the deeds of the Church community. The 'deeds' in question are worship . . . and acts performed to build up Christ's body through service to the community of faith or voluntary service in the universal mission of the Church" (*Sharing the Light of Faith* 59).

Servant

Here are some ways that you can fulfill your baptismal call to serve the Church and others.

- Volunteer to be part of a school or parish project that reaches out to people in need, for example, people needing food, clothing, or housing.
- Take part in a babysitting group in your parish.
- Help out at home without being asked.
- Tutor or coach younger children.
- Help a classmate who has been sick to catch up with schoolwork.
- Volunteer for chores that no one else wants to do.

List other ways that you can serve the Church and others.

Responses will vary.

## Faith Decision

- Work in a small group to brainstorm a list of ways to be a herald and a servant of the Gospel. Choose one suggestion from each list and decide how your group will work together to put each idea into action.
- Meet as a group after you have put the plan into action and discuss your thoughts and feelings about being a herald and about being a servant. Evaluate the outcome of your project.

In addition to working out the above action plan, this month I will work at being a herald of the Gospel by

Responses will vary.

Affirm appropriate responses.

and a servant of the Church by

Responses will vary.

Affirm appropriate responses.

67

# Day 4

## Apply

**RESPOND**

- Have the students continue working in groups to complete the first two sections of the "Faith Decision" activity.
- Remind the class that in a future session they will evaluate the success of the implementation of the plans.

**CHOOSE**

- Have everyone carefully reflect on their call to be a herald and a servant of the Gospel. Then have them write their faith decision.
- Encourage everyone to put their faith decision into practice.

**PRAY**

Have everyone imagine that they are with Jesus on the mountainside of Galilee. Ask them to close their eyes and listen as you proclaim Matthew 5:13–16.

### Teaching Tip

**Sharing Stories About Heralds and Servants.** There are many people in our Church who take being a herald quite literally by speaking openly about their faith and living in ways that demonstrate they are followers of Christ. This is one way to unite the call to be both a herald and a servant. Talk about such people with your class. Share examples of people in your own parish. Consider that service projects allow young adolescents to be both heralds and servants in a concrete way. Encourage and guide the young people in projects in which they can be both heralds and servants.

# Day 5

## Pray and Review

### FOCUS

Recall with the class that the Holy Spirit always raises up heralds and servants in the Church to proclaim the Gospel to the world. Explain that today's prayer is for heralds and servants of the Gospel in our time.

### PRAY

- Invite volunteers to be the leader and reader.
- Gather the class for prayer. Pray "A Prayer for Today's Heralds and Servants of the Gospel."

### REVIEW

- Have the young people share the meaning of the terms in "Faith Vocabulary" and compare their definitions with those in the glossary.
- Use the "Main Ideas" and "Critical Thinking" sections to clarify any questions the students may have concerning what they have learned in the chapter.
- Remind everyone to share and discuss the "Family Discussion" question with their family.

**Before Moving On . . .**

Reflect on this question before moving on to the next chapter.

*How do I model being a herald and servant of the Gospel to the young people in my class?*

# PRAY and REVIEW

## A Prayer for Today's Heralds and Servants of the Gospel

All: **In the name of the Father, and of the Son, and of the Holy Spirit.**

Leader: Before Jesus, triumphant over death, returned to you, Father, he sent the Apostles—bearers of his love and power—to proclaim the Gospel of life to all peoples

All: **We bless you, O God, and we praise your name.**

Reader: Let us listen to the Risen Jesus who said to the Eleven: *Proclaim Matthew 28:18–20.*

Leader: Silently reflect on how you are living as heralds and servants of the Gospel.

Leader: Let us pray. Father, look kindly on those whom you send forth as heralds of your salvation and peace. / Guide their steps and strengthen them. / Make their words the echo of Christ's voice. / Fill their hearts with your Holy Spirit, so that they may lead many to you. / We ask this through Christ our Lord.

All: **Amen.**

Adapted from the Blessing of Missionaries in the *Book of Blessings*



### FAITH VOCABULARY

Explain the meaning of each of these faith vocabulary terms:

1. Dark Ages
2. East-West Schism
3. mystics
4. Mendicants
5. Scholastics
6. Crusades

### MAIN IDEAS

Choose either (a) or (b) from each set of items. Write a brief paragraph to answer each of your choices.

1. (a) Describe how the rule of Charlemagne and the East-West Schism contributed to the decline and development of the Church. p. 60
   (b) Compare Saint Columba and Saint Hildegard of Bingen as heralds and servants of the Gospel. p. 61
2. (a) Describe how the Mendicants and Scholastics served the Church. pp. 62–63
   (b) Explain why the papacy of Innocent III was the climax of the temporal power of the Pope during the medieval period. p. 64

### CRITICAL THINKING

Using what you have learned in this chapter, briefly explain this statement:

The Church in the early Middle Ages shows that the Church is both human and divine.

### FAMILY DISCUSSION

How can we as a family contribute to the growth of the Church on earth?

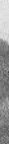

For more ideas on ways your family can live your faith, visit the "Faith First for Families" page at **www.FaithFirst.com**. Also check out "Movie Reviews" on the Teen Center.

## Evaluate

Take a few moments to evaluate this week's lesson.

I feel (circle one) about this week's lesson.

a. very pleased
b. OK
c. disappointed

The activity the students enjoyed most was . . .

The concept that was most difficult to teach was . . .

because . . .

Something I would like to do differently is . . .

# ENRICHING THE LESSON

## Creating Quizzes

**Purpose**

To reinforce the topics of the "Dark Ages" and the "Lamp of Learning" (taught on pages 60 and 61)

**Directions**

- Assign groups one of the main sections on pages 60 and 61.
- Have the groups develop a game, such as a crossword puzzle or a word search, to quiz the class.
- Explain that the quizzes could also be true/false, multiple choice, fill in the blank, matching, and so on.
- Have groups exchange games and take a quiz.

**Materials**

paper, pens or pencils

## Discovering the Doctors of the Church

**Purpose**

To reinforce the concept of a Doctor of the Church (taught on page 63)

**Directions**

- Invite the young people to choose one of the Doctors of the Church from the list on page 63.
- Have them research and write reports on these great saints and teachers.
- Encourage the young people to find the answer to this question and include it in their report: Why is this saint considered a Doctor of the Church?
- Have them report their research to the class.

**Materials**

research materials such as the Internet and the *New Catholic Encyclopedia*
paper, pens or pencils

## Creating a Good News Web Page

**Purpose**

To reinforce the concept that through the media we can share the faith of the Church with others

**Directions**

Young adolescents are technosavvy. In fact, they are members of what some call the "Digital Generation."

- Invite the students to work in small groups to create a class Good News Web page.
- Ask groups to design a page that communicates key ideas about the teaching of the Catholic Church to share with others in their school and parish.
- After they have designed their Web page, review it, and, with appropriate permission, have it posted on the school Web site.

**Materials**

computers
Web page design software

### Music Connection

- "Go Light Your World," C. Rice. *Voices As One* #26.
- "Go Make a Difference," S. Angrisano. *Gather Comprehensive (GC)* #664.
- "The Servant Song," R. Gillard. *GC* #661.
- "Vayan al Mundo/Go Out to the World," J. Cortez. *Flor y Canto* #707.

# Catholic Social Teaching

## The Overnight

The long-awaited weekend finally arrived. Josh had been looking forward to spending some time with the new players he had met on his basketball team down at the recreation center. They were not from his school, and Josh felt good spending time with them. Although he was careful not to show it on the outside, Josh was really glad they had included him in their overnight.

Several hours later, Josh found himself in an uncomfortable situation. The boys were gathered around the TV watching movies. These were not the kind of movies Josh was allowed to watch at his house or with his other friends. In fact, after his initial curiosity, he was not only stunned by the violence, but more so by the way the stars in the film treated the other characters like they were dirt, like worthless objects.

As Josh watched, he was thinking, "There must be a hidden meaning to this." But as time wore on it became clear to him that the movie's only purpose seemed to be to glorify how cool it was to put other people down and to treat people with no respect. What most bothered Josh, though, was the reaction of his new friends to the movie. They were laughing and joking at the very scenes that made Josh squirm. What Josh called the "sinning scenes" seemed to be their favorites. Should he say something? No, he could not do that . . .

"This is not right," Josh thought to himself. "Why do I feel this way? What should I do?"

### Sacredness of Life and the Dignity of the Human Person

Christians treat every person as sacred and worthy of human dignity. The creative action of God is involved in every human life, and all humans have a special relationship with God, the Creator. As Jesus did, we treat each other with respect. We acknowledge everyone to be an image of God.

# Making Connections . . .

Through his experience of watching the movies with his new friends, Josh came face-to-face with a reality: some people do not always treat others with respect. As Christians we have the responsibility to stand up for the sacredness of human life and the dignity of every person.

## WITH MATHEMATICS

Create an inventory of current popular movies. Refer to the United States Conference of Catholic Bishops Web site for news reviews and videos to create a list of movie titles, their general themes, and the values and attitudes portrayed in each. Discuss how the movies you listed portray the sacredness and dignity of human life. Using the "Movie Analysis" handout, display your findings.



## WITH SOCIAL STUDIES

The early Church found itself in a situation similar to Josh's—living in a culture where prevalent beliefs and values were very different from the values of the Gospel. Investigate topics from recent history that have needed people to take a stand for the sacredness of human life and human dignity. Share what you find out with the class.

## WITH LANGUAGE ARTS

Josh felt uncomfortable because he witnessed human life and dignity under attack. Write your own story about an experience you have had where your belief about the sacredness and dignity of people was challenged. Tell about the experience and describe how you felt, along with the reasons why you felt the way you did. What did you do?

### Faith Action

***Decide how you can stand up for the dignity of another person to whom others show disrespect.***

# LESSON PLAN

## Teach

### PRAY

Invite the young people to quiet themselves for prayer and listen and reflect as you proclaim Luke 10:25–28. Ask them to reflect on their efforts to love their neighbors and treat others with dignity and respect.

### FOCUS

Invite a volunteer to read aloud the Catholic Social Teaching principle "Sacredness of Life and the Dignity of the Human Person" on the student handout.

### ENGAGE

Invite the young people to share an experience that they have had that involved respecting the sacredness and dignity of human life. What did they do?

### DISCOVER

- Have volunteers read aloud the story about Josh.
- Find out if the students have ever been in a similar situation. Discuss: If you were Josh, what would you do? Why was he upset? How were his beliefs and values about how we should treat each other different from what they were watching on TV and different from what his friends thought was desirable behavior?

## Apply

### REINFORCE

Remind the students about what they have learned in this unit about the early Church, especially how difficult it was for Christians to live in the Roman society that held such different beliefs and values than their own.

### INTEGRATE

Ask the students to read the activities silently. Then have the young people choose the activity they wish to work on.

- **Mathematics** Distribute the handout "Movie Analysis." Have the students use the handout to research reviews and prepare a visual analysis of movies. Let them work cooperatively with partners to decide how they want to present the data.
- **Social Studies** Suggest that the students research issues or topics, such as human trafficking, slavery, racism, child labor, and anti-Semitism.
- **Language Arts** After those who choose this activity have written their own stories, have them share the stories with the class.

### CHOOSE

Discuss the "Faith Action" on page 141 of this guide. Encourage the students to make an effort to stand up for the dignity and sacredness of human life.

### PRAY

Repeat the opening prayer.

## Catholic Social Teaching

**The Equal Dignity of All People.** Chapter 3 of the *Compendium of the Social Doctrine of the Church (CSDC)* addresses the Church's teaching on the human person. It teaches "*Since something of the glory of God shines on the face of every person, the dignity of every person before God is the basis of the dignity of man before other men* [*Gaudium et Spes* 29]. Moreover, this is the ultimate foundation of the radical equality and brotherhood among all people, regardless of their race, nation, sex, origin, culture, or class" (*CSDC* 144).

# Movie Analysis

Analyze your favorite movies. Use these steps:

1. Log onto **www.usccb.org** and click on "Movies" for a list of current and recently reviewed movies.
2. Create a list of the movies by title on the chart.
3. Write a summary of the theme and the values and attitudes each portrays in the boxes next to each title.
4. Next to the Values box, rate each movie for its positive or negative portrayal of human life. Use the scale +10 for a very positive portrayal and –10 as a very negative portrayal.

| Movie Title | Themes | Values and Attitudes | -10 | -5 | 0 | +5 | +10 |
|---|---|---|---|---|---|---|---|
| | | | ⬭ | ⬭ | ⬭ | ⬭ | ⬭ |
| | | | ⬭ | ⬭ | ⬭ | ⬭ | ⬭ |
| | | | ⬭ | ⬭ | ⬭ | ⬭ | ⬭ |
| | | | ⬭ | ⬭ | ⬭ | ⬭ | ⬭ |
| | | | ⬭ | ⬭ | ⬭ | ⬭ | ⬭ |
| | | | ⬭ | ⬭ | ⬭ | ⬭ | ⬭ |

# Unit 1 Review

The review pages give you the opportunity to assess the students' understanding of the key concepts presented in each unit of the text and to affirm the young people in their growing knowledge and living of their faith in God.

Here are a few general suggestions that will help you integrate the review pages into your time with the young people.

- Stress that the two review pages are an opportunity to stop and assess what they have learned in the unit.
- Provide time for the students to ask questions.
- Be sensitive to the special needs of some learners as you process the review.

**PART A: The Best Response**

This section reviews the main concepts of unit 1. Explain to the students that if they can eliminate the obviously wrong responses, the correct response is more easily recognized. By working together on the first question, you are teaching the class an important strategy for answering this type of question.

**FAMILY CONNECTION**

Encourage the students to share the review pages with their family. This provides an excellent opportunity to involve the families in the faith formation of their children.

## UNIT ONE REVIEW

**A. The Best Response**

Read each statement and circle the best answer.

1. What is the Great Commission?
   - A. another name for the Council of Jerusalem
   - B. the descent of the Holy Spirit at Pentecost
   - (C.) Jesus' command to make disciples of all nations
   - D. God the Father's sending of his Son into the world to inaugurate the Church

2. What major decision did the Apostles make at the Council of Jerusalem?
   - A. They declared that the Holy Spirit was the Third Person of the Holy Trinity.
   - B. They changed the name of Saul to Paul and sent him on a missionary journey.
   - C. They acknowledged that the bishop of Rome was the leader of all other bishops.
   - (D.) They decided to allow Gentile converts into the community of believers in Jesus Christ.

3. Heroic people who give their lives for their faith in Christ are called ________.
   - (A.) martyrs
   - B. apologists
   - C. Mendicants
   - D. heralds

4. He reminded Emperor Theodosius that the emperor was not above the Church but within it.
   - (A.) Saint Ambrose
   - B. Saint Augustine of Hippo
   - C. Pope Saint Sylvester I
   - D. Pope Saint Leo the Great

5. Which abbot was said to carry the twelfth century on his shoulders?
   - A. Saint Columba
   - B. Saint Thomas Aquinas
   - (C.) Saint Bernard of Clairvaux
   - D. Pope Innocent III

## Teaching Tip

**Respect Learning Styles of Students.** The learning styles of students can greatly impact the outcome of an assessment. Students learn and communicate their learning in multiple ways. Some forms of communication, such as writing, come easier for some students than for others. Responding verbally to questions works better for others. Give the students the option of writing or verbally answering all or part of the unit review. The goal in all assessment is to arrive at an honest and truthful assessment of what the students have learned. The manner in which a student is invited to communicate their learning can facilitate or hinder that communication—and the value of an assessment.

# UNIT ONE REVIEW

**B. Matching Words and Phrases**

Match the faith terms in column A with the descriptions in column B.

| Column A | Column B |
|---|---|
| f 1. Gentile | a. the name of the position of leadership of the Pope |
| j 2. Council of Nicaea I | b. the first council of the Church |
| a 3. papacy | c. twelve men chosen by Jesus to accompany him and take part in his mission |
| c 4. Apostles | d. a style of communal living with an emphasis on prayer, fasting, work, and learning |
| e 5. mystic | e. one who experiences a close union or communication with God |
| i 6. apologists | f. often referred to by Scripture as anyone who is not Jewish |
| b 7. Council of Jerusalem | g. a group of individuals whose name is derived from the Latin word meaning "to beg" |
| g 8. Mendicants | h. theologians, called schoolmen, who used reason to explain the teachings of the Church |
| d 9. monasticism | i. Christian writers who wrote about their faith for nonbelievers or defended their faith against accusations |
| h 10. Scholastics | j. a gathering of Church leaders held in 325 that discussed and taught Church doctrine |

**C. What I Have Learned**

Using what you have learned in unit 1, write a reflection about each of the following statements:

1. Faithfully guarding and handing on the Deposit of Faith is one of the most sacred trusts of the Church.

   Affirm appropriate responses.

   See page 22.

2. In the first era of the Church, many believers perceived the greatest threat to the Church to be the culture of paganism that surrounded her.

   Affirm appropriate responses.

   See page 34.

**D. A Scripture Story**

On a separate sheet of paper do the following:

Recall the Gospel story of Jesus commissioning Peter by the Sea of Tiberias. In a group or on your own, put yourself in Peter's place and develop a script telling how Peter responds to Jesus. Affirm appropriate responses.

70

## Teaching Tip

**Assessment of Learners = Assessment of Teachers.** Value these reviews as an opportunity for your own assessment. Sharing the faith of the Catholic Church with the students and facilitating their growth as persons of faith is an important ministry. Listen carefully to the students' responses. Their incorrect responses or their inability to respond can give you insight into ways to improve your presentations and help you realize that the young people's growth in faith is not your work alone—the Holy Spirit is truly the primary catechist during your sessions.

**PART B:**
**Matching Words and Phrases**

This section reinforces the unit vocabulary.

- After the young people have completed the activity, have them compare their responses with the definition of the terms in the glossary.
- Have the group revisit the vocabulary words on page 8 and place a check next to the new faith words they have learned.

**PART C:**
**What I Have Learned**

This section provides the young people with the opportunity to write or talk about what they have learned.

- Have the young people write down a few key phrases for each statement. Then ask volunteers to share their responses with the group.
- Invite the students to turn to page 8 of their text and review the questions they wrote. Help the young people with unanswered questions.

**PART D:**
**From a Scripture Story**

This section is a review of the Gospel story of Jesus commissioning Saint Peter. Have the young people work with a partner to complete the activity.

**PORTFOLIO**

Help the young people select an appropriate activity or project that they completed in this unit to include in their portfolio. (See "Using Portfolios" in the *Activities and Assessment Tools* booklet for more ideas.)

# Unit 2 Opener

The opener pages are designed to assess, through a variety of questioning techniques, the students' prior knowledge and understanding of the key concepts presented in each unit of the student book. Processing these pages should not take more than ten or fifteen minutes.

### USING ILLUSTRATIONS

Pictures help stimulate the religious imagination. The first opener page contains pictures that illustrate some of the important concepts presented in this unit of the text.

- Have the young people look at and think about the three pictures to gain insight into the mysteries of faith that they portray.
- Invite volunteers to describe what each picture says to them about the faith and history of the Catholic Church.
- Ask several volunteers to share a response to the question at the bottom of the page.

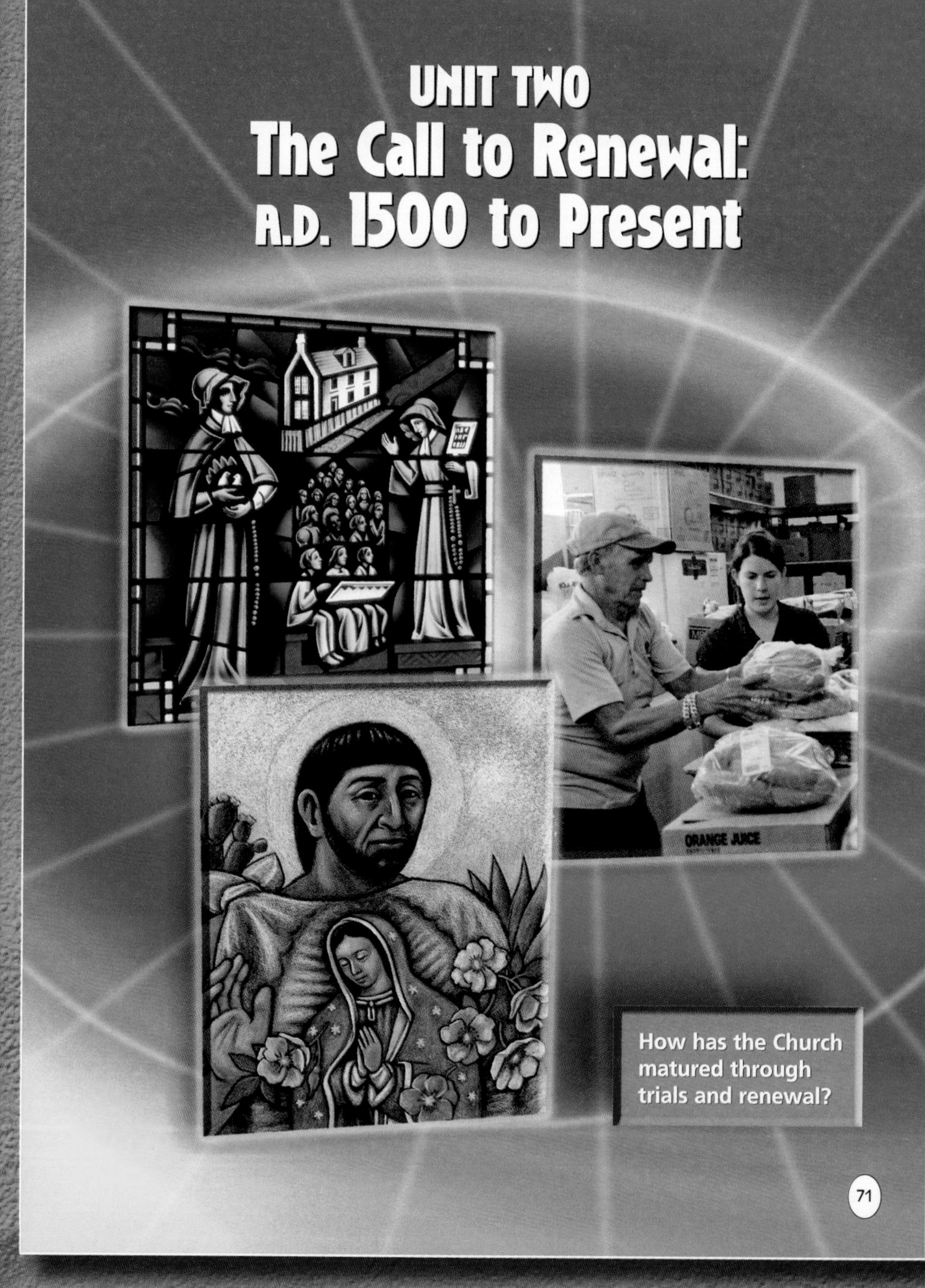


### Teaching Tip

**Begin with Prayerful Reflection.** Spend a few moments in prayerful reflection as you prepare for the teaching of unit 2 of Church History. Recall that at Baptism we receive the gift of the Holy Spirit who guides and helps us live as adopted sons and daughters of God the Father. Ask the Holy Spirit to kindle in your heart a zeal for living the Gospel and to strengthen you with courage and wisdom to witness to the difference that living the Gospel has made in your life—and the difference it will make for the young people in your class.

# Getting Ready

### Reform and Renewal

*What do you already know about the Church in the second millennium of her existence?*

The Protestant Reformation

______________________

______________________

The missionary outreach of the Church

______________________

______________________

The Popes in the twentieth century

______________________

### Faith Vocabulary

*Put an X next to the faith vocabulary terms that you know. Put a ? next to the faith vocabulary terms that you need to know more about.*

____ Protestant Reformation
____ Catholic Counter-Reformation
____ Council of Trent
____ charism
____ canonization
____ divine mission
____ Declaration of Religious Freedom
____ *aggiornamento*
____ Second Vatican Council
____ ecumenism

### Questions I Have

*What questions about the Church today do you hope the Church history chapters will answer?*

______________________

______________________

______________________

______________________

______________________

### A Scripture Story

Pentecost.

*What do you know about the Church and the Holy Spirit?*

72

## Teaching Tip

**Reviewing Catholic Social Principles.** The basic themes of the social teachings of the Catholic Church are summarized on page 143 of the text. Review these principles prior to presenting the second unit of the text. These teachings are pivotal to the development of the Church and will provide concrete statements and ways we are to live the Gospel. *From the Ground Up* (Washington, D.C.: NCEA, 1999) is a good resource for sugges-tions of a variety of ways to implement these principles.

## GETTING READY

The second opener page invites the young people to reflect on key faith concepts presented in this unit of the text and to identify questions they wish to have answered.

### *Reform and Renewal*

Brainstorm brief answers to the question in the box labeled "Reform and Renewal." List the responses on the board.

### *Faith Vocabulary*

This section is a quick assessment of the young people's familiarity with some of the faith terms used in unit 2 of the text. During the review at the end of this unit, the young people will be asked to return to this page and once again share their understanding of the words.

### *Questions I Have*

This section encourages the young people to reflect on the questions about the Church that the study of the Church history will answer. Have the young people do the activity privately. Then invite volunteers to write their questions on a chart you have prepared in advance. As you work through the text, always refer back to the chart and integrate the responses to the questions into your lessons.

### *A Scripture Story*

This section encourages the young people to reflect on the meaning of Pentecost for the life of the Church.

Chapter 7

# The Holy Spirit A Scripture Story

## CHAPTER BACKGROUND

### The Soul of the Church

The Church is the Temple of the Holy Spirit. She is "'where the Spirit flourishes'" (CCC 749).[1] The Holy Spirit is so closely linked with the Church that he is the soul of the Body of Christ, which is the Church. The Holy Spirit is inseparable from the Church, acting within her. The early Church Father Saint Irenaeus (ca.140–ca. 202) wrote, "'For where the Church is, there also is God's Spirit; where God's Spirit is, there is the Church and every grace'" (CCC 797).[2]

#### Promise of the Spirit

At the Last Supper Jesus announced the coming of the Holy Spirit. He promised to send his disciples the Advocate who would always be with them. This Advocate would stand by them, teaching them all that Jesus taught them. (See John 14:15–31.)

After Jesus' Resurrection and Ascension to the right hand of his Father, the Holy Spirit came upon the disciples as Jesus promised. Fifty days after Easter, on the feast of Pentecost, the Holy Spirit descended upon the disciples. Saint Peter and the other Apostles left the upper room where they were staying and entered the marketplace. There Saint Peter proclaimed Jesus to the Jewish pilgrims "from every nation under

heaven staying in Jerusalem" (Acts of the Apostles 2:5). From that day forward the followers of Jesus have proclaimed the Gospel to the whole world. The work of the Church had begun.

#### The Holy Spirit in Church History

In many ways Church history recounts how the Holy Spirit makes Christ present in the world through the Church. The Holy Spirit prepares men and women by his grace to go out into the world and preach the Gospel by their words and deeds.

Church history depicts the many ways that the Holy Spirit has been and continues to be integrally involved in the life of the Church. He is the guiding principle of every one of her life-giving and saving actions. He constantly helps her to be his instrument of charity in the world.

The Holy Spirit works through the Sacrament of Baptism that continues to form the Body of Christ. He works through the other sacraments to give healing and grace to the members of the Church. He gives the members of the Church charisms, or graces "which directly or indirectly benefit the Church, ordered as they are to her building up, to the good of men, and to the needs of the world" (*Catechism of the Catholic Church* 799).

The Holy Spirit resides in each member of the Body of Christ. He flows in us like "'[r]ivers of living water'" (John 7:38) as we live our faith in Jesus. He helps us pray and guides us through times of trial and persecution as Jesus, who was about to suffer and die on the cross, promised. (See John 16:1–11.)

## FOR REFLECTION

***What is my relationship with the Holy Spirit?***

***How can I help the young people include praying to the Holy Spirit in their daily lives?***

## First Thoughts

### The Giver of Life

Without the Holy Spirit, we are incapable of sharing in divine life. The Holy Spirit is the giver of life, the source of our communion with the Holy Trinity and with the Body of Christ, the Church. "The Holy Spirit, whom Christ the head pours out on his members, builds, animates, and sanctifies the Church. She is the sacrament of the Holy Trinity's communion with men" (*Catechism of the Catholic Church* 747.)

#### It's that Simple

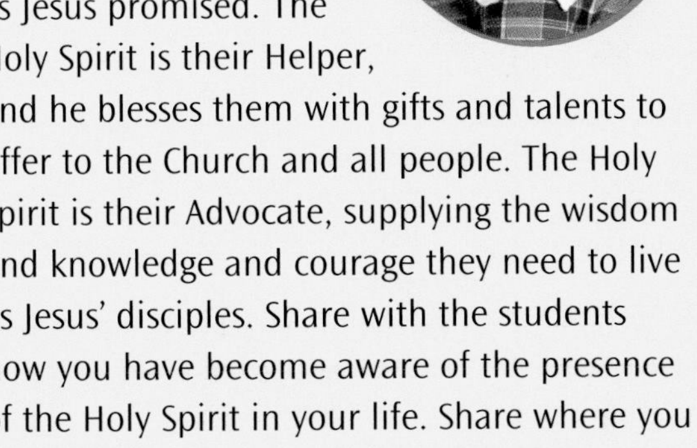

When working with your students and teaching about the Holy Spirit, let them know that the Holy Spirit is always with them just as Jesus promised. The Holy Spirit is their Helper, and he blesses them with gifts and talents to offer to the Church and all people. The Holy Spirit is their Advocate, supplying the wisdom and knowledge and courage they need to live as Jesus' disciples. Share with the students how you have become aware of the presence of the Holy Spirit in your life. Share where you see his grace at work in your life and help the young people recognize the grace of the Holy Spirit at work in their own lives.

### The Church Teaches . . .

The *National Directory for Catechesis* teaches:

> The Holy Spirit unfolds the divine plan of salvation within the Church. With Christ, the Holy Spirit animates the Church and directs her mission. . . . Thus, the Holy Spirit makes new life in Christ possible for the believers.
>
> *NDC* 28 A3, page 93

In this chapter the students will deepen their understanding of how the Holy Spirit enables the Church to continue Christ's work in the world.

#### See the Catechism . . .

For more on the teachings of the Catholic Church on the work of the Holy Spirit in the divine plan of Salvation, see *Catechism of the Catholic Church* 461–463, 659–664, 683–686, 731–732, and 737–741.

*Holy Spirit,*
*ever present, may our hearts*
*be on fire with your love.*
*May we be open to the power*
*and grace you offer us,*
*so that our lives may*
*proclaim your praise.*
*Amen.*

Footnote references may be found on page 256.

# LESSON PLANNER

**Chapter Focus**

**To learn about the work of the Holy Spirit in the history of the Church**

| Focus | Process | Materials and Options |
|---|---|---|
| **DAY 1**<br>**Engage/Teach and Apply**<br>**Pages 73–75**<br>**Focus**<br>To learn about the Holy Spirit's presence in the ministry and mission of Jesus | **Opening Prayer**<br>**Discussion**<br>How the Holy Spirit is the source of the Church's life<br>**Presentation**<br>Read, discuss, and summarize content.<br>**Scripture:** Psalm 104:30; Matthew 10:19–20; Luke 11:13; John 3:5–8, 7:38, 14:15–16, 26<br>**Activity:** List key concepts about Jesus and the Holy Spirit.<br>**Did you know:** Names for the Holy Spirit<br>**Faith Connection:** Put Jesus' words in John 3:5–8 into your own words. | **Materials**<br>pens and pencils<br>**Options**<br>***Called to Prayer and Liturgical Lessons* booklet:** See options for daily and seasonal prayers and liturgical prayers and lessons.<br>**Enriching the Lesson (TG page 161)**<br>Researching Scripture References<br>Designing a Holy Spirit Bulletin Board<br>***Additional Activities and Assessment Tools* booklet**<br>Flames of Fire: The Work of the Holy Spirit, page 19 |
| **DAY 2**<br>**Teach and Apply**<br>**Pages 76–77**<br>**Focus**<br>To explore Jesus' promise to send the Holy Spirit | **Prayer**<br>**Presentation**<br>Read, discuss, and summarize content.<br>**Scripture:** Acts of the Apostles 1:4–5, 8–9, 2:1–8<br>**Activity:** Dramatize the Pentecost event and its meaning. | **Materials**<br>Bibles<br>pens or pencils |
| **DAY 3**<br>**Teach/Apply and Connect**<br>**Pages 78–79**<br>**Focus**<br>To discover the work of the Holy Spirit in the history of the Church | **Prayer**<br>**Presentation**<br>Read, discuss, and summarize content.<br>**Activity:** Discuss why the age of the Church is the age of the Holy Spirit.<br>**Faith Connection:** Describe how the Holy Spirit is helping you fulfill your role in the Church.<br>**Our Church Makes a Difference**<br>Discover how the Holy Spirit was at work in the life of Saint Maximilian Kolbe. | **Materials**<br>pens or pencils<br>**Options**<br>***Additional Activities and Assessment Tools* booklet**<br>Crossword: The Fruits of the Holy Spirit, page 20 |
| **DAY 4**<br>**Connect and Apply**<br>**Pages 80–81**<br>**Focus**<br>To understand more about the Fruits of the Holy Spirit | **Prayer**<br>**What Difference Does Faith Make in My Life?**<br>The Fruits of the Holy Spirit reveal God's presence in your life.<br>**Activity:** Identify people from the history of the Church whose lives give witness to the Fruits of the Holy Spirit.<br>**Faith Decision:** Choose to cooperate with the Holy Spirit this week. | **Materials**<br>paper<br>pens and pencils<br>**Options**<br>**Enriching the Lesson (TG page 161)**<br>Dramatizing the Fruits of the Holy Spirit |
| **DAY 5**<br>**Pray and Review**<br>**Page 82** | **Pray**<br>Pray "Come, Holy Spirit" together.<br>**Review**<br>**Activities:** Complete the review exercises to reinforce the concepts of the chapter.<br>**Family Discussion:** Encourage the students to share and discuss the question with their family this week. | **Materials**<br>paper<br>pens and pencils<br>**Options**<br>***Additional Activities and Assessment Tools* booklet**<br>Administer the chapter 7 test.<br>**Music Connection** (TG page 161) |

**Don't Forget!** You can make lesson planning a breeze—check out the **Online Lesson Planner** at www.FaithFirst.com for additional resources to enhance this chapter.

# The Holy Spirit
## A Scripture Story

7

FAITH FOCUS

What is the work of the Holy Spirit in the history of the Church?

FAITH VOCABULARY

Holy Spirit
Advocate
Incarnation
Ascension

***Name a person from history who has played a vital role but who received little notice.***

History is filled with men and women who took a back seat to more celebrated and visible heroes. However, without their contributions, history may have taken a different course. The work of the Holy Spirit, like the work of these heroes, is also seldom noticed. The work of the Holy Spirit is made visible by the work of the members of the Church. The Holy Spirit is the source of the Church's life, of her unity in diversity, and of the richness of her gifts and charisms.

***When do you acknowledge the presence of the Holy Spirit at work in your life and in the life of the Church?***

Holy Spirit and tongues of fire, stained glass.

*When you send forth your breath, they are created, / and you renew the face of the earth.*
PSALM 104:30

73

## National Directory for Catechesis

**Implementing the *National Directory for Catechesis*: Learning by Heart.** The National Directory emphasizes that learning the principal formulations of the Church's faith by heart can "ensure an accurate exposition of the faith and foster a common language of the faith among all the faithful" (*NDC* 29F, page 102). Encourage the students to memorize the names of the twelve Fruits of the Holy Spirit discussed on pages 80 and 81. Knowing these twelve signs of the Holy Spirit's activity in our lives will help the students to be more mindful of cooperating with his grace in their daily lives.

# Day 1

## Engage

### PRAY

- Gather the class for prayer. Ask the young people to place themselves in God's presence.
- After a moment of prayerful reflection, pray Psalm 104:30 together.

### FAITH FOCUS

Read aloud and invite brief responses to the "Faith Focus" question. Explain that in this chapter the students will explore how the Holy Spirit has been present in the Church, energizing her throughout her history.

### DISCOVER

Assess the young people's prior knowledge and understanding of the role of the Holy Spirit in the Church.

- Write the "Faith Vocabulary" terms on the board. Ask volunteers to share what they already know about the meaning of the terms. Write their responses next to the appropriate terms on the board.
- Call for responses to the opening question. Then have a volunteer read the opening paragraph to the class.
- Reread the last sentence aloud, emphasizing that the Holy Spirit is the source of the Church's life, unity in diversity, and gifts and charism. Call attention to the stained-glass image of the Holy Spirit, which depicts the outpouring of the gifts and graces of the Holy Spirit upon the Church. Invite responses to the question at the end of the page.

# Day 1

## Teach

### FOCUS

Remind the young people that the Holy Spirit is the source of the Church's life, her unity in diversity, and her gifts and charisms. Tell them that today they will learn about the Holy Spirit's presence in the ministry and mission of Jesus.

### DISCOVER

- Read aloud or paraphrase the introductory paragraph, stressing that without the Holy Spirit, the third divine Person of the Holy Trinity, the Church would not exist.
- Invite volunteers to silently read "The Incarnation," "Jesus and the Holy Spirit," and "The Mission of the Holy Spirit."
- Make three columns on the board and label each column with one of the section titles from the text.
- Explore with the students what they have learned from reading the three sections by asking them to identify and name the key concepts presented in each section. List their input in the appropriate columns on the board.

## Bible Background

As you study Church history, your attention naturally becomes focused on important individuals who have played vital roles in the life of the Church. People, such as the Apostles, Popes, martyrs, and saints, quickly come to mind. There is, however, one Person without whom the Church would not exist—God, the **Holy Spirit**, the third Person of the Holy Trinity.

*Madonna and Child*, oil on canvas. Sassoferrato (1609–1685), Italian Baroque Era painter.

### The Incarnation

The work of Salvation is the work of the Holy Trinity—God the Father, God the Son, and God the Holy Spirit. When the Father sent his only Son to become man and inaugurate the Church, he also sent the Holy Spirit. This is clearly seen in the **Incarnation.** The Incarnation is the mystery of the Son of God becoming man without giving up his divinity. It is the mystery of the union of the divine and human natures in the one divine Person of Jesus. Jesus is fully divine and fully human.

It was the Holy Spirit who prepared Mary to become the Mother of God and the Mother of the Church. Through the Holy Spirit, the Blessed Virgin Mary conceived and gave birth to Jesus Christ. The name *Jesus* means "God saves," and the name *Christ* means "Anointed One," or "Messiah." Jesus Christ is the Incarnate Son of God and the long-awaited Messiah and Savior of the world.

### Jesus and the Holy Spirit

Throughout his ministry Jesus gradually revealed the Holy Spirit to his disciples. Here are some of the things that Jesus taught them:

- The Holy Spirit would flow like "rivers of living water" within those who believe in Jesus. (See John 7:38.)
- The Holy Spirit will be given by the Father to those who turn to him in prayer. (See Luke 11:13.)
- The Holy Spirit will advocate for those who are persecuted. They are not to worry about how they are to speak or what they are to say because he will speak through them. (See Matthew 10:19–20.)

74

## Background: Doctrine

**Mary, Mother of God, Full of Grace.** The Gospel proclaims Mary to be full of grace. The angel Gabriel greeted Mary, saying, "Hail, favored one! The Lord is with you" (Luke 1:28). The Church has opened up the meaning of the phrase *favored one* by designating the source of Mary's being favored by God. He has shared his life and love with her in a unique way because of her unique role in the divine plan of Salvation. Mary lives in communion with God in a way no other human person had ever lived or ever will live. Mary was always "full of grace." She was free from sin from the first moment of her conception (Immaculate Conception) and free from any personal sin during her life. (See *Catechism of the Catholic Church* 490–493.)

As the hour of his death approached, Jesus promised that the Holy Spirit would be with his disciples and with the Church. At the Last Supper he told his disciples:

> "If you love me, you will keep my commandments. And I will ask the Father, and he will give you another Advocate to be with you always." JOHN 14:15–16

Jesus was telling his disciples that the Father would send the Holy Spirit to them. Jesus was their first **Advocate**, one who stands beside a person and speaks for them. He would send them "another" Advocate, who would be their teacher and who would remind them of all that Jesus taught them. (See John 14:26.)

### The Mission of the Holy Spirit

Jesus showers the Holy Spirit upon the Church. The mission of Jesus, the Son of God, and the Holy Spirit are the same. "When the Father sends his Word, he always sends his Breath" (*Catechism of the Catholic Church* 689). The Holy Spirit is inseparable from the Father and the Son.

The Holy Spirit is the One who helps believers to believe, who gives them energy to follow Jesus, who heals them when they fail. He is the One who guides the Church to support and comfort the followers of Christ in their mission. The Holy Spirit is "'the principal agent of the whole of the Church's mission'"[1] (*Catechism of the Catholic Church* 852).

***How are the mission of the Holy Spirit and the mission of Jesus Christ the same?***

The Holy Trinity, stained glass.

## Did you Know...

The New Testament gives a variety of names and titles to the Holy Spirit. They are Paraclete, Consoler, Spirit of truth, Spirit of promise, Spirit of adoption, Spirit of Christ, Spirit of the Lord, Spirit of God, and Spirit of glory. (See *Catechism of the Catholic Church* 692 and 693.) Each of these biblical designations helps us understand the Holy Spirit and his work in the Church.

## FAITH CONNECTION

***Read John 3:5–8. Work with a partner to put Jesus' words into your own words. Describe what this passage tells you about the mission of the Holy Spirit in your life and the life of all the baptized.***

Responses will vary

Affirm appropriate responses.

75

# Day 1

## Apply

### REINFORCE

- Write the word *Incarnation* on the board. Ask a student to define the word and describe how the Holy Spirit was involved. Summarize by stating that the Incarnation is the mystery of God the Son becoming man without giving up his divinity. It is the mystery of the union of the divine and human natures in the one divine Person of Jesus. Jesus is fully divine and fully human.
- Pose the questions at the end of the sections on page 75.
- Share "Did you know" and talk about how the names for the Holy Spirit further illustrate his work in the Church.

### INTEGRATE

- Have the young people join with a partner to complete the "Faith Connection" activity.
- Invite volunteers to share their responses with the class.

### PRAY

Ask the young people to quiet themselves for prayer. Lead the class in praying the Divine Praises on page 137 of the student text.

## Background: Doctrine

**The Mission of the Holy Spirit.** The Holy Spirit has always been at work in the world. The work of the Holy Spirit is inseparable from the work of the Father and the Son. "From the beginning until the 'fullness of time' [Galatians 4:4], the joint mission of the Father's Word and the Spirit remains *hidden*, but it is at work. [The Holy] Spirit prepares for the time of the Messiah. . . . So, for this reason, when the Church reads the Old Testament, she searches there for what the Holy Spirit, 'who has spoken through the prophets,' wants to tell us about Christ"[1] (*Catechism of the Catholic Church* 702).

### *Enriching the Lesson*

The "Researching Scripture References" and "Designing a Holy Spirit Bulletin Board" activities on page 161 are related to today's content. You may wish to include them in today's lesson.

# Day 2

## Teach

**PRAY**

Invite the students to quiet themselves for prayer and proclaim Psalm 104:30 together.

**FOCUS**

Read aloud the "Faith Focus" question on page 73 and ask the young people how they would answer it based on what they have learned thus far. Remind them that the Holy Spirit was present at the Incarnation and throughout Jesus' ministry. Tell them that these pages will focus on Jesus' promise of the Holy Spirit and the fulfillment of that promise on Pentecost.

**DISCOVER**

- Have the young people work in four groups and discuss the similarities in the four images on pages 76 and 77.
- Introduce "The Promise of the Holy Spirit" and "Pentecost" and have each group read Acts of the Apostles: 1:4–5, 1:7–9, and 2:1–6.
- Invite each group to come up with a dramatization of Pentecost (Acts of the Apostles 2:1–6).

## Reading the Word of God

*Pentecost*, icon painted on wood. Artist unknown.

### The Promise of the Holy Spirit

After his Resurrection, and before his **Ascension**, Jesus appeared to his Apostles over a period of forty days and spoke to them about the Kingdom of God. The Ascension of the Risen Jesus is his glorious return to heaven from where he will return again in glory at the end of time. Luke recounts for us what happened just prior to the Ascension. He states:

> While meeting with them, he enjoined them not to depart from Jerusalem, but to wait for "the promise of the Father about which you have heard me speak; for John baptized with water, but in a few days you will be baptized with the holy Spirit." ACTS OF THE APOSTLES 1:4–5

The Apostles asked him if he was going to restore the kingdom of Israel. Jesus replied:

> "It is not for you to know the times or seasons that the Father has established by his own authority. But you will receive power when the holy Spirit comes upon you, and you will be my witnesses in Jerusalem, throughout Judea and Samaria, and to the ends of the earth." When he had said this, as they were looking on, he was lifted up, and a cloud took him from their sight.
> ACTS OF THE APOSTLES 1:7–9

Jesus' words made it clear that they would not receive political authority to rebuild the kingdom of Israel. Rather they would receive a "power," or a dynamic force, that would enable them to continue building the Kingdom of God that Jesus began and to be his witnesses to the ends of the earth.

*Pentecost*, oil on wood. Barnaba de Modena (ca. 1330–1386), Italian Byzantine-style painter.

76

### Teaching Tip

**Researching Little-Known Saints.** Help the young people recognize that they do not have to be in the spotlight in order to make a difference for good in the world. The book *We Were There, Too! Young People in U.S. History* (Phillip Hoose, Farrar Straus Giroux, 2001) is filled with stories about young people who quietly played major roles in the making of our nation. Suggest that the history of the Church is also filled with quiet deeds by amazing young people who have responded to the grace of the Holy Spirit. Have the students research those saints whose young lives made a difference.

# Day 2

## Apply

### REINFORCE

- Before the students present their dramatizations, read aloud the text that accompanies the Scripture passages on pages 76 and 77.
- Invite the groups to present their dramatizations of Pentecost.

### INTEGRATE

- Invite the students to answer the first question at the end of page 77. List their responses on the board.
- Facilitate a large group discussion about what these signs might tell us about the work of the Holy Spirit in the Church.

### PRAY

Ask the young people to quiet themselves for prayer. Pray together the Glory Prayer on page 135 of the student text, and praise God for his wonderful work among us.

*The Pentecost.* El Greco (1541–1614), Greek-born Spanish painter.

### Pentecost

After Jesus ascended to the Father, the Apostles waited in Jerusalem and devoted themselves to prayer. There they were joined by Mary, the Mother of Jesus.

> When the time for Pentecost was fulfilled, they were all in one place together. And suddenly there came from the sky a noise like a strong driving wind, and it filled the entire house in which they were. Then there appeared to them tongues as of fire, which parted and came to rest on each one of them. And they were all filled with the holy Spirit and began to speak in different tongues, as the Spirit enabled them to proclaim.
>
> Now there were devout Jews from every nation under heaven staying in Jerusalem. . . . They were astounded, and in amazement they asked, "Are not all these people who are speaking Galileans? Then how does each of us hear them in his own native language?"
>
> Acts of the Apostles 2:1–8

Peter, then, stood with the other eleven Apostles and spoke to the crowd. The power of the Holy Spirit radiated through his speech. Three thousand people accepted his message and were baptized that day.

***What are the signs that accompanied the coming of the Holy Spirit at Pentecost? What do these signs tell you about the Holy Spirit empowering you to make a difference?***

Affirm appropriate responses.

*Pentecost,* stained glass.

77

## Background: Doctrine

**The Church Is One.** In the Nicene Creed we profess faith in the "one holy catholic apostolic Church." "One, holy, catholic, and apostolic" are the four Marks, or essential characteristics, of the Church founded by Jesus Christ. The Holy Spirit is the principle of the Church's unity. "It is the Holy Spirit, dwelling in those who believe and pervading and ruling over the entire Church, who brings about that wonderful communion of the faithful and joins them together so intimately in Christ that he is the principle of the Church's unity" (Vatican II, *Decree on Ecumenism* [Unitatis Redintegratio] 2).

# Day 3

## Teach

### PRAY

Invite the students to pray the Sign of the Cross together and proclaim Psalm 104:30 to open class.

### FOCUS

Invite volunteers to summarize the signs that accompanied the coming of the Holy Spirit on Pentecost. Tell them that today's lesson will explore the work of the Holy Spirit in the Church.

### DISCOVER

- Have the young people silently read the first paragraph of "The Holy Spirit in Church History" on page 78. Point out that the work of Salvation is the work of the Holy Trinity.
- Invite volunteers to read aloud the remaining paragraphs of "The Holy Spirit in Church History."

## Apply

### REINFORCE

- Have the young people close their books, then challenge them to summarize the main points presented on page 78.
- Invite responses to the concluding question.
- Summarize by emphasizing that they first received the Holy Spirit at Baptism and that the Spirit dwells in them and in the Church.

### INTEGRATE

- Have the young people work in groups to discuss how they experience the Holy Spirit at work in their lives.
- Ask them to complete the "Faith Connection" activity.

## Understanding the Word of God

### The Holy Spirit in Church History

We speak of the age of the Church as the age of the Holy Spirit. With Jesus' Ascension to sit at the right hand of the Father in heaven, the divine plan of Salvation entered its final stage of fulfillment. The work of the Church began. "The mission of Christ and the Holy Spirit is brought to completion in the Church" (*Catechism of the Catholic Church* 737).

The Holy Spirit breathes life into the Church. He blesses members of the Church with charisms that enable them to live the Christian life and to build up the Church.

The Holy Spirit guides the Popes and bishops to faithfully fulfill their ministry and to authentically and without error teach the faith handed down from the Apostles.

The Holy Spirit is the source of the Church's holiness and unity. He helps to heal the Church in times of weakness and division.

The Holy Spirit makes Jesus present to all his followers, nourishing the Church with the Eucharist and the Word of God proclaimed in Scripture.

The Holy Spirit dwells in the Church and also in you. By giving you the courage to live as a disciple of Jesus, by acting as your teacher, by helping you to pray, and by enabling you to cooperate with his grace, the Holy Spirit is making you a vital part of the Church's history.

***What does it mean to say that the age of the Church is the age of the Holy Spirit?***

The Spirit of God dwells within you.

### FAITH CONNECTION

***Through what work is the Holy Spirit helping you to participate in the Church? Describe how you are doing that work.***

Responses will vary.

Affirm appropriate responses.

78

### Teaching Tip

**Identifying Witnesses to the Holy Spirit.** Throughout this chapter, the class has been talking about the ways the Holy Spirit works in the Church. Today's lesson emphasizes that the Holy Spirit moves in our lives too. Share an example of someone you know personally or through the media who has the Holy Spirit working in their life. Your sharing may help them identify how the same Holy Spirit is working in their own lives.

# OUR CHURCH MAKES A DIFFERENCE

Maximilian Kolbe, oil on canvas. Artist unknown.

The Holy Spirit is always at work in the Church. That presence is powerfully felt and clearly seen in the lives of those who surrender their lives to death out of love of God and others. Saint Maximilian Kolbe is such a Spirit-filled person.

### Saint Maximilian Kolbe

Maximilian Kolbe was a Franciscan priest who lived during the Nazi invasion of Poland in 1939. He lived in a large monastery that was giving shelter to 3,000 Polish refugees, two-thirds of whom were Jewish.

In May of 1941 the Nazis, intent upon exterminating the Jews and anyone who stood in their way, imprisoned Father Kolbe and many of his Franciscan brothers in Auschwitz. Assigned to a work detail run by especially abusive guards, Father Kolbe's calm and courageous faith was tested as he was given demeaning and exhausting jobs and was often severely beaten. Such abuse could not break Father Kolbe's commitment to forgive "seventy times seven" as Jesus commanded. Father Kolbe gave heroic witness to being a disciple of Jesus as he encouraged other prisoners to forgive their persecutors and to overcome evil with good.

In July 1941, a prison break caused Father Kolbe to make the greatest of all sacrifices, "no greater love does one have than to lay down his life for others" (John 15:13). It was the Nazi rule that ten men be executed for each escaped prisoner. When a married father of young children was condemned to die, Father Kolbe volunteered to take his place. On August 14, after weeks of starvation, Father Kolbe was put to death by lethal carbonic acid injection, and his body was burned in an oven, his ashes scattered.

The power of the Holy Spirit gave Father Kolbe the fortitude to resist evil and the love to give his life for a fellow man. In life and death he continued the work of Christ. On October 10, 1982, Pope John Paul II declared Maximilian Kolbe a saint, calling him a martyr of charity.

***Who do you see giving witness to the presence of the Holy Spirit at work in their life? What are some of the signs of the Holy Spirit's presence in that person's life?*** Responses will vary. Affirm appropriate responses.

Auschwitz, Poland, Nazi concentration camp.

79

# Day 3

## Connect

### HIGHLIGHT

Recall that the mission of Christ and the Holy Spirit is continued in the Church. Point out that all the baptized are empowered by the Holy Spirit to join in the work of Salvation. Saint Maximilian Kolbe is an example of a person filled with the Holy Spirit.

### DISCOVER

- Invite volunteers to read aloud about the life of Saint Maximilian Kolbe.
- Ask volunteers to share other information or stories they have heard about courageous people like Saint Maximilian.

### INTEGRATE

Invite volunteers to respond to the two questions about people giving witness to the presence of the Holy Spirit in their lives.

### PRAY

Ask the young people to quiet themselves. Pray together the Prayer to the Holy Spirit on page 137.

## Teaching Tip

**Writing in Journals.** How do we cooperate with the grace of the Holy Spirit and shape our everyday lives as disciples of Jesus? You can help the students discover the answer to this important question by encouraging them to do an in-depth study and journal reflection on the life and work of one of the heroes of the Church. In their study have them look for characteristics of faith-filled people, such as openness of heart, a vivid awareness of God's presence, a life filled with prayer and service, and an ability to see the big picture during the ups and downs of life.

# Day 4

## Connect

**PRAY**

Invite the young people to quiet themselves for prayer and place themselves in the presence of the Holy Trinity. Pray the Glory Prayer together.

**FOCUS**

Recall the life of Saint Maximilian Kolbe and how his life was filled with the Holy Spirit Tell the young people that these pages will describe the indicators, called Fruits of the Holy Spirit, that demonstrate that the same Holy Spirit is at work in our lives.

**DISCOVER**

- Paraphrase or read aloud the introductory paragraph.
- List the Fruits of the Holy Spirit on the board.
- Emphasize that if a Christian gives witness to these fruits by his or her life, then we know that the person is living as a disciple of Jesus.
- Invite the young people to silently read "Living in Communion with God."

# WHAT DIFFERENCE

## Does Faith Make in My Life?

The Church has named twelve signs of the Holy Spirit at work in the life of a person. They are love, joy, peace, patience, kindness, generosity, faithfulness, gentleness, self-control, goodness, modesty, and chastity. These twelve signs are known as the Fruits of the Holy Spirit.

### Living in Communion with God

The Fruits of the Holy Spirit are indications of God's presence at work in you. They are the result of your living in communion with God and with others. As you grow as a disciple of Christ, these Fruits of the Holy Spirit appear and radiate through you. Take a moment to reflect on how your life reflects and gives witness to these twelve signs of the Holy Spirit at work in your life.

**Charity** is loving God above all else for his own sake and loving your neighbor as yourself for the love of God. Charity helps you respect and value all people as children of God. (*Pause and reflect.*)

**Joy** is the happiness, the blessedness, that comes from your conviction of being loved by God. (*Pause and reflect.*)

**Peace** is the "work of justice and the effect of charity." True peace "cannot be attained on earth without safeguarding the goods of persons, free communication among men, respect for the dignity of persons and peoples, and the assiduous practice of fraternity" (*Catechism of the Catholic Church* 2304). (*Pause and reflect.*)

**Patience** is rooted in hope, in your conviction that all God's promises will come true. It is trusting God in every circumstance of your life, even in time of great adversity. (*Pause and reflect.*)

**Kindness** is a characteristic of mercy. Kindness, like mercy, leaves no room for revenge, hatred, or injustice of any kind. (*Pause and reflect.*)

**Goodness** is your living as a child of God, who is All-Good and the source of all that is good. Goodness brings light to the world—a light that "produces every kind of goodness and righteousness and truth" (Ephesians 5:9). (*Pause and reflect.*)

80

### Liturgy Tip

**Praying to the Holy Spirit.** While the prayer of Christians is primarily addressed to God the Father, we also pray to God the Son and to God the Holy Spirit. Encourage the students to pray to the Holy Spirit. Suggest that they learn by heart the Prayer to the Holy Spirit on page 137 of the student book and pray it daily.

### *Enriching the Lesson*

The "Dramatizing Fruits of the Holy Spirit" activity on page 161 is related to the content on this page. You may wish to include it in today's lesson.

**Generosity** is gratitude in action. It is thankfully sharing your blessings which God so "generously and ungrudgingly" gives to all (James 1:5). (*Pause and reflect.*)

**Gentleness** is connected with living the Beatitude "Blessed are the meek, for they will inherit the land" (Matthew 5:5). It is acting and speaking with reverence for yourself, others, and all creation. Followers of Jesus are to speak "with gentleness and reverence" (1 Peter 3:16) in imitation of Christ. (*Pause and reflect.*)

**Faithfulness** is keeping God first in your life. It means surrendering yourself to God in all things and following his will. (*Pause and reflect.*)

**Modesty** is being moderate in the way you present yourself to others. It is presenting yourself to others in a way that reflects the dignity with which God created you. You preserve an appearance of decency in all that you do and say. (*Pause and reflect.*)

**Self-control** is the balance in our use of created goods. It helps us develop a sense of detachment and live the Beatitude "Blessed are the poor in spirit, for theirs is the kingdom of heaven" (Matthew 5:3). (*Pause and reflect.*)

**Chastity** is the successful and proper integration of sexuality in your life. Your body is a temple of the Holy Spirit. In Baptism you "put on Christ" (Galatians 3:26), the model of chastity for all. (*Pause and reflect.*)

Think about the ways your words and deeds manifest the Fruits of the Holy Spirit. Thank the Holy Spirit for his presence in your life. The best thanks is to cooperate with the Holy Spirit who dwells within you and within the Church.

## Faith Decision

- In a small group, study each of the Fruits of the Holy Spirit. For each Fruit of the Holy Spirit suggest a name of a saint or another person from history whose life gives witness to the Holy Spirit in that way.
- As a class, brainstorm ways to cooperate with the Holy Spirit in your daily life.

This week I will cooperate with the Holy Spirit by

Responses will vary.

Affirm appropriate responses.

______________________________________________.

81

## Catholic Social Teaching

**Solidarity of the Human Family.** The Catholic Church teaches that we are all members of a single human family. This solidarity is true regardless of our national, racial, ethnic, and ideological differences. Solidarity is an awareness of the interdependence that flows from our common dignity as humans and from Jesus' command to love one another as he loves us.

**Tips:** Brainstorm a list of world problems, such as hunger, poverty, and natural disasters. Invite someone involved in the social ministry of the Church to share how they are working to serve people in need.

# Day 4

## Apply

### RESPOND

- Divide the class into small groups.
- Invite each group to study the Fruits of the Holy Spirit and suggest a name of a saint or another person from history whose life gives witness to the Holy Spirit in that way.
- Have the groups share their responses.
- Discuss as a class ways to cooperate with the Holy Spirit in our daily lives.

### CHOOSE

- Invite each young person to make a faith decision and choose a way to cooperate with the Holy Spirit this week.
- Encourage the young people to put their faith decision into practice this week.

### PRAY

Invite the students to end the session with prayer, quietly praying a personal prayer to the Holy Spirit.

# Day 5

## Pray and Review

### FOCUS

Explain that today's prayer includes the invocation to the Holy Spirit, "Come, Holy Spirit."

### PRAY

- Select a leader and a reader for the Scripture passage.
- Divide the class into four groups. Allow the students a few minutes to review their parts in the prayer.
- Gather the class for prayer.
- Pray "Come, Holy Spirit" together.

### REVIEW

- Have the young people share the meaning of the terms in "Faith Vocabulary" and compare their definitions with those in the glossary.
- Use the "Main Ideas" and "Critical Thinking" sections to clarify any questions the students may have concerning what they have learned in the chapter.
- Remind everyone to share and discuss the "Family Discussion" question with their family.

# PRAY and REVIEW

## Come, Holy Spirit

Leader: God our Father, send us the Holy Spirit, our Helper and Advocate, to fill us with light as we listen to your word.

Reader 1: A reading from the First Letter of Paul to the Corinthians. *Proclaim 1 Corinthians 12:12–13.* The word of the Lord.

All: **Thanks be to God.** *Reflect silently on the reading.*

Group 1: May the Holy Spirit help us make good decisions and avoid hurting ourselves and others.

All: **Come, Holy Spirit, fill our hearts.**

Group 2: May the Holy Spirit pray through us even when we do not know what to say.

All: **Come, Holy Spirit, fill our hearts.**

Group 3: May the Holy Spirit help us trust you in times of fear and anxiety.

All: **Come, Holy Spirit, fill our hearts.**

Group 4: May the Holy Spirit guide us throughout our life and may your care keep us safe.

All: **Come, Holy Spirit, fill our hearts.**

Leader: Father, we praise you for sending us the Holy Spirit. We give you thanks through Jesus Christ, our Lord.

All: **Amen.**

82

### FAITH VOCABULARY

Define each of these terms:

1. Holy Spirit
2. Incarnation
3. Advocate
4. Ascension

### MAIN IDEAS

Choose either (a) or (b) from each set of items. Write a brief paragraph to answer each of your choices.

1. (a) Explain the connection between the mission of Jesus and the mission of the Holy Spirit. pp. 74–75
   (b) Describe what Jesus taught his disciples about the Holy Spirit. p. 76
2. (a) Describe the events of Pentecost. p. 77
   (b) Describe ways the Holy Spirit has helped the Church during her history. p. 78

### CRITICAL THINKING

Using what you have learned in this chapter, briefly explain this statement:

The Holy Spirit is the life-force of the Church.

### FAMILY DISCUSSION

How can you and your family make the Holy Spirit central to your daily life?

For more ideas on ways your family can live your faith, visit the "Faith First for Families" page at **www.FaithFirst.com**. Also click on "Game Alley" on the Teen Center.

### Before Moving On . . .

As you finish today's lesson, reflect on the following questions before moving on to the next chapter.

*How do I recognize the Fruits of the Holy Spirit in the lives of my students? How have I affirmed them this week?*

### Evaluate

Take a few moments to evaluate this week's lesson.

I feel (circle one) about this week's lesson.

a. very pleased
b. OK
c. disappointed

The activity the students enjoyed most was . . .

The concept that was most difficult to teach was . . .

because . . .

Something I would like to do differently is . . .

# ENRICHING THE LESSON

## Researching Scripture References

**Purpose**

To reinforce the presence of the Holy Spirit in the ministry and mission of Jesus (taught on pages 74–75)

**Directions**

- Divide the class into six groups.
- Have each group read one of the following Scripture passages:
  —John 14:15–19 ("The Father will send us an Advocate who will teach us everything that Jesus told us.")
  —Acts of the Apostles 2:2–4 (Pentecost.)
  —Acts of the Apostles 2:38 (We will receive the Holy Spirit.)
  —Romans 5:5 (The love of God is poured out through the Holy Spirit.)
  —Romans 8:1–18 (Life in the Spirit.)
  —Galatians 5:16–26 (Live by the Spirit.)
- Ask them to discuss how the passage helps them understand the Holy Spirit's relationship to them.
- Invite the groups to share what they discovered with the class.

**Materials**

Bibles, one for each student

## Designing a Holy Spirit Bulletin Board

**Purpose**

To reinforce the names for the Holy Spirit (taught on page 75)

**Directions**

- Have the young people create a "Holy Spirit Bulletin Board."
- Invite them to use the "Did you know" information about the names for the Holy Spirit on page 75 and include signs, symbols, words (nouns as well as verbs), and colors that express the truths about the Holy Spirit.
- Invite them to decorate the bulletin board with their own colors, symbols, words, and shapes that describe our faith in the Holy Spirit. As you continue through the chapter, the class can add symbols that represent how the Holy Spirit is at work in their own lives.

**Materials**

pens, markers
colored paper, scissors
stapler or tacks

## Dramatizing Fruits of the Holy Spirit

**Purpose**

To reinforce the concept of the Fruits of the Holy Spirit as signs that the Holy Spirit is at work in us (taught on pages 80–81)

**Directions**

- Using twelve 3" x 5" cards, write one Fruit of the Holy Spirit on each card.
- Divide the class into groups of three or four students.
- A group comes forward and takes one card. Without telling the class what is on their card, they pantomime, role-play, or create a charade of young people living out the Fruit of the Holy Spirit that is written on their card.
- The class guesses which Fruit of the Holy Spirit is being portrayed.
- Continue until each of the twelve Fruits of the Holy Spirit have been acted out.

**Materials**

twelve 3" x 5" cards
pens, markers

## Music Connection

- "Send Down the Fire," M. Haugen. *Gather Comprehensive (GC)* #477.
- "Send Us Your Spirit," D. Haas. *GC* #476.
- "Ven, Espíritu Santo," J. Cortez. *Flor y Canto* #428.
- "We Receive Power," J. Marchionda. *Voices As One* #101.

# Chapter 8 Reformation and Renewal

## CHAPTER BACKGROUND

### The Call for Change

The dominating visual symbols in the centuries leading up to the Protestant Reformation were magnificent cathedrals and monastery churches that loomed over the landscapes of city and field. From craftsmanship, sweat, faith, and the desire of many workers to build something beautiful for God, these architectural masterpieces arose and still inspire awe and wonder today.

Now fast-forward to the present. Towering over visual landscapes are immense temples of commerce and trade that cast their shadows over the once-commanding cathedrals of an earlier time. What remarkable movements brought about this visual juxtaposition?

The most decisive event to impact the path of the Church in the second millennium was the Protestant Reformation. There was much need for renewal in the Church during the late Middle Ages. Some leaders in the Church had lived more like secular princes than servants of the Gospel. Catechesis and the training of priests were woefully inadequate. In far too many ways, spiritual decline characterized both clergy and laity alike.

Faced with this situation, many bishops, priests, religious, and laypeople called for reforms to bring the Church more in line with its apostolic origins. In 1517 an Augustinian monk named Martin Luther set in motion a movement for reform that was to effect profound and lasting changes. While his original intent was an internal renewal of the Church, Luther set in motion forces beyond his and anyone else's imagining—forces that led to tragic divisions to the unity of the Church.

### The Council of Trent

In response to these divisions brought about by Luther and other Protestant Reformers, the Catholic Church gathered for the Council of Trent from 1545 to 1563. At this council Catholic doctrine was clarified in response to the Protestant Reformers and the missionary spirit of the Church was revitalized. As a result, developments in the spiritual and devotional life of the Church were precipitated.

### Vatican Council I

By the time of the First Vatican Council (1869–70), the Church's agenda was clearly a spiritual one, attempting to respond to the materialism of society during the Industrial Revolution. In many ways, during the century between the First and Second Vatican Councils, the Church deepened her understanding that she must engage—not withdraw from—the secular world if the Gospel is to make a difference in people's daily lives.

## FOR REFLECTION

***What are some of the signs of the Holy Spirit actively working in the Church today?***

***What are some of the signs of the Holy Spirit working in the lives of the students?***

## First Thoughts

### Renewal

When we embark on a program or process of personal renewal, one of the first steps is to admit our shortcomings. The process of renewal leads us to revitalized ways of relating to ourselves and to others. One of the basic aspects of Church renewal is the ability to admit shortcomings. For that reason, Pope John Paul II apologized for the sins of Christians. During a penance service on March 12, 2000, Pope John Paul II said, "We forgive and we ask forgiveness!" This event continued the Church's ongoing desire and effort to renew herself and her efforts to be the sign and instrument of Salvation in the world.

### Faith Sharing

Consider sharing with your students an appropriate personal story about spiritual renewal. When was there a time in your life when conflict cried out for healing and forgiveness?

Remember, your faith sharing with the young people is an important element of the catechetical process. Faith sharing can help the young people recognize their own need for renewal on their own spiritual journey.

## The Church Teaches . . .

The *National Directory for Catechesis* teaches:

> [Saint] Paul exhorted the Christians at Ephesus "to preserve the unity of the spirit through the bond of peace."[1] Nevertheless there have been serious wounds to the unity of the Church through the centuries. In our age the Church must continue to "pray and work to maintain, reinforce, and perfect the unity that Christ wills for her."[2]
>
> *NDC* 51 A, page 210

In this chapter students will explore how the Church has grown through periods of reform and renewal.

### See the Catechism . . .

For more on the teachings of the Catholic Church on the Magisterium, indulgences, and Church unity, see *Catechism of the Catholic Church* 77, 88, 95, 813–822, 890, 1471–1479, and 2033–2034.

*Jesus, Savior and Redeemer, renew our hearts and minds so that we can travel as faithful pilgrims to eternal happiness. Amen.*

Footnote references may be found on page 256.

Now . . . turn the page and let's get organized!

# LESSON PLANNER

**Chapter Focus**

**To understand how God's pilgrim people have undergone reform and renewal throughout the Church's history**

| Focus | Process | Materials and Options |
|---|---|---|
| **DAY 1**<br>**Engage/Teach and Apply**<br>**Pages 83–85**<br>**Focus**<br>To explore the call for renewal within the Church in the fifteenth and sixteenth centuries | **Opening Prayer**<br>**Discussion**<br>How Saint Paul's feelings and emotions affected his work<br>**Presentation**<br>Read, discuss, and summarize content.<br>**Scripture:** Ruth 1:16, John 17:21<br>**Activity:** Write questions and answers about the Reformation.<br>**Faith Connection:** Consider your Catholic identity. | **Materials**<br>pens or pencils<br>**Options**<br>***Called to Prayer and Liturgical Lessons* booklet:** See options for daily and seasonal prayers and liturgical prayers and lessons.<br>**Enriching the Lesson (TG page 175)**<br>Researching Church Renewal Efforts |
| **DAY 2**<br>**Teach and Apply**<br>**Pages 86–87**<br>**Focus**<br>To discover the causes and effects of the Protestant Reformation and the Catholic Counter-Reformation | **Prayer**<br>**Presentation**<br>Read, discuss, and summarize content.<br>**Activity:** Describing Catholic identity<br>**Did you know:** Several reformers and their followers separated themselves from the Pope and the Catholic Church. | **Materials**<br>Bibles<br>paper<br>pens or pencils<br>**Options**<br>**Enriching the Lesson (TG page 175)**<br>Viewing a Movie<br>***Additional Activities and Assessment Tools* booklet**<br>Cause and Effect: Divisions Within the Church, page 21 |
| **DAY 3**<br>**Teach/Apply and Connect**<br>**Pages 88–89**<br>**Focus**<br>To discuss Vatican Council I and the ongoing renewal of the Church | **Prayer**<br>**Presentation**<br>Read, discuss, and summarize content.<br>**Activity:** Outline the major issues addressed by Vatican I.<br>**Faith Connection:** Reflect on what your number 1 priority for Church renewal would be.<br>**Our Church Makes a Difference**<br>Learn about the Eastern Rite Catholic Churches. | **Materials**<br>pens or pencils<br>**Options**<br>**Enriching the Lesson (TG page 175)**<br>Exploring Unity and Diversity Within the Catholic Church |
| **DAY 4**<br>**Connect and Apply**<br>**Pages 90–91**<br>**Focus**<br>To learn steps for resolving conflict | **Prayer**<br>**What Difference Does Faith Make in My Life?**<br>Learn to deal with conflict in one's life.<br>**Activity:** Practice using conflict resolution skills.<br>**Faith Decision:** Decide how you will use a conflict resolution skill this week. | **Materials**<br>pens or pencils<br>**Options**<br>***Additional Activities and Assessment Tools* booklet**<br>Expressing Faith Through Art, page 22 |
| **DAY 5**<br>**Pray and Review**<br>**Page 92** | **Pray**<br>Pray "Lord, Have Mercy" together.<br>**Review**<br>**Activities:** Complete the review exercises to reinforce the concepts of the chapter.<br>**Family Discussion:** Encourage the students to share and discuss the question with their family this week. | **Materials**<br>paper<br>pens or pencils<br>**Options**<br>***Additional Activities and Assessment Tools* booklet**<br>Administer the chapter 8 test.<br>**Music Connection** (TG page 175) |

**Don't Forget!** You can make lesson planning a breeze—check out the **Online Lesson Planner** at www.FaithFirst.com for additional resources to enhance this chapter.

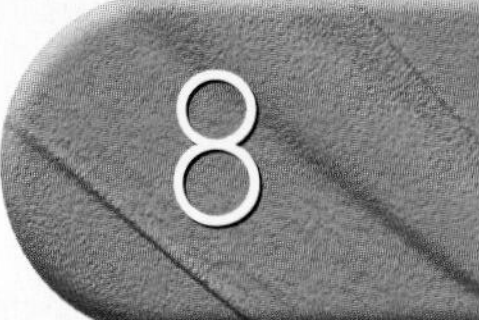

# Engage

**PRAY**

- Invite the young people to quiet themselves for prayer. Pray together the Our Father.
- Proclaim together Ruth 1:16.

**FAITH FOCUS**

Read aloud the "Faith Focus" question. Invite the students to think about how they would answer it. Share with them that in this chapter they will learn about how reform and renewal are an important part of the Church's history.

**DISCOVER**

Assess the young people's prior knowledge and understanding of periods of reform and renewal in the Church.

- Write on the board the "Faith Vocabulary" terms and ask the students to share what they already know about the terms. Write their responses next to the appropriate terms on the board. Briefly describe Zuccaro's fresco when discussing the faith vocabulary term *Council of Trent.*
- Present the opening reflection and invite responses to the two questions. Share about an experience of your own.
- Paraphrase the opening paragraph. Have the students find and underline "pilgrim people" in the text on page 83.
- Invite responses to the questions at the end of the page.

## 8 Reformation and Renewal

**FAITH FOCUS**

What can we learn about God's pilgrim people by studying the Church's history of reform and renewal?

**FAITH VOCABULARY**

| | |
|---|---|
| Protestant Reformation | Catholic Reformation |
| Council of Trent | Vatican Council I |

***Think of a time when you were on a hike or a trip with your family and discovered that you had strayed from the route you were supposed to follow. How did you discover your mistake? How did you correct your course?***

The founders of the United States set up a system of checks and balances among the different branches of government. They did this because they knew from experience how easily we can stray from the right path, and they wanted a built-in way for the nation to keep on course. The Church is sometimes called a pilgrim people. This is a way of saying that the People of God are on a journey and may at times stray from the right path toward the Kingdom of God.

***How is the Church like a pilgrim people? Where is she traveling and what is her destination?***

*Council of Trent,* detail from fresco. Taddeo Zuccaro (1529–1566), Italian painter, especially of decorative frescoes.

*"[W]herever you lodge I will lodge, your people shall be my people, and your God my God."*
RUTH 1:16

## National Directory for Catechesis

**Implementing the *National Directory for Catechesis*: Learning Within the Christian Family.** The National Directory teaches that the "Christian family is ordinarily the first experience of the Christian community and the primary environment for growth in faith" (*NDC* 29D, page 100). Invite the students to share with their families the eight strategies for resolving conflict on page 91 of the student book. Ask them to discuss with their parents and siblings how they can implement these strategies at home on a daily basis so that their family can be a source of cooperation, healing, and forgiveness for all family members.

# Day 1

## Teach

### FOCUS

Suggest that throughout her history, the Church has been challenged to renew herself. Tell the students that today's lesson will explore the challenges of the Great Western Schism and the Reformation.

### DISCOVER

- Examine the images on pages 84 and 85 of the text to prepare for the students' reading of the pages.
- Present the introductory paragraph and invite the students to silently read pages 84 and 85.
- Distribute five 3" x 5" cards to each student. Ask the students to develop one question from each of the sections of the pages. Tell them to write one question on one side of each card, and on the reverse side, write the answer to the question.

## The Pilgrimage of Renewal

Arrest of Pope Boniface VIII by the soldiers of King Philip of France in 1303. Artist unknown.

The Pope, the bishop of Rome, is the successor of Saint Peter the Apostle whom Christ chose and commissioned to be the visible foundation of the Church. He is the pastor of the universal Church to whom the keys of the Church have been entrusted. On the night before he died, Jesus prayed to his Father that his followers would always preserve unity among themselves. (See John 17:21.) "The universal Church is '. . . a people brought into unity from the unity of the Father, the Son, and the Holy Spirit' "[1] (*Catechism of the Catholic Church* 810).

84

### The Great Western Schism

The unity of the Church was challenged during the second millennium. One result of these events was the Great Western Schism. A schism "is the refusal of submission to the Roman Pontiff or of communion with the members of the Church subject to him" (*Code of Canon Law* 751).

In the beginning of the fourteenth century, the relationship between kings and the Pope was changing as kings wanted and were taking more control over their lands and other resources. When King Philip IV of France declared that the churches in his realm were under his control, Pope Boniface VIII issued the papal bull *Unam Sanctam* (One Holy) in 1302. A papal bull is a document issued by the Pope that bears his *bulla*, or official seal.

In *Unam Sanctam* Boniface reasserted the Church's teaching professed in the Nicene Creed that there is one, holy, catholic, apostolic Church. Christ named only one head of the Church, namely, Saint Peter and his successors. When King Philip tried to exert power over the Pope, placing his temporal authority over the Church, Pope Boniface responded by saying that the temporal power of the king was under the spiritual power of the Church.

In 1303 Boniface excommunicated King Philip for rejecting his teaching. What followed was a series of events in which rivals to the bishop of Rome arose, each claiming to be the successor of Saint Peter. This schism in the papacy finally came to an end at the Council of Constance (1414–1418) with the election of Martin V.

### Teaching Tip

**Affirming Positive Behaviors and Attitudes.** There may be some students who are disruptive during class time. Disruptive behavior can be a sign of a student's need for attention and recognition. Think of ways to give these young people the positive attention they need. Some ways to do this are to specifically greet the student, to discuss with them their other interests, or to invite them to help with class preparation and projects.

John Wycliffe translating Bible into English, hand-colored woodcut.

### Call for Reform

Many changes in the religious, political, cultural, and economic conditions of the fourteenth through sixteenth centuries in Western Europe sparked a desire for reform of the Church. Tragically, several of the attempts at sincere reform to help the Church to live the Gospel resulted in the establishment of churches separated from the leadership of the Pope.

#### John Wycliffe

In England John Wycliffe (1330–1384) called for a reform of the lifestyle of the clergy and the spiritual care of the laity. Among the teachings of Wycliffe that lead to his separation from the Pope was his teaching that papal authority had wrongfully usurped the authority of the Bible, and the authority of the Bible must be restored. In keeping with this position, Wycliffe advocated that the Bible should be available to all and must be read by all. He thus translated the full Bible into English. The teachings of Wycliffe that were contrary to the teachings of the Church were condemned at the Council of Constance, and he was excommunicated.

#### Desiderius Erasmus

Desiderius Erasmus (1466–1536) was a Dutch writer who became convinced that the Church needed to use a more contemporary approach to sharing the faith of the Gospel with the people. Influenced by Saint Thomas More and others, Erasmus used his literary and language gifts to translate the Bible and the writings of the early Fathers of the Church to promote the study of the Bible and living a life of virtue.

*What roles did Pope Boniface VIII, Wycliffe, and Erasmus play in calling the Church to renewal?*

Desiderius Erasmus in conversation with Thomas More, John Colet, and Thomas Linacre at Oxford, c. 1500. Seventeenth-century, English color engraving.

**FAITH CONNECTION**

*What do you consider the most important aspects of your Catholic identity?*

Responses will vary.

Affirm appropriate responses.

85

# Day 1

## Apply

### REINFORCE

- Collect the questions that the young people have written.
- Divide the group into teams. Have the teams respond to the questions as you read the questions from the cards. Tell them that they will earn points for each question answered correctly.
- Play the game to reinforce and summarize the text.
- Summarize by presenting a brief response to the question at the end of the text on page 85.

### INTEGRATE

Explain that during this time period, the Church's identity was challenged to clarify her identity. Invite the young people to join with a partner and respond to the "Faith Connection" question.

### PRAY

Invite the young people to quiet themselves for prayer and pray together the Apostles' Creed on page 137.

## Background: Doctrine

**The Church, a Pilgrim People.** The Church is both human and divine, visible and invisible. As an earthly reality that exists here and now, the Church has a past, a present, and a future. She is a pilgrim people and has a history and a story that is still being written. We are a part of that pilgrimage whose destination is the Kingdom of God, which will come about at the end of time. At the end of time all the faithful members of the Church, the Communion of Saints, will live in everlasting peace and happiness with God and with Mary and all the other saints. (See *Catechism of the Catholic Church* 769 and Vatican II *Dogmatic Constitution on the Church* [*Lumen Gentium*] 48–51.)

### *Enriching the Lesson*

The "Researching Church Renewal Efforts" on page 175 relates to the content on this page. You may want to include it in today's lesson.

# Day 2

## Teach

### PRAY

Invite the students to quiet themselves for prayer. Have them silently ask the Holy Spirit to guide them in today's lesson. Pray the Our Father together.

### FOCUS

Ask volunteers to describe to the class how the Church is like a pilgrim. Tell the class that in today's lesson they will explore how the Protestant Reformation and the Counter-Reformation, or Catholic Reformation, were part of the Church's history of renewal.

### DISCOVER

- Ask the young people to share what they already know about Martin Luther and the Catholic Church's response to him. List responses on the board.
- Present a summary of pages 86 and 87, using both the text and the four visuals.
- Have the students silently read the text. Then invite volunteers to add to the list on the board.

*Martin Luther Posting His Ninety-Five Theses.* Gustav Adolph Spangenberg (1828–1891), German painter.

### Martin Luther and the Protestant Reformation

Martin Luther (d. 1546) was a Catholic priest and Augustinian monk who called for a movement for reform within the Church, which is known as the **Protestant Reformation.** Luther began his quest for reform with no thought of leaving or dividing the Catholic Church. His initial calls for reform were directed to the authorities of the Church. Luther challenged the Pope and bishops both to correct what he saw as abuses of their authority and to better respond to the spiritual needs of the faithful. This led to a series of erroneous teachings about Sacred Scripture, grace, the authority of the Pope and ministry of priests, and the sacraments.

Copy of pre-1541 edition of a Luther Bible with margin notes and corrections made by Martin Luther.

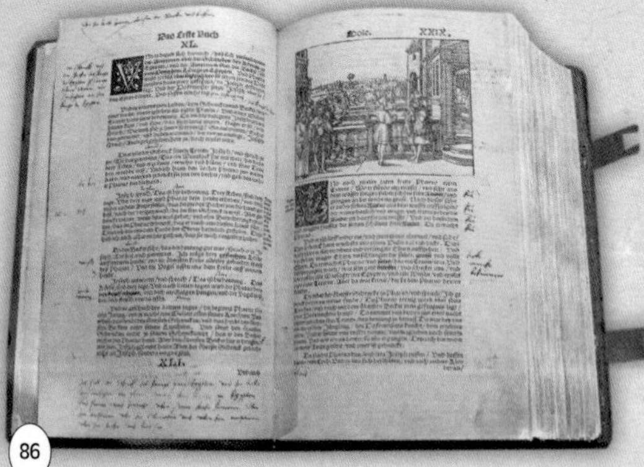

Tragically, Luther's efforts at reform started a cascade of revolts and divisions that splintered the unity of the Church. Kings, princes, and governments, for political and financial reasons, used the reformation movement set in motion by Luther to gain control over their Church lands and the temporal authority of the Church. Luther's efforts and their divisive results have left the unity of the Church splintered to this day.

### Catholic Reformation

The Counter-Reformation, or **Catholic Reformation**, is the Church's response in the sixteenth century to the Protestant Reformation. The **Council of Trent** (1545–1563) was at the center of that response. At Trent the Catholic Church developed various ways and means to renew the spiritual health of the pilgrim Church and to clarify and reassert her doctrinal teachings.

**Sacred Scripture.** In response to the Protestant reformers teaching on the interpretation of the Scriptures by individuals, Trent reasserted that the Magisterium, or living teaching office of the Church, and not individuals, has the authority to interpret authentically the Word of God, whether in its written form (Sacred Scripture) or in the form of Tradition.

**Catechisms.** In order to promote widespread understanding of authentic Catholic faith, the *Roman Catechism* was drawn up after the close of the Council of Trent. This document served as

86

### Teaching Tip

**Student Teachers.** Provide opportunities for the young people to teach part of a lesson in groups or individually. This student-centered learning style will help you learn more about the prior knowledge of your students and the new insights they have gained this year. Always encourage the young people to be creative as they prepare to teach. They can make storyboards, write stories, make up skits, draw posters, pantomime, create silent tableaux, and so on.

*Saint Charles Borromeo.* Carlo Dolci (1616–1686), Italian painter.

the basis for the *Baltimore Catechism,* which was widely used in the United States of America as a primary source for the education of the faithful.

**Formation of Priests.** The Council of Trent also mandated a complete reform of the way priests were to be trained. The seminary system which provides for the spiritual and academic formation of priests today is a direct result of Trent.

In addition to its clarification of Catholic doctrine, the Council of Trent took seriously the need for reform in other areas of the life of the Catholic Church and instituted a whole series of internal measures to reform and renew Catholic life. The Council of Trent was enormously influential in defining and shaping Catholic identity for the next four hundred years.

### Saint Charles Borromeo

In the years immediately following the Council of Trent, Charles Borromeo, (1538–1584), the bishop of Milan, supervised the composition of the *Roman Catechism* and the reform of the Church's liturgical book, implementing many efforts to instruct the people in the faith. He established seminaries for the training of priests and worked to improve the way priests celebrated the sacraments. He used the wealth he inherited from his family for the care of the poor and often personally tended to people who suffered from starvation and diseases. His death at the age of forty-six was caused, in no small measure, by the way he gave of himself in the service of his people.

***How did the Catholic Church respond to Martin Luther and the other Protestant reformers?***

### Did you Know...

By the end of the sixteenth century, the list of reformers who separated their followers from the Church of Rome included John Calvin (1509–1564), Philipp Melanchthon (1497–1560), Ulrich Zwingli (1484–1531), King Henry VIII (1491–1547), and Archbishop Thomas Cranmer (1489–1556).

*The Council of Trent.* seventeenth-century painting by an unknown artist.

87

# Day 2

## Apply

**REINFORCE**

- Draw the young people's attention to the "Did you know" feature that tells about reformers who separated from the Church.
- Invite responses to the question on page 87.

**INTEGRATE**

- Write the phrase *Catholic Identity* on the board and have the class create a word map with you by brainstorming words or phrases that come to mind that define or describe Catholic Identity.
- Have the class turn to page 136 in their books and compare what they wrote with the credal statements in the Apostles' Creed.

**PRAY**

- Ask the young people to quiet themselves. Proclaim John 17:21.
- Conclude by praying the Apostles' Creed together.

## Background: Faith-Filled People

**Saints of the Reformation.** While some people were engaged in bitter battles with the Roman Catholic Church over various issues, other reformers remained faithful to their beliefs and to the Catholic Church. One such faithful follower was author and Lord Chancellor of England, Saint Thomas More. With his refusal to take the oath of allegiance to the king of England by refusing to repudiate the Pope, Saint Thomas More was sent to the Tower of London where by order of King Henry VIII he was beheaded on July 6, 1535.

### *Enriching the Lesson*

The "Viewing a Movie" activity on page 175 is related to the content in this chapter. You may wish to include it as part of this week's experience.

# Day 3

## Teach

**PRAY**

Pray together the Act of Love on page 137.

**FOCUS**

Recall with the students key points of the response of the Catholic Church to the Protestant Reformers. Tell them today's lesson jumps forward to the nineteenth century and explores how the First Vatican Council continued the renewal of the Catholic Church begun by the Council of Trent.

**DISCOVER**

Have the students silently read page 88 and highlight key points.

## Apply

**REINFORCE**

Have the students identify and discuss the key efforts of the Catholic Church to renew herself from the sixteenth through the nineteenth centuries. Growth of religious congregations, promotion of spiritual renewal, Vatican Council I.

**INTEGRATE**

- Have the young people work in pairs to answer the "Faith Connection" question.
- Facilitate a large-group discussion about their ideas for renewal in the Church today.

### Did you Know...

In the centuries after Trent holy men and women formed a number of religious orders. Many, such as Saint Ignatius of Loyola (1491–1556) and Saint Vincent de Paul (ca. 1581–1660), devoted themselves to living the Spiritual and Corporal Works of Mercy. Others, such as Saint Teresa of Avila (1515–1582) dedicated themselves to promoting spiritual renewal and working for the reform of religious orders and congregations.

Pope Pius IX opening the First Vatican Council in 1869, chromolithograph.

The Catholic Counter-Reformation unleashed waves of energy and zeal into the Church. The efforts begun by Saint Charles Borromeo were continued by a litany of others.

### Vatican Council I

As a result of the reforms of the Council of Trent, the Church preserved the treasures of the faith handed down from previous generations. In an effort to continue the renewal of the Church and bring it up to modern times, Pope Pius IX called **Vatican Council I** (1869–70). The Council addressed a number of issues, including:

- how the Church passes on God's revelation,
- the teaching office of the Pope and of the college of bishops who have the charism, or special grace, to authentically teach in matters of faith and morals without error, and
- the relationship between the use of faith and reason in our search to understand the meaning of God's revelation.

As you know from your study of social studies, this was also a period of expansion of trade between Europe and the rest of the world. Missionaries from many religious orders accompanied explorers and brought the Gospel to the New World and other lands. We will look at the these events in chapter 9.

***What are some of the highlights of the Church's renewal of herself during the sixteenth and nineteenth centuries?***

### FAITH CONNECTION

***If you were to work for the renewal of the Church today, what would be your #1 priority?***

Responses will vary.

Affirm appropriate responses.

88

### Background: Doctrine

**Renewal in Daily Life.** The Church offers us a way to measure how we can accomplish renewal, or conversion, in our day-to-day lives. Share these ways with your students: "Conversion is accomplished in daily life by gestures of reconciliation, concern for the poor, the exercise and defense of justice and right,[1] by the admission of faults to one's brethren, fraternal correction, revision of life, examination of conscience, spiritual direction, acceptance of suffering, endurance of persecution for the sake of righteousness. Taking up one's cross each day and following Jesus is the surest way of penance."[2] (*Catechism of the Catholic Church* 1435.)

# OUR CHURCH MAKES A DIFFERENCE

Our Lady of Perpetual Help Byzantine Catholic Church. Altar and icons.

The Catholic Church is "one." The oneness or unity of the Church is expressed in diverse ways, which affirms that the Church founded by Christ is "catholic," or universal. It is the sign and instrument of Salvation for all peoples. The diversity of rites within the Catholic Church expresses both her unity and catholicity.

## The Eastern Rite Catholic Churches

The Catholic Church is the new People of God, united with the Pope both in teaching and proclaiming the faith handed down from the Apostles and in celebrating the sacraments. Although many Christians split off from Rome in the East-West Schism of 1054, a number of Eastern Churches remained in communion with the Pope. Thus, the Catholic Church today is comprised of Churches in the West and Churches in the East. The Churches in the West and in the East are grouped according to the rites they use to celebrate and live the faith they share in common. A rite is the "liturgical, theological, spiritual and disciplinary patrimony, culture and circumstances of history of a distinct people, by which its own manner of living the faith is manifested." [Code of Canons of the Eastern (Catholic) Churches, 1990]

The Eastern rite Catholic Churches are grouped according to five ancient Christian rites. The Byzantine and Alexandrian Churches are two of these Eastern rite Churches.

### The Alexandrian Church

The Alexandrian Churches trace their roots to the desert traditions of Egypt. The Alexandrian Churches include the Coptic and Ethiopian rite Churches. The origins of this community of Churches began after the Council of Chalcedon in 451. While the Alexandrian Churches recognize the bishop of Rome, the Pope, as the leader of the universal Church, they are governed by a patriarch.

### The Byzantine Church

The Churches of the Byzantine rite have their origins in the Middle East. This rite celebrates the common faith of the Catholic Church according to traditions and rites fashioned by the influence of Greek, Byzantine, and Semitic cultures. The Byzantine rite is by far the most widely used Eastern liturgical tradition.

***What are some of the ways your parish celebrates the faith?*** Responses will vary.

89

## Background: Liturgy

**Liturgical Rites of the Catholic Church.** The rites presently in use in the Catholic Church are the Latin (or Roman) rite and the Ambrosian, Byzantine, Alexandrian (or Coptic), Syriac, Armenian, Maronite, and Chaldean rites. Each of these rites is held in equal right and dignity, and the Church "wishes to preserve them in the future and to foster them in every way"[1] (*Catechism of the Catholic Church* 1203).

# Day 3

## Connect

### HIGHLIGHT

Recall with the young people the four essential characteristics, or Marks, of the Church: one, holy, catholic, apostolic. Explain to the class that within the unity of the Church there is Catholic legitimate diversity. Point out that the Church is both "one" and diverse, or "catholic."

### DISCOVER

Have the students silently read about the different rites within the Catholic Church.

### INTEGRATE

- Tell the young people that just as these rites celebrate the faith in different ways, so too do our parishes. Point out that this diversity is sometimes based on the culture and ethnic heritage of the people of the parish.
- As a group, identify some of the ways that your parish celebrates faith.

### PRAY

- Ask the young people to quiet themselves for prayer.
- Lead the class in praying this or a similar prayer: Lord, we are a pilgrim people on our journey to you. / Be with us as our guide, always. / Amen.

### *Enriching the Lesson*

The "Exploring Unity and Diversity Within the Catholic Church" activity on page 175 is related to today's content. You may wish to include it in today's lesson.

# Day 4

## Connect

**PRAY**

Invite students to gather for prayer. Have them recall Jesus' promise that he is always present with those who gather in his name. Proclaim John 17:11, 17–21, and then pray the Our Father together.

**FOCUS**

Remind the young people that during the period of history they are now studying, the Church, with the guidance of the Holy Spirit, faced many challenges in her efforts to be faithful to Jesus. Point out that these two pages will help them develop skills to face the challenges they will encounter in living the Gospel.

**DISCOVER**

- Present the introductory paragraph and have the young people read the first four paragraphs of "Dealing with Conflict" and complete the check list.
- Compare responses as a class.
- Have volunteers read aloud "What Is Conflict?" and "How Can You Resolve Conflict?"
- As a group, outline on the board the seven steps for resolving conflict.

# WHAT DIFFERENCE

## Does Faith Make in My Life?

During this period of Church history there was internal conflict and disagreement. There was a strong movement to reform the pilgrim Church and to resolve these differences so renewal could take place. The members of the Church during these centuries certainly knew what conflict was all about.

### Dealing with Conflict

Think about how you would deal with the following conflict.

Your family has one computer. You have to finish your history report. Your sister seems to be e-mailing all her friends. You ask her if you could please use the computer.

She says, "No way!" Check what you would do:

____ Get really mad.

____ Beg her, plead with her, promise her stuff, make a deal.

____ Tell your mother or father.

____ Scream at her to get off the computer, call her awful names.

____ Ask her to please let you use it and she can e-mail her friends later.

____ Try to physically move her away from the computer.

____ Walk away visibly very angry and upset.

____ Negotiate a compromise where you both will win.

____ Other

Dealing with conflict is a normal and natural part of life. Most people do not like conflict and they try to avoid it at any cost. The truth is that conflict cannot be avoided.

### What Is Conflict?

Conflicts occur when people have different opinions or opposing points of view or different needs.

It can also occur when people are being selfish and disregard the needs of others. For example, if I want what I want when I want it, and I do not care about your wants, there is a conflict. Most conflicts can be resolved peacefully if those involved are willing to work at it.

90

## Teaching Tip

**Affirming the Difference Faith Makes.** The themes that arise from the Church's history are also in many ways our own personal themes on our pilgrimages of faith. For example, this chapter's focus on reform and renewal is a very human theme, experienced by each of us. The young people can learn from the way the Church chooses to respond to internal conflict and disagreement: by addressing it, resolving it, and growing from it. The young people too can work to resolve the disagreements and conflict that arises in their own lives. They can be proud that our Church works hard to resolve conflict and to keep the Gospel alive in the world. Yes, faith *does* make a difference.

## How Can You Resolve Conflict?

Here are some suggestions to help you resolve conflicts peacefully.

1. Ask the Holy Spirit for guidance.
2. Share your opinion, state your need, make "I" statements. For example: "I need to use the computer for about an hour to finish my report. Could you please e-mail your friends later?"
3. Avoid being judgmental, sarcastic, or offensive. Statements, such as "You are so stupid. No one in their right mind would spend hours e-mailing everyone in the universe," invite conflict.
4. Focus on the specific problem or disagreement. Do not bring up stuff from the past, such as "Six months ago I let you play my video games all night."
5. Listen to the other person's point of view. Hear what they are saying. Keep your mind open and be flexible.
6. Focus on the facts. Focus on the needs that are expressed, not just your wants.
7. Be respectful. Use good manners and common courtesy. Name-calling, being stubborn, and being offensive only increase conflict.
8. Try to avoid win/lose situations. Find the best possible solution to the problem. Bring it to a win/win situation so that both your needs can be met.

### Faith Decision

- In a small group discuss how you could resolve this computer-sharing dilemma.
- How can you make it a win/win situation?

This week I will practice one of the above skills to resolve a conflict by

Responses will vary.

Affirm appropriate responses.

91

## Apply

### RESPOND

- Divide the class into small groups to work on the first two parts of the "Faith Decision" activity.
- Have each group use the steps for resolving conflict to decide how they would resolve the computer dilemma.
- Ask the groups to share how they will make resolving the conflict a win-win situation.

### CHOOSE

- Have each student choose one of the conflict resolution skills to use this week in resolving a conflict. Then have everyone make and write their faith decision.
- Encourage the young people to put their decision into practice this week.

### PRAY

Ask the young people to quiet themselves for prayer. Pray together the Act of Love on page 137 in the student text.

### Teaching Tip

**Role-Playing Conflict Resolution Skills.** Young adolescents are often challenged by conflict—be it in their families, with friends, at school, or in the neighborhood. Brainstorm with the class some common situations where they experience conflict. Then have groups role-play these situations, using the conflict resolution steps outlined on page 91.

# Day 5

## Pray and Review

**FOCUS**

Remind the class that throughout her history the Church has worked to reform and renew herself to live the Gospel of Jesus Christ. Today's prayer asks the Lord to be merciful on us, pilgrims who sometimes lose our way.

**PRAY**

- Gather the young people for prayer.
- Lead the class in praying "Lord, Have Mercy."

**REVIEW**

- Have the young people share the meaning of the terms in "Faith Vocabulary" and compare their definitions with those in the glossary.
- Use the "Main Ideas" and "Critical Thinking" sections to clarify any questions the students may have concerning what they have learned in the chapter.
- Remind everyone to share and discuss the "Family Discussion" question with their family.

# PRAY and REVIEW

## Lord, Have Mercy

**Leader:** The Church is the new People of God, a holy people journeying toward the Kingdom of God. As members of the Church, we sometimes sin. We turn away from God's love and lose sight of the end of our journey. When we do, the Holy Spirit calls us to repent, to turn toward God's love and return to the Lord's way in solidarity with our brothers and sisters everywhere. For the times we have sinned, let us pray together for God's forgiveness and mercy.

I confess to almighty God, and to you, my brothers and sisters, that I have sinned through my own fault

**All:** **Lord, have mercy.**

**Leader::** in my thoughts and in my words, in what I have done and in what I have failed to do;

**All:** **Lord, have mercy.**

**Leader:** and I ask blessed Mary, ever virgin, all the angels and saints,

**All:** **Lord, have mercy.**

**Leader:** and you, my brothers and sisters, to pray for me to the Lord our God.

**All:** **Lord, have mercy.**

92

**FAITH VOCABULARY**

Define each of these faith vocabulary terms:

1. Protestant Reformation
2. Catholic Reformation
3. Council of Trent
4. Vatican Council I

**MAIN IDEAS**

Choose either (a) or (b) from each set of items. Write a brief paragraph to answer each of your choices.

1. (a) Describe the Catholic Church prior to the Protestant Reformation. pp. 84–85
   (b) Explain what Martin Luther and the other Protestant reformers were attempting to do. p. 86
2. (a) Discuss how the Catholic Church responded to the Protestant Reformation. pp. 86–87
   (b) Describe Saint Charles Borromeo's contributions to the Church's work of renewal and reform. p. 88

**CRITICAL THINKING**

Using what you have learned in this chapter, briefly explain this statement:

> "By the power of the risen Lord [the Church] is given strength to overcome, in patience and in love, her sorrows and her difficulties, both those that are from within and those that are from without."
>
> VATICAN II, *Dogmatic Constitution on the Church* [LUMEN GENTIUM] 8

**FAMILY DISCUSSION**

Explain how your family lives out this statement: The Church is the pilgrim people of God.

For more ideas on ways your family can live your faith, visit the "Faith First for Families" page at **www.FaithFirst.com**. Also check out "Saints" on the Teen Center.

*Before Moving On . . .*

As you finish today's lesson, reflect on the following questions before moving on to the next chapter.

*How well do I resolve the conflicts in my own life? How do I help the young people experience reformation and renewal in our classroom?*

## Evaluate

Take a few moments to evaluate this week's lesson.

I feel (circle one) about this week's lesson.

a. very pleased
b. OK
c. disappointed

The activity the students enjoyed most was . . .

The concept that was most difficult to teach was . . .

because . . .

Something I would like to do differently is . . .

# ENRICHING THE LESSON

## Researching Church Renewal Efforts

**Purpose**

To further explore the reformers of the sixteenth century (taught on page 87)

**Directions**

- Using the list in the "Did you know" on page 87, invite volunteers to research one of the reformers who separated from the Catholic Church during the sixteenth century.
- Have the students present their reports to the class.

**Materials**

research materials such as the Internet and *New Catholic Encyclopedia*
paper, pens or pencils

## Viewing a Movie

**Purpose**

To reinforce the concepts of this period of renewal and reform in the Church

**Directions**

- View and discuss the movie *A Man for All Seasons,* which is about Saint Thomas More, with your class.
- Talk about the ways his life exemplifies fidelity to the Gospel and to the Church.
- Identify and name qualities of Saint Thomas More and how these same qualities can help us today live as faithful members of the Body of Christ.

**Materials**

television
VCR or DVD player
*A Man for All Seasons*

## Exploring Unity and Diversity Within the Catholic Church

**Purpose**

To reinforce the concept of oneness, or unity, of the Church and its relationship to the diversity within the Catholic Church (taught on page 89)

**Directions**

- Invite a special guest from one of the Eastern Rites of the Catholic Church to share information with your class.
- In particular, have the person share about the liturgical and prayer tradition of their Church.
- Have the class discuss the similarities and differences with the Roman rite.

**Materials**

special guest

## Music Connection

- "Abre Mis Ojos/Open My Eyes," J. Manibusan. *Flor y Canto* #499.
- "Journey for Home," E. Bolduc. *Voices As One* #50.
- "Pan de Vida," B. Hurd and P. Moriarty. *Gather Comprehensive (GC)* #811.
- "We Are Many Parts," M. Haugen. *GC* #727.

# Exploration and Evangelization

## CHAPTER BACKGROUND

### Resurgence of Faith

One of the most noteworthy aspects of the life of the Church in the period known as the Catholic Counter-Reformation was the resurgence of faith and evangelization. In the face of the Protestant Reformation and the subsequent divisions within the Church throughout much of Western Europe, the Catholic Church set out on a path of reform and emerged as an even stronger and more disciplined entity than it had been for centuries.

Challenged by legitimate demands for reform, leaders of the Church convened at the Council of Trent from 1545 to 1563 in the northern Italian city of Trent and implemented a vision of reform and renewal that was to set the tone of Church life right up to the time of the Second Vatican Council (1962–1965). Inspired by the Council's call for reform, courageous and saintly individuals abolished abuses and guided the People of God more resolutely on their earthly pilgrimage to God.

### New Era of Evangelization

During the late fifteenth century and throughout the sixteenth century, the Church began a new era of evangelization. With discoveries by such explorers as Christopher Columbus and Vasco da Gama, the vast expanse of the world came into clearer view. Saintly missionaries, such as Francis Xavier, traveled to India and Japan. Others preached the Gospel to the people in North America, Central America, and South America. In the nineteenth century, colonial expansion into Africa was similarly accompanied by missionaries who sought to preach Jesus Christ to the peoples of that vast continent.

Religious communities, such as the Franciscans, Dominicans, and Jesuits, sent missionaries to people across the globe. Other religious orders were founded, often with the sole purpose of being missionaries of the Gospel.

This was an era when the missionary Church traveled into unknown lands and established a worldwide presence. The Church was no longer a European body. Instead, people of different cultures, languages, and races from as far away as Asia and Oceania were incorporated into the Body of Christ.

### The Universal Church

The effect of this response to Jesus' command to "make disciples of all nations" (Matthew 28:19) is significant. The Church has truly

become more visibly catholic, meaning "universal."

In our own time, documents of the Second Vatican Council and subsequent papal teachings have helped to underline the Church as a people on mission to the world. Our recent Popes have focused our attention on the Church's "deepest identity" as a missionary people by calling for a renewed commitment to evangelization.

## FOR REFLECTION

***How am I living my baptismal call to proclaim the Gospel?***

***How can I encourage the young people to fulfill their call to evangelize others?***

## First Thoughts

### To the Ends of the Earth!

Jesus Christ's Gospel of compassion, justice, love, and forgiveness is meant to travel to the very ends of the earth. Indeed the Church is "catholic," that is, universal. As a religion teacher, you carry that Good News to the young people and their families. You carry that message with you wherever you go—into your home, into your school and parish, into the grocery store, into the post office, and when you travel to distant places. In a very real and practical way, you are a missionary of Jesus Christ. You are to evangelize, or "proclaim the Good News," wherever you go.

### But I'm Not Going Anywhere!

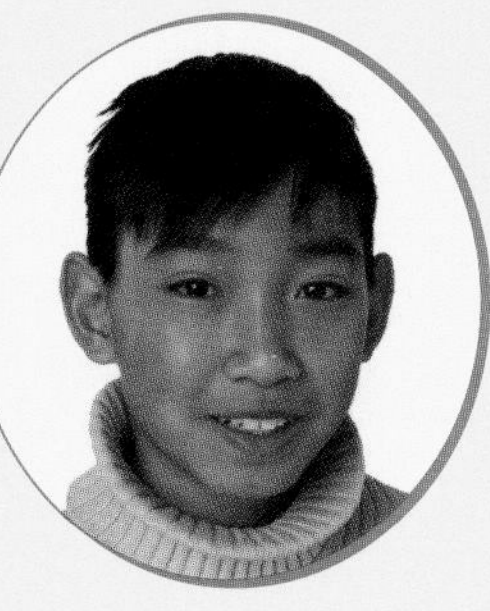

The stories of the missionaries of the Church capture the imagination of young people—distant lands, adventure, risk. Your students might be thinking, "I'm kind of stuck here. I'm not going anywhere. I am not a real missionary." But they are! It is your challenge to help them see how they can be packed and ready to go on the Christian adventure of evangelization, of proclaiming the Gospel, right here and right now.

## The Church Teaches . . .

The *National Directory for Catechesis* teaches:

> The Gospel is intended for every people and nation; it finds a home in every culture. Those who proclaim the Christian message must know and love the culture and the people to whom they bring the message in order for it to be able to transform the culture and the people and make them new in Christ.
>
> *NDC* 17A, page 46

In this chapter the students will learn how the Church has made disciples of the peoples of many nations by sharing the Good News of Jesus through its evangelizing mission.

### See the Catechism . . .

For more on the teachings of the Catholic Church on evangelization, catechumens, and the Church's call to be catholic, see *Catechism of the Catholic Church* 830–838, 849–856, 1229–1233, and 1247–1249.

*Dear Lord,*
*help me spread the*
*Good News of your love,*
*justice, forgiveness,*
*and compassion where*
*I am today.*
*Amen.*

Now . . . turn the page and let's get organized!

# LESSON PLANNER

**Chapter Focus**

**To learn that the Church proclaims Jesus Christ to the ends of the earth**

| Focus | Process | Materials and Options |
| --- | --- | --- |
| **DAY 1**<br>**Engage/Teach and Apply**<br>**Pages 93–95**<br>**Focus**<br>To discover the new energy and zeal in the Church during the fifteenth and sixteenth centuries | **Opening Prayer**<br>**Discussion**<br>How the Gospel is proclaimed globally<br>**Presentation**<br>Read, discuss, and summarize content.<br>**Scripture:** Psalm 96:3<br>**Activity:** Create a timeline of Saint Francis Xavier.<br>**Did you know:** Saint Thérèse of Lisieux<br>**Faith Connection:** Identify opportunities you have had to share the Gospel with others. | **Materials**<br>pens or pencils<br>**Options**<br>***Called to Prayer and Liturgical Lessons* booklet:** See options for daily and seasonal prayers and liturgical prayers and lessons.<br>**Enriching the Lesson (TG page 189)**<br>Depicting Spiritual Breakthroughs |
| **DAY 2**<br>**Teach and Apply**<br>**Pages 96–97**<br>**Focus**<br>To come to know Christians who exemplified the Gospel in the New World | **Prayer**<br>**Presentation**<br>Read, discuss, and summarize content.<br>**Activity:** Discuss the missionary zeal of missionaries to the New World. | **Materials**<br>pens and pencils<br>**Options**<br>***Additional Activities and Assessment Tools* booklet**<br>Map Matching: The Spread of the Gospel, page 23 |
| **DAY 3**<br>**Teach/Apply and Connect**<br>**Pages 98–99**<br>**Focus**<br>To understand the missionary efforts of the Church in modern times | **Prayer**<br>**Presentation**<br>Read, discuss, and summarize content.<br>**Did you know:** *On Evangelization in the Modern World*<br>**Faith Connection:** Share when you have defended the mistreated.<br>**Our Church Makes a Difference**<br>Learn about Pope Paul VI's and Pope John Paul II's work of evangelization. | **Materials**<br>Bibles<br>paper<br>pens and pencils<br>**Options**<br>**Faith First *Liturgy and Morality* video**<br>Segment 8: *The Visual Bible™*<br>1 Corinthians 13, "Paul's Hymn of Love" |
| **DAY 4**<br>**Connect and Apply**<br>**Pages 100–101**<br>**Focus**<br>To name and choose things to take on the Christian journey of spreading the Gospel of Jesus Christ | **Prayer**<br>**What Difference Does Faith Make in My Life?**<br>Reflect on what to take on your Christian journey to proclaim Christ to others.<br>**Activity:** Undertake your own missionary journey to build a civilization of love.<br>**Faith Decision:** Decide what to pack and what to leave behind on your faith journey. | **Materials**<br>slips of paper or 3" x 5" cards<br>pens and pencils<br>**Options**<br>**Enriching the Lesson (TG page 189)**<br>Setting Priorities<br>Creating Backpack Collages<br>***Additional Activities and Assessment Tools* booklet**<br>Planning the Pope's Evangelization Travels, page 24 |
| **DAY 5**<br>**Pray and Review**<br>**Page 102** | **Pray**<br>Pray "A Litany to the Saints" together.<br>**Review**<br>**Activities:** Complete the review exercises to reinforce the concepts of the chapter.<br>**Family Discussion:** Encourage the students to share and discuss the question with their family this week. | **Materials**<br>pens or pencils<br>**Options**<br>***Additional Activities and Assessment Tools* booklet**<br>Administer the chapter 9 test.<br>**Music Connection** (TG page 189) |

**Don't Forget!** You can make lesson planning a breeze—check out the **Online Lesson Planner** at www.FaithFirst.com for additional resources to enhance this chapter.

9

# Exploration and Evangelization

**FAITH FOCUS**

How has the Church fulfilled her mission to make disciples of all nations?

**FAITH VOCABULARY**

canonize
evangelization
patron saint

***What is an example of some really good news that you have shared with others?***

It is natural to tell others the things that are important and valuable to us. History is filled with examples of how civilizations have passed on their traditions and values to succeeding generations. The Church is no exception to this pattern. That is why one of the essential features of the Church is her missionary nature to be "catholic," to tell all nations of every age about Jesus.

***What are some of the ways you know that the Catholic Church proclaims the Gospel to all nations?***

*World #3*, computer graphic. Diana Ong (born 1940), Chinese-American artist.

*Tell God's glory among the nations; / among all peoples, God's marvelous deeds.*
PSALM 96:3

93

# Day 1

## Engage

### PRAY

Invite the young people to quiet themselves for prayer. Have the students look at and reflect on the image *World*. Pray the Sign of the Cross and proclaim Psalm 96:3 together.

### FAITH FOCUS

Read aloud and invite brief responses to the "Faith Focus" question. Share with the young people that in this chapter they will come to a fuller understanding of the universal nature of the Church and how she has proclaimed Jesus Christ to the ends of the earth.

### DISCOVER

Assess the students' prior knowledge and understanding of the Church's missionary work in the world.

- Write the terms in "Faith Vocabulary" on the board. Ask the young people to share what they know about the meaning of the faith terms. Write their responses next to the appropriate terms on the board.
- Invite responses to the opening question. Share your response to the question. Then paraphrase the opening paragraph, and write the word *catholic* on the board.
- Ask volunteers to share responses to the closing question.

## National Directory for Catechesis

**Implementing the *National Directory for Catechesis*: Learning Within the Christian Community.** The National Directory emphasizes that the parish is "the place where the Christian faith is first received, expressed, and nourished" (*NDC* 29C, page 100). Invite a member of the parish RCIA ministry team to visit your class and talk about the parish's evangelization efforts. Have the speaker include how the parish RCIA team works with people who want to become members of the Catholic Church and the process they use to help catechumens prepare to celebrate the Sacraments of Christian Initiation.

# Day 1

## Teach

### FOCUS

Draw the students' attention to the word *catholic* on the board. Ask volunteers to tell what the word means. Universal, global, worldwide. Write their responses around it. Tell them that today's lesson will explore the resurgence of faith and missionary zeal in the Catholic Church during the fifteenth and sixteenth centuries.

### DISCOVER

- Paraphrase or read aloud the introductory paragraph. Ask the young people for other examples of how close and interactive the world has become today.
- Invite a volunteer to read aloud "Resurgence of Faith" to help the students gain some insight as to how the Catholic Church expanded her missionary work beyond Europe.
- Point out that because the explosion of energy to proclaim the Gospel intersected with the age of exploration and discovery, the timing greatly aided the spread of the Gospel. Then have the students silently read "Saint Francis Xavier" and highlight the main ideas.

### Enriching the Lesson

The "Depicting Spiritual Breakthroughs" activity on page 189 is related to the content on these pages. You may want to include it in today's lesson.

## To the Ends of the Earth

*Saint Ignatius Loyola,* stained glass.

Think for a moment about the World Cup. Every four years soccer teams from around the globe gather for the world's largest, best-known competitive event. The World Cup is a symbol of how close and interactive nations around the world have become. When Jesus commanded his first disciples to take the Gospel to all nations, they had little idea of how vast the world was to which they were being sent.

### Resurgence of Faith

In the early centuries there was an intense energy within the Church to spread the Gospel and make disciples of all nations. But at that time, the Church understood her task of spreading the Gospel to be primarily to what they knew the world to be—the Roman Empire. During the later part of the fifteenth century and the early part of the sixteenth century, people's appreciation of the vastness of the world and its accessibility grew. This resulted in the Church unleashing renewed waves of apostolic energy and zeal to spread the Gospel.

This explosion of apostolic zeal intersected with the age of exploration and discovery. Transoceanic and potentially worldwide missions were opening and calling deeply to the soul of the missionary Church. The diverse cultures of Africa, China, and other eastern countries, as well as the vast reaches of the New World, beckoned men and women to journey, like the Apostles, to make disciples of all nations.

*Saint Francis Xavier,* stained glass.

94

### Background: Catholic Tradition

**Society of Jesus, the Jesuits.** The Society of Jesus, or the Jesuits as they are popularly known, was founded in 1540, during the time of the Reformation, by Saint Ignatius of Loyola (1491–1556). Today there are more than twenty thousand Jesuits serving the Church around the world. The Jesuits began their ministry in the United States of America in 1789. They now work in a wide variety of ministries, including social ministries, international ministries, pastoral ministries, the ministry of the Spiritual Exercises, communications (including education) ministries, and individual ministries (such as lawyers and physicians). More detailed information about the Jesuits in the United States can be found at www.jesuit.org.

Arrival of Saint Francis Xavier in Japan, 1549. Detail of Japanese painted paper screen, sixteenth century. Artist unknown.

### Saint Francis Xavier

Francis Xavier, who was later to be called the Apostle of India and Japan, was born in Spain on April 7, 1506. He was a hardworking student whose life was changed forever in Paris where he met Saint Ignatius of Loyola, the future founder of the Society of Jesus (Jesuits). In August of 1534, Francis joined Ignatius in the formation of the Jesuits.

Francis's first assignment as a missionary to the Middle East in 1536 fell through. The disappointed Francis had to wait until April of 1541 to finally embark on a missionary journey. From Portugal, Francis undertook a long and dangerous voyage to India. Having wintered in Mozambique, he landed in Goa thirteen months later. Francis immediately undertook the challenge of learning the language, preaching, ministering to the sick, and composing a catechism.

In July of 1547 Francis Xavier met a Japanese man named Anjiro. Francis's missionary fervor was at once aroused by all that he learned about Japan. Upon his arrival in Japan two years later, Francis learned the language and adapted himself to Japanese customs. Two years later, when he left Japan, more than 2,000 people had been baptized.

Francis Xavier next set his sights on China, a country about which he had learned much while in Japan. He reached the coast of China, near Canton, in August 1552. While trying to gain entry into the country, he grew ill with a severe fever, and on December 3 he died. In 1622 Saint Francis Xavier was **canonized**, or declared a saint of the Church. In 1748 he was declared **patron saint** of China and the other far eastern countries. Finally in 1927 he was named patron of all missions together with Saint Thérèse of Lisieux.

***How was Saint Francis Xavier a symbol of the Catholic Church's newfound energy and zeal in the sixteenth century?*** Affirm appropriate responses.

### Did you Know...

Saint Thérèse of Lisieux (1873–1897) lived only twenty-four years and never left her native Europe. Thérèse Martin entered the Carmelite monastery in Lisieux, France, at age fifteen, where she was given the name Thérèse of the Child Jesus. Thérèse was canonized a saint in 1925 by Pope Saint Pius X and declared a Doctor of the Church in 1997 by Pope John Paul II. Because of Saint Thérèse's burning love for all people and her steadfast dedication to praying for the spread of the Gospel, the Church recognizes her and Saint Francis Xavier as the patron saint of all missionaries.

### FAITH CONNECTION

***What opportunities have you had to share the Gospel with others? How did you respond? What will you do the next time you have such an opportunity?***

Responses will vary.

Affirm appropriate responses.

95

### Teaching Tip

**The Power of Using Symbols.** Sometimes while you are preparing a chapter, a particular symbol may come to mind as appropriate to use to help the young people grasp the lesson theme. For example, when talking about the age of exploration and evangelization, the use of a globe comes to mind. Use your classroom globe this week, both as a visual tool to indicate where the missionaries traveled and as a symbol for focusing prayer.

# Day 1

## Apply

### REINFORCE

- Create a timeline on the board. Invite students to come up to the board one by one and, beginning with Saint Francis Xavier's birth, create a timeline of his life.
- Have the students share what they see depicted in the images of Saint Francis Xavier on pages 94 and 95 and respond to the concluding question.
- Invite the class to read the "Did you know" feature about Saint Thérèse of Lisieux. Point out that she is recognized by the Catholic Church as a patron saint of all missionaries.

### INTEGRATE

- Invite the young people to join with one or two other students to discuss the "Faith Connection" questions.
- Have those who wish share their responses with the class.

### PRAY

Ask the young people to quiet themselves for prayer and echo after you:

> God our Father, / you will all [people] to be saved. / . . . Send workers into your great harvest / that the gospel may be preached to every creature / and your people, gathered together by the word of life / and strengthened by the power of the sacraments, / may advance in the way of salvation and love. / Amen.
>
> *Opening Prayer, Mass for the Spread of the Gospel (14), Roman Missal*

# Day 2

## Teach

**PRAY**

Invite the students to quiet themselves for prayer. Pray the Act of Faith on page 137.

**FOCUS**

Recall with the class that the renewed energy and zeal of the Catholic Church in the sixteenth century to spread the Gospel happened during the age of exploration. Point out that today they will learn about four saints who helped spread the Gospel in the New World.

**DISCOVER**

- Paraphrase or read aloud the introductory paragraph. Add Father Jacques Marquette and Blessed Junípero Serra to the list of missionaries on the board.
- Ask the class to look at the images of the four saints on pages 96 and 97. Name the saints one at a time. By a show of hands ask the students to raise their hands after you name a saint if they have heard about that saint before.
- Have the students silently read "The Church in the New World" on pages 96 and 97.
- Divide the class into groups of four students each. Ask each person in the group to assume the character of one of the saints on pages 96 and 97.
- Give the students time to reread about their saints. Have each group hold a roundtable discussion to share the contributions of each saint to the life and growth of the Church in the New World.

The fifteenth and sixteenth centuries marked the beginning of the widespread proclamation of the Gospel in the New World. Father Jacques Marquette (1637–1675), a Jesuit who helped discover the Mississippi River, and Blessed Junípero Serra (1713–1784), a Franciscan who established the California missions, were among the missionaries who did this. So significant was the work of these two missionaries, not only for the Church but also for the development of the New World, that they are among the persons honored in National Statuary Hall in the Capitol of the United States.

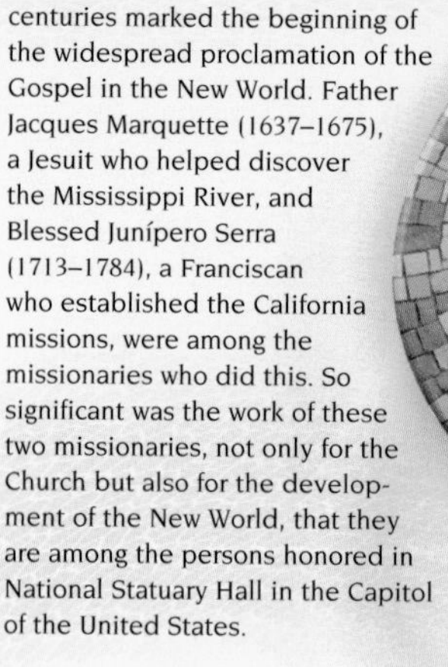

Saint Rose of Lima, detail from mosaic.

Saint Martin de Porres, also known as Saint of the Broom, stained glass.

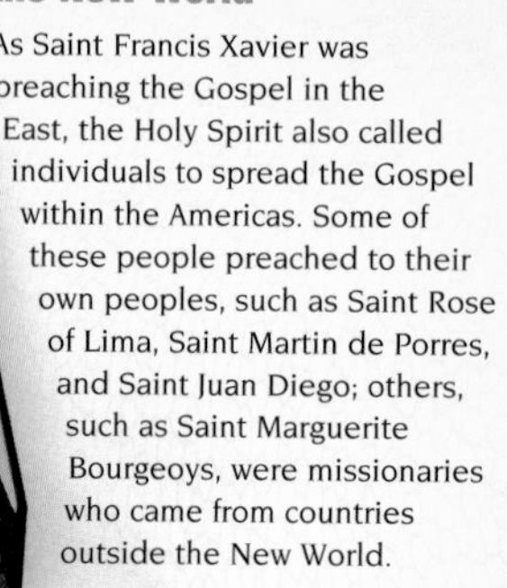

### The Church in the New World

As Saint Francis Xavier was preaching the Gospel in the East, the Holy Spirit also called individuals to spread the Gospel within the Americas. Some of these people preached to their own peoples, such as Saint Rose of Lima, Saint Martin de Porres, and Saint Juan Diego; others, such as Saint Marguerite Bourgeoys, were missionaries who came from countries outside the New World.

**Saint Rose of Lima**

Saint Rose of Lima (1586–1617), the patron saint of South America and the Philippines, is the first canonized saint of the Americas. As a teenager, Rose chose to live the Gospel by committing herself to a life of prayer, penance, and dedication to people who were sick, hungry, and suffering from other needs.

**Saint Martin de Porres**

Saint Martin de Porres (1579–1639), a close friend and collaborator with Saint Rose in Lima, is the first black American saint. Martin entered the Third Order of St. Dominic and spent the remainder of his life ministering to the suffering, just as his mother cared for African slaves. As a Dominican lay brother, Martin worked with the sick and founded an orphanage and children's hospital. The compassion of Martin was so great that he even founded a shelter for stray cats and dogs.

The lives of both these saints were so valued by their friends, neighbors, and people of Lima, that when they died, the leaders of Lima took turns carrying their bodies in procession to the grave.

96

## Background: Doctrine

**Inculturation of the Gospel.** Missionary activity must always include "a process of inculturation if the Gospel is to take flesh in each people's culture"[1] (*Catechism of the Catholic Church* 854). "[Inculturation[2] of the Gospel message] is not simply an external adaptation designed to make the Christian message more attractive or superficially decorative. On the contrary, it means the penetration of the deepest strata of persons and peoples by the Gospel which touches them deeply, 'going to the very center and roots'[3] of their cultures" (*General Directory for Catechesis* 109). For more on the inculturation of the Gospel message see *General Directory for Catechesis* 109–113.

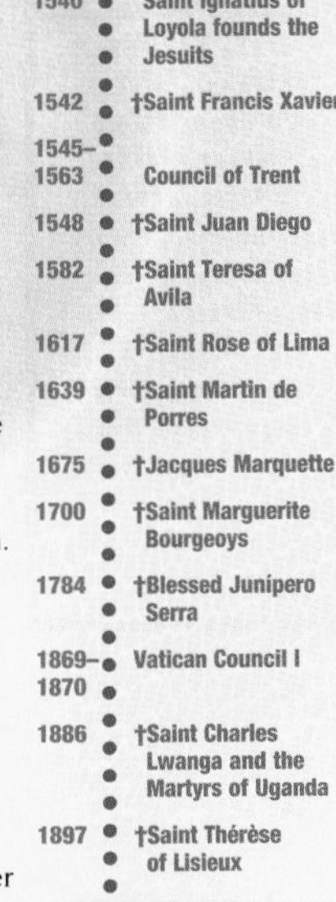

Saint Juan Diego, illustration. Julie Lonneman, contemporary American artist.

### Saint Juan Diego

Cuauhtlatoatzin (1474–1548), who described himself as a "poor Indian," was a member of the lowest and largest class of Aztec people. He was baptized with his wife between 1524 and 1529 and received the name Juan Diego. As he was walking to Mass in Tenochtitlan (Mexico City) on December 9, 1531, the Blessed Virgin Mary appeared to him, instructing him to tell the bishop to build a church on the spot of the apparition.

Juan's recounting of his vision was initially dismissed by the bishop, probably because Juan was only a "poor Indian." Eventually the bishop listened to Juan when he opened his cloak, revealing a miraculous image of the "Lady" imprinted on it. In his homily at the canonization of Saint Juan Diego on July 31, 2001, Pope John Paul II prayed to Juan Diego, saying:

> We ask you to accompany the Church on her pilgrimage in Mexico, so that she may be more evangelizing and more missionary each day.

Saint Juan Diego is a symbol of the way that God works through the poor and lowly to bring relief and comfort to those who suffer and to announce the Gospel through them.

### Saint Marguerite Bourgeoys

Marguerite Bourgeoys (1620–1700) came to Montreal in New France (Canada) in 1653. Because of her commitment to building strong families, Marguerite, in 1658, opened the first school in a stable in Montreal. She later expanded her work among young women and girls on whom the education of children so much depended. So vital was Marguerite's work that she became known as "Mother of the Colony." The work that Sister Bourgeoys began in the seventeenth century is continued today by the community she founded, Sisters of the Congregation de Notre-Dame. Pope John Paul II canonized Marguerite Bourgeoys on October 31, 1982, giving the Church in Canada its first woman saint.

***How did the missionary zeal of members of the Church in the New World help build the Church in the New World?***

Affirm appropriate responses.

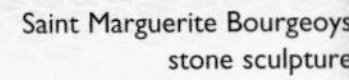

Saint Marguerite Bourgeoys, stone sculpture.

97

# Day 2

## Apply

### REINFORCE

- Review the "Timeline" with the class.
- Ask each group of "saints" to come up with a response to the question at the end of page 97, using specific examples from what they have just discussed. Invite the groups to share their responses with the class.

### INTEGRATE

Ask the young people to quietly reflect on how their attitudes, words, and actions during the past week may have helped someone come to know Christ better.

### PRAY

Conclude the lesson by leading the young people in praying the Act of Faith on page 137.

## Teaching Tip

**Contact Diocesan Mission Office.** Most dioceses in the United States have an office dedicated to fostering the missionary work of the Catholic Church. Consider inviting a representative from your diocesan mission office to visit with your class and share with the students the diocese's current missionary efforts in various parts of the world. The young people can explore the United States Conference of Catholic Bishops' Web site, http://www.usccb.org/, to find out more about both home missions and world mission efforts.

# Day 3

## Teach

**PRAY**

Pray together the Act of Hope on page 137 of the student text.

**FOCUS**

Invite the students to recall some of the names and deeds of the saints that they learned about in the previous lesson who spread the Gospel in the Americas. Point out that they will now move forward in history to learn about the missionary efforts of the Catholic Church in Africa in the nineteenth century.

**DISCOVER**

- Write the word *evangelization* on the board and brainstorm key words or phrases that define the Catholic Church's work of evangelization, or spreading the Gospel.
- Invite the students to silently read the introductory paragraph on page 98 and the "Did you know" feature. Then invite volunteers to add words that describe evangelization to the words that are already on the board.
- Have the students silently read about "Saint Charles Lwanga and the Martyrs of Uganda."

## Apply

**REINFORCE**

As a class, discuss the closing question. Emphasize how the martyrs of Uganda were executed for living out the Catholic belief in the dignity of the human person.

**INTEGRATE**

- Have the students work in small groups to discuss the "Faith Connection" questions.
- Invite volunteers to share their stories with the class.

### Did you Know...

In 1995 Pope Paul VI promulgated his apostolic exhortation *On Evangelization in the Modern World*. In this document Pope Paul VI describes and gives direction to the Church's mission of evangelization. "Evangelizing is in fact the grace and vocation proper to the Church. . . . She exists in order to evangelize" (14).

During the nineteenth and twentieth centuries the Church intensified her **evangelization** of the native populations in Africa. The word *evangelization* means "the proclamation of Christ [and his Gospel] by word and testimony of life," in fulfillment of Christ's command (*Catechism of the Catholic Church* 905).

Pilgrims at tomb of Saint Charles Lwanga, Basilica of the Uganda Martyrs, Namugongo, Uganda.

### Saint Charles Lwanga and the Martyrs of Uganda

The Society of Missionaries of Africa, also known as the White Fathers, was founded in 1868 to help the Church fulfill her mission of evangelization of Arab and black people in Africa. After only six years in Uganda, the White Fathers had built up a Church community unwavering in faith and capable of bringing the Gospel to their fellow countrymen. Saint Charles Lwanga (1865–1886), was one of the people evangelized by the White Fathers.

Charles Lwanga was both an official in the royal court and a leader and catechist in the local Church. When he and others tried to protect the young boys from the king's attempts to sexually abuse them, Mwanga turned his wrath on them, and on June 3, 1886, thirteen Catholics and eleven Protestants were executed at the order of Mwanga. As the blood of martyrs in the early Church did, the blood of Charles Lwanga and his companions nourished the growth of the Church in Africa.

***What does the missionary effort of the Church in Africa teach us about the importance of the Church fulfilling her commission to preach the Gospel to all nations?*** Affirm appropriate responses.

### FAITH CONNECTION

***When have you ever stepped forward to protect or defend someone who was being mistreated? What happened?***

Responses will vary.

Affirm appropriate responses.

98

### Teaching Tip

**Encourage but Do Not Force Sharing.** Some young people will choose not to share about spiritual matters they find personal. Always respect a student's privacy when your class is having faith-sharing conversations. Never force a young person to participate in faith sharing and other discussions that reveal "personal" information.

# OUR CHURCH MAKES A DIFFERENCE

Christ sends the Church to all peoples. The Church speaks to all peoples. She encompasses all times. She is "missionary of her very nature"[1] (*Catechism of the Catholic Church* 868). Both Pope Paul VI and Pope John Paul II were evangelizing, or missionary, Popes. Both traveled the world proclaiming Jesus Christ.

Pope Paul VI, Kampala, Uganda, July 31, 1969.

### Pope Paul VI

When Giovanni Cardinal Montini was elected Pope on June 21, 1963, he chose his name, Paul VI, very deliberately. Like his namesake, Saint Paul the Apostle, this missionary Pope would undertake nine pilgrimages around the world between 1964 and 1970. Pope Paul VI's eighth pilgrimage was to Uganda in July-August 1969, making him the first Pope to visit Africa. In his greeting of the people upon his arrival at Entebbe International Airport, he said that working for justice among the peoples is part of the work of evangelization.

### Pope John Paul II

The missionary travels that began with Pope Paul VI became one of the defining features of the papacy of Pope John Paul II. During his 26 years as Pope, he made 104 trips outside Rome, stopping in more than 129 countries that spanned every continent except Antarctica. These travels, he said in 1980, were designed "to announce the Gospel, to consolidate the Church, to meet the people." Speaking to the Catholic youth in his homily at Mass on World Youth Day in Paris in 1997, he encouraged the youth to take part in the Church's work of evangelization and build a "civilization of love." He said:

> Dear young people, your journey does not end here. Time does not come to a halt. Go forth now along the roads of the world, along the pathways of humanity, while remaining ever united in Christ's Church! . . . help our brothers and sisters to see the world transfigured by God's eternal wisdom and love.

***If the Pope visited your parish and school and you had a chance to interview him, what would you ask him?*** Responses will vary. Affirm appropriate responses.

Pope John Paul II, Human Rights Square, Paris, France, August 21, 1997, during the twelfth World Youth Day celebration.

99

## Teaching Tip

**Questions! Questions!** The young people may have questions they want to ask the Pope that you (or they) will not be able to answer in the class discussion. In your role as religion teacher, you are not expected to have all the answers. However, you are expected to join with the young people on their journey of discovery about the faith and help them find the answers to their questions about the Church. Save the questions from today's lesson and invite your parish priest or another qualified person to visit with the class and respond to their questions.

# Day 3

## Connect

### HIGHLIGHT

- Recall with the class the meaning of *evangelization* and how the evangelizing efforts of the Catholic Church spread to Africa in the nineteenth and twentieth centuries.
- Point out to the young people that two of the Church's recent Popes are known as evangelizing, or missionary, Popes because of the zeal with which they traveled to bring the Gospel to the world.

### DISCOVER

- Present the introductory paragraph on page 99. Then divide the class into two groups and give each group a sheet of newsprint and markers.
- Assign one group "Pope Paul VI" and the other "Pope John Paul II."
- Have each group read the section about the Pope assigned to them, and together create an outline of the key facts presented in the text.
- Invite the groups to present what they learned to each other.

### INTEGRATE

Invite the young people to write down on slips of paper or 3" x 5" cards several interview questions that they would like to ask the Pope if he visited their parish and school. Collect the questions and use them to facilitate discussion about the Church.

### PRAY

Invite the students to quiet themselves for prayer. Pray together the prayer on page 181 of this teacher guide.

# Day 4

## Connect

**PRAY**

Invite the students to quiet themselves and pray the Act of Love on page 137.

**FOCUS**

Remind the students that Pope Paul VI said the Church's reason for existing is evangelization, the spread of the Gospel. Recall the "Faith Focus" question on page 93. Ask the students to answer it, using what they learned in this chapter. List responses on the board. Point out that these two pages will explore skills that will help them fulfill their baptismal call to proclaim the Gospel.

**DISCOVER**

- Read aloud the introductory paragraph. Tell the young people that today's lesson will give them time for reflection and prayer.
- Ask the students to assume comfortable positions in the classroom. Then have them silently read "Building a Civilization of Love."
- Invite them to spend time reflecting on the questions and on deciding what they need to pack or unpack for their journey.

# WHAT DIFFERENCE

## Does Faith Make in My Life?

One of the four Marks, or essential characteristics, of the Church is "apostolic." The Church today is rooted in the Apostles and shares the same commission Christ gave to the Apostles, namely, "Go, therefore, and make disciples of all nations" (Matthew 28:19). In this chapter you learned about several ways that the Church carried out that commission during the fifteenth through nineteenth centuries. As a member of the Catholic Church, you have the responsibility to proclaim Jesus Christ to others.

### Building a Civilization of Love

Like the youth gathered in Cologne in 2005 for the twentieth World Youth Day, you are always on a journey building a civilization of love, the Kingdom of God announced by Jesus. Before you make this journey and strive to live as a follower of Jesus, you will need to make sure your bags are properly packed.

First, carefully evaluate how prepared you are to go on your journey. Take time to respond to these questions:

- How ready are you to follow Jesus, the Good Shepherd, along the path he is leading you? Why?
- How determined are you to walk this path? How willing are you to do whatever it takes to be a true missionary? Why?
- How well do you recognize and appreciate the gifts and talents that the Holy Spirit gives you to guide and strengthen you for this journey? Give examples.
- How heavy are your bags? What things in them, for example, attitudes that might hold you back from living as a faithful follower of Jesus, might be obstacles to your successfully making the journey?

100

## Teaching Tip

**Provide a Miniretreat Experience.** Encourage a retreat-type atmosphere to the lesson by changing the classroom environment just a little. Consider dimming lights and playing music that facilitates reflection. Invite the young people to leave their desks and find a comfortable spot on the floor or other area. If possible, take them to another place on the school grounds, such as the chapel.

**Time to Pack/Unpack Your Bags**

To undertake this Christian journey you will need to pack your bags with certain values and beliefs and fill yourself with certain strengths and virtues. You will also have to eliminate certain things from your baggage that would hold you back from making good choices.

Check the things you will need to help you be a true follower of Jesus. Cross out the obstacles that will hold you back on the journey. Add anything else you believe you will need.

- Courage
- Peace
- Riches
- Fear
- Integrity
- Dishonesty
- Love
- Acceptance
- Intolerance
- Prejudice
- Commitment
- Respect
- Dignity for yourself and others
- Self-esteem
- Resentment
- Jealousy
- Gratitude
- Compassion

Add other items that you would pack:

- __________
- __________
- __________

**Faith Decision**

- In a small group discuss the things listed that you identified would help you successfully make your journey. Be sure to give reasons for your choices.
- Work independently and name what you think might be the biggest obstacle that would prevent you personally from successfully making your journey. Be sure to identify ways that you might overcome that obstacle.

This week I will use the following qualities or values that will help me successfully make my journey, namely,

Responses will vary.

Affirm appropriate responses.

I will unpack the following baggage that is holding me back on my Christian journey, namely,

Responses will vary.

Affirm appropriate responses.

101

## Day 4

## Apply

### RESPOND

After a period of quiet time for reflection, have the students gather in small groups to discuss the first part of the "Faith Decision" activity. Then have everyone work independently to complete the second part of the activity.

### CHOOSE

- Allow the young people more quiet time to make and write their faith decision independently.
- Encourage the young people to put their decision into practice this week.

### PRAY

Lead the young people in a brief intercessory prayer for one another asking the Holy Spirit to strengthen them for their Christian journey. Conclude by praying the Our Father together.

### Teaching Tip

**Encourage Trust in the Holy Spirit.** Life can get very complicated and busy these days. Our journey of faith can seem to be difficult at times. Remind the young people that the Holy Spirit is always there, ready, and willing to guide and strengthen them for the journey. Share Matthew 11:28–30, which records words of Jesus that will guide them as they make their journey of faith.

### *Enriching the Lesson*

The "Setting Priorities" and the "Creating Backpack Collages" activities on page 189 are related to today's content. You may wish to include them in today's lesson.

# Day 5

## Pray and Review

### FOCUS

Explain that today's prayer is a litany focused on the missionary saints of the Church. Share how a litany is prayed and select a volunteer to be the leader of the prayer.

### PRAY

Gather the class for prayer. Pray "A Litany to the Saints" together.

### REVIEW

- Have the young people share the meaning of the terms in "Faith Vocabulary" and compare their definitions with those in the glossary.
- Use the "Main Ideas" and "Critical Thinking" sections to clarify any questions the students may have concerning what they have learned in the chapter.
- Remind everyone to share and discuss the "Family Discussion" question with their family.

# PRAY and REVIEW

## A Litany to the Saints

**Leader:** Let us pray for all missionaries—for those in foreign lands and for those who carry the Gospel to others here at home:

**Leader:** Saint Francis Xavier,
**All:** **pray for us.**

**Leader:** Saint Rose of Lima,
**All:** **pray for us.**

**Leader:** Saint Martin de Porres,
**All:** **pray for us.**

**Leader:** Saint Juan Diego,
**All:** **pray for us.**

**Leader:** Saint Marguerite Bourgeoys,
**All:** **pray for us.**

**Leader:** Saint Charles Lwanga and the Martyrs of Uganda,
**All:** **pray for us.**

**Leader:** Let us pray.
God our Father, in your care and wisdom / you extend the kingdom of Christ to embrace the whole world / and to give all people the offer of salvation. / May the Catholic Church be the sign of our salvation, / may it reveal for us the mystery of your love, / and may that love become effective in our lives. We ask this through Christ the Lord.

**All:** **Amen.**

Adapted from the Roman Missal, Opening Prayer, Mass for the Universal Church

102

### FAITH VOCABULARY

Define each of these faith vocabulary terms:

1. canonize
2. patron saint
3. evangelization

### MAIN IDEAS

Choose either (a) or (b) from each set of items below. Write a brief paragraph to answer each of your choices.

1. (a) Describe the background for the resurgence of faith after the Council of Trent. p. 94
   (b) Discuss the life and mission of Saint Francis Xavier. p. 95
2. (a) Describe the spread of the Gospel in the Americas in the sixteenth and seventeen centuries. pp. 96–97
   (b) Explain the nineteenth-century evangelization of Africa. p. 98

### CRITICAL THINKING

Using what you have learned in this chapter, briefly explain these words:

"The Church . . . exists in order to evangelize."

### FAMILY DISCUSSION

How are the members of your family missionaries?

For more ideas on ways your family can live your faith, visit the "Faith First for Families" page at **www.FaithFirst.com**. Also check out "Make a Difference" on the Teen Center.

### Before Moving On . . .

Reflect on this question before moving on to the next chapter.

*How conducive is the classroom environment to reflection and prayer?*

## Evaluate

Take a few moments to evaluate this week's lesson.

I feel (circle one) about this week's lesson.

a. very pleased
b. OK
c. disappointed

The activity the students enjoyed most was . . .

The concept that was most difficult to teach was . . .

because . . .

Something I would like to do differently is . . .

# ENRICHING THE LESSON

## Depicting Spiritual Breakthroughs

**Purpose**

To reinforce the experience of renewed zeal and commitment to living the Gospel (taught on pages 94–95)

**Directions**

- Distribute art paper and markers to the students.
- Ask the young people to recall a moment of spiritual breakthrough in their lives when they felt renewed and energized about the living Gospel.
- Have them use symbols and words to depict a time or event in their personal spiritual lives that brought about a wave of new energy, discovery, and zeal to live the Gospel.
- Invite volunteers to share their completed pictures with the entire group.
- Respect the privacy of those young people who want to keep these times in their lives personal.

**Materials**

art paper, markers

## Setting Priorities

**Purpose**

To reinforce that we make choices about what we take with us on our Christian journey (taught on page 101)

**Directions**

- Facilitate this activity as a large group.
- Have the young people prioritize the items on page 101 that they will take with them for the journey of their Christian life, as well as the items they will leave behind.
- Have the students use a scale of 1 = Very important to pack or unpack, 2 = Somewhat important, and 3 = Not very important to prioritize the items.
- Make two columns on newsprint and label one column "Pack" and the other "Unpack." Ask volunteers to list the items on their lists in the appropriate columns.
- Invite the students to summarize the results and try to come to a consensus about what the most important items are to take on one's faith journey.

**Materials**

newsprint, markers

## Creating Backpack Collages

**Purpose**

To reinforce the concept that as travelers on the Christian journey we carry values and beliefs with us (taught on page 101)

**Directions**

- Provide the students with art paper, markers, and scissors. Have them draw and cut out an outline of a backpack.
- Instruct them to create a collage using the outline of the backpack and include images of the things they will pack for the Christian journey. Tell them that they may cut pictures or phrases from magazines as well as incorporate their own words and drawings of symbols.
- Invite students to share their completed collages with the group.

**Materials**

construction paper, scissors, markers

### Music Connection

- "All That is Hidden," B. Farrell. *Gather Comprehensive (GC)* #654.
- "Anthem," T. Conry. *GC* #681.
- "Pescador de Homres/Lord, You Have Come," C. Gabaráin. *Flor y Canto* #709.
- "We Are the Hope," P. Tate. *Voices As One* #97.

# Chapter 10 The Missionary Church A Scripture Story

## CHAPTER BACKGROUND

### Salvation History

Church history is part of the sweeping story of Salvation History. The story and history of Salvation begins at creation and coincides with the Covenant God entered into with humankind. The Bible speaks of God's covenants with Noah and his descendants; with Abraham and his descendants, the Israelites who were named after Israel (Jacob), one of the sons of Abraham; and with Moses and the Israelites at Mount Sinai. Through the prophets, God reaffirmed his fidelity to the Covenant and his chosen people and prepared the way for the Salvation of all peoples in Jesus, the new and everlasting Covenant and Savior of the world. (See *Catechism of the Catholic Church* 54–67.)

### Jonah and the Ninevites

The Book of Jonah is a gently amusing but unmistakably pointed tale that underlines the universality of Salvation. It proclaims the truth that God's forgiveness is meant for all people, as are his justice and mercy.

As such, the Book of Jonah is a cautionary tale against a narrow-minded interpretation and limitation of God's love and mercy. Like many people of his time, Jonah had a proprietary attitude toward God. He felt God was the property of the Israelites, and God's blessings were meant for them alone. Additionally, Jonah felt that the enemies of the Israelites were also God's enemies, deserving nothing but God's wrath and destruction. Jonah did not understand that God was not working for the Israelites as much as he was working through them to offer and bring Salvation to all people, including Israel's worst enemies.

### New People of God

Like the Israelites, the new People of God, the Church, live in covenant with God. The Church is the sign and instrument through which God brings Salvation to the whole of humanity. This means that the Church by her very nature is missionary. As members of the Church we are called by God to spread the Gospel by our words and deeds. The Book of Jonah teaches us that no one is excluded from this outreach. Jesus Christ is the Savior of all people, even those who may not have yet come to know him. The Church at the Second Vatican Council reminded us of this truth:

> Those who, through no fault of their own, do not know the Gospel of Christ or his Church, but who nevertheless seek God with a sincere heart, and, moved by grace, try in their actions to do his will as they know it through the dictates of their conscience—those too may achieve eternal salvation.
>
> Dogmatic Constitution on the Church *[Lumen Gentium 16]*.

## FOR REFLECTION

***How do my words and deeds express my faith in the universality of Salvation?***

***What can I do to help the students know that God extends his mercy and love to everyone?***

## First Thoughts

### God for All People

God's love is universal. He invites all people to share in the gift of divine life and to live in communion with him. God's love for all people is echoed in the command of Jesus to his disciples to "make disciples of all nations." The Old Testament Scripture story in this chapter teaches that God's love for people included those who Jonah and the Israelites considered to be wicked and their adversaries.

#### A Story that Comes Alive

A story that comes alive for the young adolescents is the kind of story that they will most appreciate. In this chapter you have great material to work with in the story of Jonah. To deepen the students' appreciation, help them understand what we would expect of Jonah who God chose and called to be one of his prophets—certainly not what we end up reading: that he takes off running when God calls him and pitches major temper tantrums to boot. Jonah is supposed to act one way, but he acts the opposite of what we expect. The bonus for us is that, at his expense, we learn an important lesson about how God is the God of all people—not just the people we happen to like.

## The Church Teaches . . .

The *National Directory for Catechesis* teaches:

> Christ [is] "the center of the history of salvation."[1] He came "in the fullness of time."[2] As the definitive Revelation of God, he is the point in salvation history toward which the created order proceeds from the beginning of time and the final event toward which it converges.
>
> *NDC* 25A, page 76

As the students study the story of Jonah in this chapter, they will learn the importance of responding to the call we first received at Baptism.

### See the Catechism . . .

For more on the teachings of the Catholic Church about missionaries, our baptismal call, and Salvation History, see *Catechism of the Catholic Church* 430–432, 668, 849–856, 1080, and 1265–1274.

*God of all people,
help me see that your
love is for everyone
without exception!
Amen.*

Footnote references may be found on page 256.

Now . . . turn the page and let's get organized!

# LESSON PLANNER

**Chapter Focus**

**To learn what the Book of Jonah prefigures about the missionary nature of the Church**

| Focus | Process | Materials and Options |
|---|---|---|
| **DAY 1**<br>**Engage/Teach and Apply**<br>**Pages 103–105**<br>**Focus**<br>To explore the work of the prophets and the background of the Book of Jonah | **Opening Prayer**<br>**Discussion**<br>What the unique mission of the Old Testament prophets was<br>**Presentation**<br>Read, discuss, and summarize content.<br>**Scripture:** Exodus 3:10, Jeremiah 1:7, Romans 9:26<br>**Did you know:** Nineveh<br>**Faith Connection:** Look up and describe the mission of the Old Testament prophets. | **Materials**<br>Bibles<br>pens or pencils<br>**Options**<br>***Called to Prayer and Liturgical Lessons* booklet:** See options for daily and seasonal prayers and liturgical prayers and lessons.<br>***Additional Activities and Assessment Tools* booklet**<br>A Faith-Sharing Recipe, page 25 |
| **DAY 2**<br>**Teach and Apply**<br>**Pages 106–107**<br>**Focus**<br>To discover what the Book of Jonah teaches about who God invites to Salvation | **Prayer**<br>**Presentation**<br>Read, discuss, and summarize content.<br>**Scripture:** Jonah 1:1–2, 4–5, 11–12, 3:1–4, 4:10–11<br>**Activity:** Act out a dramatic presentation of the story of Jonah. | **Materials**<br>Props for melodrama<br>**Options**<br>**Enriching the Lesson (TG page 203)**<br>Writing a Screenplay<br>**Faith First *Liturgy and Morality* video**<br>Segment 1: Interviews with young people about faith |
| **DAY 3**<br>**Teach/Apply and Connect**<br>**Pages 108–109**<br>**Focus**<br>To understand that the Church is a sign and instrument of Salvation | **Prayer**<br>**Presentation**<br>Read, discuss, and summarize content.<br>**Scripture:** Matthew 5:6<br>**Faith Connection:** Create advertising copy for a movie based on the Book of Jonah.<br>**Our Church Makes a Difference**<br>Discover how volunteers work full time for peace and justice. | **Materials**<br>pens or pencils<br>**Options**<br>**Enriching the Lesson (TG page 203)**<br>Choosing a Class Mission<br>***Additional Activities and Assessment Tools* booklet**<br>Billboard: The Mission of Jesus Christ Today, page 26 |
| **DAY 4**<br>**Connect and Apply**<br>**Pages 110–111**<br>**Focus**<br>To reflect on our mission as Catholics | **Prayer**<br>**What Difference Does Faith Make in My Life?**<br>Consider ways to pray, learn, and act in order to live the mission of a disciple.<br>**Scripture:** John 3:5<br>**Activity:** Surface ideas for how to fulfill the call to be a living sign of Christ.<br>**Faith Decision:** Complete a mission statement and choose to act on it. | **Materials**<br>paper<br>pens or pencils<br>**Options**<br>**Enriching the Lesson (TG page 203)**<br>Praying Around the World |
| **DAY 5**<br>**Pray and Review**<br>**Page 112** | **Pray**<br>Pray "The Prayer of Jonah" together.<br>**Review**<br>**Activities:** Complete the review exercises to reinforce the concepts of the chapter.<br>**Family Discussion:** Encourage the students to share and discuss the question with their family this week. | **Materials**<br>pens or pencils<br>**Options**<br>***Additional Activities and Assessment Tools* booklet**<br>Administer the chapter 10 test.<br>**Music Connection** (TG page 203) |

**Don't Forget!** You can make lesson planning a breeze—check out the **Online Lesson Planner** at www.FaithFirst.com for additional resources to enhance this chapter.

# The Missionary Church
## A Scripture Story

10

### FAITH FOCUS

What does the Book of Jonah teach us about the missionary mandate of the Church?

### FAITH VOCABULARY

Salvation History
prophet
parable
mission
exile

***Name some examples from today's news that report the work of people who have been sent on "special assignment."***

Throughout your life you will be sent on assignments. A parent may send you to the store to purchase groceries. A teacher may send you to the library or to a computer to look up some specific information. A coach may send you into the game to help the team in a way that you do best. As you grow older, your company may send you on a business trip, or your country may send you to a foreign land to help bring assistance to others. The Bible tells us many stories about God sending people on "special assignment."

***Give an example of someone who the Scriptures tell us God sent on a special assignment, or mission.***

*Jonah*, stained glass.

*"And in the very place where it was said to them, 'You are not my people,' / there they shall be called children of the living God."*
Romans 9:26

103

# Day 1
## Engage

**PRAY**

Invite the young people to quiet themselves for prayer and recognize God's presence in their lives today. Proclaim Romans 9:26 together.

**FAITH FOCUS**

Read aloud and invite brief responses to the "Faith Focus" question. Explain that in this chapter the students will focus on the Book of Jonah and explore what it prefigures about the missionary nature of the Church.

**DISCOVER**

Assess the students' prior knowledge and understanding of the Book of Jonah and the mission God gave Jonah the Prophet.

- Write on the board the "Faith Vocabulary" terms as the headings of five columns. Ask the class to share what they already know about the meaning of each of the terms. Write their responses in the appropriate columns.
- Invite volunteers to share what it means when one is sent on "special assignment."
- Ask for examples from today's news that report the work of people on "special assignment."
- Paraphrase the opening paragraph and ask for an example of someone from Scripture who God sent on a special assignment, or mission.
- Draw the students' attention to the stained-glass image of Jonah and point out that Jonah the Prophet was one of these people.

## National Directory for Catechesis

**Implementing the *National Directory for Catechesis*: Making a Commitment to Live the Christian Life.** The National Directory teaches that "the private practice and the public witness of knowledgeable and committed Christians are indispensable factors in the sanctification of the world, a responsibility to which all the baptized are called" (*NDC* 29G, page 104). Invite the students to make booklets illustrating the story of Jonah that they can share with primary students during an upcoming session. This activity will give them the opportunity to be on "special assignment" to announce God's plan for the Salvation of all people.

# Day 1

## Teach

**FOCUS**

Remind the young people that throughout the history of Salvation God has chosen people and given them a special work, or mission, to accomplish. Point out that in today's lesson they will discover more about these people.

**DISCOVER**

- Invite a volunteer to read aloud the introductory paragraph on page 104. Point to the "Faith Vocabulary" term *Salvation History* on the board and have the students add to the words in the column that describe it.
- Have volunteers read aloud "The Prophets: God's Envoys." Ask the class to follow along and underline key points.
- Address the remaining four vocabulary words on the pages, namely, *mission, prophets, exile,* and *parable* by having the young people add to their descriptions of the terms listed in the columns on the board.
- Invite volunteers to respond to these questions:
  —Why were the prophets of the Old Testament key figures among all those whom God chose and sent? Prophets were chosen by God to speak in his name.
  —What was the prophet's unique mission? To announce and remind God's people of his saving love at work among them.
- Have the students respond to the question that concludes the text on page 104. The work of the prophets tells us that God has always been involved with his people, calling them to friendship with him.



## Bible Background

**Salvation History** is the history of God working among his people, restoring humanity to friendship with God. This story begins when God promised the Covenant and Salvation to our first parents after the Fall. It includes God's promises to Noah, Abraham, and Moses, and the account of God choosing a special people through whom he would reveal himself and his work. The Israelites were the first people God chose for this mission. The Church is the new People of God whom God has gathered in Jesus Christ, the new and everlasting Covenant.

### The Prophets: God's Envoys

Salvation History contains the stories of both individuals and groups who received a special assignment, or **mission,** from God to help accomplish the divine plan of Salvation. The word *mission* comes from a Latin word meaning "to send."

The **prophets** of the Old Testament were key figures among those whom God chose and sent. A prophet is a person chosen by God to speak in his name. The prophets had the mission to announce and remind God's people of his saving love at work among them. Moses and Jeremiah are examples of such prophets.

#### Moses

Moses was called by God with these words: "Come, now! I will send you to Pharaoh to lead my people, the Israelites, out of Egypt" (Exodus 3:10). Initially, Moses was not sure he could accept this mission and complained to God that he was not up to the challenge. He argued with God and tried to wriggle out of the mission. In the end Moses obeyed God and accepted the unique mission entrusted to him.

#### Jeremiah

Jeremiah was called by God in this way, "To whomever I send you, you shall go; / whatever I command you, you shall speak" (Jeremiah 1:7). Jeremiah was also reluctant to accept the mission God had given him. He insisted that he was too young and did not know what to say. God then touched Jeremiah's mouth and said, "See, I place my words in your mouth!" (Jeremiah 1:9). The Book of Jeremiah shares with us the specifics of Jeremiah's mission.

***What does the work of the prophets tell us about Salvation History?*** Affirm appropriate responses.

Prophet Jeremiah, detail from Sistine Chapel, Vatican City. Michelangelo Buonarroti (1475–1564), Italian painter and sculptor.

104

## Background: Scripture

**Prophets Prepare for the Coming of Christ.** The Old Testament prophets lead us to the Messiah, to Christ. Throughout the days of the Old Testament, the Holy Spirit prepared the people for the time of the Messiah. "So, for this reason, when the Church reads the Old Testament, she searches there for what the Spirit, 'who has spoken through the prophets,' wants to tell us about Christ"[1] (*Catechism of the Catholic Church* 702).

Assyrian royal palace at Nineveh on Tigris River, destroyed in 612 B.C., hand-colored woodcut.

### The Book of Jonah

The Old Testament book that tells about Jonah was probably written in fifth century B.C. It was a time when the Israelites had suffered through periods of **exile**, during which many of them had been uprooted from their homeland and forced to live in Babylon or Assyria. The memory of living in exile, along with the oppression and suffering that accompanied living in exile, was still fresh in the minds of the Israelites. They had become a somewhat separatist and narrow-minded nation. Many of the people, feeling that God's justice and mercy extended only to the chosen people, spurned cultures outside of their own.

The Book of Jonah is a **parable** that addresses this situation. A parable is a story that compares one thing to another and invites the reader or listener to make a decision about how to follow God. For example, Jonah may be a stand-in for the Israelites. Nineveh, the legendary city of Assyria and the traditional enemy of Israel, may represent all the nations whose cruelty and wickedness had oppressed Israel.

The Book of Jonah is a literary masterpiece that contains elements of humor and irony. It is also a cautionary tale with a definite message: God's call for repentance extends to all people as do his justice and mercy.

***How does the Book of Jonah help us understand Salvation History?***

### Did you Know...

The prophet Nahum called Nineveh "the bloody city, all lies, / full of plunder, whose looting never stops!" (Nahum 3:1). It was the last capital of the Assyrian Empire that at one time was a dominant power in the known world. In 612 B.C. the Babylonian army destroyed Nineveh so completely that, by the time the Book of Jonah appeared, the city may have been only mounds of rubble under drifting sands. The site of ancient Nineveh is now part of Mosul, the second largest city in modern Iraq.

### FAITH CONNECTION

***In small groups look up other Old Testament prophets and describe their mission in Salvation History.***

Responses will vary.

Affirm appropriate responses.

105

# Day 1

## Apply

### REINFORCE

- Ask the class to describe the message of the Book of Jonah. God's call for repentance extends to all people, as do his justice and mercy.
- Have the students use all five "Faith Vocabulary" terms to respond to the question that concludes the text on page 105.
- Call the the students' attention to the woodcut of Nineveh and present the "Did you know" feature about Nineveh.

### INTEGRATE

- Ask the young people to form small groups and use their Bibles to work on the "Faith Connection" activity.
- Have the groups share their work with the class.

### PRAY

Ask the young people to quiet themselves and lead the class in praying the Prayer to the Holy Spirit on page 137 of the student text.

## Background: Catholic Tradition

**The Missionary Work of the Church.** In the *Decree on the Church's Missionary Activity (Ad gentes)* promulgated by the Second Vatican Council in 1965, the Church calls upon all those who do missionary work to respect "those elements of truth and grace which are found among peoples, and which are, as it were, a secret presence of God" (*AG* 9). That is why many missionaries today are told that when they bring the Gospel to people for the first time, they should remember that they stand on holy ground, for God is already present there. The missionary's role is to "consolidate, complete, and raise up the truth and the goodness that God has distributed among men and nations" (*CCC* 856).

# Day 2

## Teach

### PRAY

Invite the young people to quiet themselves for prayer and consider God's desire to touch their lives by inviting them into a deeper friendship with him.

### FOCUS

Ask volunteers to share with the class the meanings of the terms listed in "Faith Vocabulary" on page 103. Tell them that in today's lesson they will explore how the story of Jonah the Prophet helps us know about who God invites to Salvation.

### DISCOVER

- Encourage the students to sit in a comfortable position with their books open to pages 106 and 107.
- Present the introductory paragraph. Then read aloud "God's Persistence" and "God's Mercy and Justice."
- Pause throughout the story to reiterate and use the illustrations on the pages to emphasize key points.

## Reading the Word of God

Being chosen by God to be a member of his people is indeed a privilege, but, more than a privilege, it is a responsibility. All God's people have the mission to announce that God invites all people to Salvation. The Old Testament Book of Jonah helps us understand that Revelation.

### God's Persistence

The Book of Jonah begins:

> This is the word of the LORD that came to Jonah, son of Amittai: "Set out for the great city of Nineveh, and preach against it; their wickedness has come up before me." JONAH 1:1–2

This was an unnerving message for Jonah to hear. Jonah hated Nineveh in the east and wanted nothing to do with God's mission. God's call so jarred him that he boarded a ship and headed to the west. We read:

> The LORD, however, hurled a violent wind upon the sea, and in the furious tempest that arose the ship was on the point of breaking up. Then the mariners became frightened and each one cried to his god. . . . Meanwhile, Jonah had gone down into the hold of the ship, and lay there fast asleep. JONAH 1:4–5

While the mariners pleaded to their gods for deliverance, they eventually realized that Jonah was not calling upon his God and that, in fact, he was fleeing from him.

> "What shall we do with you," they asked, "that the sea may quiet down for us?" For the sea was growing more and more turbulent. Jonah said to them, "Pick me up and throw me into the sea, that it may quiet down for you; since I know it is because of me that this violent storm has come upon you." JONAH 1:11–12

Since it was apparent to the mariners that Jonah's God was punishing him, they decided to cooperate with his God and accepted Jonah's suggestion. They threw him overboard, and the raging seas calmed down.

Jonah cast forth by the whale (Jonah 2:11), wood engraving. Gustave Doré (1832–1883), French book illustrator.

106

### Teaching Tip

**Multiple Intelligences.** In the "Catechist Workshop" at the front of this teacher's guide, you learned some of the many ways in which young people learn best. Some students learn best by listening, some by seeing, others by doing. Some are more logical and others more intuitive. Some even learn best when concepts are put to music or rhyme. If you notice that a young person is having trouble grasping a concept, vary your presentation, using a variety of techniques.

# Day 2

## Apply

### REINFORCE

- The story of Jonah presents a wonderful opportunity for dramatic presentation. Assign parts to the class for a melodramatic reading of pages 106 and 107. Characters include Jonah, God, the mariners, the people of Nineveh, the whale, and a narrator who directs the melodrama.
- Encourage the young people to be creative with props as they act out the melodrama.

### INTEGRATE

After the class has presented the drama, discuss the question at the end of page 107.

### PRAY

- Ask the class to pause and reflect on God's desire for them to live in friendship with him. Lead the class in proclaiming Psalm 67:2–3:

  May God be gracious to us and bless us; / may God's face shine upon us. / So shall your rule be known upon the earth, / your saving power among all the nations.
- Conclude by praying the Glory Prayer together.

God, however, was not about to let Jonah drown and thereby escape from his mission. The Book of Jonah tells us that God sent a large fish that swallowed Jonah, who remained in the fish's belly for three days and nights. Jonah prayed soulfully to God, God relented, and the fish spewed Jonah out onto dry ground.

Jonah taking shelter under a tree outside Nineveh, eighteenth-century print. Artist unknown.

#### God's Mercy and Justice

The Book of Jonah continues, telling that God then tried again!

> The word of the LORD came to Jonah a second time: "Set out for the great city of Nineveh, and announce to it the message that I will tell you." So Jonah made ready and went to Nineveh, according to the LORD's bidding. Now Nineveh was an enormously large city; it took three days to go through it. Jonah began his journey through the city, and had gone but a single day's walk announcing, "Forty days more and Nineveh shall be destroyed."
>
> JONAH 3:1–4

Much to Jonah's dismay, the people believed God. Nineveh's king, its people, and even its cattle fasted and were covered in sackcloth and ashes. Seeing their repentance, God chose not to punish the city. Jonah saw what God had done and was so angry at him for sparring Nineveh that he wanted to die.

Jonah then went off into the hills to sulk, and God provided him a shade plant for his comfort. The plant died, and this once again angered Jonah. And God said to Jonah,

> "You are concerned over the plant which cost you no labor and which you did not raise. . . . And should I not be concerned over Nineveh, the great city, in which there are more than a hundred and twenty thousand persons?"
>
> JONAH 4:10–11

***What does this story tell you about the extent of God's forgiveness and his desire for people to live in friendship with him?*** Affirm appropriate responses.

107

### Teaching Tip

**Preparing a Melodrama.** A melodrama is a drama—a play, film, or television program—characterized by exaggerated emotions, stereotypical characters, and interpersonal conflicts. To present the story of Jonah melodramatically, the narrator, as he or she tells the story, is instructing the characters on what to say and what to do "on stage." In other words, the narrator will read what Jonah says, then the character playing Jonah will repeat the dialogue. When the narrator describes a particular action, the character(s) involved actually does the action. It is a fun and interactive way to retell a story, particularly a story with comic undertones and satire.

### *Enriching the Lesson*

The "Writing a Screenplay" activity on page 203 is related to today's content. You may wish to include it in today's lesson.

# Day 3

## Teach

**PRAY**

Begin the lesson by praying the Sign of the Cross and the Our Father together.

**FOCUS**

Recall with the students that the Book of Jonah teaches that God's call for repentance and his invitation to Salvation extend to all people. Explain that in today's lesson they will learn more about the Church as the sign and instrument of Salvation.

**DISCOVER**

- Paraphrase the introductory paragraph, emphasizing our baptismal call to announce to all people the good news of Salvation in Christ.
- Have the young people read "The Missionary Church: Sign and Instrument of Salvation" to discover that as Christ reached out to all so does the Church.

## Apply

**REINFORCE**

Have the students discuss with a partner what the Book of Jonah reveals about how we are to live our Baptism. Invite volunteers to share one idea from their discussion and list these ideas on the board.

**INTEGRATE**

- Have the students work in small groups to complete the "Faith Connection" activity.
- Have the groups share their advertising copy with the class.

## Understanding the Word of God

The Book of Jonah helps us understand that God wishes all people to be saved and to live in communion with him. All people who seek God with a sincere heart and, moved by his grace, follow his will as they understand it may achieve Salvation.

### The Missionary Church: Sign and Instrument of Salvation

God sent Jonah on a mission to people who were so evil in Jonah's eyes that he did not want to go near them. After first refusing God, Jonah begrudgingly gives in, and his mission has unexpected results—all of Nineveh repents.

Recall for a moment the stories of Saint Maximilian Kolbe and Saint Charles Lwanga and the martyrs of Uganda. What do the lives of these saints tell us? Throughout her history, the Church has been sent by the Father and assisted by the Holy Spirit to preach the Gospel of Jesus, even among those whom the world considers the most evil of people.

By her very nature the Church is the sign and instrument of Salvation for all people. As Christ reached out to all, including those who put him to death on the cross, so does the Church.

> All [people] are called to belong to the new People of God. This People therefore, [while] remaining one and only one, is to be spread throughout the whole world and to all ages in order that the design of God's will may be fulfilled: he made human nature one in the beginning and has decreed that all his children who were scattered should be finally gathered together as one.[1]
>
> Vatican II, *Dogmatic Constitution on the Church* [Lumen Gentium] 13

***How does the Book of Jonah help us understand how we are to live our Baptism?***

**FAITH CONNECTION**

***Imagine that the Book of Jonah is to be made into a movie and that you have been hired to promote it. What advertising copy would you write?***

Responses will vary.

Affirm appropriate responses.

108

### Background: Doctrine

**Christ as Prophet.** The word *Christ* comes from the Greek translation of the word *Messiah*, which means "Anointed." Jesus was the Messiah, anointed and consecrated for God's mission. "This was the case for kings, for priests and, in rare instances, for prophets.[1] This had to be the case all the more so for the Messiah whom God would send to inaugurate his kingdom definitively.[2] It was necessary that the Messiah be anointed by the Spirit of the Lord at once as king and priest, and also as prophet.[3] Jesus fulfilled the messianic hope of Israel in his threefold office of priest, prophet, and king" (*Catechism of the Catholic Church* 436).

# OUR CHURCH MAKES A DIFFERENCE

Jesuit volunteers packing food to be given to families in need, Guadalupe Center, Houston, Texas.

The social teachings of the Catholic Church guide the members of the Church in showing the universality of God's saving love in many ways. Living these principles is not always easy and often brings about both misunderstanding of the Church's work among people and suffering for those who implement these principles. Remember Christ's words, "Blessed are they who hunger and thirst for righteousness, / for they will be satisfied" (Matthew 5:6).

### Jesuit Volunteer Corps

The Jesuit Volunteer Corps (JVC) offers women and men an opportunity to work full-time for justice and peace. Jesuit volunteers are called to the mission of serving the poor directly and working for structural change in the United States. They also accompany people in developing countries in places as diverse as the coastal desert of Peru, the Pacific Islands of Micronesia, South Africa, and throughout Belize.

The challenge to Jesuit volunteers is to integrate Christian faith into society by working and living among the poor and marginalized, by living simply and in community with other Jesuit Volunteers, and by examining the causes of social injustice. The Jesuit Volunteer Corps offers the volunteers a year or more of experience that will open their minds and hearts to live always conscious of the poor and committed to the Church's mission of promoting justice in the service of faith.

The Jesuit Volunteer Corps operates within the spiritual Tradition of the Roman Catholic Church, which provides the foundation for JVC's mission and vision. Catholic theology, liturgy, and social teaching give form to the life and prayer of the volunteers. Whether Catholic or of another Christian tradition, volunteers must be open and ready to respond to the Gospel.

***How are the members of the Jesuit Volunteer Corps living signs of God's love for all people? What are other ways the Church fulfills this mission?***

Responses will vary. Affirm appropriate responses.

Jesuit volunteer working with reading group, Good Shepherd School, New Orleans, Louisiana.

109

## Day 3

## Connect

### HIGHLIGHT

Remind the young people that the Church is the sign and instrument of Salvation. Paraphrase the first paragraph on page 109. Emphasize that the social teachings of the Catholic Church guide us in sharing God's love for all people.

### DISCOVER

Invite the young people to read about the Jesuit Volunteer Corps silently.

### INTEGRATE

- Have volunteers use the photo images on page 109 to summarize the mission of the Jesuit Volunteer Corps.
- Ask the group to brainstorm different ways the Church works for people whose needs are ignored or even forgotten by society.

### PRAY

Invite the young people to sit quietly for a minute and reflect on the love God has for them and for all people. Conclude by praying together this or a similar prayer:

> Come, Holy Spirit, / fill our hearts / and the hearts of all people / with the fire of your love. Amen.

### Teaching Tip

**The Values Guiding the Jesuit Volunteer Corps.** The cornerstones of the Jesuit Volunteer Corps are the four values of social justice, simple living, community, and spirituality. Each member of each JVC community, whether located in the United States or elsewhere in the world, focuses on these four values in their lifestyle and their work. The majority of the JVC volunteers are young adults. Encourage the young people to visit JVC's Web site at www.jesuitvolunteers.org to find out more about how these people answer their baptismal call through service. If your parish or community has any JVC volunteers (past or present), invite them to come talk with your students about their experiences.

### *Enriching the Lesson*

The "Choosing a Class Mission" activity on page 203 is related to today's content. You may wish to include it in today's lesson.

# Day 4

## Connect

### PRAY

Ask the young people to take a few moments to center themselves in God's presence and reflect on ways that they are taking part in the mission of Christ and his Church. After a moment of reflection, invite them to thank God for entrusting that work to them.

### FOCUS

Present the introductory paragraph on page 110. Tell the young people that today they will consider their own mission as members of the Church.

### DISCOVER

- Have volunteers read aloud "Taking Part in the Mission of the Church" on pages 110 and 111.
- Number the students in the class 1, 2, and 3. Assign 1s "Pray," 2s "Learn," and 3s "Act." Invite each student to read their assigned section and explore ideas for a specific way to accept and fulfill the call to be a living sign of Christ.
- Have the young people gather in triads so that each triad has a 1, 2, and 3. Have the students in each triad share with each other ways that they can accept and fulfill the call to follow Christ through prayer, learning, and actions.

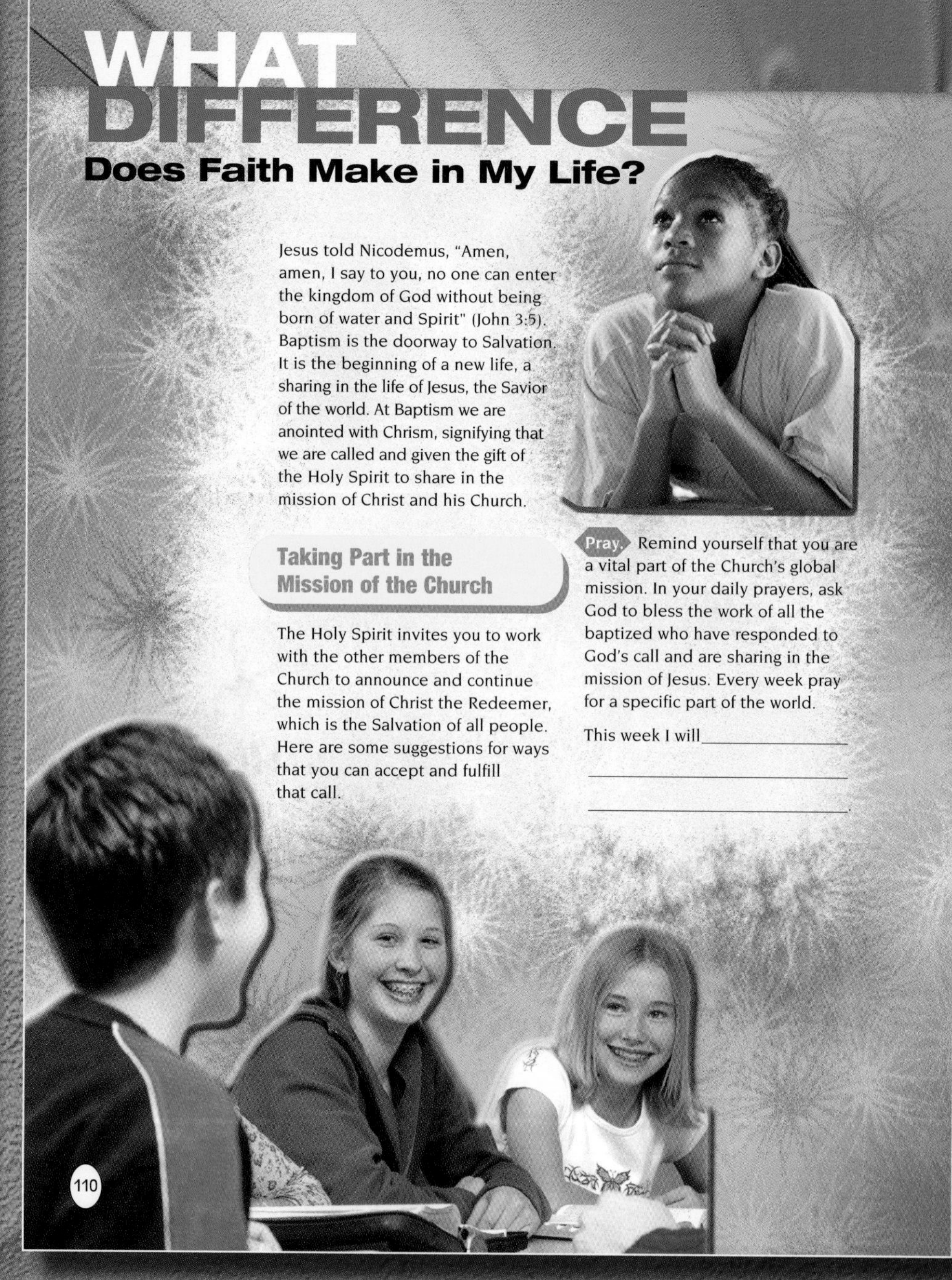


## Background: Doctrine

**The Church's Missionary Mandate.** The Church's missionary mandate is to make all people "share in the communion between the Father and the Son in their Spirit of love"[1] (*Catechism of the Catholic Church* 850). The love of Christ urges the Church on, and God wills that everyone be saved through knowledge of the truth. The Church must go out and bring the truth to people. "Because she believes in God's universal plan of salvation, the Church must be missionary" (*Catechism of the Catholic Church* 851).

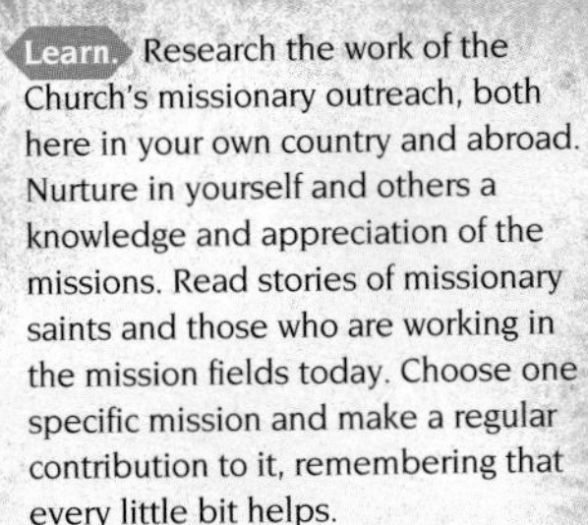

**Learn.** Research the work of the Church's missionary outreach, both here in your own country and abroad. Nurture in yourself and others a knowledge and appreciation of the missions. Read stories of missionary saints and those who are working in the mission fields today. Choose one specific mission and make a regular contribution to it, remembering that every little bit helps.

This week I will________________________

**Act.** Let your life be a witness. Your honesty, decency, kindness, and generosity are a daily witness to your belief in Jesus and help you share in the Church's saving mission. Develop a missionary spirit by finding a project you can perform today. You may choose to assist an elderly neighbor, help your parents, tutor a younger child, or in some way use your time and talent to help another.

This week I will________________________

## Faith Decision

- Quietly reflect on how your Baptism was the beginning of a new life, life in Christ and in his Body, the Church.
- On a piece of paper, write a mission statement for your life. Complete these and similar statements and include them in your mission statement:

*I will use my mouth to . . .* ____________________.

*I will use my hands to . . .* ____________________.

*I will use my talent of* __________ *to . . .* ____________________.

This week I will be a missionary bringing the good news of Salvation in Jesus by

Responses will vary.

Affirm appropriate responses.

111

## Teaching Tip

**Mission Statement Resource.** A great resource for guiding young people in writing their own personal mission statements is the book *The 7 Habits of Highly Effective Teens* by Sean Covey. In particular, Habit #2, "Begin with the end in mind," helps the young person focus on their mission and goals in life.

# Day 4

## Apply

### RESPOND

- Review the activities outlined in the "Faith Decision" feature with the young people.
- Have the young people prayerfully reflect on their Baptism.

### CHOOSE

- Invite the young people to work independently to write their mission statements. Then have them make and write their faith decisions.
- Encourage the young people to put their faith decision into practice this week.

### PRAY

For closing prayer, ask the young people to hold their mission statements in their hands and silently ask the Holy Spirit to guide them in living out their commitment to share the good news of Salvation.

### Enriching the Lesson

The "Praying Around the World" activity on page 203 is related to today's content. You may wish to include it in today's lesson.

# Day 5

## Pray and Review

### FOCUS

Tell the young people that today's prayer is from the Book of Jonah.

### PRAY

- Invite a volunteer to be the prayer leader and assign the two groups.
- Pray "The Prayer of Jonah" together.
- End by offering one another a sign of God's peace.

### REVIEW

- Have the young people share the meaning of the terms in "Faith Vocabulary" and compare their definitions with those in the glossary.
- Use the "Main Ideas" and "Critical Thinking" sections to clarify any questions the students may have concerning what they have learned in the chapter.
- Remind everyone to share and discuss the "Family Discussion" question with their family.

## PRAY and REVIEW

### The Prayer of Jonah

**Leader:** Lord God, you call us to announce to all people the good news of your saving love. Sometimes we resist your call because of our fear. Hear our prayer, as you heard the prayer of Jonah. Give us the courage to respond to you.

**Group 1:** Out of my distress I called to the LORD, / and he answered me; /

**Group 2:** From the midst of the nether world I cried for help, / and you heard my voice.

**All:** **Out of the depths**
**I cry to you, Lord.**

**Group 1:** For you cast me into the deep, into the heart of the sea, / and the flood enveloped me;

**Group 2:** All your breakers and billows passed over me.

**All:** **Out of the depths**
**I cry to you, Lord.**

**Group 1:** When my soul fainted within me, / I remembered the LORD;

**Group 2:** My prayer reached you in your holy temple.

**All:** **Out of the depths**
**I cry to you, Lord.** JONAH 2:3–4, 8

**Leader:** Let us share a sign of peace as a sign of our support of one another to respond to God's call to share in the mission of the Church.

#### FAITH VOCABULARY

Define each of these faith vocabulary terms:

1. Salvation History
2. mission
3. prophet
4. exile
5. parable

#### MAIN IDEAS

Choose either (a) or (b) from each set of items. Write a brief paragraph to answer each of your choices.

1. (a) Describe the role of prophets in Salvation History. p. 104
   (b) Describe the message of the Book of Jonah. p. 105
2. (a) Retell the story of Jonah in your own words. pp. 106–107
   (b) Explain what the Book of Jonah tells about the divine plan of Salvation. p. 107

#### CRITICAL THINKING

Using what you have learned in this chapter, briefly explain this Scripture passage:

"Those who were not my people I will call 'my people,' / and her who was not beloved I will call 'beloved.'" ROMANS 9:25

#### FAMILY DISCUSSION

How can you and your family be living signs of God's love for all people?

For more ideas on ways your family can live your faith, visit the "Faith First for Families" page at **www.FaithFirst.com**. Also check out "Saints" on the Teen Center.

### Evaluate

Take a few moments to evaluate this week's lesson.

I feel (circle one) about this week's lesson.

a. very pleased
b. OK
c. disappointed

The activity the students enjoyed most was . . .

The concept that was most difficult to teach was . . .

because . . .

Something I would like to do differently is . . .

### *Before Moving On . . .*

Reflect on this question before moving on to the next chapter.

*How have I emphasized with the young people that God's love reaches to everyone, even our enemies?*

# ENRICHING THE LESSON

## Writing a Screenplay

**Purpose**

To reinforce the teachings in the Book of Jonah (taught on page 107)

**Directions**

- Form small groups and have them work cooperatively to write a screenplay of the Book of Jonah.
- Be sure they include the various scene descriptions, actions of the characters, and dialogue.
- Invite the groups to present their screenplays to the class.

**Materials**

Bibles, writing paper, pens or pencils

## Choosing a Class Mission

**Purpose**

To reinforce the concept that all the baptized, both individually and as a communion of believers, are called to live out their baptismal call (taught on page 109)

**Directions**

- Start a discussion about how the group can take part in the mission of the Church through prayer, learning, and action.
- Print the headings "Pray," "Learn," and "Act" on each of three pieces of newsprint and post them around the room.
- Have the students rotate around the room writing down ideas for what the class can do together in each of the areas.
- Have a large-group discussion about the ideas on the newsprint and decide on one or two things that the class can do in each area.

**Materials**

newsprint, tape, markers

## Praying Around the World

**Purpose**

To reinforce the concept that praying for people everywhere is an important part of our baptismal commitment (taught on page 111)

**Directions**

- Display a map of the world in the classroom and tell the young people that this is the class's prayer map.
- Choose a part of the world to start with and, using a marker or map flags, label it with the week's dates.
- Tell the students that each week they will pray for people living in a particular part of the world.
- Incorporate a short prayer for the people living in a country or region, in your class's daily prayers.
- The following week, have a student choose another part of the world.
- Continue this over a period of weeks until the class has prayed for people living in every part of the world.

**Materials**

large map of the world
markers or map tacks

### Music Connection

- "All Are Welcome," M. Haugen. *Gather Comprehensive* #741.
- "Bread for the World," B. Farrell. *Glory & Praise* #528.
- "Id y Enseñad/Go and Teach," C. Gabaráin. *Flor y Canto* #703.
- "We Are the Hope," P. Tate. *Voices As One* #97.

Chapter 11

# The Church in the New World

## CHAPTER BACKGROUND

### The Church in the United States

Catholic citizens of the United States are accepted members of society. Catholics have even been president of the United States, Supreme Court justices, and members of both the House of Representatives and the U.S. Senate. Catholics lead large corporations, serve at the highest echelons of the military, preside over major academic institutions, and play major roles in health care and other organizations that make a difference in the lives of people.

### Seventeenth and Eighteenth Centuries

But it was not always so. The early history of the Catholic Church in the United States is a sobering story of religious persecution and bigotry. Many of the earliest settlers of what is today the United States came to the New World to escape religious persecution in their European homelands. But they brought with them many of the prejudices and "old ways" of thinking about and acting toward those of religious faiths different from their own.

In the early days of our country, the first settlers came mostly from Protestant backgrounds, harboring deep suspicions about Catholics and their "papist" loyalties to the bishop of Rome. In many places Catholics were not allowed to practice their faith openly, and even after the Constitution guaranteed that right to all, many generations of Catholics were regarded with suspicion and even hostility by the Protestant majority.

### Nineteenth Century to Present

The massive numbers of immigrants who arrived on our shores in the nineteenth and twentieth centuries numbered a high percentage of Catholics in their ranks. This swelling of a Catholic presence exacerbated the tensions in many places. Riots and cross-burnings that aimed to intimidate Catholic Americans were the more overt expressions of this tension. More quiet but extremely pervasive were the subtler forms of discrimination and prejudice that Catholics encountered in the larger society.

What was it that resulted in the assimilation of Catholics into mainstream American culture and the widespread acceptance of Catholics at every level of our society? No single factor has been more influential than the leadership of a series of strong and vigorous bishops over many generations who were determined to demonstrate to the Protestant majority that Catholics are equal partners in our democracy and fully committed to the ideals of the American social system. These bishops founded Catholic schools that fostered values of public service and commitment to the common good. They also encouraged religious communities that started hospitals, orphanages, and other charitable institutions open to every citizen.

## FOR REFLECTION

***What are the values I have learned as a Catholic that help me to be a productive member of American society?***

***What can I do to enable the young people to grow in the virtue of citizenship?***

## First Thoughts

### Living Signs of Christ

How are you a living sign of Christ to the world? This question may be one on which we do not often reflect. In the day-to-day routine of our lives, it is easy to forget that what we say and do manifests to others what it means to be a Christian. How well do our words and actions point to Christ? This is an important question for us to ask ourselves.

#### My Life, a Gospel?

Someone once said, "You may be the only Gospel someone will ever read." What an amazing and challenging statement. The truth is that our lives have the power to speak loudly and clearly to others. Remind the young people that because of their Baptism their words and actions are meant to have special meaning—they are meant to echo and proclaim the Gospel. What a responsibility and calling. Help the young adolescents in your class see how they point people to Christ by the way they live every day.

### The Church Teaches . . .

The *National Directory for Catechesis* teaches:

> Just as all races, ethnicities, and cultures in the world are represented in the population of the United States, so too do they find a home within the Catholic Church. Each group brings its own language, history, customs, rituals, and traditions "for building up the body of Christ."[1]
>
> *NDC* 11C1, page 29

In this chapter the students will examine the development of the Catholic Church in the United States.

#### See the Catechism . . .

For more on the teachings of the Catholic Church on catechesis, the common good, love for the poor, and the ministry of the bishops, see *Catechism of the Catholic Church* 4–12, 873, 894–896, 1560, 1897–1904, 1905–1912, and 2443–2449.

*Lord Jesus,*
*by the way I live my life*
*every day, I want to be*
*a living sign of you.*
*May your presence*
*fill me and inspire me*
*to a life of service*
*in your name.*
*Amen.*

Footnote references may be found on page 256.

Now . . . turn the page and let's get organized!

# LESSON PLANNER

## Chapter Focus

**To learn how the Catholic Church in the United States has been a sign and instrument of God's saving presence**

| Focus | Process | Materials and Options |
|---|---|---|
| **DAY 1**<br>**Engage/Teach and Apply**<br>**Pages 113–115**<br>**Focus**<br>To discover how the early seeds of faith were sown in the Americas | **Opening Prayer**<br>**Discussion**<br>Who the missionaries were who planted the seeds of faith in the New World<br>**Presentation**<br>Read, discuss, and summarize content.<br>**Scripture:** Acts of the Apostles 1:8<br>**Activity:** In small groups present profiles of missionaries.<br>**Faith Connection:** Research and report on missionaries in the New World. | **Materials**<br>pens or pencils<br>**Options**<br>***Called to Prayer and Liturgical Lessons* booklet:** See options for daily and seasonal prayers and liturgical prayers and lessons. |
| **DAY 2**<br>**Teach and Apply**<br>**Pages 116–117**<br>**Focus**<br>To understand the growth of the Catholic Church in the United States | **Prayer**<br>**Presentation**<br>Read, discuss, and summarize content.<br>**Did you know:** Saint Frances (Mother) Cabrini<br>**Activity:** Describe what moves you to give witness to your faith in Jesus. | **Materials**<br>pens or pencils<br>**Options**<br>**Enriching the Lesson (TG page 217)**<br>Researching Church Statistics<br>***Additional Activities and Assessment Tools* booklet**<br>Word Search: Missionaries in the Americas, page 27 |
| **DAY 3**<br>**Teach/Apply and Connect**<br>**Pages 118–119**<br>**Focus**<br>To explore the work of the Church in the United States during the Vatican II era | **Prayer**<br>**Presentation**<br>Read, discuss, and summarize content.<br>**Activity:** List important features of the Church in the United States during the Second Vatican Council.<br>**Faith Connection:** Research social teachings of the bishops of the Catholic Church in the United States.<br>**Our Church Makes a Difference**<br>The bishops in the United States proclaim the Gospel and guide the faithful to live according to God's law. | **Materials**<br>pens or pencils<br>**Options**<br>**Enriching the Lesson (TG page 217)**<br>Exploring the USCCB<br>***Additional Activities and Assessment Tools* booklet**<br>Collage: The Church in the World Today, page 28 |
| **DAY 4**<br>**Connect and Apply**<br>**Pages 120–121**<br>**Focus**<br>To reflect on how you are the only Gospel some people will ever read | **Prayer**<br>**What Difference Does Faith Make in My Life?**<br>You are a living sign of Christ to those you meet.<br>**Activity:** Commit to living as a sign of Christ.<br>**Faith Decision:** Decide how you will continue to develop the faith qualities of a Christian. | **Materials**<br>pens or pencils<br>**Options**<br>**Enriching the Lesson (TG page 217)**<br>Writing Profiles in Faith |
| **DAY 5**<br>**Pray and Review**<br>**Page 122** | **Pray**<br>Pray "Prayer of Praise and Thanksgiving."<br>**Review**<br>**Activities:** Complete the review exercises to reinforce the concepts of the chapter.<br>**Family Discussion:** Encourage the students to share and discuss the question with their family this week. | **Materials**<br>pens or pencils<br>**Options**<br>***Additional Activities and Assessment Tools* booklet**<br>Administer the chapter 11 test.<br>**Music Connection** (TG page 217) |

**Don't Forget!** You can make lesson planning a breeze—check out the **Online Lesson Planner** at www.FaithFirst.com for additional resources to enhance this chapter.

# The Church in the New World

## FAITH FOCUS

How has the Catholic Church in the United States of America been a sign and instrument of God's saving presence?

## FAITH VOCABULARY

plenary councils

Third Plenary Council of Baltimore

***Who are some of the people who played a vital role in the development of the Americas?***

The history and growth of the Americas can be retold from the life stories of key people. Each country in the Americas has its founders and heroes who have helped their country grow. The story of the growth and expansion of the Catholic Church in the New World is inextricably bound up with the history of the people of the Americas. Knowing that story and the heroes who made it happen helps us grow in our identity as Catholics.

***Describe a person from the history of the Catholic Church in the United States who inspires you.***

*"[Y]ou will be my witnesses in Jerusalem, throughout Judea and Samaria, and to the ends of the earth."*
ACTS OF THE APOSTLES 1:8

113

## National Directory for Catechesis

**Implementing the *National Directory for Catechesis*: Learning Through the Witness of the Catechist.** The National Directory states: "For catechesis to be effective, catechists must be fully committed to Jesus Christ. They must firmly believe in his Gospel and its power to transform lives" (*NDC* 29E, page 101). This chapter presents you with the opportunity to reflect on how you can redouble your efforts to be a living example of God's saving presence in your interaction with students, faculty, and parents.

# Day 1

## Engage

### PRAY

- Invite the young people to quiet themselves for prayer. Pray the Sign of the Cross together.
- Ask the students to reflect for a moment on their experience of the ways their parish lives the Gospel. Then proclaim Acts of the Apostles 1:8 together.

### FAITH FOCUS

Read aloud the "Faith Focus" question and invite the students to think about how they might respond to it. Share that in this chapter they will explore how the Catholic Church in the United States is a witness to God's saving presence in the world.

### DISCOVER

Assess the young people's prior knowledge of the Catholic Church in the Americas.

- Focus the students' attention on the terms in "Faith Vocabulary." Ask if anyone knows what these terms mean.
- Ask the opening question. List some of the people the young people mention on the board.
- Paraphrase or read aloud the paragraph.
- Invite partners to describe to each other one person in the history of the Catholic Church in their country who has inspired them.
- Have volunteers share with the class who they talked about.

# Day 1

## Teach

**FOCUS**

Remind the young people that throughout the history of the Church, missionaries have traveled the world to spread the Gospel. Tell them that on these two pages they will learn about missionaries and other Catholics who played an important part in the growth of the Catholic Church in North America.

**DISCOVER**

- Paraphrase or read aloud the introductory paragraph on page 114.
- Create four groups. Assign one of the four sections on pages 114 and 115 to each group: "Blessed Fray Junípero Sierra," "Saint Isaac Jogues and His Companions," "Lord Baltimore," and "Charles Carroll/John Carroll."
- Have each group read the section assigned to it and create a presentation for the class based on the key points of the text.

## The Gospel in the New World

The early seeds of faith were sown in North America by missionaries from three different national backgrounds and languages, namely, Spanish, French, and English. Spanish missionaries brought the Gospel to our south and southwest. French missionaries evangelized in the north central and northeastern United States, as well as in New France, which would eventually be called Canada. English missionaries operated primarily in the original British colonies.

### Blessed Fray Junípero Serra

The zeal of the early Spanish missionaries is typified in the tireless efforts of Blessed Junípero Serra (1713–84). Father Serra was a Spanish Franciscan priest, explorer, and colonizer of California, where he established and laid the foundation for the California missions.

In 1749 Father Serra responded to the call for Franciscan missionaries to serve in the New World. After several assignments in Mexico, he was sent to present-day California, where he established a series of nine missions along the California coast, each a one-day walk apart (about 30 miles). Biographers estimate that he walked more than 24,000 miles in California alone—more than the journeys of Marco Polo and Lewis and Clark combined. After Father Serra died on August 28, 1784, the 9 missions grew to 21 missions. Today, more than 60 percent of California's total population lives in areas surrounding the missions. Junípero Serra was beatified by Pope John Paul II in September 1988.

### Saint Isaac Jogues and His Companions

The story of Isaac Jogues (1607–1646) and his companions, Rene Goupil and Jean de Brebeuf, is a chronicle of almost incredible courage in the face of hardship and torture. In 1636, at the age of 29, Isaac Jogues joined the Jesuit mission in what was then known as New France. He worked first among the Huron Indians, but in 1642 he was captured by the Mohawks and underwent constant torture. With the assistance of Dutch settlers, he

Junípero Serra with Gaspar de Portola, governor of Las Californias (1768–1770), expedition at San Diego, California, in 1769.



### Teaching Tip

**Map It!** Use a large wall map of North America during your class's study of the Catholic Church in North America. For today's lesson, use the map when you present the introductory paragraph on page 114 and show the students where the missionaries proclaimed the Gospel. Encourage the students to use the map during their group presentations about the growth of the Catholic Church in the New World.

escaped and returned to France where he recuperated for a short time, only to return in 1644 and give his life in martyrdom in 1646. Saint Isaac Jogues and his companions are venerated as the first of the North American Martyrs.

***What roles did Blessed Junípero Serra and Isaac Jogues and his companions play in proclaiming the Gospel in North America?***

### Lord Baltimore

The history of Catholicism in the English colonies began in Maryland. There Lord Baltimore in the early 1600s succeeded in establishing a place where religious tolerance allowed people of every faith to worship according to their conscience. Lord Baltimore's experiment in religious tolerance ended fifty years later, when political upheavals resulted in Catholics once more becoming a persecuted minority in Maryland.

Thanks to the spirit of tolerance in neighboring Pennsylvania, however, Catholics were able to continue practicing their faith, free from persecution for the next 100 years. But it was not until after the Revolutionary War, when the Constitution and the Bill of Rights were enacted, that the principle of universal religious liberty guaranteed Catholics the right to openly practice their faith everywhere in the new nation.

### Charles Carroll, John Carroll

The patriotism that prominent Catholics such as Charles Carroll, one of the signers of the Declaration of Independence, showed at the time of the Revolutionary War helped pave the way for a greater acceptance of Catholics in the new nation. A turning point in the history of the Catholic Church in what is today the United States of America was reached in 1790, when John Carroll, a distant cousin of Charles Carroll, was ordained the first Catholic bishop in the United States. John Carroll expressed his hope for the United States of America, writing:

> If we have the wisdom and temper to preserve, America may come to exhibit a proof to the world, that general and equal [religious] toleration . . . is the most effectual method to bring all denominations of Christians to a unity of faith.

***How did the Catholic Church begin in the English colonies?***

Statue of John Carroll, Georgetown University, Washington, D.C.

### FAITH CONNECTION

***Work with a partner and learn more about the missionaries who first preached the Gospel in the New World. Identify where the missionaries worked and what virtues strengthened them for their work.***

| Missionary | Location of Work | Virtue |
|---|---|---|
| | Responses will vary. | |
| | Affirm appropriate responses. | |

115

# Day 1

## Apply

### REINFORCE

- Invite the four groups to give their presentations to the class.
- After the presentations, facilitate a large-group discussion using the questions on pages 114 and 115 to assess what the students have learned.
- Refer to the images on the pages and summarize the students' responses.

### INTEGRATE

- Have the young people work in pairs to complete the "Faith Connection" activity.
- Ask the pairs to join with another pair and share their work with each other.

### PRAY

- Invite the students to open their Bibles to Acts of the Apostles 1:1–8, place themselves in God's presence, and silently read and reflect on the passage.
- Conclude by leading the class in praying:

  Lord, fulfill your promise. / Send your Holy Spirit to make us witnesses before the world / to the good news proclaimed by Jesus Christ our Lord. / Amen.

  *Roman Missal*, Alternative Opening Prayer, Ritual Masses, Confirmation

## Teaching Tip

**Missionaries Where My Ancestors Settled.** Have the young people share with the class where in the New World their ancestors first settled. Let them use a map as a visual. Some of the students may be from families who are first- or second-generation immigrants to the United States. Invite the young people to join with a partner whose ancestors first settled in the same general area of the New World as their ancestors did to complete the "Faith Connection" activity. Tell them to research a missionary who spread the Gospel in that area of the New World and to discover the roots of Catholicism in that part of the country.

# Day 2

## Teach

### PRAY

Invite the young people to quiet themselves for prayer and lead them in praying:

> Lord, fulfill your promise. / Send your Holy Spirit to make us witnesses before the world / to the good news proclaimed by Jesus Christ our Lord. / Amen.
>
> *Roman Missal*, Alternative Opening Prayer, Ritual Masses, Confirmation

### FOCUS

Invite volunteers to recall the names of some of the first missionaries to the New World. Tell them that on the next two pages they will learn how the Catholic Church in the United States grew during the nineteenth and twentieth centuries.

### DISCOVER

- Ask the young people to recall their study of American history, in particular the history of the state in which they live. Then have the class brainstorm what was happening in the United States or in the state in which they live from around 1800 to the late 1960s.
- Present the introductory paragraph and the first paragraph of "Growth and Development." Then have the class silently read the two sections on page 116.
- Create two columns on the board, labeling one "Saint Elizabeth Seton" and the other "Saint John Neumann." List the class's responses to the question on page 116 under the appropriate saint's name.
- Invite volunteers to read aloud "The Immigrant Church."

Saint Elizabeth Ann Seton (Mother Seton), educator, detail from stained glass.

One hundred and fifty years was to pass between the death of Bishop John Carroll in 1815 and the close of the Second Vatican Council in 1965. During that century and a half, the Catholic Church in the United States of America underwent a remarkable period of growth and development. The growth was paralleled, in many ways, by the dramatic expansion and growth of the United States itself.

#### Growth and Development

On the East Coast, major metropolitan areas such as Boston, New York, and Philadelphia became flourishing centers of Catholicism. In these areas, many of the establishments, including parishes, schools, and hospitals, still remain today and have become signs of the vitality of Catholic life. Two saints, Elizabeth Ann Seton (1774–1821) and John Neumann (1811–60), are examples of the combination of spiritual energy and the spirit of innovation that marked this era.

**Saint Elizabeth Ann Seton**

Elizabeth Ann Bayley Seton was a New York socialite, a devoted wife, and a mother of five. After being widowed, she converted to Catholicism and founded the first new community for religious women in the United States, the Sisters of Charity of Saint Joseph. Saint Elizabeth Ann Seton is the first native-born North American to be canonized. Her life and work have inspired the founding of six religious communities, hundreds of schools, social service centers, and many hospitals.

**Saint John Neumann**

John Neumann emigrated to the United States of America from Bohemia. After his ordination, Father Neumann was assigned to rural New York State where he worked among immigrants from many countries. In 1840 he joined the Redemptorists and served the Church in Maryland, Virginia, Ohio, and Pennsylvania. After he was consecrated bishop of Philadelphia in 1852, he built fifty churches and nearly twice as many schools.

***How did Saint Elizabeth Ann Seton and Saint John Neumann contribute to the growth of the Catholic Church in the United States of America?***

Saint John Neumann, bishop of Philadelphia, from 1852 to 1860, detail from stained glass.

116

FAITH WORDS

### Faith Vocabulary

**Plenary Councils.** The word *plenary* means "complete in every respect" and "fully attended or constituted by all entitled to be present" (*Merriam-Webster's Collegiate Dictionary,* Eleventh Edition). A plenary council of the Church is a council which is fully attended by all qualified members, such as the bishops of a particular country or geographical region. A plenary council cannot be called in the Catholic Church without the approval and authority of the Apostolic See.

### The Immigrant Church

As millions of immigrants flooded into the country from Europe throughout the nineteenth century, Catholicism in the United States of America continued to grow at an extraordinary rate. One of those immigrants, Saint Frances Cabrini (1850–1917), exemplifies how the Catholic Church ministered to the spiritual and corporal needs of these immigrant populations.

Concerned about the rapid growth of the Church and creation of a unified Catholic presence in the United States, the bishops in the United States of America called **plenary councils** in 1852, 1866, and 1884 in Baltimore, Maryland. At the **Third Plenary Council of Baltimore** in 1884, the bishops ordered the use of the *Baltimore Catechism*. The *Baltimore Catechism* was a basic textbook of religious instruction that was used nearly everywhere in the United States, right up until the time of the Second Vatican Council (1962–1965).

In 1908 the Vatican removed the Church in the United States from the supervision of its missionary office, declaring it sufficiently mature to flourish on its own. In the first half of the twentieth century the Catholic Church in the United States continued to grow. This was true not only in numbers, but also in other indices that measure the vitality of a religious organization. For example:

- Vocations to the priesthood and religious life flourished.
- The number of institutions, such as schools and hospitals, continued to grow. Catholics were increasingly taking on important roles in the larger society.
- Interest by Catholics in the spiritual life was also evident in the number of centers of prayer and contemplation and apostolic service.

***What moves you to give witness to your faith in Jesus Christ?***
Affirm appropriate responses.

#### Did you Know...

Frances Cabrini emigrated from Italy to serve as a missionary in the United States. After founding the Missionary Sisters of the Sacred Heart in Italy to work with poor children in hospitals and schools, she moved to the United States in 1889, where she later became a naturalized citizen. Canonized in 1946 by Pope Pius XII, Frances Cabrini is the first citizen of the United States to be named a saint of the Church. She is the patron saint of immigrants and orphans.

Saint Frances Xavier Cabrini (Mother Cabrini), stained glass.

117

# Day 2

## Apply

### REINFORCE

Point out the "Did you know" feature about Mother Cabrini. Use the stained-glass image on page 116 to discuss how the work of Mother Cabrini reflects the work of the Church in the United States.

### INTEGRATE

- Allow the young people quiet time to reflect on the closing question on page 117.
- Incorporate the faith sharing of their reflections into the closing prayer for the lesson.

### PRAY

- Invite the young people to quiet themselves for prayer.
- Have volunteers share their reflections to the closing question.
- End by praying this or a similar prayer:

  Lord, / bless our efforts to give witness / to our faith in you today. / Amen.

## Background: Catholic Tradition

**Catechisms.** The *Catechism of the Catholic Church,* which was published in 1992, "brings to catechesis 'the great tradition of catechisms[1]' " (*General Directory of Catechesis* 130). To help make the *Catechism of the Catholic Church* more accessible Pope Benedict XVI in 2005 approved the publication of the *Compedium of the Catechism of the Catholic Church.* The *Compendium* is a series of 598 questions and answers, presenting "the essential and fundamental elements of the Church's faith" ("Moto Propio" for the *Compendium*).

### Enriching the Lesson

The "Researching Church Statistics" activity on page 217 is related to today's content. You may wish to include it in today's lesson.

# Day 3

## Teach

### PRAY

Invite the young people to quiet themselves for prayer. Begin by praying the Sign of the Cross and the Our Father together.

### FOCUS

Remind the young people that during the last two hundred years, a hallmark of the Catholic Church in the United States has been her tremendous growth. On the next two pages, they will learn about the Catholic Church in our country during the era of Vatican II and about how the bishops in the United States of America shepherd the Church.

### DISCOVER

- Present the introductory paragraph on page 118.
- Have the young people silently read "The U.S. Catholic Church in the Vatican II Era," underlining or highlighting the main ideas.

## Apply

### REINFORCE

Read the question at the end of page 118 and list the students' responses on the board.

### INTEGRATE

Have the students work independently to complete the "Faith Connection" activity.

The involvement and influence of the Catholic Church in the United States at the First Vatican Council (1869–1870) was quite limited. Nearly a century later, at the Second Vatican Council (1962–1965), bishops and theologians from the United States were deeply involved in all of the Council's most important deliberations.

Blessed Pope John XXIII, recording radio and television speech about the upcoming Second Vatican Council, September 11, 1962.

### The U.S. Catholic Church in the Vatican II Era

Nowhere was the American influence stronger or more decisive than in the writing of and deliberation on the *Declaration on Religious Freedom.* An American Jesuit theologian, Father John Courtney Murray, was the principle advisor who helped the bishops at the Council understand and accept a breakthrough vision of religious liberty as an inalienable right that every government must protect.

During the time of the Council, Catholics in the United States were also coming of age politically, as was proven by the 1960 election of a Catholic president, John F. Kennedy, for the very first time in the nation's history. It is hard to appreciate now what a remarkable accomplishment that was in a nation that had harbored many fears and bigoted ideas about Catholics in public life. The bishops of the United States wrote important documents on war and peace and on principles that guide our economic life. Catholic Social Teaching became increasingly respected by religious and civic leaders even outside of the Catholic Church.

***What were some of the important features of the Catholic Church in the United States of America during the Vatican II era?***

Cover of *LIFE* magazine, December 17, 1965, depicting assembly ending Second Vatican Council.

#### FAITH CONNECTION

***Name three things that you can do to learn about the social teachings of the bishops of the Catholic Church in the United States.***

Responses will vary.

Affirm appropriate responses.

118

### Catholic Social Teaching

**Call to Participation in Family and Community.** All people have the obligation and the responsibility to participate in society and to work to promote the common good. As the one People of God, the Church lives the Works of Mercy and promotes the equitable, just, and fair participation of all peoples in community life.

**Tip:** Help your students recognize some of the ways their families are living the Gospel. Point out the different things families do for the community, such as volunteering in school or in the broader community, taking part in the Rice Bowl and Angel Tree projects, helping at a local food bank, or participating in a community clean-up day.

# OUR CHURCH MAKES A DIFFERENCE

The bishops are the successors of the Apostles. At their ordination they share in the fullness of the Sacrament of Holy Orders. They are the visible head and shepherd of the particular Church entrusted to their care. Together with the Pope and under his authority they share in the responsibility and mission Jesus entrusted to the Apostles.

### United States Conference of Catholic Bishops

Bishops throughout the world proclaim the Gospel and remind the people of the Church and society in general of their responsibility to live according to God's law. In the United States of America the bishops do this together through the United States Conference of Catholic Bishops (USCCB). The USCCB is the assembly of bishops of the United States working to guide Catholics who live in this country in understanding the teachings of the Church and in living the Gospel.

The creation of a council of bishops started during World War I. Under the leadership of James Cardinal Gibbons of Baltimore, the National Catholic War Council was formed. This council demonstrated the value of the national collaboration of bishops. Further encouragement arrived from the Pope at that time.

In a 1919 letter Pope Benedict XV urged the U. S. hierarchy to join him in working for peace and social justice. The bishops responded by deciding to meet annually and to set up the National Catholic Welfare Council (later called Conference). Over the years the bishops addressed many national concerns through this organization.

After the close of the Second Vatican Council, the bishops set up two organizations for the Catholic Church in America to continue the work that the bishops began in 1917. In the National Conference of Catholic Bishops (NCCB) they attended to the Church's own affairs in this country in fulfillment of the Vatican Council's mandate that bishops "exercise their pastoral office jointly" (VATICAN II, *Decree on Pastoral Office of the Bishops in the Church*, 38). In the United States Catholic Conference (USCC) the bishops collaborated with other Catholics to address issues that concerned the Church as part of the larger society.

In 2001 the NCCB and the USCC were combined to form a single organization, the United States Conference of Catholic Bishops (USCCB). Today this Conference continues all of the work formerly done by the NCCB and the USCC.

***Pretend you are an advisor to a bishop. What national issues would you want him to address with his fellow bishops?*** Responses will vary. Affirm appropriate responses.

119

## Background: Catholic Tradition

**Work of the Church in the World.** The Church has an obligation and a responsibility to be involved in economic and social matters " 'when the fundamental rights of the person or the salvation of souls requires it.' "[1] The Church is concerned with the common good, and "she strives to inspire right attitudes with respect to earthly goods and in socio-economic relationships" (*Catechism of the Catholic Church* 2420).

# Day 3

## Connect

### HIGHLIGHT

Tell the young people that in the United States of America Catholic bishops work together to carry out their responsibility to proclaim the Gospel.

### DISCOVER

Paraphrase the introductory paragraph and invite volunteers to read aloud "United States Conference of Catholic Bishops."

### INTEGRATE

- Have the class work in small groups to role-play the scenario of serving as advisors to their bishop. Tell the students that they are to decide on three issues they want their bishop to address with his fellow bishops.
- Challenge the young people to explain the importance of their selected issues for the Catholic Church.
- Have each group share the results of its discussion with the class.
- List on the board the issues named by the young people.

### PRAY

Conclude the lesson by asking the students to pause and silently pray for the bishops.

### *Enriching the Lesson*

The "Exploring the USCCB" activity on page 217 is related to today's content. You may wish to include it in today's lesson.

# Day 4

## Connect

### PRAY

Invite the young people to quiet themselves for prayer. Prayerfully proclaim Matthew 5:13–16 to the class.

### FOCUS

Remind the students that the Church is a living Gospel, a living sign of Christ and instrument of Salvation in the United States and throughout the world. Write the sentence "You may be the only Gospel some people will ever read" on the board. Tell the students that today's lesson will explore this statement.

### DISCOVER

- Present the introductory paragraph and the first two paragraphs of "Living with Courage" on page 120.
- Have the students read "A Living Profile of Faith" aloud. Then ask volunteers to provide concrete examples for living each of the twelve characteristics of a person of faith.

Affirm appropriate responses.

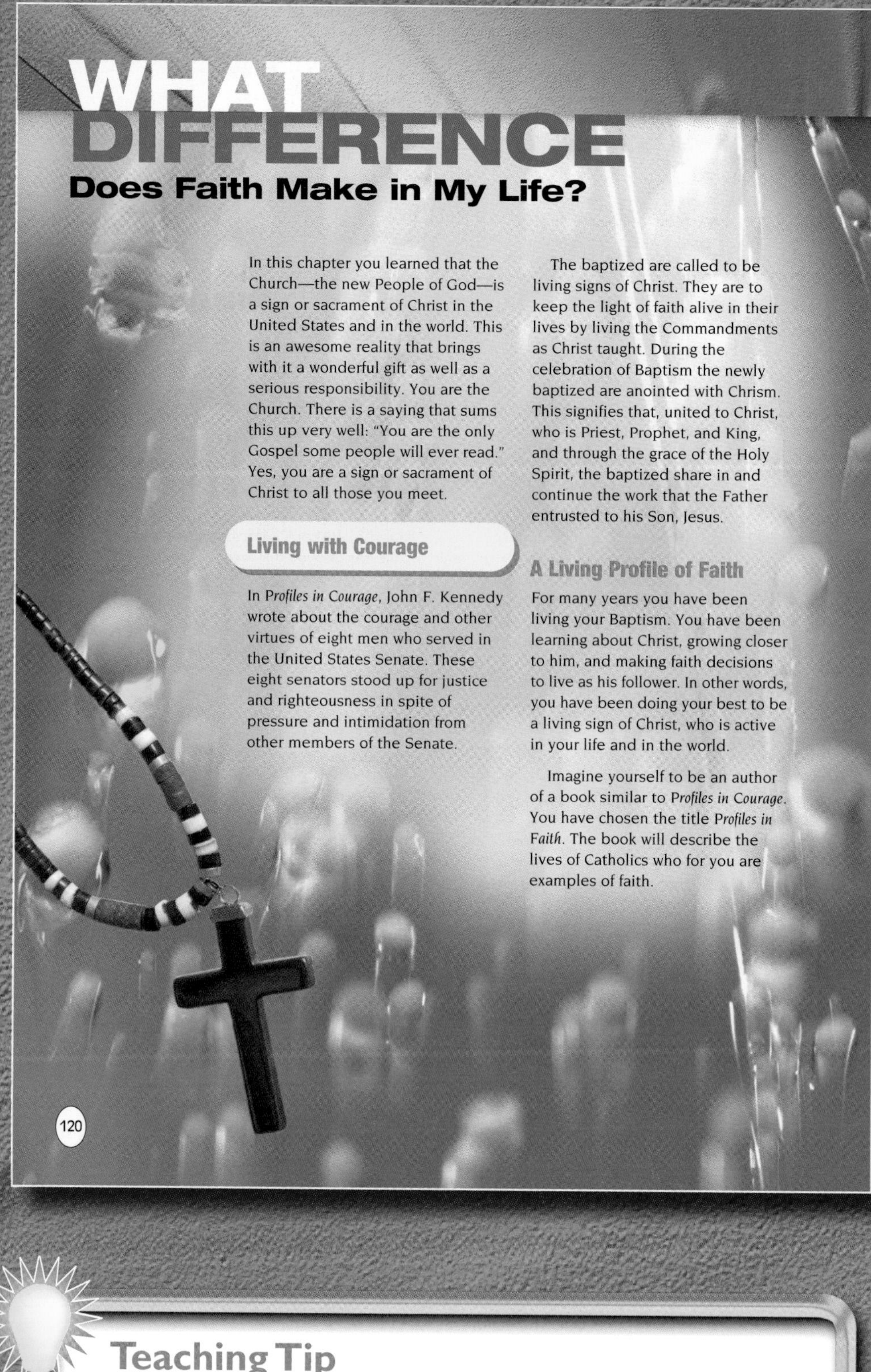

# WHAT DIFFERENCE Does Faith Make in My Life?

In this chapter you learned that the Church—the new People of God—is a sign or sacrament of Christ in the United States and in the world. This is an awesome reality that brings with it a wonderful gift as well as a serious responsibility. You are the Church. There is a saying that sums this up very well: "You are the only Gospel some people will ever read." Yes, you are a sign or sacrament of Christ to all those you meet.

## Living with Courage

In *Profiles in Courage*, John F. Kennedy wrote about the courage and other virtues of eight men who served in the United States Senate. These eight senators stood up for justice and righteousness in spite of pressure and intimidation from other members of the Senate.

The baptized are called to be living signs of Christ. They are to keep the light of faith alive in their lives by living the Commandments as Christ taught. During the celebration of Baptism the newly baptized are anointed with Chrism. This signifies that, united to Christ, who is Priest, Prophet, and King, and through the grace of the Holy Spirit, the baptized share in and continue the work that the Father entrusted to his Son, Jesus.

## A Living Profile of Faith

For many years you have been living your Baptism. You have been learning about Christ, growing closer to him, and making faith decisions to live as his follower. In other words, you have been doing your best to be a living sign of Christ, who is active in your life and in the world.

Imagine yourself to be an author of a book similar to *Profiles in Courage*. You have chosen the title *Profiles in Faith*. The book will describe the lives of Catholics who for you are examples of faith.

120

## Teaching Tip

**Living Signs of Christ.** Encourage the students to value that each of us is a living sign of Christ to the world. Share concrete examples of how, in the classroom, you see them putting the teaching of the Gospel into action. Affirm them for living out their responsibility to be signs of Christ to one another and to you.

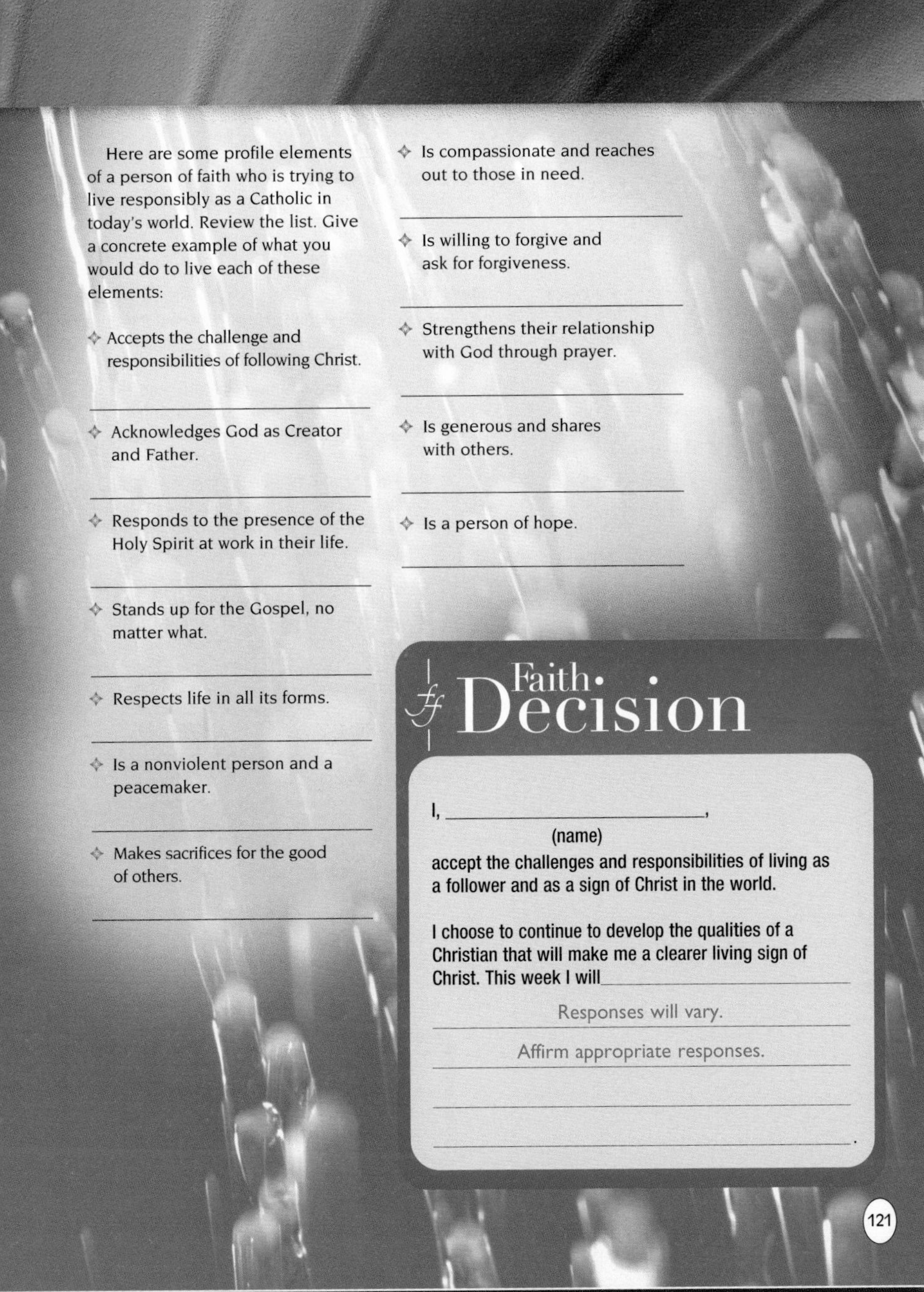

Here are some profile elements of a person of faith who is trying to live responsibly as a Catholic in today's world. Review the list. Give a concrete example of what you would do to live each of these elements:

- Accepts the challenge and responsibilities of following Christ.
- Acknowledges God as Creator and Father.
- Responds to the presence of the Holy Spirit at work in their life.
- Stands up for the Gospel, no matter what.
- Respects life in all its forms.
- Is a nonviolent person and a peacemaker.
- Makes sacrifices for the good of others.
- Is compassionate and reaches out to those in need.
- Is willing to forgive and ask for forgiveness.
- Strengthens their relationship with God through prayer.
- Is generous and shares with others.
- Is a person of hope.

Faith Decision

I, ______________________,
(name)
accept the challenges and responsibilities of living as a follower and as a sign of Christ in the world.

I choose to continue to develop the qualities of a Christian that will make me a clearer living sign of Christ. This week I will______

Responses will vary.

Affirm appropriate responses.

121

# Day 4

## Apply

### RESPOND

- Give the students quiet time to reread the twelve characteristics of a person of faith.
- Have them select a concrete example of how they would live each of the elements and write them on the lines provided in the text.

### CHOOSE

- Have the students complete the "Faith Decision" activity independently.
- Challenge them to be specific and concrete about how they will develop the qualities of a person of faith. Then have them make and write their faith decisions.
- Encourage everyone to put their faith decision into practice this week.

### PRAY

Lead the class in praying a prayer of intercession based on the twelve characteristics of a person of faith that are enumerated on page 121. Conclude by praying together the Prayer to the Holy Spirit on page 137 of the student text.

### Liturgy Tip

**Suggestions for the Closing Prayer.** The characteristics of a person of faith that are enumerated on page 121 are wonderful meditations for your class's closing prayer. As an alternative closing prayer, use the twelve characteristics as a prayer of meditation. Have the young people pause for a moment after each element. Look for other opportunities throughout the year when your class can actually pray what it is learning.

### *Enriching the Lesson*

The "Writing Profiles in Faith" activity on page 217 is related to today's content. You may wish to include it in today's lesson.

# Day 5

## Pray and Review

**FOCUS**

Share that today's prayer is a prayer of praise of God and thanksgiving for his blessings.

**PRAY**

- Have a volunteer be the leader for the prayer.
- Pray the "Prayer of Praise and Thanksgiving" together.

**REVIEW**

- Have the young people share the meaning of the terms in "Faith Vocabulary" and compare their definitions with those in the glossary.
- Use the "Main Ideas" and "Critical Thinking" sections to clarify any questions the students may have concerning what they have learned in the chapter.
- Remind everyone to share and discuss the "Family Discussion" question with their family.

# PRAY and REVIEW

## Prayer of Praise and Thanksgiving

**Leader:** The heavens declare the glory of God, and every creature extols God's goodness. Let us together with praise and thanksgiving call upon God by saying:

**All:** **Glory to you, O Lord, for all your gifts to us.**

**Leader:** Father most generous, in Christ Jesus, your Son, you have given us all things; grant that we may never fail to sing your praises.

**All:** **Glory to you, O Lord, for all your gifts to us.**

**Leader:** You have told your disciples to share what they have with others; grant that our neighbors may share in your gifts to us, so that they may also share in our joy.

**All:** **Glory to you, O Lord, for all your gifts to us.**

**Leader:** Almighty Father, you are lavish in bestowing all your gifts, and we give you thanks for the favors you have given to us. We ask that you continue to protect us and shelter us in the shadow of your wings. We ask this through Christ our Lord.

**All:** **Amen.**

ADAPTED FROM *Book of Blessings*, BLESSING IN THANKSGIVING

122

**FAITH VOCABULARY**

Define each of these faith vocabulary terms:

1. plenary council
2. Third Plenary Council of Baltimore

**MAIN IDEAS**

Choose either (a) or (b) from each set of items. Write a brief paragraph to answer each of your choices.

1. (a) Describe the influence of Blessed Junípero Serra and Saint Isaac Jogues on the growth of the Church in North America. pp. 114–115
   (b) How have Catholics "come of age" in U. S. society in the twentieth century? p. 117
2. (a) Describe the contribution that Saint Elizabeth Ann Seton and Saint John Neumann made to the Church in the United States of America. p. 116
   (b) Write a brief paragraph explaining the special contribution to the Second Vatican Council that was made by Father John Courtney Murray. p. 118

**CRITICAL THINKING**

Using what you have learned in this chapter, briefly explain this statement:

The early seeds of faith were sown in North America by missionaries from three different national backgrounds and languages, namely, Spanish, French, and English.

**FAMILY DISCUSSION**

How does your family keep the flame of faith alive in its life so that it is a living sign of Christ in the community in which you live?

For more ideas on ways your family can live your faith, visit the "Faith First for Families" page at **www.FaithFirst.com**. Also check out the interactive story on the Teen Center.

### Evaluate

Take a few moments to evaluate this week's lesson.

I feel (circle one) about this week's lesson.

a. very pleased
b. OK
c. disappointed

The activity the students enjoyed most was . . .

The concept that was most difficult to teach was . . .

because . . .

Something I would like to do differently is . . .

### *Before Moving On . . .*

Before moving on to the next chapter, reflect on this question.

*How am I a living sign of Christ to the students in my class?*

# ENRICHING THE LESSON

## Researching Church Statistics

**Purpose**

To reinforce the students' learning about the growth of the Catholic Church in the United States of America over the past century (taught on page 117)

**Directions**

- Have interested students do some sociological work by researching the current demographics and membership trends in the Catholic Church in the United States.
- Have the students begin with the local diocese and find out how many Catholics there are presently in the diocese, how many Baptisms there were in the past year, and so on.
- Encourage them to use the Center for Applied Research in the Apostolate, http://cara.georgetown.edu, to gather national statistics and trends.
- Have the young people report back to the class about what they discover.

**Materials**

Internet access, paper, pens or pencils

## Exploring the USCCB

**Purpose**

To learn about the ministries of the United States Conference of Catholic Bishops (taught on page 119)

**Directions**

- Invite volunteers to prepare a report on the work of the United States Conference of Catholic Bishops.
- Emphasize the comprehensive nature of the Conference's ministry.
- Have them explore what kinds of issues the bishops address, what the various departments of the Conference are, and what their ministries involve.
- Point out that they will find the Web site www.usccb.org a helpful resource in gathering their information.
- Have the students report back to the class.

**Materials**

Internet access, paper, pens or pencils

## Writing Profiles in Faith

**Purpose**

To reinforce that the faithful are living signs of Christ to all those they meet (taught on page 121)

**Directions**

- Invite volunteers to label posters, one for each of the twelve characteristics of a person of faith listed on page 121.
- Lay out the posters so that students can add their concrete examples of what they would do to live each of the elements to the posters.
- Give the young people time to move to each of the posters and add their ideas.
- Display the completed posters in the room as a reminder of how we are living signs of Christ.

**Materials**

poster boards, markers

### Music Connection

- "Danos un Corazón," J. Espinosa. *Flor y Canto* #686.
- "Gathered As One," P. Tate and D. Light. *Voices As One (VAO)* #25.
- "I Will Choose Christ," E. Bolduc. *Gather Comprehensive* #683.
- "Rain Down," E. Bolduc. *VAO* #76.

# Chapter 12 The Second Vatican Council . . . and Beyond

## Chapter Background

### The Church in the Modern World

On December 4, 1962, Leon-Joseph Cardinal Suenens (1904–1996), archbishop of Malines-Brussels, Belgium, addressed the members of the Second Vatican Council. He raised the question of how the Church viewed herself in relation to the modern world. On December 5 and 6, Giovanni Battista Cardinal Montini (1897–1978), later Pope Paul VI, and Giacomo Cardinal Lercaro (1891–1976), archbishop of Bologna, Italy, raised similar concerns. The Second Vatican Council's response to these concerns is found in the *Pastoral Constitution on the Church in the Modern World* (also known by its Latin title, *Gaudium et Spes*), which the Council promulgated three years later on December 7, 1965.

#### Daily Responsibilities of the Followers of Christ

Through this document the Church encourages the People of God to "be aware of and understand the aspirations, the yearnings, and the often dramatic features of the world in which we live" (4). This accent on the responsibilities of the Church to respond to the "ever recurring questions which [people] ask about the meaning of this present life and of the life to come, and how one is related to the other" (4) carries over into the Church's relationship with other Christian Churches. The Constitution warmly advises that, whenever it is appropriate, Catholics should join with other Christians in distributing and collecting aid to benefit those in need. (See 88.)

The Council teaches that the life of faith is not separate and cannot be separated from the daily responsibilities of the followers of Christ. "The Christian[s] who shirk [their] temporal duties shirk [their] duties towards [their] neighbor, neglect God himself, and endanger their eternal salvation" (43).

#### Living the Gospel in the World

In the *Pastoral Constitution on the Church in the Modern World*, the Council gives the People of God a vision and direction for living the Gospel in the world. This vision clearly focuses on the attainment of the spiritual mission of the Church and warns against the misdirection of the past that identified the Church too closely with the political order.

In this document the Church teaches: "[T]here are close links between the things of earth and those things in [the human] condition which transcend the world, and the Church utilizes temporal realities as often as its mission requires it. But it never places its hopes in any privileges accorded to it by civil authority . . . With loyalty to the Gospel in the fulfillment of its mission in the world, the Church . . . consolidates peace among [peoples] for the glory of God" (76).

### For Reflection

***How can I be faithful to the mission of the Church in the world in which I live?***

***What can I do to help the young people assume their daily responsibilities to live the faith?***

## First Thoughts

### History Gives us Hope

The chapters in this book have emphasized the difference that faith makes in our lives. The gift of faith enables us to see and appreciate history with a sense of hope for the future. Through faith we can understand that Jesus calls us to take responsibility for re-creating the earth and preparing the way for the coming of the Kingdom of God.

#### This Moment

The absence of faith in a person's life can lead them to say that the state of the world allows for little reason to be hopeful about its future. Seeing historical events with the eyes of faith strengthens our hope and motivates us to live the commandment of love taught by Jesus: "[L]ove one another. As I have loved you, so you also should love one another. This is how all will know that you are my disciples, if you have love for one another" (John 13:34–35). Remind the young people that God is with them, at this moment, loving them, guiding them, and helping them bring the Gospel of Jesus Christ to the world.

### The Church Teaches . . .

The *Pastoral Constitution on the Church in the Modern World (Gaudium et Spes)* teaches:

> At all times the Church carries the responsibility of reading the signs of the time and of interpreting them in the light of the Gospel, if it is to carry out its task.
>
> *Gaudium et Spes* 4

In this chapter the students will examine the importance of the Second Vatican Council and how the Catholic Church is an effective sign of Jesus' presence in the world today.

#### See the Catechism . . .

For more on the teachings of the Catholic Church on the unity and renewal of the Church, charisms, and Catholic social teaching, see *Catechism of the Catholic Church* 670–671, 798–800, 820–821, 827, 1428, 1928–42, 2003, 2425–26, and 2832.

*God of hope and history, help me see your presence at this moment in time. Help me participate in bringing about your kingdom. Amen.*

Now . . . turn the page and let's get organized!

# LESSON PLANNER

**Chapter Focus**
**To learn about the importance of the Second Vatican Council**

| Focus | Process | Materials and Options |
|---|---|---|
| **DAY 1**<br>**Engage/Teach and Apply**<br>**Pages 123–125**<br>**Focus**<br>To explore Blessed Pope John XXIII's call for an ecumenical council | **Opening Prayer**<br>**Discussion**<br>How the Church is a sign of Christ in every age and culture<br>**Presentation**<br>Read, discuss, and summarize content.<br>**Scripture:** Isaiah 34:1<br>**Did you know:** *aggiornamento*<br>**Activity:** Discuss the four goals of the Second Vatican Council.<br>**Faith Connection:** Describe how young Catholics can implement the goals of the Second Vatican Council. | **Materials**<br>pens or pencils<br>**Options**<br>***Called to Prayer and Liturgical Lessons* booklet:** See options for daily, seasonal, and liturgical prayer and lessons.<br>**Enriching the Lesson (TG page 231)**<br>Researching the Second Vatican Council |
| **DAY 2**<br>**Teach and Apply**<br>**Pages 126–127**<br>**Focus**<br>To examine the work and documents of the Second Vatican Council | **Prayer**<br>**Presentation**<br>Read, discuss, and summarize content.<br>**Activity**<br>Create a mind map for the Second Vatican Council.<br>**Did you know:** Communion of Saints | **Materials**<br>pens or pencils<br>**Options**<br>**Enriching the Lesson (TG page 231)**<br>Preparing a Homily |
| **DAY 3**<br>**Teach/Apply and Connect**<br>**Pages 128–129**<br>**Focus**<br>To discover the Catholic Church's efforts to work for the unity of all Christians | **Prayer**<br>**Presentation**<br>Read, discuss, and summarize content.<br>**Activity:** Discuss the role of the *Catechism of the Catholic Church* in your faith formation.<br>**Faith Connection:** Discuss ways to promote understanding and dialogue with other Christian churches.<br>**Our Church Makes a Difference**<br>Learn about the contributions of the Church's Catholic Social Teaching. | **Materials**<br>pens or pencils<br>**Options**<br>**Enriching the Lesson (TG page 231)**<br>Looking Through the Eyes of the Church<br>***Activities and Assessment Tools* booklet:** Scavenger Hunt: The Second Vatican Council, page 29 |
| **DAY 4**<br>**Connect and Apply**<br>**Pages 130–131**<br>**Focus**<br>To explore how you are a part of the Church's continuing history | **Prayer**<br>**What Difference Does Faith Make in My Life?**<br>Identify the virtues that help you keep the flame of faith alive.<br>**Activity:** Write down virtues you want strengthened in yourself.<br>**Faith Decision:** Decide what you will do to make a difference. | **Materials**<br>slips of paper<br>pens or pencils<br>**Options**<br>***Activities and Assessment Tools* booklet:** Prayer Card: Keeping God at the Center of Our Life, page 30 |
| **DAY 5**<br>**Pray and Review**<br>**Page 132** | **Pray**<br>Pray together "Prayer of Blessed Pope John XXIII."<br>**Review**<br>**Activities:** Complete the review exercises to reinforce the concepts of the chapter.<br>**Family Discussion:** Encourage the students to share and discuss the question with their family this week. | **Materials**<br>pens and pencils<br>**Options**<br>***Activities and Assessment Tools* booklet:** Administer the chapter 12 test. Plan for the unit 2 review.<br>**Music Connection** (TG page 231) |

**Don't Forget!** You can make lesson planning a breeze—check out the **Online Lesson Planner** at www.FaithFirst.com for additional resources to enhance this chapter.

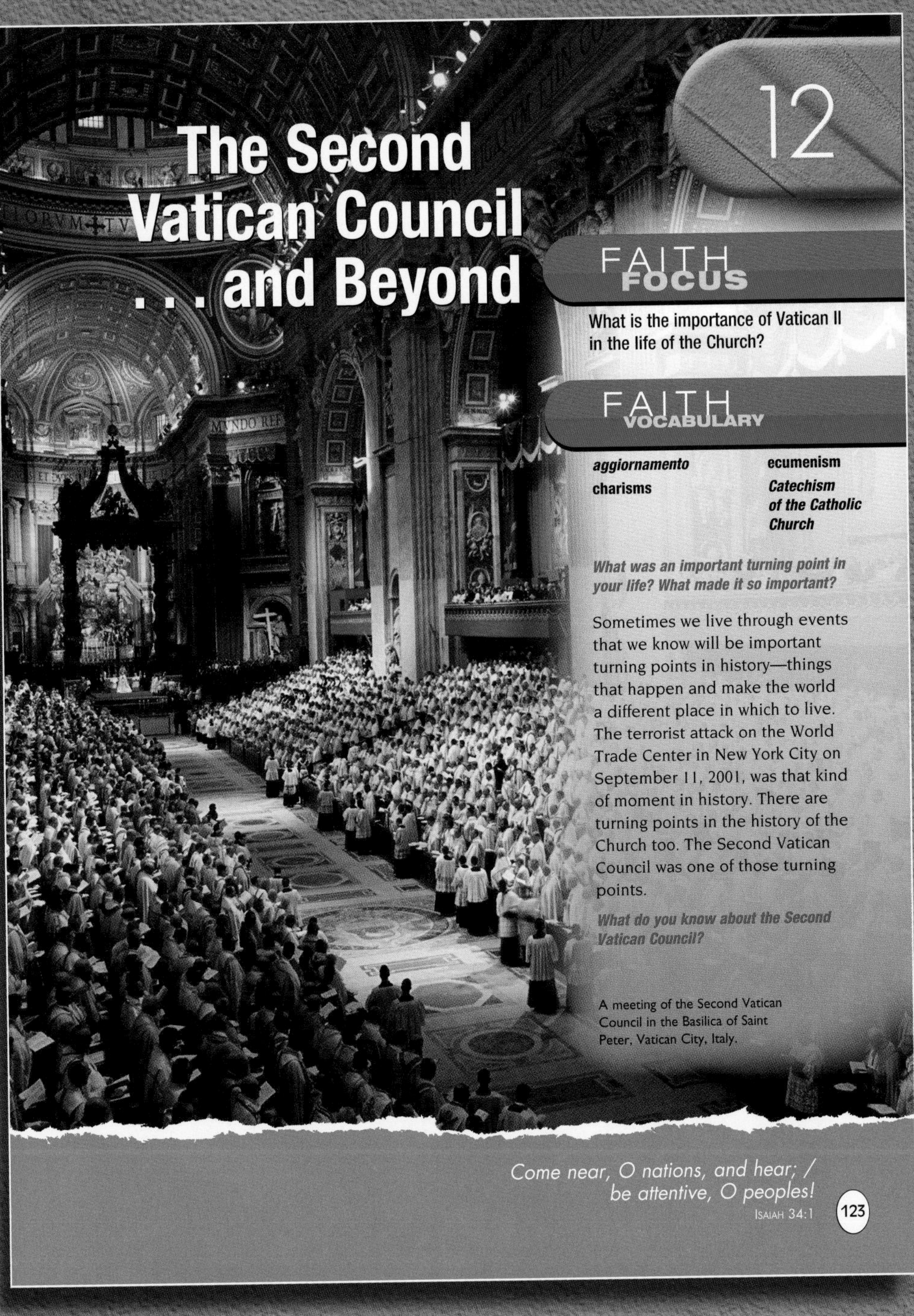


## National Directory for Catechesis

**Implementing the *National Directory for Catechesis*: Learning Through Human Experience.** The National Directory teaches that human experiences are the "means through which human beings come to know themselves, one another, and God" (*NDC* 29A, page 97). To help the students better understand the Catholic Church's work for unity among all Christians, invite the pastor or a member of your diocese's ecumenical ministry to visit with the students and discuss the ecumenical ministry of the Church in your area. You might also work with a staff person of a neighboring non-Catholic Christian Church to plan a community service project the youth may do together to make a difference in your community.

# Day 1

## Engage

### PRAY

Invite the young people to quiet themselves for prayer. Lead the group in praying the Sign of the Cross. Proclaim Isaiah 34:1 together.

### FAITH FOCUS

Read aloud and invite brief responses to the "Faith Focus" question. Call the students' attention to the image on page 123 and share with the class that in this chapter they will learn about the Second Vatican Council and its importance in the history of the Church.

### DISCOVER

Assess the young people's prior knowledge and understanding of the Second Vatican Council.

- Write the "Faith Vocabulary" terms on the board. Ask the young people to share what they already know about the meanings of the terms. Write key words or phrases from their responses next to the appropriate term on the board.
- Ask the opening question. Let the students respond. Share an appropriate turning point in your life.
- Share with the class a summary of the introductory paragraph aloud.
- Ask volunteers to tell what they know about the Second Vatican Council.

# Day 1

## Teach

**FOCUS**

Remind the students that the Church exists to be a living sign of Christ in the world. Tell them that on these two pages they will explore how the Church is a living sign of Christ in every age and culture.

**DISCOVER**

- Ask the students to name ways that the Church acts as a sign of the love and unity of God revealed by Christ. After they respond, invite a volunteer to read aloud the introductory paragraph.
- Invite a volunteer to read the opening paragraph of "The Second Vatican Council" aloud. Pause throughout to emphasize key points, particularly emphasizing the Catholic Church's responsibility to apply the Gospel in every age and in every society.
- Have students silently read "Announcement," "Preparations," and "The Four Sessions" to learn more about the Second Vatican Council.

## A Sign of God's Love

The Church exists to be a sign of Christ's presence to people in every age and culture. She acts like a sign of God's love to all humanity. Like a giant neon marquee, she must be visible for all to see. How, then, does the Church act as a sign of God's love and unity? The Church does so by acting like Christ in a concrete way to the men and women of every age, race, and social condition. Just as Christ was visible and active among the people of his age, the Church does the same and is an effective sign that makes Jesus come alive today.

### The Second Vatican Council

Not quite a century would pass after the close of the First Vatican Council (1870) before Blessed Pope John XXIII (1958–1963) called the twenty-first and latest ecumenical council of the Church, the Second Vatican Council, or Vatican II. The period between the two councils was packed with numerous developments that significantly affected the life of the Church and the world. The challenge of making the Christian message meaningful to the secular, industrialized, and technological world of the twentieth century was something of which the Church became more and more aware.

#### Announcement

On January 25, 1959, just three months after having been elected, Pope John XXIII announced to a small group of cardinals gathered in Rome that he had decided to call an ecumenical (universal) council of the Church. His announcement stunned not only the cardinals present but eventually the entire religious world. Everyone had expected that the early actions of the elderly Pope would be minor and transitional in nature.

#### Preparations

In calling for an ecumenical council of the Church, Pope John said that one of its primary purposes was ***aggiornamento***, that is, bringing the Church up to date. He consulted bishops throughout the world about what they thought the agenda of the

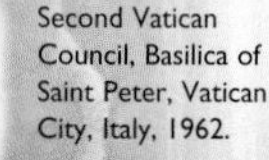

Second Vatican Council, Basilica of Saint Peter, Vatican City, Italy, 1962.



### Teaching Tip

**Second Vatican Council Resources.** *The Faithful Revolution: Vatican II* is a five-tape video series produced by RCL that documents the Council. Set against a dramatic backdrop of world events, *The Faithful Revolution* documents the Council, its decisions, and its profound impact on all of humanity through the eyes of many men and women who took part in and experienced firsthand the Council and the changes in Church life stimulated by the Council. *Vatican II in Plain English* is a three-book series that provides an overview of the Council (Book 1) and paraphrases the documents of the Council in engaging sense lines (Books 2 and 3).

Blessed Pope John XXIII.

council should include. The pilgrim Church was on the verge of another major renewal.

### The Four Sessions

The actual work of the Second Vatican Council took place over a period of four years, beginning with Blessed Pope John XXIII in 1962 and ending with Pope Paul IV in 1965. During this time there were working sessions held in the fall of each of the four years that the Council was held.

The Council's work, as specified by Pope John XXIII, was primarily to address the pastoral renewal of the Church. He repeatedly urged Catholics to pray that the Council would be a "new Pentecost." He hoped the Council would foster the internal reform and renewal of the Church as well as the unity of all Christians.

When Pope John died in the summer between the first and second sessions of the Council, many thought the Council would die with him. However, his successor, Pope Paul VI, proved to be a staunch promoter of the vision of John XXIII and the work of the Second Vatican Council. The new Pope immediately announced his intention to continue the work of the Council.

In his opening address at the second session, Pope Paul VI listed four goals that he saw for the Council:

- Deepen people's understanding of the nature of the Church, especially the collaboration between the bishops and the Pope.
- Promote reform of the Church, especially in the Church's liturgy.
- Foster the cause of Christian unity.
- Enter into dialogue with the modern world.

The sessions of the Second Vatican Council under his leadership worked diligently to provide the direction for the Church to achieve these goals.

***How did the goals for the Second Vatican Council named by Pope Paul VI reinforce the goal of aggiornamento set by Pope John XXIII?*** Affirm appropriate responses.

## Did you Know...

By using the Italian word *aggiornamento*, which means "bringing up to date," to describe the work of Vatican II, Blessed Pope John XXIII renewed and deepened our understanding of the Church's relationship to the world. He said that the Church must "open the windows" and let in the fresh air of renewal if it is to preach the Gospel effectively to the men and women of the modern world.

## FAITH CONNECTION

***Work in small groups to describe one way young Catholics can work at implementing the goals of the Second Vatican Council.***

Responses will vary.

Affirm appropriate responses.

125

## Teaching Tip

***Destination Vatican II.*** Make available the CD-ROM *Destination Vatican II* for class use during your presentation of this chapter. This CD-ROM is an interactive exploration of the Second Vatican Council. The CD-ROM contains the sixteen documents of the Council; presents the Council in historical perspective with an interactive timeline, video clips, and archival photographs of the Council and its legacy; and offers many other interactive features. *Destination Vatican II* was produced by and is available from RCL.

# Day 1

## Apply

### REINFORCE

- Have a volunteer read "Did you know." Invite another student to explain why "opening the window" is a good image for the goals of the Second Vatican Council.
- Discuss the question at the end of page 125, drawing the correlation between *aggiornamento* and the four goals of the Council.

### INTEGRATE

- Divide the class into four groups.
- Assign each group one of the four goals of the Second Vatican Council and have them complete the "Faith Connection" activity.
- Have the groups report back to the class on the ways Catholic teens can work at implementing the goals of the Second Vatican Council.

### PRAY

Ask the young people to quiet themselves for prayer. Lead the class in praying:

> God our Father, / may the Catholic Church be the sign of our salvation, / and may it reveal for us the mystery of your love, and may that love become effective in our lives. / Amen.

From "Opening Prayer, Mass for the Universal Church A" *Roman Missal.*

### *Enriching the Lesson*

The "Researching the Second Vatican Council" activity on page 231 is related to today's content. You may wish to include it in today's lesson.

# Day 2

## Teach

**PRAY**

Invite the young people to quiet themselves for prayer. Recall with the students the Church's vocation to announce the Gospel by words and deeds. Pray the Prayer to the Holy Spirit on page 137 together.

**FOCUS**

Invite volunteers to remind the class about the four goals of the Second Vatican Council. Share that in the next two pages the students will look more closely at the work of the Second Vatican Council.

**DISCOVER**

- Ask the class if they think that all of the bishops gathered for the Council agreed with each other on everything all the time.
- After listening to their responses, paraphrase the introductory paragraph on page 126.
- Have the students silently read "The Documents of the Second Vatican Council" on pages 126 and 127. Encourage them to highlight the key points.

Soon after the opening of the Council it became clear that there were many differences of opinion among the bishops. Nonetheless, the climate of dialogue and debate that characterized Vatican II was extraordinarily invigorating. The results of this dialogue and debate were formulated in the sixteen documents promulgated by the Council.

### The Documents of the Second Vatican Council

Among the documents of the Council, four major documents, called Constitutions, were promulgated, or officially adopted. These were the *Constitution on the Sacred Liturgy* [Sacrosanctum Concilium], the *Dogmatic Constitution on the Church* [Lumen Gentium], the *Dogmatic Constitution on Divine Revelation* [Dei Verbum], and the *Pastoral Constitution on the Church in the Modern World* [Gaudium et Spes.] In addition, the Council approved twelve other documents, namely, nine Decrees and three Declarations.

#### Dogmatic Constitution on the Church

The *Dogmatic Constitution on the Church* is also called "Lumen Gentium," which is Latin for "Light of the Nations," the opening words of the document. In this Constitution the bishops gathered at the Council taught that the work of the Church is the responsibility of all the baptized—laypeople, the ordained, and members of the consecrated life. All the baptized are to be witnesses for Christ.

The Holy Spirit generously distributes **charisms** to all the baptized. A charism is "a specific gift or grace of the Holy Spirit which directly or indirectly benefits the Church, given in order to help a person live out the Christian life, or to serve the common good in building up the Church" ("Glossary," *Catechism of the Catholic Church*).

By cooperating with the Holy Spirit and using our own gifts we contribute in our unique way to build up the Church on earth and prepare for the coming of the Kingdom of God at the end of time when Christ's and the Church's mission will be completed. It is in

126

## Background: Catholic Tradition

**Naming of Church Documents.** In many cases, the official name of council documents, papal documents, and other forms of Catholic Church teaching are derived from the first two or three words of the original Latin text. For instance, the various documents from the Second Vatican Council are referred to in this country by an English title and a Latin title: *The Dogmatic Constitution on Divine Revelation* is also called *Dei Verbum*, the Latin title, which means "The Word of God."

# Did you Know...

The Church is the Communion of Saints. "We believe in the communion of all the faithful of Christ, those who are pilgrims on earth, the dead who are being purified, and the blessed in heaven, all together forming one Church" (Pope Paul VI, *Credo of the People of God* 40).

family homes, in workplaces, in schools, and on the streets that the Church must let its light shine. How can the world see Christ if it does not see him in those who bear his name? How can the Church be an instrument and effective sign of God's love if the members of the Church do not act charitably wherever they are each and every day?

### Constitution on Divine Revelation

Vatican Council II taught that:

> Access to sacred Scripture ought to be open wide to the Christian faithful. . . . "Ignorance of the Scriptures is ignorance of Christ."
>
> Vatican II, *Dogmatic Constitution on Divine Revelation* [Dei Verbum] 22, 25

While the reforms of the Council of Trent did not result in any marked increase in the laity's reading and study of Sacred Scripture, the reforms of the Second Vatican Council did.

Scripture is the truth that God "for the sake of our salvation, wished to see confided to the sacred Scriptures" (*Dogmatic Constitution on Divine Revelation* 11). The Bible is to be read prayerfully and carefully, and with the intent to search out "the meaning which the sacred writers really had in mind" (*Dogmatic Constitution on Divine Revelation* 12). We do this by studying the language and types of writing the human authors of the Bible used to get their inspired message across to their readers. We can better understand the meaning of the Scripture when we read it, study it, and pray over it with the Church.

***How do the* Dogmatic Constitution on the Church *and the* Constitution on Divine Revelation *guide you in living your Baptism?***
Affirm appropriate responses.

127

## Teaching Tip

**Mind Map.** Mind maps are a great way to review, summarize, and assess learning. The mind map you create with the class in this lesson will have many words and phrases that the young people can further define by connecting other words and phrases to them. Challenge them to keep going with the activity until they have exhausted all the possibilities for connections to the Second Vatican Council based on what they have learned to this point in the chapter.

# Day 2

## Apply

### REINFORCE

- Write *Second Vatican Council* on the board.
- Create a mind map with the students by asking them to brainstorm everything that they can remember about the Second Vatican Council.
- Write their words and phrases around *Second Vatican Council.* Expand the mind map by having the young people add to the words you put on the board.
- Let the students use their texts so that they can make the mind map as comprehensive as possible.

### INTEGRATE

- Paraphrase the "Did you know" feature about the Communion of Saints.
- Ask the young people to reflect on what is portrayed in the photos on pages 126 and 127. Then invite the young people to share how the *Dogmatic Constitution on the Church* and the *Constitution on Divine Revelation* help them live their Baptism.
- Conclude by reviewing "Basic Principles of the Church's Teaching on Social Justice" on page 143 in the student text.

### PRAY

Invite the young people to reflect on their efforts to learn about and live the Catholic faith. Conclude by praying together the Apostles' Creed.

### Enriching the Lesson

The "Preparing a Homily " activity on page 231 is related to today's content. You may wish to include it in today's lesson.

# Day 3

## Teach

**PRAY**

Call the young people to prayer. After a moment of quiet prayer, proclaim John 17:20–21.

**FOCUS**

Remind the young people about the lack of unity within the Church that has arisen as a result of the East-West Schism and the Protestant Reformation. Tell them that on these two pages they will learn about efforts of the Catholic Church to bring about the unity of all Christians to which the Church is called by the Holy Spirit.

**DISCOVER**

- Summarize the introductory paragraph highlighting that working for the unity of the whole Church is a goal of the Catholic Church.
- Present "Ecumenism," then have a volunteer read aloud "Synod of Bishops and *Catechism of the Catholic Church*."

## Apply

**REINFORCE**

- Discuss the importance of all Christians to dialogue and work together.
- Ask the students to describe the role that the *Catechism of the Catholic Church* plays in their faith formation.

**INTEGRATE**

Invite partners to discuss and respond to the "Faith Connection" activity and share their ideas with the class.

One of the hallmarks of the twentieth century was the beginning of the ecumenical movement. This is the effort to bring about unity among all Christians. At the Second Vatican Council efforts were initiated to work more diligently at healing the divisions within the Church.

Pope Benedict XVI greeting Metropolitan Chrisostomos, representing Christian Orthodox Church at meeting of ecumenical leaders at the Vatican.

### Ecumenism

**Ecumenism** is the dedicated work of restoring "unity among all Christians, the unity which is a gift of Christ and to which the Church is called by the Holy Spirit. For the Catholic Church, the Decree on Ecumenism of the Second Vatican Council provides a charter for ecumenical efforts" (Glossary, *Catechism of the Catholic Church*). Considerable ecumenical progress is unfolding now and will continue to unfold in the centuries to come.

### Synod of Bishops and *Catechism of the Catholic Church*

Pope John Paul II convoked, or called together, the 1985 Synod of Bishops on the twentieth anniversary of the Second Vatican Council. One of the responsibilities of a synod of bishops is the study and promotion of the teachings of the Second Vatican Council. To achieve this goal the bishops at the 1985 Synod recommended that a new catechism of the teachings of the Catholic Church be developed. The work of developing the new catechism began in 1986 and concluded in 1992 with the publication of the ***Catechism of the Catholic Church***. The *Catechism of the Catholic Church* is divided into four parts. It systematically presents the teachings of the spiritual heritage of the faith of the Catholic Church.

***What role does the Catechism of the Catholic Church play in your faith formation?*** Affirm appropriate responses.

**FAITH CONNECTION**

***What can you do to promote understanding and dialogue with other churches?***

Responses will vary.

Affirm appropriate responses.

128

### Background: Liturgy

**Unity of the Church.** Each year the Church celebrates a week of prayer for Christian unity, beginning on January 18 and concluding on January 25, the Feast of the Conversion of Saint Paul. Your class can prepare a prayer service for Christian unity, perhaps one in which the whole school can participate.

# OUR CHURCH MAKES A DIFFERENCE

The work of the Second Vatican Council and its goal of entering into dialogue with the contemporary world is historic and decisive. The Church continues to critique both the positive and the negative elements of our modern world in light of the Gospel. The overall relationship between the Church and the world is changing dramatically and irreversibly from that of previous generations. There is simply no question about the goodness of God's creation and the role of the Church in promoting human development.

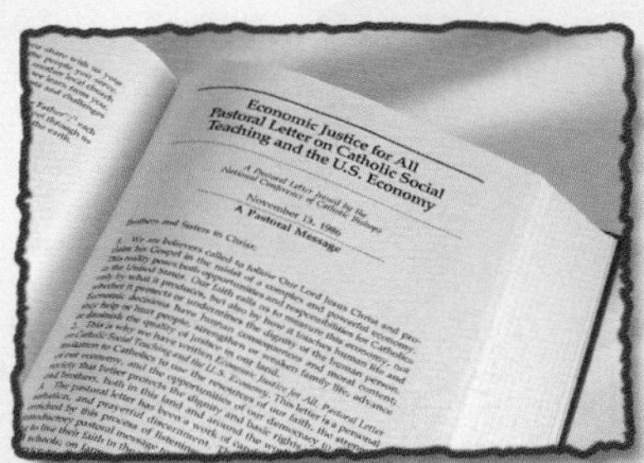

### Catholic Social Teaching after the Second Vatican Council

In the decades since the Second Vatican Council, the Catholic Church has worked at engaging the world. One way she has done this is through a body of official social teachings written both by Popes and bishops. These teachings apply the Gospel to the changing situations of contemporary life.

Especially under Pope Paul VI and Pope John Paul II, the Church has led the way in opening up the dialogue between the Church and various sectors of contemporary society. In his work promoting the Great Jubilee opening the third millennium, Pope John Paul II made explicit efforts to continue to deepen the dialogue between the Church and the entire human family.

The bishops of the Catholic Church in the United States of America are prominent among the world's bishops in promoting social justice. They have written important pastoral letters that both proclaim Gospel values and guide Catholics in integrating these values into their personal lives and the life of the nation. These pastoral letters include *The Challenge of Peace: God's Promise and Our Response* (1983) and *Economic Justice for All: Catholic Social Teaching and the U.S. Economy* (1986).

***What are some of the important social issues the world faces today? How can the Church guide you in dealing with those issues in an appropriate way?***
Affirm appropriate responses.

129

## Teaching Tip

**Pray the News.** Praying is one essential way we can take part in building and preparing for the coming of the Kingdom announced by Jesus. A group of Carmelite sisters in Indiana make it their life's work to pray the news. They have a Web site, www.praythenews.com, where they offer a prayer for something currently happening in the world that needs our prayers. Encourage your students to develop the daily habit of praying the news. This is one sure way that everyone can take part in the work of the Church.

# Day 3

## Connect

### HIGHLIGHT

Share the significance the Second Vatican Council placed on addressing contemporary issues facing the world in light of the Gospel. Tell the students that the Catholic Church continues to promote the goodness of God's creation and human development.

### DISCOVER

- Have the young people silently read "Catholic Social Teaching after the Second Vatican Council."
- Share that the Catholic Church stands for the human rights of all people regardless of race, gender, religion, or culture.

### INTEGRATE

Facilitate a large-group discussion using the questions at the end of page 129 as your guide.

### PRAY

Invite the young people to quiet themselves for prayer. Proclaim John 17: 20–23. Then together pray:

Almighty and eternal God, / Father of all, / make us one in fullness of faith / and keep us one in fellowship of love. / Amen.

From "Opening Prayer," "Mass for Unity of Christians," *Roman Missal.*

### Enriching the Lesson

The "Looking Through the Eyes of the Church" activity on page 231 is related to today's content. You may wish to include it in today's lesson.

# Day 4

## Connect

**PRAY**

Invite the young people to pause and pray the Our Father together to open the class.

**FOCUS**

Present the introductory paragraph and share with the students that the history of the Church on earth continues. Point out that they are a part of that continuing history.

**DISCOVER**

- Read aloud "Continuing the Story of the Church" on pages 130 and 131 to the class as a meditation. (See the Teaching Tip below.)
- Have the students form small groups and do the first section of "Faith Decision." Ask the groups to discuss what they have learned about the history of the Church and how what they learned will help them be more active and responsible members of the Church.

# WHAT DIFFERENCE

## Does Faith Make in My Life?

This year we have explored the history of the Catholic Church. We have discovered some of the key events, issues, and people who have shaped the Church as we know it today. But the history of the Church on earth continues and will continue until the work of Christ is completed, when he comes again in glory at the end of time. You are part of that continuing history.

### Continuing the Story of the Church

We study the history of the Church to learn about our roots and to recognize that the work of the Holy Spirit has always been present within our Church. We take from the past that which will help us continue to know, love, and serve God and his people today. The 2,000-year history of the Church, beginning with the first Pentecost, tells us where we have been. The struggles, challenges, reforms, accomplishments, joys, and sorrows of the new People of God throughout history make up the heritage of the Church today.

You are a member of the Church of today. The virtues and qualities that our Catholic ancestors needed in order to keep their faith alive, especially in times of great conflict, are the same virtues you need today. You are living in a world where certain teachings, values, and beliefs stand in contradiction to the Gospel and the teachings of the Catholic Church. This may at times make it difficult for you to practice your faith. You need to ask yourself: What will help me continue to face and overcome the challenges to keeping the flame of faith alive in my life each day?

### Past and Present

You may have heard the expression "Carpe diem," which means "Seize the day." You may also have heard the expression "Live today as if it were the first day of the rest of your life." A few of the virtues that will help you keep the flame of faith alive in your life are wisdom, courage, and perseverance.

#### Wisdom

Wisdom is one of the seven Gifts of the Holy Spirit. Wisdom helps you see the world through the eyes of faith, to see the world as God sees it. Ask, How can I grow in wisdom?

130

### Teaching Tip

**Meditation for Today.** Read the text on pages 130 and 131 in advance so that you will know where you want to put emphasis and where you will pause to allow the young people time for reflection. This text is motivational and challenging and calls young people beyond themselves. Read it with the passionate conviction that young people today can make a difference in our world. They do not easily forget inspirational moments such as this, if you put your heart into what you are telling them.

#### Courage

Courage, or fortitude, is also one of the seven Gifts of the Holy Spirit. You need courage to really live your faith. Courage is the moral and mental strength to choose what is right. It strengthens you to live the Gospel and the faith of the Church, even when doing so is unpopular or causes you ridicule. Ask, How can I overcome fears and risk living my life as a follower of Christ, no matter what the cost?

#### Perseverance

Perseverance is a moral virtue, or habit, of making choices to live as a child of God. Perseverance flows from the virtues of courage and faith. It is the steadfast persistence in your commitment to be a follower of Jesus Christ. It is having the courage, in spite of pressure or obstacles, to keep your eye on your ultimate goal—eternal life and happiness with God. Ask, What obstacles to living the Gospel do I regularly face that demand perseverance?

### Future

It has been said that young people make up 50 percent of our population and 100 percent of our future. You are part of the Church now and part of the Church of the future. You make a difference in the life of the Church. So believe and trust and hope in God, who dwells within you. Believe in yourself and your God-given gifts and strengths. Believe that you are a messenger of hope and love in the world.

## Faith Decision

- In a small group discuss something each member of the group has learned about the history of the Church. Describe how what you have learned will help you be a more active and responsible member of the Church today.
- Think about faith, wisdom, courage, and perseverance. Reflect on your life and name which of these virtues are already strong within you. Give examples. Which do you need to strengthen?

As an important member of the Church of today and tomorrow, I believe I can make a difference. I will begin by

Responses will vary.

Affirm appropriate responses.

131

## Teaching Tip

**Affirm the Students' Growth in Faith.** Take the time to recall and celebrate the efforts of the students. Ask them to share some of the important key faith concepts they learned and list them on the board. Remind the students of the good prayer habits they have been forming and encourage them to continue those habits.

# Day 4

## Apply

### RESPOND

- Tell the groups to complete the second part of "Faith Decision." Have them spend several minutes quietly considering the virtues of faith, wisdom, courage, and perseverance.
- Ask them to reflect on and discuss the place of these virtues in their life and to identify which virtues they need to strengthen.
- Have them write the virtues they have identified on a slip of paper and fold it.
- Collect the papers to use in the closing prayer for today's lesson.

### CHOOSE

- Have the young people complete the last section of "Faith Decision" independently.
- Encourage the young people to put their faith decision into practice this week.

### PRAY

Lead the class in a prayer in which they ask God for his blessings on one another. Have them echo this or a similar prayer after you:

> May almighty God bless us. / May he strengthen our faith / with proofs of his love, / so that we will persevere in good works. / May he show us how to walk in charity and peace. / Amen.

BASED ON "SOLEMN BLESSINGS, ORDINARY TIME III," *ROMAN MISSAL*

# Day 5

## Pray and Review

**FOCUS**

Share that the prayer today invokes the Holy Spirit to join us on our journey of faith.

**PRAY**

- Assign a volunteer to be the reader. Give the class time to silently read the prayer in preparation.
- Pray "Prayer of Blessed Pope John XXIII" together.

**REVIEW**

- Have the young people share the meaning of the terms in "Faith Vocabulary" and compare their definitions with those in the glossary.
- Use the "Main Ideas" and the "Critical Thinking" sections to clarify any questions the students may have concerning what they have learned in the chapter.
- Remind everyone to share and discuss the "Family Discussion" question with their family.

# PRAY and REVIEW

## Prayer of Blessed Pope John XXIII

**Leader:** Come, Holy Spirit,
Advocate and Teacher,
open our minds and hearts
to hear and live the Gospel.

**Reader:** A reading from the Acts of the Apostles.
*Proclaim Acts of the Apostles 2:1–4.*
The word of the Lord.

**All:** **Thanks be to God.**

**Leader:** Let us all pray together the prayer that Blessed Pope John XXIII gave to us in his opening address to the Second Vatican Council:

**All:** **Renew your wonders in our time,
as though for a new Pentecost,
and grant that the holy Church,
preserving unanimous and continuous prayer,
together with Mary the Mother of Jesus,
and also under the guidance of Saint Peter,
may increase the reign of the Divine Savior,
the reign of truth and justice,
the reign of love and peace.
Amen.**

132

### FAITH VOCABULARY

Define each of these faith vocabulary terms:

1. *aggiornamento*
2. charisms
3. ecumenism
4. *Catechism of the Catholic Church*

### MAIN IDEAS

Choose either (a) or (b) from each set of items. Write a brief paragraph to answer each of your choices.

1. (a) Describe the goals of the Second Vatican Council. pp. 124–125
   (b) Discuss the work of the Church as described in the *Dogmatic Constitution on the Church*. pp. 126–127
2. (a) Explain the importance of all Christians working for the unity of the Church. p. 128
   (b) Describe how the *Catechism of the Catholic Church* guides Catholics in understanding, celebrating, and living their faith. p. 128

### CRITICAL THINKING

Using what you have learned in this chapter, briefly explain this statement:

The Church brings the light of Christ to the people of all nations.

### FAMILY DISCUSSION

How are we as a family making the light of Christ visible to our neighbors?

For more ideas on ways your family can live your faith, visit the "Faith First for Families" page at **www.FaithFirst.com**. Also check out "Make a Difference" on the Teen Center.

## Evaluate

Take a few moments to evaluate this week's lesson.

I feel (circle one) about this week's lesson.

a. very pleased
b. OK
c. disappointed

The activity the students enjoyed most was . . .

The concept that was most difficult to teach was . . .

because . . .

Something I would like to do differently is . . .

### *Looking Back . . .*

As you finish today's lesson, reflect on the following question.

*How clear a sign of Christ am I at this moment in my life?*

# ENRICHING THE LESSON

## Researching the Second Vatican Council

**Purpose**

To reinforce the importance of the Second Vatican Council in the history of the Church (taught on pages 124–128)

**Directions**

- Invite students to do some further research on the Second Vatican Council to discover why the Council is one of the most significant religious events of the twentieth century.
- Suggest that the students research information on the Internet, in reference books, or by talking to people who remember the events of the Council.
- Have the students interview older Catholics who were young adults or older during the 1960s. Have them ask these people to describe how the teachings of the Council affected life in their parish.
- Be sure to have the students share what they find out with the class.

**Materials**

paper, pens or pencils

## Preparing a Homily

**Purpose**

To reinforce the importance of reading the Scriptures (taught on page 127)

**Directions**

Share that two ways we learn about the Scriptures are by hearing the Word of God proclaimed at Mass and by listening to the Sunday homily.

- Invite the pastor or parish deacon to visit the class and explain the process they use in preparing a homily.
- Perhaps they can show the students some of the resources that they use to help in researching and writing their homilies.
- Have the students write their own brief reflections on the Gospel for the upcoming Sunday.

**Materials**

paper, pens or pencils

## Looking Through the Eyes of the Church

**Purpose**

To reinforce that the Catholic Church helps us understand contemporary issues in light of the Gospel (taught on page 129)

**Directions**

- Distribute art paper to the students.
- Have each student draw a large magnifying glass on their paper. Tell them to think of this magnifying glass as the Church.
- Have them illustrate in the magnifying glass various issues in the world today that they are better able to see or understand because they view it through the eyes of the Church.
- Invite volunteers to share their illustrations with the class.

**Materials**

art paper, markers, scissors

### Music Connection

- "Bring Forth the Kingdom," M. Haugen. *Gather Comprehensive (GC)* #640.
- "Gather Your People," B. Hurd. *GC* #742.
- "Great One in Three," P. Tate and P. Berrell. *Voices As One* #30.
- "Somos el Cuerpo de Cristo/We Are the Body of Christ," J. Cortez. *Flor y Canto* #576.

# Catholic Social Teaching

## How Can We Help?

Mr. and Mrs. Salvatore did not know what to do. At the beginning of every year they designated a certain amount of their income for charities. There were some charities they always included and once in awhile there were new ones. But lately the phone had been ringing off the hook and the mailbox was filled with requests from organizations for donations to deal with natural disaster relief, a major outbreak of famine in Africa, as well as all other issues that were perpetually present.

"I wish we could help," Mrs. Salvatore sighed one night to her husband as she got off the phone with another solicitor. "But we just don't have enough money to send everybody something!"

At that point the Salvatore children, Ginny and Jack, came in from the kitchen. "We have an idea!" they blurted out.

"We probably should be helping out," Ginny started, "since we're part of this family, too."

Jack interrupted, "So we've decided that we're going to buy chickens for a family or maybe even a goat!"

Ginny continued, "We were talking at school about how we have to stand in someone else's shoes to know what their lives are like, and then figure out how we can help. Our teachers were telling us about how you can buy chickens and other animals to give to families living in poverty. The families who receive the gift learn the skills to raise the animals. They then share both the offspring of their animals and the skills they learned to raise the animals with other families who, in turn, do the same with other families."

"Maybe we have enough money to buy a flock of chickens for a family on the other side of the world, and maybe it will help that family survive!" Jack exclaimed.

"Yeah, and we'll think of some other stuff we can do to help, too!" added Ginny.

### Solidarity of the Human Family

We all live on the same planet. We are all members of one body of people in this world. Christians always look for ways to use the blessings God has given them to build a better world for all people.

# Making Connections . . .

Catholics have the responsibility to help people secure the things all people need to satisfy basic human needs. When we walk in another's shoes, we realize the great responsibility we have to reach out to the human family.

## WITH SCIENCE

Distribute the handout on page 235. Identify the kinds of animals that can best help families in need and state the reasons. Use information from Heifer International (www.heifer.org) to find out what kinds of animals are sent to help families around the world. Choose four of the animals and research the food the animals will provide and other ways the animals can help families.



## WITH LANGUAGE ARTS

Become a pen pal with a young person your age who lives in another part of the world. With your teacher or another adult, investigate how to find a pen pal. Write your pen pal an introductory letter telling him or her about yourself. Continue the correspondence to stay connected to your global friend.

## WITH SOCIAL STUDIES

Use a globe or world map, recent newspapers, magazines, or the Internet, to research the various areas of the world that have significant needs at this time. Identify the issues and ways the global community is working to address the needs. Report what you find out to your class.

### Faith Action

***Learn about a global need or issue, and decide on a simple way you can respond. Put your decision into action.***

# LESSON PLAN

## Teach

**PRAY**

Place a globe or map of the world in the classroom prayer area. Invite the young people to quiet themselves for prayer, and listen and reflect as you read aloud Psalm 96. Ask the class to join with you and pray for the needs of people around the globe.

**FOCUS**

Invite a volunteer to read aloud the Catholic Social Teaching principle feature, "Solidarity of the Human Family," on the student "Catholic Social Teaching" handout page.

**ENGAGE**

Ask the young people to tell about what countries and parts of the world they have heard about in the news whose people are suffering from the need for food, medicine, or some other basic need. List the parts of the world on the board where the young people have heard that great need exists.

**DISCOVER**

- Point out and read aloud the title of the story on the student page. Ask how many of the young people have heard someone ask that question, or have asked it themselves.
- Then invite volunteers to read the story aloud. Explain that the children Jack and Ginny in the story are talking about participating in the "Passing on the Gift" program of Heifer International. (For more information go to www.heifer.org.)

## Apply

**REINFORCE**

Let the young people tell what they know about some of the needs mentioned in the story.

**INTEGRATE**

Ask the students to read the activities silently. Invite and answer any questions. Then have the young people choose the activity they wish to work on.

- **Science:** Distribute the handout on page 235. Be sure to have the students report what they find out to the class.
- **Language Arts:** Help the young people establish pen pal relationships with young people around the world by guiding them to the appropriate resources. Encourage them to share about their pen pals with one another.
- **Social Studies:** Invite students to research where there are significant issues and needs around the world and have them report to the class what they find out.

**CHOOSE**

Invite a volunteer to read aloud "Faith Action" on the handout on page 233 of this guide. Encourage the students to make an effort to raise their own awareness of global issues and needs.

**PRAY**

Repeat the opening prayer.

## Catholic Social Teaching

**Solidarity and the Common Growth of Humanity.** Chapter 4 of the *Compendium of the Social Doctrine of the Church (CSDC)* teaches: "The term 'solidarity,' widely used by the Magisterium,[1] expresses in summary fashion the need to recognize in the composite ties that unite men and social groups among themselves. . . . *The principal of solidarity requires that men and women of our day cultivate a greater awareness that they are debtors of the society of which they have become part.* They are debtors because of those conditions that make human existence livable, and because of the indivisible and indispensable legacy constituted by culture, scientific and technical knowledge, material and immaterial goods and by all that the human condition has produced" (*CSDC* 194, 195).

# Provide an Animal for a Family

Choose four animals. Fill out the information requested on the chart to find out if they would be good resources to send to a family in need. Write your conclusions on the lines below.

| Type of Animal | How will this animal help a family? | How much will it cost? |
|---|---|---|
| | | |
| | | |
| | | |
| | | |

______________________________________________

______________________________________________

______________________________________________

______________________________________________

______________________________________________

______________________________________________

# Unit 2 Review

These review pages provide the opportunity to assess the young people's understanding of the key faith concepts presented in the unit and to affirm them in their growing knowledge of and living their faith in God.

Here are a few general suggestions that will help you integrate the review pages into your time with the young people.

- Emphasize that these pages are an opportunity to stop and review what they have learned.
- Provide time for the class to ask questions.
- Be sensitive to the special learning needs of some of your learners as you proceed.

**PART A:**
**The Best Response**

This section reviews the main faith concepts of the unit. Explain to the students that if they can eliminate the obviously wrong response or responses, then the correct response is more easily recognized. By working together on the first question, you are teaching them a strategy for answering these types of questions.

## UNIT TWO REVIEW

### A. The Best Response

Read each statement and circle the best answer.

1. What is the name for the sixteenth-century event that resulted in disunity in the Church?
   A. Great Western Schism
   B. Council of Trent
   (C.) Protestant Reformation
   D. Catholic Counter-Reformation

2. Who is the saint who is called the Apostle to India and Japan?
   (A.) Francis Xavier
   B. Martin de Porres
   C. Juan Diego
   D. Charles Lwanga

3. To which saint did the Blessed Virgin Mary appear in 1531?
   A. Francis Xavier
   B. Martin de Porres
   (C.) Juan Diego
   D. Charles Lwanga

4. Who was the Jesuit missionary martyred in 1646 in North America?
   A. John Carroll
   (B.) Isaac Jogues
   C. Junípero Serra
   D. John Neumann

5. Which Pope called the Second Vatican Council?
   A. Pius IX
   (B.) Blessed John XXIII
   C. Paul VI
   D. John Paul II

133

### Teaching Tip

**Affirmation of Good Effort.** Assessment is a time of affirmation. Be sure to point out to the young people their many efforts of living the faith that they have been learning. Encourage them to look for the many opportunities that arise each day to learn about the faith of the Church and to come to know Jesus more and more. Encourage everyone to pray to the Holy Spirit for guidance and zeal to live the Gospel and make a difference.

# UNIT TWO REVIEW

**B. Matching Words and Phrases**

Match the terms in column A with the descriptions in column B.

| Column A | Column B |
|---|---|
| d 1. Protestant Reformation | a. a power given by the Holy Spirit for the benefit of the Church |
| j 2. Catholic Counter-Reformation | b. the nineteenth-century council that taught about the nature of the Church |
| g 3. Great Western Schism | c. the twentieth-century council that was a global gathering of two thousand bishops |
| f 4. Council of Trent | d. the sixteenth-century event that divided the Church in the West |
| c 5. Second Vatican Council | e. a saint honored as a special protector or intercessor |
| a 6. charism | f. the sixteenth-century council that emphasized the Church's authority to interpret authentically the meaning of God's word |
| i 7. canonization | g. the period when no less than three bishops claimed to be Pope |
| e 8. patron saint | h. a dedicated search to bring all Christians into unity |
| b 9. First Vatican Council | i. a solemn declaration by the Pope that a person can be venerated as a saint |
| h 10. ecumenism | j. the sixteenth-century event that spiritually, institutionally, and intellectually renewed the Church |

**C. What I Have Learned**

Using what you learned in unit 2, write a two-sentence reflection about each of these statements.

1. The Church would not exist without the Holy Spirit.

Affirm appropriate responses.

2. As a member of the Church you are a living sign of Christ in the world.

Affirm appropriate responses.

**D. From a Scripture Story**

On a separate sheet of paper do the following.

Describe the descent of the Holy Spirit at Pentecost. Tell how he influences your life today.

134

## Teaching Tip

**Good Job.** Use this final review to deepen the young people's sense of accomplishment this year. Share how much they have learned, and what a difference they have made for your life of faith. Take time to remind them that Jesus spent many years in Nazareth as a teenager and young adult with Mary and Joseph and the people of their synagogue and village learning the teachings, prayers, and practices of the Jewish religion. Encourage the young people to pray each day during the summer that they might come to know and love Jesus more and more.

**PART B:**
**Matching Words and Phrases**

This section reinforces the unit vocabulary.

- After the young people have completed the activity, have them compare their responses with the definition of the terms in the glossary.
- Have the group revisit the faith vocabulary words on page 72 and place a check next to the new faith words they have learned.

**PART C:**
**What I Have Learned**

This section provides the young people with the opportunity to write or talk about what they have learned.

- Have the young people write their reflections for each statement. Then ask volunteers to share their responses with the group.
- Invite the students to turn to page 72 of their text and review the questions they wrote. Help the young people with unanswered questions.

**PART D:**
**From a Scripture Story**

This section is a review of one of the unit Scripture chapters.

- Have the young people work with a partner to complete the activity.
- Invite volunteers to share their responses with the whole group.

**FAMILY CONNECTION**

Encourage the students to share the unit 2 review pages with their family. This provides an excellent opportunity to involve the families in the faith formation of their children.

# Catholic Prayers and Practices

## Sign of the Cross

In the name of the Father,
and of the Son,
and of the Holy Spirit. Amen.

## Signum Crucis

In nómine Patris,
et Filii,
et Spíritu Sancti. Amen.

## Glory Prayer

Glory to the Father,
and to the Son,
and to the Holy Spirit:
as it was in the beginning, is now,
and will be for ever. Amen.

## Gloria Patri

Glória Patri
et Filio
et Spirítui Sancto.
Sicut erat in princípio,
et nunc et semper
et in sæcula sæculórum. Amen.

## Lord's Prayer

Our Father, who art in heaven,
hallowed be thy name;
thy kingdom come;
thy will be done on earth
as it is in heaven.
Give us this day our daily bread;
and forgive us our trespasses
as we forgive those who trespass
against us;
and lead us not into temptation,
but deliver us from evil. Amen.

## Pater Noster

Pater noster, qui es in cælis:
sanctificétur nomen tuum;
advéniat regnum tuum;
fiat volúntas tua, sicut in cælo, et in terra.
Panem nostrum cotidiánum
da nobis hódie;
et dimítte nobis débita nostra,
sicut et nos dimíttimus debitóribus nostris;
et ne nos indúcas in tentatiónem;
sed líbera nos a malo. Amen.

## Hail Mary

Hail Mary, full of grace,
the Lord is with you!
Blessed are you among women,
and blessed is the fruit
of your womb, Jesus.
Holy Mary, Mother of God,
pray for us sinners,
now and at the hour of our death.
Amen.

## Ave, Maria

Ave, María, grátia plena,
Dóminus tecum.
Benedícta tu in muliéribus,
et benedíctus fructus ventris tui, Jesus.
Sancta María, Mater Dei,
ora pro nobis peccatóribus,
nunc et in hora mortis nostræ. Amen.

The four prayers on this page are in English and in Latin. Latin is the universal language of the Roman Catholic Church.

## Nicene Creed

We believe in one God,
the Father, the Almighty,
maker of heaven and earth,
of all that is, seen and unseen.

We believe in one Lord, Jesus Christ,
the only Son of God,
eternally begotten of the Father,
God from God, Light from Light,
true God from true God,
begotten, not made, one in Being
with the Father.
Through him all things were made.
For us men and for our salvation
he came down from heaven:

by the power of the Holy Spirit
he was born of the Virgin Mary, and
became man.

For our sake he was crucified under
Pontius Pilate;
he suffered, died, and was buried.
On the third day he rose again
in fulfillment of the Scriptures;
he ascended into heaven
and is seated at the right hand
of the Father.
He will come again in glory to judge
the living and the dead,
and his kingdom will have no end.

We believe in the Holy Spirit, the Lord,
the giver of life,
who proceeds from the Father
and the Son.
With the Father and the Son he is
worshiped and glorified.
He has spoken through the Prophets.
We believe in one holy catholic and
apostolic Church.
We acknowledge one baptism for the
forgiveness of sins.
We look for the resurrection of the dead,
and the life of the world to come.
Amen.

*The Holy Trinity,*
stained glass.

## Apostles' Creed

I believe in God,
the Father almighty,
creator of heaven and earth.

I believe in Jesus Christ,
his only Son, our Lord.
He was conceived by the power
of the Holy Spirit
and born of the Virgin Mary.
He suffered under Pontius Pilate,
was crucified, died, and was buried.
He descended to the dead.
On the third day he rose again.
He ascended into heaven,
and is seated at the right hand
of the Father.
He will come again to judge
the living and the dead.

I believe in the Holy Spirit,
the holy catholic Church,
the communion of saints,
the forgiveness of sins,
the resurrection of the body,
and the life everlasting. Amen.

## Morning Prayer

Dear God,
as I begin this day,
keep me in your love and care.
Help me to live as your child today.
Bless me, my family, and my friends in all we do.
Keep us all close to you. Amen.

## Evening Prayer

Dear God,
I thank you for today.
Keep me safe throughout the night.
Thank you for all the good I did today.
I am sorry for what I have chosen to do wrong.
Bless my family and friends. Amen.

## Grace before Meals

Bless us, O Lord,
and these your gifts
which we are about to receive
from your goodness.
Through Christ our Lord. Amen.

## Grace after Meals

We give you thanks for all your gifts,
almighty God,
living and reigning now and for ever. Amen.

## The Divine Praises

Blessed be God.
Blessed be his holy name.
Blessed be Jesus Christ, true God and true man.
Blessed be the name of Jesus.
Blessed be his most sacred heart.
Blessed be his most precious blood.
Blessed be Jesus in the most holy sacrament
of the altar.
Blessed be the Holy Spirit, the Paraclete.
Blessed be the great mother of God, Mary
most holy.
Blessed be her holy and immaculate
conception.
Blessed be her glorious assumption.
Blessed be the name of Mary, virgin and mother.
Blessed be Saint Joseph, her most chaste spouse.
Blessed be God in his angels and in his saints.

## Prayer to the Holy Spirit

Come, Holy Spirit, fill the hearts
of your faithful.
And kindle in them the
fire of your love.
Send forth your Spirit and
they shall be created.
And you will renew the
face of the earth.

## Act of Faith

My God, I firmly believe that you are one God in three divine Persons, Father, Son, and Holy Spirit; I believe that your divine Son became man and died for our sins, and that he will come to judge the living and the dead. Amen.

## Act of Hope

My God, relying on your infinite goodness and promises, I hope to obtain pardon of my sins, the help of your grace, and life everlasting, through the merits of Jesus Christ, my Lord and Redeemer. Amen.

## Act of Love

My God, I love you above all things, with my whole heart and soul, because you are all good and worthy of all my love. I love my neighbor as myself for the love of you. I forgive all who have injured me and I ask pardon of all whom I have injured. Amen.

*The Holy Trinity,* stained glass.

## Magnificat

My soul proclaims the greatness
  of the Lord,
my spirit rejoices in God my Savior
for he has looked with favor
  on his lowly servant.

From this day all generations
  will call me blessed:
the Almighty has done great things
  for me,
and holy is his name.

He has mercy on those
  who fear him
in every generation.

He has shown the strength
  of his arm,
he has scattered the proud
  in their conceit.

He has cast down the mighty
  from their thrones,
and has lifted up the lowly.

He has filled the hungry
  with good things,
and the rich he has sent away empty.

He has come to the help
  of his servant Israel
for he has remembered
  his promise of mercy,
the promise he made to our fathers,
to Abraham and his children for ever.

BASED ON LUKE 1:46–55
FROM CATHOLIC HOUSEHOLD BLESSINGS AND PRAYERS

## Memorare

Remember, most loving Virgin Mary,
never was it heard
that anyone who turned to you for help
was left unaided.

Inspired by this confidence,
though burdened by my sins,
I run to your protection
for you are my mother.

Mother of the Word of God,
do not despise my words
  of pleading
but be merciful and
  hear my prayer.
Amen.

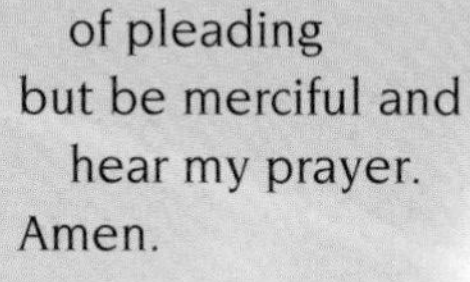

Our Lady of the Rosary, stained glass.

## Rosary

Catholics pray the Rosary to honor Mary and remember the important events in the life of Jesus and Mary. We begin praying the Rosary by praying the Apostles' Creed, the Lord's Prayer, and three Hail Marys. Each mystery of the Rosary is prayed by praying the Lord's Prayer once, the Hail Mary ten times, and the Glory Prayer once. When we have finished the last mystery, we pray the Hail, Holy Queen.

## Joyful Mysteries

1. The Annunciation
2. The Visitation
3. The Nativity
4. The Presentation
5. The Finding of Jesus in the Temple

## Mysteries of Light

1. The Baptism of Jesus in the Jordan River
2. The Miracle at the Wedding at Cana
3. The Proclamation of the Kingdom of God
4. The Transfiguration of Jesus
5. The Institution of the Eucharist

## Sorrowful Mysteries

1. The Agony in the Garden
2. The Scourging at the Pillar
3. The Crowning with Thorns
4. The Carrying of the Cross
5. The Crucifixion

## Glorious Mysteries

1. The Resurrection
2. The Ascension
3. The Coming of the Holy Spirit
4. The Assumption of Mary
5. The Coronation of Mary

Symbol for Mary, Queen of the Rosary, stained glass.

## Hail, Holy Queen

Hail, holy Queen, mother of mercy,
hail, our life, our sweetness,
and our hope.
To you we cry, the children of Eve;
to you we send up our sighs,
mourning and weeping
in this land of exile.
Turn, then, most gracious advocate,
your eyes of mercy toward us;
lead us home at last
and show us the blessed fruit
of your womb, Jesus:
O clement, O loving, O sweet
Virgin Mary.

## Stations of the Cross

1. Jesus is condemned to death.

2. Jesus accepts his cross.

3. Jesus falls the first time.

4. Jesus meets his mother.

5. Simon helps Jesus carry the cross.

6. Veronica wipes the face of Jesus.

7. Jesus falls the second time.

8. Jesus meets the women.

9. Jesus falls the third time.

10. Jesus is stripped of his clothes.

11. Jesus is nailed to the cross.

12. Jesus dies on the cross.

13. Jesus is taken down from the cross.

14. Jesus is buried in the tomb.

Some parishes conclude the Stations by reflecting on the Resurrection of Jesus.

## The Great Commandment

"You shall love the Lord,
your God, with all your
heart, with all your soul,
and with all your mind. . . .
You shall love your neighbor as yourself."

MATTHEW 22:37, 39

## The Ten Commandments

1. I am the LORD your God: you shall not have strange gods before me.
2. You shall not take the name of the LORD your God in vain.
3. Remember to keep holy the LORD'S Day.
4. Honor your father and your mother.
5. You shall not kill.
6. You shall not commit adultery.
7. You shall not steal.
8. You shall not bear false witness against your neighbor.
9. You shall not covet your neighbor's wife.
10. You shall not covet your neighbor's goods.

## Precepts of the Church

1. Participate in Mass on Sundays and holy days of obligation and rest from unnecessary work.
2. Confess sins at least once a year.
3. Receive Holy Communion at least during the Easter season.
4. Observe the prescribed days of fasting and abstinence.
5. Provide for the material needs of the Church, according to one's abilities.

## The Beatitudes

"Blessed are the poor in spirit,
for theirs is the kingdom of heaven.
Blessed are they who mourn,
for they will be comforted.
Blessed are the meek,
for they will inherit the land.
Blessed are they who hunger
and thirst for righteousness,
for they will be satisfied.
Blessed are the merciful,
for they will be shown mercy.
Blessed are the clean of heart,
for they will see God.
Blessed are the peacemakers,
for they will be called children of God.
Blessed are they who are persecuted for the
sake of righteousness,
for theirs is the kingdom of heaven.

Blessed are you when they insult you and persecute you and utter every kind of evil against you [falsely] because of me. Rejoice and be glad, for your reward will be great in heaven."

MATTHEW 5:3–12

The Beatitude window, stained glass.
Jerry Sodorff, photographer.

## Theological Virtues

Faith
Hope
Love

## Cardinal, or Moral, Virtues

Prudence
Justice
Fortitude
Temperance

## Works of Mercy

Jesus proclaimed, "Blessed are the merciful, for they will be shown mercy" (Matthew 5:7). The Corporal and Spiritual Works of Mercy guide us in living as a "merciful" people. One of the chief witnesses to our love for another is the giving of alms to the poor, or sharing our material and spiritual blessings with others. (See *Catechism of the Catholic Church* 2447.)

### Corporal Works of Mercy

Feed people who are hungry.
Give drink to people who are thirsty.
Clothe people who need clothes.
Visit prisoners.
Shelter people who are homeless.
Visit people who are sick.
Bury people who have died.

### Spiritual Works of Mercy

Help people who sin.
Teach people who are ignorant.
Give advice to people who have doubts.
Comfort people who suffer.
Be patient with other people.
Forgive people who hurt you.
Pray for people who are alive and for those who have died.

## Gifts of the Holy Spirit

Wisdom
Understanding
Right judgment (Counsel)
Courage (Fortitude)
Knowledge
Reverence (Piety)
Wonder and awe (Fear of the Lord)

## Fruits of the Holy Spirit

| | |
|---|---|
| Charity | Joy |
| Peace | Patience |
| Kindness | Goodness |
| Generosity | Gentleness |
| Faithfulness | Modesty |
| Self-control | Chastity |

Symbols for faith (anchor), hope (cross), and love (heart), stained glass.

## Basic Principles of the Church's Teaching on Social Justice

The Church's teaching on social justice guides us in living lives of holiness and building a just society. These principles are:

1. All human life is sacred. The basic equality of all people flows from their dignity as human persons and the rights that flow from that dignity.
2. The human person is the principle, the object, and the subject of every social group.
3. The human person has been created by God to belong to and to participate in a family and other social communities.
4. Respect for the rights of people flows from their dignity as persons. Society and all social organizations must promote virtue and protect human life and human rights and guarantee the conditions that promote the exercise of freedom.
5. Political communities and public authority are based on human nature. They belong to an order established by God.
6. All human authority must be used for the common good of society.
7. The common good of society consists of respect for and promotion of the fundamental rights of the human person, the just development of material and spiritual goods of society, and the peace and safety of all people.
8. We need to work to eliminate the sinful inequalities that exist between peoples and for the improvement of the living conditions of people. The needs of the poor and vulnerable have a priority.
9. We are one human and global family. We are to share our spiritual blessings, even more than our material blessings.

Based on the *Catechism of the Catholic Church*

## The Seven Sacraments

Jesus gave the Church the seven sacraments. The sacraments are the main liturgical signs of the Church. They make the Paschal Mystery of Jesus, who is always the main celebrant of each sacrament, present to us. They make us sharers in the saving work of Christ and in the life of the Holy Trinity.

### Sacraments of Initiation

#### Baptism

We are joined to Jesus Christ, become members of the Church, receive the gift of the Holy Spirit, and are reborn as God's adopted children. Original and all personal sins are forgiven.

#### Confirmation

Our Baptism is sealed with the gift of the Holy Spirit.

#### Eucharist

We receive the Body and Blood of Christ who is truly and really present under the appearances of bread and wine. We share in the one sacrifice of Christ. Sharing in the Eucharist most fully joins us to Christ and to the Church.

### Sacraments of Healing

#### Reconciliation, or Penance

We receive God's gifts of forgiveness for the sins we commit after we are baptized and of peace.

#### Anointing of the Sick

Jesus' work of healing is continued in our lives and strengthens our faith and trust in God when we are seriously ill or dying.

### Sacraments at the Service of Communion

#### Holy Orders

A baptized man is ordained and consecrated to serve the Church as a bishop, priest, or deacon.

#### Matrimony

A baptized man and a baptized woman are united in a lifelong bond of faithful love. They become a sign of God's love for all people and of Christ's love for the Church.

# Celebrating the Mass

## The Introductory Rites

The Entrance
Greeting of the Altar and
of the People Gathered
The Act of Penitence
The Gloria
The Collect

## The Liturgy of the Word

The First Reading from the Bible (Usually from the Old Testament)
The Responsorial Psalm
The Second Reading from the Bible (Usually from New Testament Letters)
Acclamation
The Gospel
The Homily
The Profession of Faith
The Prayer of the Faithful

## The Liturgy of the Eucharist

The Preparation of the Gifts
The Prayer over the Offerings
The Eucharistic Prayer
The Communion Rite
- The Lord's Prayer
- The Rite of Peace
- The Fraction, or the Breaking of Bread
- Communion

The Prayer After Communion

## The Concluding Rites

Greeting
Blessing
Dismissal of the People

# Celebrating Reconciliation

## Individual Rite of Reconciliation

Greeting
Scripture Reading
Confession of Sins
Act of Contrition
Absolution
Closing Prayer

## Communal Rite of Reconciliation

Greeting
Scripture Reading
Homily
Examination of Conscience with Litany of Contrition and the Lord's Prayer
Individual Confession and Absolution
Closing Prayer

## Act of Contrition

My God,
I am sorry for my sins with all my heart.
In choosing to do wrong
and failing to do good,
I have sinned against you
whom I should love above all things.
I firmly intend, with your help,
to do penance,
to sin no more,
and to avoid whatever leads me to sin.
Our Savior Jesus Christ
suffered and died for us.
In his name, my God, have mercy.

# Time LINE

|  |  |
|---|---|
| c. 4 B.C. | Jesus of Nazareth born |
| c. A.D. 28/29 | Jesus' public ministry |
| c. 30–33 | Jesus crucified and raised from the dead |
| c. 42–62 | Paul's missionary journeys |
| c. 51 | Council of Jerusalem |
| c. 64/65 | † Apostles Peter and Paul martyred |
| c. 70 | Saint Mark's Gospel written |
| 70 | Romans destroy Jewish Temple in Jerusalem |
| 90 | Emperor Domitian persecutes the Church |
| c. 100 | Saint John's, the final Gospel, written |
| c. 107 | Saint Ignatius of Antioch martyred |
| c. 156 | Polycarp martyred |
| c. 164 | Oldest Mayan monuments |
| 229–50 | Emperor Decius persecutes the Church |
| 292 | Roman Empire divided into East and West |
| 303–305 | Emperor Diocletian tries to destroy the Church |
| 312–337 | Reign of Emperor Constantine I |
| 313 | Edict of Milan issued |
| 314–335 | Papacy of Pope Saint Sylvester I |
| 325 | Council of Nicaea |
| 361 | Saint Martin of Tours begins missionary work |
| 374 | Saint Ambrose becomes Bishop of Milan |
| 430 | † Saint Augustine, Bishop of Hippo |
| 452 | Attila the Hun invades Italy |
| 440–61 | Papacy of Pope Saint Leo I |
| 476 | Last emperor in the West deposed |
| 528 | Saint Benedict of Nursia founds monastery at Monte Cassino |
| 563 | Saint Columba arrives in Scotland |
| 570 | Birth of Muhammed |
| 590 | Islam takes over in the Middle East |
| 622 | Book printing starts in China |
| 790–870 | Vikings invade Europe |
| 800 | Charlemagne crowned Holy Roman Emperor |
| 979 | China unified under the Sung Dynasty |
| 1000 | Climax of the Mayan civilization on the Yucatan Peninsula |
| 1054 | Schism of Eastern and Western Churches |
| 1096–99 | First Crusade |
| 1153 | † Saint Bernard of Clairvaux |
| 1160– | Cathedral building booms in the West |
| 1174 | † Saint Hildegard of Bingen |
| 1198–1216 | Papacy of Innocent III |
| 1209 | Saint Francis of Assisi establishes the Franciscans |
| 1215 | Magna Carta in England |
| 1216 | Saint Dominic de Guzman founds Dominican Order |
| 1265–72 | Saint Thomas Aquinas writes *Summa Theologica* |
| 1337–1453 | Hundred Years' War between France and England |
| 1347–1351 | Europe's Black Death |
| 1378–1417 | Great Schism of the papacy |
| 1438 | Incas rule in Peru |
| 1440 | Gutenberg introduces movable-type printing |
| 1450–1550 | Spanish and Portuguese missionaries come to New World |
| 1462 | Ivan the Great begins rule as first Russian czar |
| 1492 | Christopher Columbus is first European in the Caribbean |
| 1495–1498 | Leonardo da Vinci's *Last Supper* |
| 1501 | First black slave in America |
| 1517 | Luther initiates the Protestant Reformation |
| 1531 | Saint Juan Diego sees vision of the Blessed Virgin Mary |
| 1535 | King Henry VIII makes himself head of the English Church |
| 1540 | Saint Ignatius Loyola founds the Jesuits |
| 1542 | Saint Francis Xavier arrives in India |
| 1545–1563 | Council of Trent |
| 1548 | † Saint Juan Diego |
| 1558 | Elizabeth I becomes Queen of England |
| 1584 | † Saint Charles Borromeo |
| 1614 | St. Peter's Basilica in Rome completed |
| 1617 | † Saint Rose of Lima, first canonized saint of the Americas |
| 1639 | † Saint Martin de Porres |
| 1620 | Pilgrims land in New England |
| 1643 | Taj Mahal completed in India |
| 1646 | † Saint Isaac Jogues martyred |
| 1700 | † Saint Margaret Bourgeoys, first woman Canadian saint |
| 1769 | Blessed Junípero Serra establishes first California mission |
| 1776 | Declaration of Independence |
| 1789 | French Revolution |
| 1790 | John Carroll ordained bishop of Baltimore, first bishop in the United States |
| 1815 | Napoleon defeated at Waterloo |
| 1821 | † Saint Elizabeth Ann Seton, first native-born American to be canonized |
| 1660 | † Saint John Neumman, bishop of Philadelphia |
| 1861–1856 | American Civil War |
| 1869–70 | First Vatican Council |
| 1884 | Third Plenary Council of Baltimore |
| 1885–86 | † Saint Charles Lwanga and the Martyrs of Uganda |
| 1914–18 | World War I |
| 1917 | † Saint Frances Cabrini, first citizen of the United States to be canonized |
| 1939–45 | World War II |
| 1948 | Mahatma Gandhi assassinated in India |
| 1952 | Elizabeth II becomes Queen of England |
| 1962–65 | Second Vatican Council |
| 1963 | † Blessed Pope John XXIII |
| 1969 | Humans walk on the moon |
| 1979 | Pope John Paul II visits the United States of America, Mexico, Dominican Republic, and Bahamas |
| 1980 | Pope John Paul II visits Africa and Brazil |
| 1983 | Pope John Paul II visits Central America and Caribbean |
| 1984 | Pope John Paul II visits Canada |
| 1990 | *Catechism of the Catholic Church* |
| 1992 | Pope John Paul II promulgates *Catechism of the Catholic Church* |
| 1999 | Pope John Paul II Visits Mexico and St. Louis |
| 2001 | Terrorists destroy World Trade Center in New York City |
| 2005 | † Pope John Paul II |
| 2005 | Benedict XVI elected Pope |
| 2005 | Hurricane Katrina devastates U.S. Gulf Coast |
| 2006 | Pope Benedict XVI promulgates his first encyclical |

**Note:** The symbol † on the timeline indicates the year of the death of the person or persons.

# Glossary

## A-B

**Advocate**
The Holy Spirit, the third Person of the Holy Trinity.

***aggiornamento***
The Italian word, meaning "bring up to date," used by Blessed Pope John XXIII to describe the work of the Second Vatican Council.

**apologist(s)**
Christian writers in the early Church who explained the faith of the Church and defended it against false teachers and teachings.

**Apostles**
The Twelve called by Jesus, the chosen witnesses of the Resurrection and the foundation on whom the Church is built, those chosen by Jesus himself to preach the Gospel to the whole world.

**apostolic succession**
The unbroken connection between the Popes and bishops with the Apostles; bishops are the successors of the Apostles.

**Ascension**
The return of the Risen Jesus' humanity into divine glory to his Father, to God's heavenly domain, forty days after his Resurrection.

**Body of Christ** (Church)
An image for the Church used by Paul the Apostle that teaches that all the members of the Church are one in Christ, the Head of the Church, and that all members have a unique and important work in the Church.

## C-D

**call narrative(s)**
A literary genre, or form, used by the biblical writers to teach that God had entrusted to a person a special work, or mission.

**canonize**
To officially name one of the faithful a saint of the Church.

***Catechism of the* Catholic *Church***
The official summary of the teachings of the Catholic Church promulgated for use in 1992 by Pope John Paul II.

**Catholic Church**
The Church under the leadership of the bishop of Rome, the Pope, founded by Christ on the Apostles, who profess the same faith, and in the seven sacraments, and in whom is found the fullness of the means of Salvation.

**Catholic Reformation**
The response of the Catholic Church to the Protestant Reformation.

**charisms**
Gifts or graces freely given to individual Christians by the Holy Spirit for the benefit of building up the Church.

**Christendom**
The growth of the Church in territory and in both temporal, or political, and spiritual authority resulting in the Pope's authority exceeding that of the emperor, and eventually that of the kings, in the West.

**Church**
The word *church* means "convocation, those called together." The Church is the sacrament of Salvation—the sign and instrument of our reconciliation and communion with God and with one another. The Church is the Body of Christ, the people God the Father has called together in Jesus Christ through the power of the Holy Spirit.

**consecrated life**
The life of the baptized who promise or vow to live the evangelical counsels of poverty, chastity, and obedience in a way of life approved by the Church.

**Council of Jerusalem**
The first council of the Church held around A.D. 51 to discuss and settle the controversy over whether a Gentile had to first become a Jew before being baptized.

**Council of Trent**
The ecumenical council of the Church held in Trent in Northern Italy from 1545 to 1563 at which the Catholic Church developed various ways to renew the spiritual health of the Church and clarify and reassert her doctrinal teachings.

**Dark Ages**
The term used to mistakenly characterize the early Middle Ages (ca. 476–ca. 1100) as a time of decline of the many institutions of culture and learning.

**Deposit of Faith**
The source of faith that is drawn from to pass on God's Revelation to us; it is the unity of Scripture and Tradition.

**Divine Revelation**
God making known the hidden mystery of who he is and the divine plan of creation and salvation known over time so that we can get to know him and love him better; God's free gift of making himself known and giving himself to us by gradually communicating his own mystery in deeds and words.

**dogma of faith**
A truth of faith taught by the Church as revealed by God.

## E-F

**East-West Schism**
The division in the Church in 1054 between the Churches under the leadership of the patriarch of Constantinople and the Churches under the leadership of the bishop of Rome.

# Glossary

**ecumenical council**
The gathering of all the bishops of the world called by the Pope or approved by him in the exercise of their collegial authority to shepherd the Church.

**ecumenism**
The dedicated search to draw all Christians together to manifest the unity that Christ wills for his Body, the Church, on earth.

**Edict of Milan**
The edict issued in A.D. 313 by the Emperor Constantine, granting Christianity legal status in the Empire and the freedom to gather and worship publicly.

**Eucharist**
The sacrament in which we are made sharers in the Paschal Mystery of Christ and receive the Body and Blood of Christ, who is truly present under the appearances of bread and wine; the word *eucharist* is from a Greek word meaning "thanksgiving" or "gratitude."

**evangelization**
The proclamation of the Gospel by words and deeds in fulfillment of Jesus' command to make disciples of all nations and to teach all people to live as he taught.

**exile**
To force a person or group of people to live outside of their homeland.

**Exile**
Period in the history of the Israelites when their leaders and others were forced to live in Babylonia from 587 B.C. to 537 B.C.

**Fathers of the Church**
Bishops and other writers during the first eight centuries of the Church whose teachings were acknowledged as the authentic, or orthodox, teaching of the Church.

## G-H

**Gentiles**
The biblical identification of all people who are not Jewish.

**Great Commission**
The Risen Jesus sending forth the Apostles "to make disciples of all nations, baptizing them in the name of the Father, and of the Son, and of the holy Spirit, teaching them to observe all that I have commanded you" (Matthew 28:19–20).

**heresies**
Religious opinions contrary to the teachings of the Apostles and the Church, a post-baptismal denial of some truth which must be believed with divine and catholic faith.

**Holy Spirit**
The third divine Person of the Holy Trinity sent to us by the Father in the name of his Son, Jesus.

**Holy Trinity**
The mystery of one God in three divine Persons—God the Father, God the Son, God the Holy Spirit.

## I-J

**Incarnation**
A word meaning "take on flesh"; the term the Church uses to name that the Son of God truly became human while remaining truly God; Jesus is true God and true man.

**infallibility**
The charism of the Holy Spirit given to the Church that guarantees that the official teaching of the Pope, or Pope and bishops, on matters of faith and morals is without error.

## K-O

**Kingdom of God**
The image used in the Bible for eternal life to describe all people and creation living in communion with God when Christ comes again in glory at the end of time.

**Magisterium**
The teaching authority and office of the Church, guided by the Holy Spirit, to authentically and accurately interpret the Word of God, Scripture, and Tradition.

**Marks of the Church**
One, holy, catholic, and apostolic; the four attributes and essential characteristics of the Church and of the mission of the Church.

**martyr(s)**
A word meaning "witnesses"; the martyrs of the Church are those who witness to their faith in Christ by suffering death.

**Mendicants**
The word *mendicant* comes from a Latin word meaning "to beg"; Mendicants dedicate themselves to living the Gospel ideal of poverty and belong to a way of living and preaching the Gospel approved by the Church, which includes "begging" for food and whatever else is needed to support their work.

**mission**
A work done in someone else's name; the work Christians carry out in the name of Jesus Christ.

**missionary**
A Christian who travels to places in their own country and in other countries to live and preach the Gospel.

**monasticism**
A way of living the Gospel in which men and women live in community and devote themselves to prayer, work, and learning.

**mystic(s)**
People who receive the gift of an intense experience of union and communication with God.

## P-Q

**paganism**
A term used in the early Church to designate a religion other than Christianity or Judaism, whose values are contrary to the teachings of Sacred Scripture.

**papacy**
The office and authority of the Pope, the bishop of Rome.

**parable(s)**
A type of story Jesus used to teach, comparing one thing to another, inviting his listeners to make a decision to live for the Kingdom of God.

**Paschal Mystery**
The saving events of the Passion, death, Resurrection, and glorious Ascension of Jesus Christ; the passing over of Jesus from death into a new and glorious life; the name we give to God's plan of saving us in Jesus Christ.

**patron saint(s)**
A saint to whom a person, a group of people, a city, country, a church or diocese has a special veneration as their protector and intercessor.

**Pentecost**
The fiftieth day of the Jewish celebration of Passover on which the Holy Spirit came upon the disciples and was given to the Church as Jesus promised.

**Petrine ministry**
The unique mission of Saint Peter the Apostle and his successors, the bishops of Rome, or Popes.

**plenary council(s)**
A gathering of bishops of a country that has the authority to enact legislation for the dioceses of a country.

**polytheism**
The belief in many gods.

**presbyters**
Leaders in the early Church chosen by the Apostles to be their co-workers. Today the designation refers to those who have been ordained to the priesthood in the Sacrament of Holy Orders.

**prophet(s)**
A Greek word meaning "those who speak before others"; those people whom God has chosen to speak in his name.

**Protestant Reformation**
The sixteenth-century attempt at the reform of the Church which resulted in the Protestant reformers separating themselves and their followers from the authority of the Pope.

## R-S

**Resurrection**
Jesus being raised from the dead to a new glorified life.

**Resurrection stories**
Accounts in the Gospels that give testimony of the Church to the fact of and the apostolic Church's faith in Jesus' Resurrection.

**sacrament(s)**
Effective signs of grace, instituted by Christ and entrusted to the Church, by which divine life is shared with us; the seven main liturgical actions of the Church.

**Sacred Scripture**
The collection of all the writings God has inspired authors to write in his name that are collected in the Bible.

**Sacred Tradition**
The passing on of our faith in Christ by the Church through the power and guidance of the Holy Spirit.

**Salvation History**
The history, or events, of God working among his people, restoring humanity to friendship with God in Jesus Christ, the Savior of the world.

**schism**
The refusal of submission to the Roman Pontiff (the Pope) or of communion with the members of the Church subject to him.

**Scholastics**
A term meaning "schoolmen"; twelfth- and thirteenth-century theologians who used the discipline of philosophy to create new syntheses of Christian teaching.

## T-Z

**Temple of the Holy Spirit**
New Testament image used to describe the indwelling of the Holy Spirit in the Church and within the hearts of the faithful.

**Third Plenary Council of Baltimore**
Plenary council held in Baltimore, Maryland, in 1884 in which the *Baltimore Catechism* was adopted for use by the Catholic Church in the United States of America.

**Vatican Council I**
The twentieth ecumenical council of the Church held between December 8, 1869, and September 1, 1870, whose teachings addressed Divine Revelation, the teaching authority of the Pope and bishops, and the relationship between faith and reason.

# Index

# Credits

**Cover design: Kristy Howard**
**Cover illustration: Amy Freeman**

**PHOTO CREDITS:**

**Abbreviated as follows: (bkgd) background, (t) top, (b) bottom, (l) left, (r) right, (c) center.**

**Frontmatter:** Page 5, © Photodisc/Gettyimages; 6, © The Crosiers/Gene Plaisted, OSC. Chapter 1: Page 9, © The Crosiers/Gene Plaisted, OSC; 10, © Julie Lonneman/The SpiritSource; 11, © Lars Justinen/ Goodsalt; 12, © The Crosiers/Gene Plaisted, OSC; 13, © Leonid Bogdanov/Superstock; 14, © Erin Moroney/Imageworks; 15, Courtesy of the Propagation of the Faith.org; 16 (t), © AFP/Gettyimages; 16 (b), © Associated Press/APWideworld.

**Chapter 2:** Page 19, © Charlie Waite/Stone; 20 (t), © Musee des Beau-Arts, Lyon, France/Bridgeman Art; 20 (b), © Carol-Anne Wilson; 21, © Elio Ciol/ Corbis; 22, © Ann Ronan Picture Library/Imageworks; 23, © Archivo Iconografico, S. A./Corbis; 24, © Mary Evans Picture Library/Imageworks; 25 (tl), © AP/ Wideworld Photos; 25 (br), © Danny Lehman/Corbis; 26 (tl), © Randy Faris/Corbis; 26 (c), © Bob Daemmrich/ Photoeditinc; 26 (br), © Nancy Richmond/Imageworks; 27, © Matthias Kulka/zefa/ Corbis.

**Chapter 3:** Page 29, © The Granger Collection/ Granger; 30 (t), © A.K.G., Berlin/Superstock; 30 (b), © Ronald Sheriden/Ancient Art & Architecture Collection, Ltd.; 31, © The Granger Collection/Granger; 32, © The Crosiers/Gene Plaisted, OSC; 33, © Palazzo del Bo, Padua, Italy/Mauro Magliani/SuperStock; 34 (tr), © Ann Ronan Picture Library/Imageworks; 34 (bl), © Graham Salter/Lebrecht/Imageworks; 35 (t), © 1991 Br. R. Lentz, ofm/ Courtesy of Trinity Stores, www.trinitystores.com ; 35 (r), © Associated Press/ APWideworld; 35 (b), Courtesy of Pax Christi USA; 36, © Leon Zernitsky/Images.com; 37, © James Endicott/Images.com.

**Chapter 4:** Page 39, © The Crosiers/Gene Plaisted, OSC; 40 (all), © The Crosiers/Gene Plaisted, OSC; 41 (t), © Josef Polleross/Imageworks; 41 (r), © North Wind/North Wind; 42 and 43, © SuperStock, Inc./ SuperStock; 44, © Getty Images/Getty Images; 45 (cl), © Vittoriano Rastelli/Corbis; 45 (cr), © Associated Press/L'Osse/APWideworld; 46, © Judy Glasel/Imageworks; 46, © Joe Sohm/Imageworks; 47, © Getty Images/Gettyimages.

**Chapter 5:** Page 49, © Bridgeman Art Library; 50, © Nancy Carter/North Wind; 51, © Archivo Iconografico, S.A./Corbis; 52, © Scala/Art Resource, NY; 53, © Cameraphoto-Arte, Venezia/Art Resource, NY; 54, © Archivo Iconografico, S.A./Corbis; 55, ????; 56 (bl), © SW Productions/Gettyimages; 56 (tr), © Robert Cushman Hayes; 57, © Leon Zernitsky, Images.com.

**Chapter 6:** Page 59, © SuperStock, Inc./Superstock; 60 (tl), © Scala/Art Resource, NY; 60 (cl), © New York Public Library, New York/SuperStock; 61, © Michael Nicholson/Corbis; 62 (tl), © Elio Ciol/Corbis; 62 (br), © The Crosiers/Gene Plaisted, OSC; 63 (tl), © The Granger Collection/Granger; 63 (br), © Bridgeman Art Library; 64, © The Granger Collection/Granger; 65, © Images.com/Corbis; 66, © Design Pics Inc./ Design Pics 67 (all), © Michael Newman/ Photoeditinc.

**Chapter 7:** Page 73, © Angus Imagers/Angus Images; 74, © Superstock Inc. Superstock; 75, © The Crosiers/Gene Plaisted, OSC; 76, © Francis G. Mayer/ Corbis; 77 (t), © National Gallery Collection; by kind permission of the Trustees of the National Gallery, London/Corbis; 77 (b), © The Crosiers/Gene Plaisted, OSC; 79 (tl), © The Crosiers/Gene Plaisted, OSC; 79 (br), © Topham Picturepoint/Imageworks; 80 (bl), © Jose Luis Palaez, Inc/Corbis; 80 (tr), © Bill Varie/Corbis; 81, © Ian Shaw/Gettyimages.

**Chapter 8:** Page 83, © Archivo Iconografico, S.A./ Corbis; 84, © SuperStock, Inc./Superstock; 85 (tl), © North Wind/North Wind Pictures; 85 (cr), © The Granger Collection/Granger; 86 (t), © National Gallery Collection; by kind permission of the Trustees of the National Gallery, London/Corbis; 86 (b), © James L. Amos/Corbis; 87 (tl), © Bettmann/ Corbis; 87 (bl), © Scala Art Resource, NY; 88, © Ann Ronan Picture Library/Imageworks; 89, © Chris Claus, Our Lady of Perpetual Help Byzantine Catholic Church, Albuquerque, New Mexico; 90 (tl), © Paul Anderson/Images.com; 90 (br), © Yves Lefevre/ Images.com; 91, © Campbell Laird/Images.com.

**Chapter 9:** Page 93, © Diana Ong/Superstock; 94 (all), © The Crosiers/Gene Plaisted, OSC; 95, © The Granger Collection/Granger; 96 (bl), © Angus-Images/AngusImages; 96 (tr), © The Crosiers/Gene Plaisted, OSC; 97 (tl), © Julie Lonneman/ TheSpiritSource; 97 (br), © The Crosiers/Gene Plaisted, OSC; 98, © Chip Somodevilla/Gettyimages; 99 (tl), © APWideworld/APWideworld; 99 (br), © Associated Press, AP/APWideworld; 100, © PhotoDisc, Inc; 101, © Jack Hollingsworth/ Gettyimages.

**Chapter 10:** Page 103, © The Crosiers/Gene Plaisted, OSC; 104, © Bridgeman Art Library Superstock; 105, © North Wind/North Wind Pictures; 106, © The Granger Collection/Granger; 107, © Historical Picture Arcihves/Corbis; 108, The Crosiers/Gene Plaisted, OSC; 109, (all) Courtesy of Jesuit Volunteer Corps South; 110 (b), © Design Pics Inc./Design Pics; 110 (tl), © Brand X Pictures/Punchstock; 111 (br), © Robin Nelson/Photoeditinc; 111 (tr), © Bill Wittman/Wittman.

**Chapter 11:** Page 113, © 1994 N. Carter/North Wind Pictures; 114, © The Granger Collection/Granger; 115, © North Wind/North Wind Pictures; 116 (all), © The Crosiers/Gene Plaisted, OSC; 117, © The Crosiers/Gene Plaisted, OSC; 118 (bl), © Ralph Crane/ Gettyimages; 118 (tr), © Associated Press/ APWideworld; 119, © Catholic News Service.

**Chapter 12:** Page 123, © David Lees/Corbis; 124, © Franklin McMahon/Corbis; 125, © David Lees/ Corbis; 126 (tl), © David Young-Wolff/Photoeditinc; 126 (bl), © Left Lane Productions/Corbis; 127 (t), © Spencer Grant/Photoeditinc; 127 (br), © AP/ Wideworld Photos; 128, © L'Osservatore Romano/ AP Wideworld; 129 (all), © Tricia Legault/RCL; 130, © Chris Cheadle/Gettyimages; 131, © Vickie Wehrman/Images.com.

# Footnotes

**Page 44**

1 Cf. *Matthew* 16:18–19; John 21:15–17.

2 Second Vatican Council, *Lumen gentium*: The Dogmatic Constitution on the Church 23.

**Page 58**

1 Cf. *Matthew* 5:13–16.

**Page 75**

1 John Paul II, *Redemptoris Missio*, On the Permanent Validity of the Church's Missionary Mandate 21.

**Page 84**

1 Second Vatican Council, *Lumen gentium*: The Dogmatic Constitution on the Church 4 citing St. Cyprian, *De Dom. orat.* 23: PL 4, 553.

**Page 99**

1 Second Vatican Council, *Ad Gentes*: Decree on Missionary Activity in the Church 2.

# Guide Credits

**Cover design: Kristy Howard**
**Cover illustration: Amy Freeman**

**PHOTO CREDITS:**

**Abbreviated as follows: (bkgd) background, (t) top, (b) bottom, (l) left, (r) right, (c) center.**

Page 26 (all), © Photodisc; 27 (bl), © Tony Freeman/Photoeditinc; 27 (br) © Bill Wittman; 28 (tr), © Arnold Gold/News Haven Register/The Image Works; 28 (b), Corbis Images/Picturequest; 29 © John Newbauer/Photoeditinc; 30, Bill Wittman; 32, © Rob Crandall/PictureQuest; 38 (br), © Banana Stock; 38 (all others), © Creatas; 39 (all) © Comstock; 40 (tr), Christopher M. Wingo; 40 (b), © Arthur Tilley/Gettyimages; 41, © Image 1000/Punchstock; 44© Corbis Images/Picturequest; 56, © The Crosiers/Gene Plaisted, OSC; 70, © Archivo Iconografico, S. A./Corbis; 84 (bl), © Graham Salter/Lebrecht/Imageworks; 98, © SuperStock, Inc./SuperStock; 112, © Archivo Iconografico, S.A./Corbis; 126, © Elio Ciol/Corbis; 148, © The Crosiers/Gene Plaisted, OSC; 162, © Scala Art Resource, NY; 176, 190, 204, © The Crosiers/Gene Plaisted, OSC; 218, © David Young-Wolff/Photoeditinc.

# Footnotes

**Front Matter**
Page 30
1 Cf. *John* 17:4

Page 42
1 *Redemptoris Missio*, On the Permanent Validity of the Church's Missionary Mandate, no. 3.

**Chapter 2**
Page 71
1 *Catechesis Tradendae*: Catechesis in Our Time 27.

Page 79
1 *Lumen Gentium*: Dogmatic Constitution on the Church 44 § 4.

Page 81
1 Cf. Second Vatican Ecumenical Council, Pastoral Constitution *Gaudium et Spes*: On the Church in the Modern World 75: AAS 58 (1996), 1097–1099.
2 Cf. *Catechism of the Catholic Church*, 1913–1917.

**Chapter 6**
Page 133
1 Cf. John Paul II, Post-synodal Apostolic Exhortation, *Christifideles Laici*: On the Laity (30 December 1988): AAS 81 (1989) pp. 393–521, 62; cf. John Paul II, Post-synodal Apostolic Exhortation, *Familaris Consortio* (22 November 1981): AAS 73 (1981) pp. 81–191, 38.

**Chapter 7**
Page 148
1 Saint Hippolytus, *Trad. Ap.* 35: SCh Sources Chretiennes (Paris: 1942-) 11, 118.
2 Saint Irenaeus, *Adv. haeres.* 3, 24, 1: PG7/1, 966.

Page 153
1 Cf. 2 *Corinthians* 3:14; *John* 5:39, 46.

Page 163
1 Ephesians 4:3
2 *Catechism of the Catholic Church*, no. 820.

**Chapter 8**
Page 170
1 Cf. *Amos* 5:24; *Isaiah* 1:17.
2 Cf. Luke 9:23.

Page 171
1 *Sacrosanctum Concilium*: Second Vatican Council, Constitution on the Sacred Liturgy 4.

**Chapter 9**
Page 182
1 Cf. *Redemptoris Missio* 52-54.
2 The term "inculturation" is taken from diverse documents of the Magisterium. See CT 53; RM 52-54. The concept of culture, either in a general or an ethnological or sociological sense is clarified in GS 53. Cf. also ChL 44a.
3 *Evangelii nuntiandi*: On Evangelization in the Modern World 20; cf. EN 63; John Paul II, Encyclical Letter, *Redemptoris Missio* 52.

Page 191
1 *General Catechetical Directory*, no. 41.
2 *Ephesians* 1:10.

Page 194
1 Cf. 2 *Corinthians* 3:14; *John* 5:39, 46.

**Chapter 10**
Page 198
1 Cf. *Exodus* 29:7; *Leviticus* 8:12; 1 *Samuel* 9:16; 10:1; 16:1, 12-13; 1 *Kings* 1:39; 19:16.
2 Cf. *Psalm* 2:2; Acts 4: 26-27.

3 Cf. *Isaiah* 11:2; 61:1; *Zechariah* 4: 14; 6: 13; *Luke* 4: 16-21.

Page 200
1 Cf. John Paul II, *Redemptoris Missio* 23.

Page 205
1 *Ephesians* 4:12.

**Chapter 11**
Page 213
1 *Gaudium et Spes*, On the Church in the Modern World 76 § 5.

Page 234
1 Solidarity, though not yet with that explicit name, is on of the basic principles of *Rerum Novarum* (cf. John XXIII, Encyclical Letter *Mater et Magistra*: AAS 53 [1961], 407). "What we nowadays call the principle of solidarity . . . is frequently stated by Pope Leo XIII, who uses the term 'friendship' a concept already found in Greek philosophy. Pope Pius XI refers to it with the equally meaningful term 'social charity'. Pope Paul VI, expanding the concept to cover the many modern aspects of the social question, speaks of a 'civilization of love'" (John Paul II, Encyclical Letter *Centesimus Annus*, 10: AAS 83 [1991], 805). Solidarity is one of the basic principles of the entire social teaching of the Church (cf. Congregation for the Doctrine of the Faith, Instruction Libertatis Conscientia, 73: AAS 79 [1987], 586). Starting with Pius XII (cf. Encyclical Letter Summi Pontificatus: AAS 31 [1939], 426-427), the term *solidarity* is used ever more frequently and with ever broader meaning: from that of "law" in the same encyclical to that of "principle" (cf. John XXIII, Encyclical Letter *Mater et Magistra*: AAS 53 [1961], 407), that of "duty" (cf. Paul VI, Encyclical Letter *Populorum Progressio*, 17, 48: AAS 59 [1967], 265-266, 2810 and that of "value" (cf. John Paul II, Encyclical Letter *Sollicitudo Rei Socialis*, 38: AAS 80 [1988], 564-566), and finally that of "virtue" (cf. John Paul II, Encyclical Letter *Sollicitudo Rei Socialis*, 38, 40: AAS 80 [1988], 564-566, 568-569).